Confronting
HATE

Confronting HATE

THE UNTOLD STORY OF THE RABBI WHO STOOD UP FOR HUMAN RIGHTS, RACIAL JUSTICE, AND RELIGIOUS RECONCILIATION

DEBORAH HART STROBER & GERALD S. STROBER

Skyhorse Publishing

Skyhorse Publishing books may be purchased in bulk at special discounts for sales promotion, corporate gifts, fund-raising, or educational purposes. Special editions can also be created to specifications. For details, contact the Special Sales Department, Skyhorse Publishing, 307 West 36th Street, 11th Floor, New York, NY 10018 or info@skyhorsepublishing.com.

Skyhorse® and Skyhorse Publishing® are registered trademarks of Skyhorse Publishing, Inc.®, a Delaware corporation.

Visit our website at www.skyhorsepublishing.com.

10 9 8 7 6 5 4 3 2 1

Library of Congress Cataloging-in-Publication Data is available on file.

Cover design by Brian Peterson
Cover photo credit © 1981, Oregonian Publishing Co. All rights reserved. Used with permission of The Oregonian.

ISBN: 978-1-5107-4539-1
Ebook ISBN 978-1-5107-4540-7

Printed in the United States of America

To Joshua-Marc Bennett Tanenbaum
That he may know the father he never met

Contents

*This title is taken from *A Prophet for Our Time: An Anthology of the Writings of Rabbi Marc H. Tanenbaum*, Fordham University Press, 2002.

Preface

MORE THAN A QUARTER CENTURY has passed since Rabbi Marc Tanenbaum died in 1992, but his legacy endures. Indeed, his remarkable life provides a roadmap for transcending these troubled times. Fascinating, featuring intimate encounters with the religious, political, and communal leaders who shaped our contemporary world, it is a guide for anyone seeking to live according to the principle of *Tikkun Olam*—the Jewish imperative to fix what is broken in the world.

In his daily life, Rabbi Tanenbaum challenged the status quo, understanding that bringing about lasting change required tenacity and struggle. His actions were as bold and transformative as his words; he fought the good fight. His legacy lives on in the bridges he built, the conflicts he mediated, and the advances in human rights for which he fought. He played a historic role in the removal of systemic anti-Semitism from Catholic liturgy. He catalyzed Jews and evangelicals to overcome their mutual suspicion and find common ground. He made common cause with Muslims, Sikhs, and any others willing to join forces with him in pursuit of justice. He was active in the American civil rights struggle. He mobilized support for Vietnamese boat people, starving Biafrans, and anti-apartheid forces in South Africa. And he was a key player in liberating Soviet Jews.

His deep involvement in all of these game-changing undertakings was highly visible as they were unfolding over the course of Rabbi Tanenbaum's career. As a result, he became widely known as "the human rights rabbi," "the foremost apostle to the gentiles," and the "Secretary of State of the Jews."

Much has been written about Rabbi Tanenbaum's work, but this is the first account to focus on his life in its entirety, presenting a multidimensional and holistic portrait of this iconic individual. Our goal in publishing this work is not merely to memorialize Marc Tanenbaum, but to enable the lessons of his leadership to inspire those who want to bring about lasting social and political change.

Many hands and minds shaped this work. Extensive research was conducted by Gerald Strober, who worked closely with Marc at the American Jewish Committee. Strober and his wife, Deborah, drew on extensive oral and written histories compiled by the AJC as well as numerous interviews they themselves conducted with many individuals who worked with Rabbi Tanenbaum in a variety of his causes. Most of the facts and stories, the tales and quotations, that form the corpus of this volume are drawn from those histories. This historical record was supplemented by the vast trove of material in the Tanenbaum collection at the American Jewish Archives in Cincinnati. In addition, the rabbi's widow, Georgette Bennett, also gave generously of her time, not only by offering her recollections, but also by providing original source materials.

The text was further shaped and edited by Harvey Shapiro, an experienced writer with a keen understanding of the issues and themes animating the Jewish world and the American polity during Marc Tanenbaum's distinguished career.

For more than a quarter century, the Tanenbaum Center for Interreligious Understanding, founded after the rabbi's death by his widow, has worked to sustain and advance his objectives and aspirations. The Center's focus has not been on buffing its namesake's reputation, but on building upon his achievements.

Those who want to go beyond what's recounted in this book and learn more about Rabbi Tanenbaum and his work can visit The Rabbi Marc H. Tanenbaum Collection at the American Jewish Archives (https://fa.americanjewisharchives.org/tanenbaum/).

Introduction

"We had no food and water. We began to drink the seawater and eat seaweed. Our children became deathly sick and feverish and we were certain that we would die. Rabbi, you as a Jew, will understand this better than most people. . . . The worst thing of all was the awareness that we were abandoned by the world, that our lives meant absolutely nothing to anybody—that human life had become worthless."

> —Nguyen Than, one of thousands of Vietnamese
> boat people fleeing tyranny, describing his and his
> immediate family's ordeal to Rabbi Marc Tanenbaum

FEBRUARY 1978, SOUTHEAST ASIA. IT is a typically hot, humid day on the banks of the South China Sea. As jeering Indonesian officials massed on the shore to look on, a Westerner of patrician bearing in his early fifties plunges fully clothed into the choppy waters and swims toward a group of small boats adrift within sight of land.

The craft are overloaded with starving men, women, and children. Struggling against the strong current, their would-be rescuer grabs hold of one after another of the flimsy boats and pushes them with all his might toward the shore—and, he hopes, to safety.

This courageous—and perhaps quixotic—effort is being undertaken by Rabbi Marc Tanenbaum, an expression of his sense of innate human decency and compassion—and his embodiment of Leviticus

19:16: *Thou shalt not stand by idly while the blood of your brother cries out from the earth*. Tanenbaum is being taunted by the scoffing authorities. Not content with merely shouting down the frightened mass of humanity fighting for their very lives, the onlookers attempt to push the fragile boats back into the water.

But the rabbi does not desist. The director of the American Jewish Committee's Department of Interreligious Affairs, Tanenbaum has journeyed many thousands of miles from his comfortable life in New York to participate in a two-week-long humanitarian mission to Southeast Asia organized by the International Rescue Committee. He is not one to stand by, immune to the human suffering before him.

Among those traveling with the rabbi are such luminaries as film and stage star Liv Ullmann, folksinger Joan Baez, former Soviet refusenik and Prisoner of Zion Alexander Ginzburg, civil rights activist Bayard Rustin, and Holocaust survivor and scholar Elie Wiesel. They are bearing witness and offering humanitarian assistance to refugees housed in camps throughout the region.

It is during their stop in Jakarta that Rabbi Tanenbaum has walked purposefully onto a rotting pier and plunged into the city's teeming harbor. Continuing his very personal rescue mission, he climbs into a leaky craft he recalled as having been "no larger than an oversized rowboat." It is crammed "in sweltering closeness" with fifteen Vietnamese boat people, among them Nguyen Than, his wife, and their eight children.

As the rabbi sat with the Than family on their decrepit boat, struggling to keep from falling back into the water, he learned of the family's odyssey following the events of April 30, 1975. On that day, victorious Vietcong forces had overrun Saigon, the South Vietnamese capital, bringing to an ignominious end America's long presence in that nation. On April 30, 1975, iconic television footage would focus on the roof of the US embassy, the scene of a chaotic evacuation of American personnel as well as of those Vietnamese lucky enough to be able to climb onto the hovering helicopters.

Nguyen Than and his family would not be among the fortunate

ones. The Communist regime in Hanoi, which would become the new capital of Vietnam, had ordered the Thans to the rural countryside for "reeducation." Than was dismissed from his position as a teacher and ordered to perform agricultural work in a rural collective, while the regime confiscated the family's meager property. Through bribery and stealth, however, the family escaped from their rural prison. Making their way through the Vietnamese forest, they reached the coast. There, Than and his brother purchased the leaky boat on which they would escape under the cover of darkness and sail for four weeks across the roiling China Sea.

On reaching land, the Thans would be turned away by border patrols in both Singapore and the Philippines. Soon, their supplies of food and water exhausted, the starving families were forced to drink seawater and eat seaweed in order to survive. Recalling their ordeal, Nguyen Than says, "We were certain that we would die."

But suddenly, there was someone in their boat trying to help. Gazing intently into the rabbi's eyes, this beleaguered refugee said, "I now understand what it meant to be a Jew in Nazi Germany in the 1930s, when the world knew that the Jewish people were being destroyed and you were abandoned." The rabbi, in turn, would later say that Than's description of his family's ordeal would "penetrate my heart."

In years to come, Marc Tanenbaum's heart would continue to absorb the travails of others, not only as he served as a fierce advocate for *his* people, the Jewish people around the world, but also on behalf of victims of oppression in dozens of countries. Hillel, the ancient Jewish sage, poised this question: "If I am not for myself, who will be? If I am only for myself, what am I?" Rabbi Marc Tanenbaum sought to resolve this dilemma by working tirelessly on behalf of Jews and gentiles and, above all, bringing together people of diverse beliefs.

He is best remembered for his significant role in helping to bring about *Nostra Aetate*, the Vatican II declaration that laid to rest long-embedded Catholic doctrines blaming the Jews for the crucifixion of Christ and condoning anti-Semitism. While he sought to improve relations between these two great religions, Marc Tanenbaum also played an integral role in enhancing relations among the Jewish community, evangelicals, and Muslims. He was a vigorous proponent of the downtrodden throughout the world. He was animated by the core value of Tikkun Olam: the imperative to fix our broken world.

This is his story.

PART I
IN THE BEGINNING

CHAPTER 1

Baltimore:
Living above the Store

Every spring, as the Passover and Easter holidays approached, Sadie
Tanenbaum [Marc's mother] would prepare extra food—matzo balls
and other kosher-for-Pesach delicacies—and distribute them to their
Jewish and Gentile neighbors alike, a gesture toward the less fortunate that had "quite an impact on" on young Marc Tanenbaum.

—Sima Scherr, Marc's sister

MARC TANENBAUM'S STORY BEGINS IN Baltimore, a city with an important past in early American history. Given Baltimore's excellent natural
resources and the development of major shipping and rail lines, it is not
surprising that the city became a magnet for immigrants from nations
throughout Europe seeking economic opportunities and, in the case of
Eastern European Jews, freedom from anti-Semitism.

While there had been a Jewish presence in major eastern seaboard
cities from New York to Savannah since the late seventeenth century,
Jewish settlement in Baltimore dated back only to the mid-eighteenth
century. Among the city's earliest-known Jewish residents was a mer-
chant named Jacob Hart, a native of Fürth, Germany, who supplied the
Marquis de Lafayette with war matériel during the American Revolution.

One explanation for the relatively belated arrival of Jews to Baltimore was that during the administration of Cecil Calvert, the second Lord Baltimore, in 1649 the Toleration Act was promulgated, granting freedom of religion to Catholics and Protestants—but not to Jews. Following the American Revolution, a further hindrance to Jewish settlement in the city may have been a clause in the state of Maryland's Constitution limiting the rights of non-Christians. In 1826, however, legislation known as "The Jew Bill" was enacted, nullifying the religion-based restrictions, and Jewish settlement in the city began to increase.

The Jewish population grew, particularly during the great Jewish migration from Eastern Europe at the end of the nineteenth century. By 1925, Baltimore was home to approximately 65,000 Jews. While the first to arrive were mainly immigrants from Germany, a much larger group came later, composed of those fleeing the virulent anti-Semitism and pogroms that had erupted throughout Eastern Europe.

Much of Baltimore's Jewish population would be concentrated in East Baltimore, where a number of significant Jewish institutions would be developed, including synagogues and day schools . In 1850, Baltimore would become home to the first YMHA to be established in the United States. Baltimore Hebrew College was founded in 1919 and the Ner Israel Rabbinical College in 1933.

Early in the twentieth century, the stream of immigrants arriving from Ukrainian shtetls would include Sadie Baumsiger, from Olita, and Abraham Tanenbaum, from Dimidivka, near the Bug River. Sadie, born in 1900, was sixteen years old when she arrived at Ellis Island. Sadie was acutely aware that those seeking a better life in America could be turned back at the whim of an immigration officer. And so, she prepared carefully for her arrival. While she had been wearing her auburn hair fashioned in a long pigtail that made her look younger, she thought she would stand a better chance of passing muster by cutting it off and, thus, appearing more mature, as well as looking very healthy.

Sadie's careful preparations paid off; she was admitted to the United States without incident. But she almost didn't arrive when she intended to. Sadie's older brother, Harry—she was the middle child, and Max was the youngest of the three siblings—had sent money intended to purchase a ticket, but for *Max*. But the high-spirited Sadie declared, "Oh, no! *I'm* going next!" She arrived in America in the middle of World War I and quickly went to work sewing clothing for soldiers. Max made it to America not long afterward, but not before witnessing fierce fighting during the war between Red and White Russian factions. He was at one point forced to hide behind tombstones in a cemetery while bullets were flying back and forth.

Meanwhile, Abraham Tanenbaum was witnessing terrible acts of anti-Semitism in Dimidivka. During a Good Friday sermon at a local church, the priest raged about the Jews as Christ killers. Soon after, Abraham's brother, Aaron, was abducted, taken to a bridge, and thrown into the Bug River, where he perished. This was the unambiguous signal for Abraham that it was time to leave for America. Arriving in New York in 1907, he joined the city's Jewish immigrant community on Manhattan's Lower East Side and found work in a sweatshop there.

After a time, Abraham made his way to Baltimore, where a *landsman*—someone from his village—named Grossblatt and his family were living. The Grossblatts not only offered Abraham temporary lodging in their home, they introduced him to the young woman with beautiful auburn hair who had so carefully prepared herself for inspection at Ellis Island.

Soon thereafter, Sadie Baumsiger and Abraham Tanenbaum would be married. The newlyweds would operate a series of grocery stores at various locations in Baltimore before moving into a modest 2,200-square-foot brick-and-stucco corner house built at 1850 Light Street in 1905. It was across the way from a factory that manufactured metal buckets in what was then a largely Italian, German, and Irish neighborhood not far from the city's Inner Harbor.

Assuming that the local streetcar line would one day extend as far as 1850 Light Street, the Tanenbaums opened a shop on the ground floor, reasoning that people getting off the streetcar in front of their store would shop there on their way home. But the streetcar extension never materialized, and the family would always struggle to make ends meet.

The Tanenbaums lived behind and above their store. Their dining room was in back of the store, and at the rear of the building, there was a kitchen, in which there was a small sofa. There were three bedrooms on the second floor: Sadie and Abraham's at the front, overlooking Light Street; another one next to theirs, then a hallway; and at the back of the house, another bedroom.

It was in this house that Herman Marc Tanenbaum, the second of Sadie and Abraham's three children, was born on Tuesday, October 13, 1925. His Hebrew name was Chaim Mordechai, which pays homage to the hero of the Purim story. He would later adopt "Marc" as his first name because he never liked his original first name, and he would relegate Herman to serving as his middle name. Herman's older brother, Ernest—everybody called him Ernie—had been born three years earlier, and his sister Sima would come along in 1928.

As the three Tanenbaum children were growing up, their father, whom Herman would later recall as having been "more the dreamer of the family, the poet," loved to tell stories about Sholem Aleichem. But he also told his American-born children about the dark side of shtetl life—the terrible acts of anti-Semitism and the horrific pogroms. Abraham provided his children with plenty of love, but it was impossible to shelter them from the growing awareness that he had a serious heart condition.

Still, the Tanenbaum home was full of life. While Abraham was deeply rooted in Orthodox Jewish observance, he enjoyed secular pursuits, among them keeping up with current events. And so he would begin each day by switching on his radio and listening to the news of the world.

When it came to their children's education, Abraham and Sadie believed in a strong grounding in Jewish tradition. And so they enrolled Herman in the city's Talmudical Academy, which at that time provided students through the eighth grade with both a secular and Jewish education. Its students began their school day with prayer and the study of the Bible as well as other Jewish texts. Then came secular subjects, including languages—Hebrew, English, French, and Latin—as well as mathematics, sciences, and history.

Following Herman's years at the Talmudical Academy, he attended Baltimore City High School. An excellent student, he would graduate from high school at the age of fifteen.

As the Tanenbaum children grew into adolescence, Herman and Ernie would often wrestle in their back bedroom. Sima, who could hear their horseplay, was both angry and resentful because she longed to share in the fun. But the boys would have none of her. As Sima would recall many decades later, "I felt like I missed out on that part of our youth."

Despite that grievance, Sima looked back with great affection at her brother Herman, whom she at that time called by his Hebrew name, Chaim. "He was the serious one, the academic, always sitting at the dining room table, studying," she recalled. Ernie, four years Herman's senior, was tall, handsome, and gregarious, she recalled, adding he was "more outgoing, the comedian, an actor and a performer." By contrast, Sima described Herman as being "short, plump, and pimply."

Herman would adopt a very protective attitude toward his sister, helping her academically and also helping her to understand the physiological changes wrought by adolescence—developments that Sadie, due to her own upbringing and modesty, wasn't able to discuss with her daughter. "At that time," Sima would recall many years later, "immigrant parents didn't speak too easily about such things." When Herman became a rabbinical student, she said, "I felt free to ask him what was happening. And he did an excellent job, and I always appreciated that."

Herman, Ernest, and Sima were true children of the Depression. After school and during vacations, they helped out in their parents' small grocery store, where credit was always extended to their mostly poor customers. One day, when Herman opened the cash register, he found only a single quarter in the change section. He recalled feeling intense panic, because he couldn't understand how the Tanenbaum family could possibly survive.

But survive they *did,* and every spring, as the Passover and Easter holidays approached, Sadie, the major businesswoman of the family, would prepare extra food—matzo balls and other kosher-for-Pesach delicacies—and distribute them to their Jewish and gentile neighbors alike, a gesture toward the less fortunate that Sima said had "quite an impact on Herman." Moreover, at Christmastime, Sadie would fill baskets with food for their needy neighbors, because she felt that they could not be without food on their big holiday. Herman would accompany his mother as she distributed these gifts.

While the Tanenbaums managed to support their family on the income from the store, Abraham urged his son Herman to become a physician, because, as he liked to say, "There will always be sick people," and therefore, Herman would always be able to make a living. Being able to say "my son the doctor" was, of course, hardly an unfamiliar aspiration among Jewish immigrant parents. Sadie, however, despite being the more practical parent, wanted Herman to become a rabbi. Herman would later conclude that one reason for this aspiration was that she felt that she had to prove her own orthodoxy to her parents, and there was no better way to do so than to produce a rabbi for the family.

Initially, Herman's father's wish seemingly prevailed. As Herman began to contemplate going to medical school in Baltimore, he and his Uncle Max Baumsiger, who regarded Herman as the son he never had, began to explore the possibility of Herman obtaining a scholarship. And so Herman applied to both the University of Maryland and Johns Hopkins University for financial assistance.

In the 1930s, however, such preeminent institutions had stiff quotas for Jewish students, and Herman's prospects for admission seemed shaky. And so a bit of a conspiracy was hatched: the principal of the Baltimore Hebrew Academy and Sadie joined forces to obtain Herman a scholarship to study at Yeshiva College—it was not until 1945 that this college would become the liberal arts division of the larger Yeshiva University—in New York City. There, Herman was assured, in addition to religious training in the Orthodox tradition, he could take science and premed courses in preparation for medical school later on.

While resisting that idea for several months, Herman went on to enroll in several individual premed courses at Johns Hopkins. Herman was also interested in literature, and he took several courses in Shakespearean plays, all the while realizing that he was merely avoiding a major decision about his future.

Herman's scholarship came through, and Sadie and Abraham escorted their reluctant teenager up to New York and handed him over to Yeshiva's registrar. Herman, six months shy of his fifteenth birthday, cried "like a baby," because, as he told an interviewer nearly forty years later, "I *was* a baby." Indeed, he was still wearing children's knee pants on the day he reported for classes at Yeshiva College.

Despite Herman's reluctance to confront his future and leave his loving family, his college experience in New York City would profoundly affect his life.

CHAPTER 2

A Rebel in New York City

"I sensed from the minute I met him that he was a very curious person, he was very open; he was very pluralistic. He was different than most of the people I was meeting at that time."
—Myron Fenster, rabbi emeritus, Shelter Rock Jewish Center, Roslyn, New York; schoolmate of Herman Tanenbaum at Yeshiva College and the Jewish Theological Seminary

IMAGINE HERMAN'S SENSE OF WONDER on the day in 1940 that he first eyed one towering skyscraper after another as he and his parents arrived in New York City en route to the campus of Yeshiva College in the Washington Heights section of Manhattan!

And imagine Herman's amazement as he caught sight of Yeshiva's main building, a massive, four-storied edifice at 500 West 185th Street, replete with such architectural features as a soaring corner tower, turrets, minarets, arches, buttresses, and balconies. Its walls were infused with surprising orange-hued and marble striping reminiscent of Byzantine architecture.

The building had been erected in 1929 as the epicenter of the Rabbi Isaac Elchanan Theological Seminary and Yeshiva College, America's oldest and largest Jewish-sponsored institution of higher learning.

At the time of Herman's enrollment, classes in which the students studied Talmud began in the morning and continued until 3 p.m. The remainder of the day and the early evening hours were devoted to liberal arts, including Jewish history, literature, and philosophy.

Once Herman had gotten over the initial shock "of being thrown into this whole different kind of world," he adjusted well to his new surroundings. Loving dormitory life, he made friends with "some wonderful guys, a bunch of very bright, very gifted people," and he experienced "a real sense of continuity and family." He did so despite being several years younger than most of his classmates.

Herman thrived academically, receiving A's in all his courses that first year. Best of all, however, Yeshiva's biological sciences program was proving to be as excellent as Uncle Max had promised—a fortunate situation, given Abraham's hopes for his son's future success as a doctor.

Despite the demands of Herman's coursework, he managed to find time to pursue his budding interest in a number of extracurricular activities, among them journalism. He joined the staff of the campus newspaper, *The Commentator*, as a news editor and went on to become the publication's editor during his senior year. There, Herman met and became friends with another future rabbi, Myron Fenster. Several years younger than Herman, Myron would serve as *The Commentator*'s sports editor. Herman, an avid reader of that section of the paper, was by then also a stringer for the Denver, Colorado–based *Intermountain Jewish News*, an English-language weekly. He was so impressed with Myron's sports stories that he sought him out.

"He like *spotted* me when I was a freshman," Rabbi Fenster recalled. "I started writing sports stories as soon as I came to Yeshiva College, and he apparently was reading them—I hope others were too—but he came up to me one day and said, 'I like what you're writing. I have a job for you. I said I had just decided to become a rabbi a short time before, and I was very into it, so I said, 'A *job*?'"

"He said, 'I'd like you to write some stories'—he wanted *me* to be a stringer for the *Intermountain Jewish News*, as well—and he would say to me every once in a while, 'Hey, there's a good story downtown today; so-and-so is coming, and you go there and write up that story. I'll see to it that it gets in.' And I would very often say to him, 'I can't *do* that; I don't have time for that right now!'"

Myron's family lived in Brooklyn, so he would stay during the week in a room near the campus and join his family for Shabbat. Herman remained on campus, only rarely going home to Baltimore, but the two young students bonded and remained friends until Herman's death. Myron, who, unlike his schoolmate, would spend most of his career as a congregational rabbi, appreciated Herman's openness to a wide range of differing views. "Most of the people I was meeting at that time would ask a lot of questions—what books I was reading, and that kind of thing," Rabbi Fenster recalled. But Herman "never did that; he accepted you for what you were. He was interested in what you were and wanted you to tell him about it, but that was the extent of his intrusion into your personal life. I respected that in him."

Another fellow student whose life was positively impacted by Herman Tanenbaum was Ted Comet, of Cleveland, Ohio. Like Herman, he was a dormitory resident, in contrast to most of Yeshiva's approximately 250 students, who were commuters. A year behind Herman at Yeshiva, Comet would go on to a distinguished career in Jewish communal service. "If you ask me whose presence was very much felt," he said, "I saw him more as an activist, which he later became, rather than as a pastoral type. He was a fulsome, fully developed man with enormous energy, a lot of ambition and drive." Comet found Herman to be charming, but with "a strong ego that needed to be fed." Yet Comet never sensed that personality trait overrode Herman's essential human decency. As Comet put it, "He was well rounded, well put together, smart, focused, and ambitious, and in some ways, driven too."

Despite the intense atmosphere at Yeshiva, there could be light-hearted moments, too, with students sometimes playing boisterous pranks.

In one Hebrew class, the teacher was describing the use of dots that serve as vowels in the Hebrew language. Noticing that Herman did not seem to be paying attention, the instructor asked him to describe what the teacher had just explained. "You just made a vowel movement," Herman replied.

When Herman decided to pursue collegiate politics, he was elected president of his class. At this time, he was also beginning to realize that his curiosity about the greater world would likely preclude a career as a congregational rabbi. While Herman found his coursework in general history, Jewish history, and Biblical studies to be stimulating, he was beginning to sense that some aspects of his Talmudic studies were not readily applicable to day-to-day life.

For example, he disdained discussion of such subjects as sacrifice or whether an egg is kosher or not or how a slaughtered chicken can be plucked so as to locate its veins. "What the hell has that got to do with real life?" he asked rhetorically during an interview conducted more than thirty-five years later by an AJC lay leader. While acknowledging that "For every Orthodox Jew it meant a great deal," Herman was discovering that "the rabbinical school in Yeshiva was becoming increasingly repressive, increasingly fundamentalist orthodox."

He attributed that development to the influx of faculty members from Eastern Europe, notably Poland. Among them was one professor Herman regarded as being "a spiritual KGB operative who was given keys to open rooms to look in and see what the boys were doing, whether they were shaving with a straight razor, which was forbidden, and that sort of thing."

Herman was beginning to sense that he was not suited for life as an Orthodox Jew—indeed, intuited that he "was not Orthodox in my guts." Despite the fact that many Conservative rabbis of his day had been born into the Orthodox tradition, moving to a more liberal form of observance was no small consideration for him. His decision was not just an affront to the values of his home, but upended the role he was expected to play in Sadie's desire to confirm her own religious bona fides to *her* parents.

Though fully aware of the consequences for his parents, Herman was not one to withdraw from Orthodoxy quietly. He decided to use

The Commentator as his bully pulpit. He would write what he later called "angry editorials of a veiled nature." While he didn't cite what he described as the KGB-like atmosphere of the institution, he questioned whether Yeshiva "was going to create a synthesis for science or technology in the real world that we were living in."

While the adolescent Tanenbaum struggled with his religious identity in New York City, the early 1940s saw a world engulfed in a war raging from Europe to Africa to Asia to Australia. Even more ominously for Jews, news of the methodical roundup, ghettoizing, deportation, and annihilation of European Jewry—the Nazi genocide that would go down in history as the Holocaust, the Shoah in Hebrew—was beginning to reach the United States. Horror vacillated with skepticism; the stories seemed too horrific to be true. Important newspapers, such as the *New York Times*, failed to report the truth until far too late, and yet the truth trickled out. American Jews watched the slaughter of their brethren from afar, powerless. There was only one bit of positive news for world Jewry during those terrible years: some of those European Jews who had managed to escape before the Nazi implementation of the "final solution" had made their way to Palestine. There they joined previously arrived Zionists who had already established communities and were engaged in an epic struggle to end the British Mandate and establish a modern Jewish state in the historic land of Israel.

On May 8, 1945, the war in Europe was officially at an end. Six million Jews had been murdered, together with many million of other innocents. The world stood in shock as the scope of these crimes was revealed. Finally, the Nazi killing apparatus had been dismantled, and Nazi war criminals were on the run. But the war against the Jews would continue, especially in Poland. There, on July 4, 1946, more than a year after the cessation of hostilities in Europe, a pogrom would take place in the town of Kielce, where forty Jews were murdered by a furious mob of anti-Semites, likely at the instigation of Communist security forces.

During the spring of 1945, as Herman's senior year was coming to an end, the formerly knickers-clad weepy adolescent had matured into a poised collegian, as shown in a stately photograph he would publish in *Masmid*, his college yearbook.

Upon graduating with a bachelor of science degree, Herman was still grappling with his resistance to the strict demands of Orthodox observance. At this time, Herman began to seriously contemplate identifying with the more liberal Conservative branch of Judaism, which was gaining momentum among American Jews. As Herman rethought his identity, he decided to follow his father's advice to pursue a career as a physician, thus avoiding drawing any denominational lines in the sand. He applied to—and was accepted by—the Essex County Medical School in New Jersey.

Herman's acceptance to medical school was no easy feat given the ongoing restriction imposed by medical schools under the *numerus clausus,* which barred many Jewish students from attending American institutions of higher learning. It was the same quota system under which Herman had earlier been rejected by the Johns Hopkins University School of Medicine. This time, however, Uncle Max Baumsiger intervened, pulling strings to assure Herman's acceptance at the New Jersey school.

It did not take long for Herman to realize that he was not destined for life as a physician. On his very first day of studies, upon walking into the cadaver room, he exclaimed: "My God! What am I *doing* here? I'm not going to spend my life cutting up people!" Dashing out of that room, his medical career came to a abrupt end.

Herman now was in possession of a bachelor of science degree that he would likely never use. He also knew that he would never become an Orthodox rabbi. As he would say years later, "I was completely at sea." Not yet nineteen, he pondered his future.

The only other thing that really interested Herman was writing. Given his success at *The Commentator,* he began to pound the pavements in Manhattan in the hopes of landing any kind of editorial position. His dedication finally paid off in the form of employment, for the very modest sum of $35 a week, as an assistant to the editor of a newsletter, *Current Events,* which, as he observed, had "a kind of elitist

Jewish circulation in the United States and in Israel." Herman's boss, a "brilliant" journalist named Grossman, was a member of the movement headed by the right-wing Israeli underground leader Menachem Begin, and Grossman's daughter Rena wrote for *Time* magazine.

Despite Herman's good fortune in being able to work in his field of choice rather than being reduced to odd jobs like many other aspiring writers, he was virtually penniless. All he could afford for lodgings was a room in somebody else's apartment. He found one on 42nd Street and 8th Avenue for only $10 a week—only to discover that his German-born husband-and-wife landlords were most likely Nazis and definitely heavy drinkers. Every night after dinner, they would argue. Worst of all, the husband would beat his wife. Fearing for his own safety as his landlords fought, Herman would lock the door of his room, get into bed, and lie there in terror until he fell asleep.

There were two consolations, however: the cheap rent and the fact that the *Current Events* office, on 42nd Street and Sixth Avenue, was only two blocks east of his living quarters.

One day in 1946, while strolling up Broadway, Herman ran into a friend from Yeshiva College, Harold Shulweis. Like Herman, he had begun to question his Orthodox roots. He said that he was planning to take the entrance exam for admission to the Jewish Theological Seminary of America (JTS), a Conservative institution.

This was a life-changing encounter.

"I'm going with you!" Herman told his friend.

CHAPTER 3

Seeking God in Morningside Heights and Beyond

"It was a very congenial atmosphere in many ways . . . it was an
atmosphere in which you had a chance to grow and find yourself."
—Rabbi Marc H. Tanenbaum, reminiscing in 1980
about the Jewish Theological Seminary

THE MOMENT THE IDEA OCCURRED to him, Herman Tanenbaum was
eager to take the entrance exam for the Jewish Theological Seminary of
America (JTS), the nation's preeminent Conservative Jewish seminary.
It had been founded in 1887 in several rooms of an Orthodox institution, Congregation Shearith Israel, also known as the Spanish and
Portuguese Synagogue, on 19th Street, just west of Fifth Avenue. After
a few subsequent relocations, JTS was ultimately moved to its present
site at 3080 Broadway. Its grand Georgian-style buildings, designed by
the architectural firm Gehron & Ross, reflected the seminary's stature
as a spiritual and academic center of Conservative Judaism.

At 8:30 on the morning of September 9, 1946, Herman made
his way to the seminary's Teachers Institute Building, located on the
northeast corner of Broadway and 122nd Street, to begin the rigorous
admission examinations.

Both he and his friend Harold Shulweis did well on those examinations and were accepted as rabbinical students by the seminary, the flagship institution of Conservative Judaism in the United States. Classes for the academic year 1946–1947 would begin following the High Holy Days. They were enrolling at the beginning of what would come to be referred to as the seminary's "Finkelstein era." From 1940 to 1972, the noted Cincinnati-born rabbi and scholar Louis Finkelstein—himself a graduate of the seminary and successor as chancellor to such notable rabbi-scholars as Sabato Morais, Solomon Schechter, and Cyrus Adler—made numerous innovations.

This was the beginning of Conservative Judaism's golden age. The leadership of the movement were superstars—brilliant, articulate, modern, charismatic. Rabbi Finkelstein made a priority of reaching out to and engaging the American public via broadcast media. The seminary developed *The Eternal Light*, a dramatic series that began in 1945 and for several decades was aired every Sunday afternoon on radio and later on television. Scripts were written initially by the highly regarded author and dramatist Morton Wishengrad, with the participation of major Jewish personalities of the day. *The Eternal Light* explored Judaism and the religion's holy days in the context of history, literature, and social issues. It was designed to be accessible and interesting to people of other faiths. Herman, who by this time had significant experience as a writer, would become one of the program's research assistants and, for four years, its scriptwriter.

Rabbi Finkelstein also made major academic appointments to the faculty, including the Talmudic scholar Saul Lieberman, who joined such distinguished scholars as Boaz Cohen, H. L. Ginsberg, Louis Ginzberg, Robert Gordis, Alexander Marx, and Mordechai Menahem Kaplan. Moshe Davis was appointed to the faculty in 1942; Shalom Spiegel in 1943; and, most significantly for Herman Tanenbaum, the eminent Polish-born scholar and theologian Rabbi Abraham Joshua Heschel, in 1945.

JTS classes began at nine o'clock each weekday morning and ran through the late afternoon, except on Friday, when students prepared for the Jewish Sabbath, which begins at sundown. Each student was required to participate in a minimum of two elective seminars and submit two term papers during his year of study. Herman reveled in what he would call "an intellectually free atmosphere," one devoid of the oppression that he felt had dogged his days at Yeshiva College. While there were religious services, attendance was not mandatory. "Nobody was going to hit you over the head if you didn't go," he would observe years later. "You weren't looked on as an infidel by the faculty members."

Herman would retain vivid memories of his residence in the seminary's comfortable living quarters, consisting of two-bedroom suites. His roommate was Harold Weisberg, "a brilliant philosophy major who turned out to be a radical socialist." Harold spent his spare time traveling to Union Square to stand on a soapbox and preach to the masses. He was fond of buttonholing Herman in the bathroom and challenging him to prove the existence of God. Their freewheeling discussions often degenerated into screaming matches that would last until three or four o'clock in the morning. One night, during a verbal joust between the roommates, a visiting novelist who was bunking next door barged through their door, shouting, "Will you people please go to sleep? You are not going to solve that problem tonight *in the john*! Get the hell out of there; I want to go to sleep!"

Repeating his Yeshiva College pattern, Herman concentrated on the subjects that really interested him, namely, Jewish history, philosophy, and literature. Meanwhile, he continued to regard Talmudic studies as being remote from contemporary life and human needs, and he paid less attention to that discipline.

Herman also found time then to explore the art of poetry writing. A number of his verses were subtly romantic in nature, likely the result of his having met and dated the young relatives of his classmates or young women from other schools in the area, including Barnard College and the City College of New York (CCNY). For example, in December 1946, in a verse titled "Frustrate," Herman reveals conflicted emotions regarding sexual stirrings and the necessity of observing religious proscriptions against acting on one's desires.

Another of his poems, written the following spring, was titled "Labyrinthine Heart." The original text was embellished with Herman's handwritten inscription, "To the partner of an astonishingly wonderful relationship!" The poem suggested that he may have become involved in a meaningful relationship:

I took my heart in hand
and looked through it.
Nothing could be seen
for inflamed, festered tissue
Enveloped, beveiled the
Pumping soul.

With scalpel's shimmering edge
I incised the veiling, opaque tissue
Thru the rent aperture I peered
To fathom the mystery of
Passion, heart, mind.

Probed, I probe
And widen the breach did I.
But more did I gaze an' seek
Less did I know
Less could I comprehend the maze.

Mending temporarily the cut
I placed the torn heart
Within the bosom well
Leaving it to heal with time,
Leaving it till mind could comprehend
the incised, festering heart.

(Conceived wistfully on a
morbid morn sprinkled abundantly
with lurid moonlight . . . 4/6/47)

In "Anvil Tones," an undated verse on a totally different theme, Herman
seemed to be pondering the impact of the Holocaust, and he invoked
Jewish and Christian imagery:

Peace, called they, and
Good will bellowed lustily
But hollow the sham
Did din on crushed souls.

The prince prophecy glorious
On page engraved
But in disciples' soul
Sham—lip mockery.

O, how long must
Circumcised hearts
Smart under blessures
Chiseled with Christian love?

Abraham's sires turned
The cheek over and o'er
Yet butchered the Pius sword
To the anvil-ring:
"Peace, good-will".

In sepulchrous grave,
The prince, if he be,
Muttered: The words are mine
But thine the hypocrisy.

Meanwhile, Herman's next major academic achievement came in spring 1947, when he was one of two students given awards during the seminary's commencement exercises on June 8.

His burgeoning rabbinic career was unfolding alongside significant historical markers. Less than six months later, on November 29, 1947, the UN General Assembly approved Resolution 181, which called for the partition of Palestine into Jewish and Arab states. As the delegates cast their voice votes, Jewish families throughout the world, including the Tanenbaums in Baltimore and their son Herman in New York, sat by their radio consoles tabulating the results. Finally, with thirty-three nations voting in favor, thirteen opposed, and ten abstaining, the resolution, known as the Partition Plan, was passed. Six months after that, on the warm afternoon of May 14, 1948, David Ben-Gurion, the leader of the Mandate-era Yishuv, ascended the dais at the Tel Aviv Museum of Art to read the new Jewish state's declaration of independence.

The destiny of the Jewish people would be forever changed. The creation of the Jewish state led almost immediately to armed attacks by the armies of Egypt, Iraq, Jordan, Lebanon, Saudi Arabia, and Syria. That conflict would go down in history as Israel's War of Independence.

Surprisingly, the events of November 1947 through the following spring did not necessarily resonate positively among the administration and faculty of the JTS. For example, the singing of "Hatikvah," Israel's national anthem, was not permitted at that year's graduation ceremonies, or for some years to come, according to Herman's schoolmate Myron Fenster. Many years later, in 2012, Myron, now Rabbi Fenster, acknowledged that inquiries regarding the post–Independence War banning of the singing of "Hatikvah" on campus raise certain "very delicate questions." He added, "This was the decision and the students didn't like it! And they always spoke of various rebellions."

This reflected a theological tension at JTS that mirrored a concern in Orthodox circles. As Rabbi Fenster explained, "Religious Jewry always had a strain of (being) very pro-Israel—part of the daily prayers of every Jew are: 'We build, O God Jerusalem; help us to rebuild

Jerusalem, Amen; God help us to rebuild Jerusalem with compassion, with peace.'" The view that the creation of the State of Israel should await the coming of the Messiah was not only an article of faith among very Orthodox Jews, it also infused the thinking of some Conservative Jews, as well. "And, also," Rabbi Fenster said, "who was rebuilding Palestine in those days? It was the secular element, the kibbutz movement, *Halutzim*, not known for their religious fervor. Many people saw that as an antithesis to what they had dreamt about and hoped for, as to what would be the nature of the new Jewish State."

During the 1948–1949 academic year, Herman's weekly schedule of courses was taught by professors who constitute a Who's Who of 20th Century American Jewish life. For those who knew the world of Conservative Jewish thinkers, Herman's schedule was the theological equivalent of an All-Star team.

Herman took a course in medieval Jewish history, which was taught by Rabbi Abraham Joshua Heschel. During that academic year, Professor Heschel's scholarship and personal values had a profound impact on Herman's worldview. At a time when Herman should have been exhilarated by the intellectual ferment surrounding him, he was despondent because his beloved father's health was steadily deteriorating. During Herman's senior year, Abraham had suffered a heart attack. The young rabbinical student—who had forsaken his father's dream—was overcome with concern for his father's health and with guilt for being in New York, instead of at home in Baltimore to comfort Sadie and Sima.

On the morning that he learned of his father's heart attack, Herman happened to encounter Rabbi Heschel as they were both entering an elevator. The great scholar, sensing his student's distress and wanting to ease his pain, said, "Something is bothering you; come into my office." As soon as teacher and student were alone, Herman broke down and cried as he told Rabbi Heschel of his father's heart attack and of his concern for his mother and sister. The rabbi immediately picked up his telephone and called Sadie in Baltimore to comfort her. "It was like *God* calling!" Herman said. Thus began the enduring bond between teacher and student. As Herman would one day recall, "I fell in love with him."

Rabbi Heschel's daughter, Dr. Susannah Heschel, said that her father's gesture toward his troubled student was "very typical of how he was—he knew how to be a rabbi; he knew how to comfort someone, to be attentive, to be what nowadays we call 'pastoral,' to be a '*Seelsorge*,' someone who takes care of your soul, as they used to say in Germany."

Susannah Heschel remembers Herman as "a very *warm* person, tall, handsome, smart, very polite, and very well-mannered, very dignified." Herman would become very much a presence in her family's life. "My father often referred to him and met with him and talked to him; he was devoted to my father and was a good friend," she recalled.

Herman's despondency over Abraham's ongoing health problems was relieved by visits from Sima. She was now grown and living in Greenwich Village, the center of New York City's vibrant bohemian culture. Aspiring to a career in the visual arts, she had taken a course at the Maryland Institute in Baltimore. Then, wishing to spread her wings, she moved to Manhattan, where she made and wore a red cape befitting her new identity as an artist.

Sima was torn, however, because of her mother's opposition to her decision to pursue a career. While charitable and friendly with her Gentile neighbors, Sadie had feared that having grown up in a largely Christian neighborhood, her only daughter would become romantically involved with a non-Jew. She wanted Sima to marry as soon as possible, settle down, and have children.

Sima, aware of Sadie's hopes for her future yet determined to realize her dream, turned to Herman for advice. He understood both her yearning to express herself artistically and their mother's concern. Sima believed that her brother possessed "the wisdom of the ages," a virtue that had enabled him to reorder his religious identity. "Do what you feel is the right thing," Herman said. Sima did precisely that. She became a jewelry designer and then returned to Baltimore and married a Jewish lawyer named Herbert Scherr, with whom she would have two children, Abby and Adam.

During Sima's stay in New York, there were often lighthearted moments between sister and brother. One Sunday, while waiting to move into the apartment she had rented, Sima appealed to Herman for help. His next-door neighbor at the seminary happened to be away for the weekend, and so he said that Sima could stay in his room. "So we're walking down the hallway of the dormitory—he's carrying my suitcase and I'm walking behind him—and doors start opening up," Sima recalled. "And I thought: 'Oh, my, he's going to get it tomorrow!'"

While Sima enjoyed Herman's company enormously, she was concerned about his smoking and black coffee consumption—excesses she attributed to "a lot of pressure in all his various writings and demands," including his scriptwriting for *The Eternal Light*. Herman was living with that pressure at the time in the hope of "getting this writing thing out of my system." Rather than affording him the opportunity to do so, however, his four-year span of creativity with Morton Wishengrad and *The Eternal Light* was leading to his further immersion in literary pursuits. He became a contributor of articles to Jewish newspapers and was hired as the *Jewish Post*'s New York bureau chief, two opportunities he thought would provide him "entrée to study Jewish life and the important things that were happening" in that community.

The very industrious rabbinical student was also doing public relations for the seminary, as well as for major Jewish organizations including the Mizrachi Organization of America, the Rabbinical Assembly (the association of Conservative Rabbis), the Jewish Reconstructionist Foundation, the National Women's League (composed of women in the Conservative movement), and the New York Board of Rabbis.

Not all of Herman's time was being spent in pursuit of academic excellence, extracurricular activities, and employment as a publicist, however. Having shed the baby fat of his childhood—he was now nearly six feet tall and slender—he was becoming more confident and outgoing.

As Herman approached his graduation from JTS, he was still dogged by the same issues he had grappled with while an undergraduate at Yeshiva College. These centered around his very serious doubts, "theologically and religiously, about the relevance of the ritualistic parts of the tradition." Only this time he was questioning the Conservative branch of Judaism instead of Orthodoxy.

So ambivalent was Herman that he had written a paper on the ancient ritual of sacrifice, which, in his words, "upset one of my professors terribly." Among the questions he raised was: "Is [sacrifice] really essential to the faith, this primitive stage of development we had to pass through?" Herman said that his questioning attitude caused certain faculty members "to feel that they were raising a heretic" and that it would be "better to take care of him beforehand." And so, according to Herman, "Rabbi Finkelstein used to call me in occasionally to give me a long lecture about the importance of religious observance and being a religious leader to your people, and all that."

Despite Herman's theological rebelliousness, on the afternoon of June 18, 1950, on the occasion of the Jewish Theological Seminary's fifty-sixth annual commencement ceremony, he was one of seventeen graduating students ordained as "Rabbi, Teacher and Preacher" with the degree of Master of Hebrew Literature. During the ceremony, the honorary degree of Doctor of Hebrew Letters was conferred on Harry J. Carman, Dean of Columbia College, and Simon H. Rifkind, a former federal judge. Both Simon Rifkind and his son, the prominent attorney Robert Rifkin—the latter having dropped the final "d" from the family surname—would one day work closely with Herman at the American Jewish Committee, the judge as a lay leader of the agency and his son as its president.

Herman celebrated his graduation in a unique manner. He had long disliked his first name, and after graduation from the seminary, he decided to style himself as "Marc." In consideration of his parents, however, he retained Herman as his middle name.

Marc went on to work for about a year as the religion correspondent of *Time* magazine, writing several cover stories. One of them was about Rabbi Finkelstein. At *Time*, Marc encountered genteel anti-Semitism, as well as a social culture replete with drug and alcohol excesses and alleged wife swapping, and he soon decided to move on.

After establishing his own firm, Marc H. Tanenbaum and Associates, he joined the publishing house of Henry Schuman, where he served as both public relations director and literary editor. Marc proved to be unusually gifted in his latter role. He had an eye for fine literature, and one of his major acquisitions was the manuscript of Rabbi Heschel's *The Earth Is the Lord's*, his close friend and mentor's first book written in the English language.

Rabbi Heschel had sent Marc the manuscript, which he read and liked. Going to Schuman, Marc said, "Henry, you absolutely must publish this book!" and the receptive publisher agreed to do so. Marc served as Rabbi Heschel's editor and commissioned an artist to illustrate *The Earth Is the Lord's* with woodcuts. Marc also arranged for the eminent Protestant theologian Reinhold Niebuhr to review *The Earth Is the Lord's*. That effort not only contributed to the book's success, but also marked the beginning of Niebuhr's enduring relationship with Rabbi Heschel.

By fall 1952, however, Marc's multifaceted endeavors were beginning to take their toll. He was simply exhausted, and, as Sima recalled, "He was smoking too many cigars," a new passion. Marc's workload was overwhelming, and his father was increasingly ill. As a devoted son and a rabbi, how could he possibly continue to pursue his very stimulating life in New York when he felt responsible for helping Sadie and Sima care for Abraham? It was becoming abundantly clear to Marc that he needed a sabbatical so that he could return to Baltimore, at least temporarily.

There was yet another reason for Marc's homecoming at that moment: he yearned to write a fictionalized account of life in Depression-era Baltimore. In order to do so, this first-generation American who had achieved so much at such a young age needed to return to his roots in what he called "this poor neighborhood, surrounded by incredible stimuli."

CHAPTER FOUR

The Return
of the Prodigal Son

"I thought I had a novel in my belly."
                —Rabbi Tanenbaum in 1980, on his literary ambitions

MUCH HAD CHANGED IN THE Tanenbaum family's circumstances besides Abraham's medical condition by the time of Marc's return to Baltimore. His older brother, Ernie, was now the manager of radio station WGAY in Silver Springs, Maryland. He had changed his last name to "Tannen" and had gone into show business prior to World War II as a member of the Alliance Players. Later, he would marry Ada Rhea Cohen, a member of that little theater troupe. As for Sadie, Abraham, and Sima, they had moved from the house on Light Street where they had lived and worked for more than a quarter century to 4012 Hilton Road. Marc joined them there in the fall of 1952.

In addition to assisting his mother and sister in caring for Abraham, the ever-industrious young rabbi also had to earn money, so he taught Hebrew at Temple Beth El, which was conveniently located near Hilton Road. Marc would become a close colleague of the congregation's prominent spiritual leader, Rabbi Jacob B. Agus.

Marc was also eager to begin to fulfill his ambitions as a writer.

But at that juncture in his life, he received a letter with an intriguing offer. Dated November 24, 1952, it was from Abraham Rockmore, the first vice president of the Northeast Hebrew Congregation, in nearby Washington, D.C. Writing as the chairman of this Conservative congregation's "Committee to Engage a Rabbi," Rockmore was offering Marc the pulpit there. The Korean War had broken out two summers earlier, and the Congregation's temporary rabbi, Louis Barish, was awaiting orders to go to the Far East as an Army chaplain.

Rockmore informed Marc that Rabbi Wolfe Kelman of the seminary's Commission on Rabbinic Placement had proposed Rabbi Tanenbaum. He suggested that Marc join the congregation for Friday night and Shabbat as a visiting rabbi on the weekend of December 25–26.

Marc was indeed eminently qualified, even at a young age, to serve a major urban congregation. After all, he had conducted services or served as a weekend rabbi at several prestigious synagogues, including Temple Beth El in Baltimore, under Rabbi Agus's supervision; Temple Beth El, in Easton, Maryland; Congregations Adath Jeshurun and Beth Am, both in Philadelphia; Temple Beth El, in Utica, New York; Kehilath Jeshurun, in Boston; and the Park Avenue Synagogue on Manhattan's Upper East Side. A Baltimore luminary, Judah Nadich, had become the senior rabbi there, and Marc conducted the overflow High Holy Day services. (He almost didn't make it. Park Avenue Synagogue had booked him a room in a nearby hotel so that he could walk to services. Just as he was preparing to leave, he got locked in the bathroom and couldn't get out. He did make it to services and apparently was deemed to have done a good job despite his unnerving experience.)

Marc was willing to consider Rockmore's offer, albeit with several caveats. Replying to the synagogue chairman's letter four days later, he wrote:

> I am currently involved in writing a book and am therefore only
> free to accept a weekend position. I am not clear whether your

congregation is considering this type of candidacy or only that of full-time candidates. If the former, I shall be glad to visit with you on the stipulated date of December 26.

He added, "Forgive me, but I do not easily discuss 'salary' and much less so in a letter. Could we save this for a conversation?"

More correspondence between the search committee chairman and the young rabbi followed. On December 11, Marc told Rockmore he would conduct Shabbat services, but ultimately, he begged off on the original date because of ill health. He did eventually preside over the Congregation's Shabbat services, an experience he said was "singularly enjoyable." Nonetheless, in one of two letters written to Rockmore on January 21, 1953, he reiterated that he was not willing to assume a full-time position.

The Northeast Hebrew Congregation's Board of Directors accepted his conditions, and Marc celebrated his first Shabbat there on February 3, 1953. According to the terms of Marc's agreement with the Congregation, his compensation would be $200 per month for the conducting of services from February through May 31. Furthermore, it was agreed that shortly before the conclusion of Marc's three-month commitment, the Congregation would consider whether to retain him as its full-time rabbi. But even if no such agreement were to be reached, Marc would agree to conduct the Congregation's 1953 High Holiday services for the fee Marc requested: $600.

Given Marc's long-held interest in interfaith relations, he was pleased to learn that on February 20, the Congregation would observe National Brotherhood Week, and the guest sermonizer would be the Rev. Carl G. Howie, pastor of the Sherwood Presbyterian Church.

Meanwhile, at the age of twenty-seven, Marc was nominated for inclusion in both *Who's Who in America* and *Who's Who in World Jewry*.

While Marc's work with the synagogue seemed to be going well, on May 12, Marc wrote to A. B. Kapplin, an official of his new shul, saying that he wished to spare his frequent weekend hosts, "the wonderful Claymans," the inconvenience of having him share their home every Shabbat, and that he was requesting funds amounting to "12–15 dollars" weekly for a hotel room and food. "Now for me the most difficult part of this writing," Marc went on:

> I've been trying to see my way clear to dispose of my complicated and personally distressing family situation, to finish my increasingly neglected book, and to accept the position with your wonderful people.
>
> The more I have tried to work this out, the less I am able to see how I can manage it. It is a certainty that I cannot make a final dissolution of my family affairs before the next six or eight months, if then. Knowing how trying all of this has been until now, I am quite convinced that when, please God, I have finally unraveled this, I shall be more emotionally drained than I already am, which is hardly a background out of which to launch immediately into such an important effort as the developing and helping grow of a new congregation.

Marc, clearly anguishing over his decision, wrote that had circumstances been different, he and the Hebrew Congregation "would have made a first-rate *shidduch*." But given Marc's personal situation at that difficult time in his life, he felt that it would be unfair of him to "have me attached to you while a heavy umbilical cord tugs me elsewhere."

Having given up his pulpit, in the summer of 1953, Marc was free to concentrate on his novel. And so, despite his commitment to his family, he was prepared to embark on a more concentrated process of self-discovery. He needed a distraction-free place where he could concentrate. Luckily, Ernie knew a farmer who owned a shack on the side of a mountain in western Maryland and who agreed to rent it out. While the rustic place lacked both running water and electricity, it would be the ideal place for Marc to work for a time.

Camping there in not-so-splendid isolation, he would be awakened every morning by the mooing of cows roaming around outside. Leaving the shack, he would trek down the hill to a gas station, relieve himself in the men's restroom, fill a large can with water for washing and drinking, purchase enough food for that day's meals, and then make his way back to his primitive aerie. Then he would devote the remainder of the day to writing. Later, his sister Sima would recall, "I vividly remember taking a pot of cooked food which my mother prepared so that her 'Chaimie' would not starve."

Within a week of Marc's arrival on the mountain, however, he was facing an all-too-familiar dilemma: he was virtually penniless. But this time, unlike the moment years earlier when he had been so traumatized on opening a nearly empty cash register in the family store in Baltimore, he felt empowered: he could earn some quick money writing short stories, for which there was a still a flourishing magazine market in the early 1950s.

One of these stories, which was undated, was semiautobiographical and revelatory. It clearly reflected Marc's attitude about the strictures of religious orthodoxy as well as his feelings about the power of prayer. As the story begins, the narrator, at times appearing more the protagonist, reflecting Marc's experience as a scriptwriter for *The Eternal Light*, explains to the reader: "To begin with, I'm not suggestible. My friends accuse me of having no imagination and that's alright with me, I plead guilty. What's more, I want to stay that way and that's why I think the story I have to tell has its point."

His character goes on to explain that three years earlier, while spending the night in his younger brother Harry's dormitory room in an orthodox Jewish seminary—"He's not like me at all"—at about three o'clock in the morning he was awakened by loud pounding on the door—"Someone was knocking as if he wanted to break the door down, enough to wake my kid brother up, which means it was only slightly less than earthquake proportions."

The door-pounding individual turns out to be "a short youngster with red hair" who says that his mother, who lives in Cincinnati, is sick and in a coma. Wishing to assemble a minyan, the quorum of ten Jews needed so that prayers can be said for his mother, he invites Harry and his visiting brother to join him in his own room. They oblige, and as they

make their way to the anxious student's room in the chill night air—
the younger boy suggests that the heat be turned off after 11 o'clock—
Harry's brother asks, "Aren't you supposed to do this at the bedside?" He
wonders: will prayer work "if we're in NY and his ma's in Cincinnati?"

Harry shoots his big brother "a dirty look," and the visitor thinks:
"All right, don't answer. You can be a rabbi if you want to, but I still
can't take this voodoo seriously." The brothers arrive in the distraught
boy's room to find it filled with very sleepy boys ranging from the ages
of fourteen to sixteen. The sick woman's son then leads the group in
prayer. The skeptical older brother is touched by their ardent entreaties.
As he observes in an aside to the reader:

> There is something about reading the psalms in the middle of
> the night, in a hushed voice; it leaves you with a kind of sober
> excitement, in spite of myself this thing was getting through
> to me.

The hours pass. At four o'clock, a "wild-eyed kid" rushes into the room
and hands a telegram to the red-headed boy. He tears it open, sobs, and
then reads:

> The doctors say mother will get well.
> Father

What is the older brother's conclusion?

> You may think it was penicillin but I know that it was the 10
> kids in bathrobes in a room on Washington Heights. But, of
> course, I don't expect you to believe me.

Marc's summertime sojourn on that rural mountain—his Walden—
permitted him to write the novel he had been determined to produce.
In this revelatory effort, which survives in manuscript form, Marc
clearly drew inspiration for his characters from the plight of gentile

newcomers to the Light Street neighborhood of his youth—people he knew while living opposite the bucket factory because they shopped in the Tanenbaum family's store.

In Marc's detailed five-page-long typewritten synopsis of the manuscript—direct quotes are reproduced here with *his* punctuation—he described a family "happy on farm (secure in food material, content in being producers, united in common effort)." Their lives begin to come unglued, however, when, as Marc described the downward trajectory of their existence, they "Come to the city (to establish a 'future' for growing children, to ease the work of farm-life, to educate children, to get them wives, to enjoy civilized blessings—cars, toilets, radio, gas, electricity, washing machines).

"To survive in the city," Marc's synopsis continued, "they must get jobs in factory." When Willie, the father in Marc's story, worked, "there was great hope for future (children went to school but quickly fed up because they were in lower classes, they were outdoor kids and couldn't stand indoors)." Marc's story ended in tragedy: Willie, the family's breadwinner, is laid off from work, the family seems to fall apart, Willie dies, and the bruised survivors' wistful dreams of returning to the farm are ended.

While Marc was writing about the lives of rural gentiles, he is obviously expressing the aspirations of immigrants like his parents—absent, of course, any hint of despair or the specter of anti-Semitism that had impelled the Jews' migration from shtetl to city.

In a separate four-page-long addendum, Marc provided intriguing descriptions of his main characters. Gracie, "about 45, who lives in the corner house near the bucket factory, supervises gate entrance for trucks"; Willy, her husband; their eldest son, Albert, 26, "lean, wide-nostrils, blond, blue-eyes, false teeth," resembles Britain's King George VI; the middle son, the "headstrong" Henry, 24; the "superstitious, stringy, nervous, jumping, sly, honest" Robbie, 21; their blonde kid sister, Margie, 16, "with black teeth from cavities"; and Howard, 50, the new garage mechanic, and Gracie's love interest, "Appealing to office women (left impression of exciting, freshman), cover up of vacuum of loneliness and want of companionship and home-maker."

One other character, Mrs. Levin, the neighborhood's kindly Jewish storekeeper—obviously modeled on Sadie Tanenbaum—is mentioned in the synopsis. One day when Gracie comes into the store, Mrs. Levin notices that she "looks troubled." She listens as Gracie unburdens herself: she had wanted to leave Willie "long ago." And now she can't pay her store bill because she has to buy medicine for her ailing, underachieving husband.

Marc, too, may have been concerned with finances as he sketched out Gracie's traits. At the top of page one of his handwritten version of "Character Descriptions," he has scrawled the number 75,000, divided by 20, equaling 3,750. Was he trying to figure out a twenty-month budget should he sell his novel?

At summer's end, his sojourn on the mountain over, Marc seemed to have put aside his literary ambitions. He does not seek to get his manuscript published. Instead, Marc was turning his attention to yet another interest: his growing belief in the importance to humanity of better interfaith understanding and harmony. He had begun working as the public relations director of the Synagogue Council of America, the central Jewish religious agency in the United States whose purpose was to promote fellowship and cooperation among the Orthodox, Conservative, and Reform movements and to represent the Jewish community to the government as well as to Christian organizations.

In early 1954, Rabbi Meyer Passow was resigning his position as the executive director of the Synagogue Council of America. Passow would go on to become the general manager of the New York and Tel Aviv offices of the Israel Tourist Service, and Rabbi Tanenbaum was asked to become the Synagogue Council's "acting executive director." On March 4, 1954, the council issued a press release from its headquarters at 110 West 42nd Street, in Manhattan, announcing Marc's appointment to that post. He would go on to assume the title of "executive director" in 1955. At the age of twenty-eight, Marc was the youngest professional leader in the agency's history.

He was ready to begin his quest of fulfilling the Biblical admonition: To Be a Light unto the Nations.

PART II

THE BRIDGE BUILDER WHO SERVED AS "SECRETARY OF STATE FOR THE JEWS"

CHAPTER 5

Shaking up the Synagogue Council of America

"The Orthodox were not opposed to having social action cooperation with Christians, but they didn't want any 'God-talk' and Marc
believed it was necessary to have so-called God-talk—to be able to
talk religion with Christians—and he couldn't do it at the Synagogue
Council."

—Judith Banki, former assistant director,
Interreligious Affairs, American Jewish Committee

WHILE THE YOUNG RABBI MARC Tanenbaum was half the age of many
of those who headed major Jewish community organizations, he possessed an indispensable attribute for attaining both personal harmony
and professional achievement: self-knowledge. He had the courage
during his student days at Yeshiva College to contemplate the world
beyond the Orthodox community he had been born into. Even then,
he realized that he could not remain within that world. And, having
briefly held a variety of pulpits, he realized that his true calling lay in
ecumenical outreach. He felt so passionately about his destiny that he
summoned the courage to go against the grain of the expectations of
those dearest to him: his parents, Sadie and Abraham.

Now, on assuming his new position at the Synagogue Council, he knew exactly what he wanted to accomplish. And he knew how to go about realizing his goal. Being the executive director of the Synagogue Council, he believed, would afford him the platform to convince the leadership of the American Jewish community that it must take an active role in public life. Otherwise, he feared that the community would be even more marginalized than it had been prior to the establishment of the modern State of Israel, and anti-Semitism would not decrease.

On assuming his seemingly ideal leadership position, he thought that he would flourish, but this would not turn out to be the case. In fact, his tenure at the Synagogue Council of America may have been compromised almost from its very inception by the organization's roots. The Synagogue Council had been established early in 1926 by a small number of individuals who had highly ambitious— but also highly unrealistic—goals of bridging the rabbinical and congregational interests of its constituent groups and of speaking with a united voice, while not interfering with the constituents' individual autonomy.

Two years earlier, in January 1924, Rabbi Abram Simon, president of the Central Conference of American Rabbis, a Reform group, had suggested that there should be cooperation among all of American Jewry's religious movements. Then in January 1925, Rabbi Simon offered a resolution during a gathering at the Union of American Hebrew Congregations, calling for a meeting to be held to discuss the disparate groups' commonalities.

Their disagreements, however, would frequently outweigh their commonalities. Thus, Marc's nearly seven-year-long tenure at the Synagogue Council would be fraught with frustration, particularly for someone so open to a broad range of concepts. In fact, the cleavages were deep, particularly between the Orthodox and Reform movements (and those tensions continue into the present day).

Nonetheless, foreshadowing what the rabbi would one day achieve as the American Jewish Committee's director of Interreligious Affairs,

Marc had several meaningful achievements during his tenure at the Synagogue Council. Within the context of 1950s Christian-Jewish relations, for example, he succeeded in reaching out to several of the more controversial Christian leaders, including televangelists and primates of the Greek Orthodox Church. And in an early demonstration of his passionate belief in justice for the African American community, he made common cause with Dr. Martin Luther King Jr.

Marc was a strong believer in the separation of church and state, but he was also a strong believer in utilizing the intersection of religion and public policy as fertile ground for interreligious understanding. Rabbi Tanenbaum served as a presidential adviser during the first Eisenhower Administration (and he would go on to offer counsel to subsequent administrations).

The rabbi's early months as the Synagogue Council's executive director were marked by a burst of energy that would be characteristic of his career. He initiated creative programs to revitalize the largely moribund agency; no issue was too small to attract his attention or too formidable to be addressed. In addition to producing a variety of boilerplate statements for the High Holy Days, as well as for Labor Day, a Religion and Press Day, and a Day of Prayer on September 22, he organized a daylong "General Assembly" in which leaders of the Orthodox, Conservative, and Reform rabbinic and lay movements met under Synagogue Council auspices to discuss "areas of agreement on major moral, social, and religious issues."

He was not shy about announcing these activities. In a memorandum circulated just before Thanksgiving titled "In Less Than Eleven Weeks the Synagogue Council of America Represented *You* in These Ways," the new executive director informed constituent organizations of the agency's accomplishments. They included meetings between Synagogue Council representatives and officials of the National Council of Churches and the National Catholic Welfare Conference in order to develop a trifaith approach for the implementation of local community relations projects, "with special emphasis on problems of Negroes in (the) South."

The memo also noted that the Synagogue Council expressed its opposition to a proposed amendment to the US Constitution "to recognize the authority and law of Jesus Christ." Other Synagogue Council initiatives mentioned included a reception scheduled to honor a Danish schoolmaster who had helped save the lives of Jewish refugees during the Holocaust as well as cosponsorship of a three-day conference on religion and the public schools and a "blueprinted" nationwide movement to encourage synagogue and church attendance in cooperation with non-Jewish religious leaders. The Synagogue Council also advised the national Boy and Girl Scouts movements regarding religious programs for Jewish children, planned a January 1955 conference of twenty-five Synagogue Council–sponsored prison chaplains to "help improve religious services to Jewish inmates in correctional institutions," and began preparations for a radio program to be produced by Rabbi Tanenbaum and aired on the Mutual Network, one of the major national radio networks.

The Synagogue Council's new executive director, as if to reinforce in readers' minds the singularity of the agency, concluded this communication with the words: "The Synagogue Council of America is the only central national Jewish Agency which represents American Jewry as a religious community." To underscore that point—and perhaps to convince *himself* that he has made the correct career decision—Rabbi Tanenbaum wrote: "IF THE SYNAGOGUE COUNCIL DID NOT EXIST, WE WOULD HAVE TO CREATE IT."

As the rabbi continued the Synagogue Council's public relations and outreach campaigns, he was also dealing with the myriad internal Synagogue Council organizational duties required of an executive director. They included policy making, speechmaking, writing book reviews and articles on Jewish themes, and fund-raising. An adept promoter of the agency, he significantly strengthened its financial base.

The Synagogue Council's executive director's many responsibilities and pressures were leaving him scant time to pursue personal matters. Aware of his parents' solid partnership in the face of many financial and health-related issues, he understood the importance of having the companionship of a loving helpmate.

So, in 1955, one year into his sojourn with the agency, the thirty-year-old bachelor decided that the time had come to turn his attention to marrying and starting a family of his own. He had two years earlier met a woman he thought would be the ideal companion and helpmate with whom to share his life.

In 1953, Helga Weiss, who was four and a half years younger than Marc, was a school psychologist-in-training with the Bureau of Child Guidance at the New York City Board of Education. Marc was taken at that time not only with Helga's good looks, but with her intellect. She had been elected to Phi Beta Kappa at Hunter College in Manhattan, where she had graduated cum laude before earning a master's degree at Columbia University. (Years later, she would go on to earn a PhD at Columbia's Teachers College.) Marc's life was very full at that time. Not only was he administering the Synagogue Council's many programs and grappling with the agency's increasingly apparent problems, he was serving as a member of the Board of Directors of both Religion in American Life and the United Seamen's Service. He was also running his public relations firm, Marc H. Tanenbaum & Associates, with offices at 140 West 42nd Street, Suite 907, just west of the Synagogue Council's headquarters, and he was serving as a partner in Galtran Associates, another public relations firm, located not far away, at 489 Fifth Avenue.

Nevertheless, he found time to woo Helga. They became engaged on February 3, 1955. A little more than three months later, on May 22, they were married at the Hotel Riverside Plaza. The young couple moved into an apartment at 83–06 Vietor Avenue, in Elmhurst, Queens, just across the East River from Manhattan and an easy subway commute to their respective weekday destinations. Later on, in the 1960s, they would relocate to an apartment on a tree-lined street in nearby Jackson Heights.

Helga Weiss's journey to the United States is worth noting, as it is illustrative of the journeys of many European-born Jews of that era. She had been born to Dr. and Mrs. Harry Weiss on February 6, 1930, in Cologne, Germany. Less than three years later, the Weimar government collapsed, and Adolf Hitler became chancellor and führer. As the Nazis' persecution of Jews increased, Helga's parents managed to send her, by herself, to safety in the United States via the Netherlands and Britain.

Helga was nine years old when, on November 10, 1939, exactly one year after the devastating attacks of Kristallnacht, she finally reached New York. Although Helga and her parents would be reunited after the war, it may well be that she never really recovered from the trauma of their long separation.

Marc was smitten with Helga. In his typical fashion of linking his work and his private life, Marc Tanenbaum & Associates issued a press release in 1954 enthusing about the appearance of "the lovely and youthful New York City schoolteacher, 24-year-old Helga Weiss," who would be appearing "before the cameras of WNBC (Channel 4) to introduce the 'The Fourth R.'"

Following their marriage, when Marc's rapidly increasing out-of-town commitments required his absence for extended periods of time, he sought to include Helga in his travels. In the late spring of 1956, he was invited by Rabbi Gershon Hadas, the spiritual leader of Congregation Beth Shalom, in Kansas City, Missouri, to officiate over the Congregation's Rosh Hashanah "Assembly Service" as well as over certain Yom Kippur services during the coming High Holy Days.

In his letter of invitation, Rabbi Hadas stated, "I have been authorized to allow $1,650.00 for your services which amount is to include all expenses"—including, of course, travel expenses. Ten days later, on June 25, Rabbi Tanenbaum asked about "providing for the travel of my wife." Given that Helga, then on the faculty of Queens College, could not remain in Kansas City for the duration of the High Holy Days, he was seeking additional funds to cover what he referred to as her "one-voyage out and back for Rosh Hashanah."

Driving his point home with a dramatic flourish, he mixed a little Yiddish with an allusion to a Shakespearean character in *Much Ado About Nothing*: Benedict, a longtime bachelor now newly married. The rabbi wanted his wife to join him, he said, "because being a Benedict of one year in the expensive process of establishing a homestead presses this matter of '*kemah*' home with singular poignancy." (Replying on

August 8 to Rabbi Tanenbaum's imaginative request for additional funds, Rabbi Hadas said it would be impossible to go back to the shul's committee and get additional travel money.)

Meanwhile, Rabbi Tanenbaum also stated that he "should like very much to take advantage of your kind offer to arrange for a meeting with the Rabbinical Association in your area during the course of my visit." The rabbi added that he wanted to do so in the hope of "getting across the concept of the Synagogue Council, its program, and its current 'Back to the Synagogue' movement." In turn, he wrote, he hoped to benefit from the Rabbinical Association's input.

One of the major issues that aroused the concern of the Synagogue Council was that a relatively small proportion of American Jews were involved in a meaningful way in their respective synagogues. Thus, a major Synagogue Council project was launched early in 1956 with the commissioning of a report from Columbia University's Bureau of Applied Social Research on "The Place of the Synagogue in Contemporary Life." The purpose of the study, as stated in the Bureau's preface to the proposal, would be to undertake "a comprehensive study of the factors motivating and inhibiting the meaningful involvement of the Jewish population in the life of the synagogue."

The Synagogue Council's objective in commissioning the expensive study—the bureau estimated that it would cost between $60,000 and $100,000, a substantial sum in 1950s dollars, and require intensive research, perhaps lasting as long as eighteen months—was to learn why relatively few Jews were synagogue-affiliated, and among those who were, why their attendance was so sporadic.

In March of that year, the Synagogue Council, under Marc's guidance, launched its "Back to the Synagogue" campaign. In a letter announcing the initiative, the Synagogue Council stated: "In this dramatic campaign, the Orthodox, Conservative and Reform branches of Jewry—marking a new level of in American Jewish cooperation and program—have joined together to bring 1,500,000 unaffiliated Jews back to the Synagogue, and to uplift every Jew in the United States to a deeper sense of piety and pride."

In 1957, the Synagogue Council of America's Second Annual Assembly, focusing on "Jewish Religious Renewal," took place on March 24–25 on the campus of Columbia University in New York City. The agency's executive director spoke on the theme "The Synagogue Council Looks Ahead." Among the other presenters were the eminent scholars Nathan Glazer, Will Herberg, and Rabbi Arthur Hertzberg, as well as the educational leader Rabbi Emanuel Rackman.

During that year, Marc also spoke at numerous organizational dinners and participated in various synagogues' adult education programs. While the minimum fee per appearance he sought was $50, he did not always receive that amount. As he learned from Rabbi Sanford H. Hahn, the spiritual leader of the Jewish Community Center of Mount Kisco, New York, when he attempted to negotiate his honorarium there, "as $30 is the normal fee we can afford to pay for a lecture, it would be awkward for me to request more."

Under Marc's professional leadership, the Synagogue Council's sphere of interest was hardly limited to religious matters. In fact, in the wake of the emergence of newly independent nations amid the rapid decline of colonialism, the agency was deeply concerned with America's global responsibilities.

An open letter addressed to "The Congress of the United States" attested to their concern. Signed by thirty-four American religious leaders, the letter was made public on July 16, 1958, by Rabbi Tanenbaum, Dr. Kenneth Maxwell, representing the National Council of Churches, U.S.A., and the Reverend James L. Vizzard of the National Catholic Rural Life Conference during a joint press conference held in the Capitol Hill office of Senator Leverett Saltonstall, a Republican from Massachusetts. The letter began:

> The undersigned view with dismay and concern the heavy cuts made by the House of Representatives in the appropriation to carry out our Mutual Security program for the next fiscal year. Particularly are we concerned over the drastic reduction made in the funds for economic development of the new and

emerging nations of Asia, Africa, the Middle East and Latin America.

The open letter noted that the Mutual Security program "is designed to cope with the world-wide revolution which is the outstanding political fact of our age." It also observed that the program is based "firmly on moral values which are common to the major religious faiths of our country it has been supported consistently by many religious organizations and spokesmen representing Protestants, Catholics and Jews throughout the nation."

Later in 1958, alarming news landed on Marc's desk: The National Council of Churches, never a friend of the Jewish people, had embarked on a Missionary Program on the Middle East. That program put forward a slanderous view of Jews and Judaism as well as Israel and Zionism, in which many observers felt more than five thousand years of Jewish history were distorted and an entire people maligned. On October 24, reacting to this deeply troubling development, Marc sent a "confidential and urgent" letter to the Synagogue Council's constituent movements regarding what he described as the "Protestant Community's Mission Study Program on the Middle East."

One week later, on the thirty-first, the Synagogue Council executive director sent out a six-page, single-spaced "Statement by the Synagogue Council of America on the Current Middle East Study Program." This memorandum offered a stinging point-by-point critique of the Middle East Study Program of the National Council of Churches.

Marc, in his introduction, wrote that

hundreds of thousands, perhaps millions of Protestant men, women and young people are being called upon to study books and to look at films and filmstrips dealing with the Middle East which, in the judgment of responsible Rabbinical and other Jewish leaders, misrepresent the Jewish religion, distort Jewish history, impugn the loyalty of Jews to America, and present unfairly the case of the State of Israel and its relationships with its Arab neighbors.

The memorandum was promptly distributed by J. Allan Ranck, the general director of the Commission on Missionary Education–Friendship Press to nine hundred local councils of churches and churchwomen.

The following year proved to be equally eventful. Marc published a major article on religion in the *American Jewish Year Book*. On May 11, 1959, the rabbi, in his capacity as a vice-chairman of the Religious Advisory Council of the President's Commission on Government Contracts, participated in a Religious Leaders Conference at the Sheraton Park Hotel in Washington, D.C. Following this conference, the Synagogue Council's executive director would deepen his relationship with another participant, the Reverend Martin Luther King Jr., the pastor of the Dexter Avenue Baptist Church in Montgomery, Alabama.

In November, during the twenty-eighth annual General Assembly of the Council of Jewish Federations and Welfare Funds (CJFWF) held at the Fairmont Hotel, in San Francisco, Marc presented a paper on Federation-Synagogue Relationships. And that fall, the Synagogue Council, in an initiative conceived by Marc in the hope of broadening the agency's financial base and thus achieving greater visibility in the American Jewish community, established a National Advisory Council (NAC).

The NAC held its first meeting on December 3 at the Harmonie Club, the Manhattan social club founded by wealthy German Jews. The meeting was chaired by Benjamin Lazarus, of Cincinnati, whose family controlled the Federated Department Stores chain. The group's advisory board included such luminaries as Orin Lehman and Maurice Tempelsman of New York, Nathan Cummings of Chicago, Kivie Kaplan of Boston, Joseph Meyerhoff of Baltimore, and Benjamin H. Swig of San Francisco, all prominent figures in their respective communities.

During Marc's presentation at the Harmonie Club meeting, he noted that although the Synagogue Council had been invited to participate in several major national programs, due to lack of budget and staff, the newly formed group had not been able to do so. Former US Senator Herbert Lehman, the NAC's honorary chairman, was, according to the meeting's minutes, "obviously moved by Rabbi Tanenbaum's comments," and he stated:

> It is my great hope that this Council will grow into a really useful organization. I think it can. It will not be easy. It will mean convincing a lot of people. I hope it will be carried forward. No one here can doubt the validity and value of this Council and the work it has undertaken. I hope it will grow in size, and power and resources.

Meanwhile, on the morning of December 16, 1960, Marc, utilizing his White House contacts, escorted a select Synagogue Council delegation to the Oval Office. There, the group presented the soon-to-be outgoing president, Dwight D. Eisenhower, with the agency's first-ever "Judaism and World Peace" award. The agency's citation read in part: "to signal the climax of his stewardship of our nation and of the free world during his eight years of sacrificial devotion and leadership as president of the United States, and of his public service career."

That afternoon, President Eisenhower wrote to Rabbi Max Davidson, the Synagogue Council's president: "I am deeply complimented that, in your opinion, my efforts to advance the cause of peace these past eight years merited the 'Judaism and (World) Peace' Award. I shall lastingly value the sentiments you and the others conveyed to me." In honoring the President of the United States, of course, it was not lost on Marc that the award was also promoting the name of the Synagogue Council.

During Marc's seven-year tenure with the Synagogue Council of America, he was involved in a a diverse set of hot-button issues. They ranged from equal employment opportunity to foreign aid to interfaith relations to racial and religious prejudice to ritual slaughter to traffic safety to United Nations affairs.

Meanwhile, he also served on various boards of directors. One was devoted to self-help programs in Latin America involving literacy, health, and agriculture; the National Safety Council; and Religion in American Life. In addition, in 1958, he was appointed vice-chairman of the President's National Committee for the 1960 White House Conference on Children and Youth and also served on the conference's "Theme and Focus" committee. Later, the rabbi served as chairman of the Planning Committee on Religion in preparation for a meeting of the White House Conference on Aging, held from January 9 to 12, 1961.

He was making a meaningful contribution to all of these organizations, and establishing himself as a *macher*, a significant figure in the American Jewish community. But the inner tensions of the Synagogue Council were taking their toll. Despite Marc's many accomplishments as the Synagogue Council of America's innovative, bridge-building executive director, when the opportunity arose to work in a more congenial atmosphere, he decided to leave, joining the prestigious American Jewish Committee.

The AJC, founded in 1906, was, a half century later, still closely associated with German Jews. The Kuhns and Loebs, the Schiffs and Lehmans, and other German-Jewish immigrants and their offspring, had become prominent as investment bankers and merchants. As they prospered in America, they sought not only to improve the lot of their coreligionists, but also to advance intergroup relations. In 1960, this pioneering American human relations agency, whose mandate has been to protect and advance the civil and religious rights of Jews throughout the world, offered Marc Tanenbaum the position of director of Interreligious Affairs.

In his letter of resignation from the Synagogue Council, written on December 31, 1960, Marc diplomatically cited "Compelling personal needs" for his decision to move on. He observed that the Synagogue Council's recent growth had left him with "little time and opportunity for self-growth through serious study and writing." More pointedly, he added that the American Jewish Committee's offer "enables me to devote myself in greater measure to creative intellectual activity."

On January 25, 1961, barely three weeks following the conclusion of the White House Conference on Aging, the rabbi, writing to his colleagues at a number of organizations "in both my personal and professional capacities," confided that as of March 1 he would be leaving the Synagogue Council of America.

On March 3, 1961, the Synagogue Council held a testimonial dinner for Marc at the Olcott Hotel, on West 72nd Street, in Manhattan. In the presence of his family, as well as prominent rabbis and community leaders, Marc was presented with an illuminated scroll bearing the words:

> His stewardship of the council has been marked by consummate statesmanship and his contribution to its growth has been without parallel in the organization's history. He has enhanced the name and prestige of the Synagogue Council in his work with U.S. government agencies, the White House, the United Nations, and the Protestant and Catholic communities.

In the years after he left the Synagogue Council, Rabbi Marc Tanenbaum would go on to become an increasingly significant figure in the Jewish world and beyond.

CHAPTER 6

Arriving at the American Jewish Committee at the Right Moment

"Is it not time to put an end to the un-Christian use of the Jews as a scapegoat people?"
—A question posed in a memorandum prepared at the request of Cardinal Augustin Bea for submission to Vatican Council II

IN THE AMERICAN JEWISH COMMUNAL world, a newly appointed executive normally enjoyed a brief honeymoon period and even a leisurely shakedown cruise. But Rabbi Marc Tanenbaum had no such luxury. The AJC's new director of Interreligious Affairs knew that for years the agency had been engaged in efforts to address anti-Semitism in Christian education through research and dialogue, and it needed to take the initiative vis-à-vis the upcoming Vatican Council that had recently been announced.

On October 28, 1958, the College of Cardinals had elected Cardinal Angelo Roncalli, a son of peasants who would later serve as the Patriarch of Venice, to succeed Pope Pius XII. Cardinal Roncalli, who, from his post in Turkey during the Holocaust, played an important role in rescuing Jews, had also served for twenty years as a papal representative in the Balkans and the Near East. At the time of his election as pope, when he became Pope John XXIII, the new pontiff was considered to be serving a *transitional* role. But three months after his election, on January 25, His Holiness, in the spirit of aggiornamento, or adaptation to the modern world, stunned many Church officials by announcing his intention to convene an ecumenical council, the twenty-first such convocation in the annals of the Roman Catholic Church. This twentieth-century conclave, the first since 1869–1870, would go down in history as Vatican Council II.

Even as Marc was grappling with "God-talk" issues during his tenure at the Synagogue Council, he had recognized the momentous potential for Catholic-Jewish relations created by John XXIII's announcement. In fact, as Marc would recall in 1980:

> When I'd put on the agenda the Vatican Council and that the Jewish community should respond to it, we should find out about it and see whether we ought to relate to it, it was vetoed. The Orthodox community said—and I respect this judgment, but I think it was a wrong judgment—they said: "It's an internal Christian meeting, we're to have nothing to do with it.

During the run-up to the Council, the committee was invited by high Church officials to submit suggestions and findings to the convocation's preparatory commission. That overture was based on the AJC's promotion of interreligious understanding from its very founding in 1906, as well as its subsequent, extensive research bearing on Christian-Jewish relations.

The study of religious education as a source of prejudice had been a priority for the committee as early as 1932. At that time, the agency had joined with the Drew Theological Seminary and the National Conference of Christians and Jews in a pioneering review of Protestant teaching materials aimed at replacing stereotypes about Jews with accurate information. Under the AJC's auspices, that research would later be expanded to embrace self-studies of Protestant, Catholic, and Jewish textbooks examining the ways in which each of those religious groups viewed one another.

In 1960, the year before Marc's arrival at the committee, Judith Banki, then Judith Hershcopf, the agency's assistant director of Interreligious Affairs, was assigned to meet with researchers, familiarize herself with their studies, highlight their findings, and make them known to the religious community.

At the same time, Zachariah "Zach" Shuster, director of the committee's European office, was consulting privately with Jewish and Christian experts on interreligious issues in anticipation of the convening of the Council. Among Shuster's religious advisers were two friends of long standing: Paul Démann, the author of *La Catéchèse Chrétienne et le Peuple de la Bible*, a study of the portrayal of Jews in Catholic education in France that had been published in 1952 and was analogous to committee-sponsored investigations in the United States; and James Parkes of Britain, a Protestant authority on Christianity and the Jews, whose book *Anti-Semitism* would be published in 1963.

Committee-sponsored studies in the United States, as well as the work of European scholars, revealed that both anti-Semitic stereotypes and toxic language remained entrenched in Christian thinking. In response, the agency's leadership undertook an initiative to place these issues on the agenda of Vatican Council II.

A key element in this undertaking was the committee's association with the Rome-based Pro Deo University. It was through this relationship that entrée would be gained to influential members of the Roman hierarchy. The university was not run directly by the Catholic Church, but its educational philosophy was based on Catholic religious values. It was also inspired by American-style democratic ideals. Pro Deo specialized in the training of future public administrators, business entrepreneurs, industrial managers, and labor experts, mostly from developing nations. In the political context of the mid-twentieth century, the university sought to provide Italy with a bulwark against Communism.

Pro Deo—"the International University of Social Studies"—was not primarily funded by Catholics, nor were its faculty and student body recruited from within that religious denomination. Rather, financing, as well as faculty and students, came from a variety of sources and nations, and it operated under an international, interdenominational board of trustees. Nonetheless, it was known to be close to Vatican officials. Thus, the university appeared singularly suited to serve as the liaison among the different groups concerned with the outcome of Vatican Council II.

The committee's fruitful relationship with Pro Deo dated back to 1950, when the university's founder, a Belgian-born Dominican priest named Félix A. Morlion, sought the committee's assistance in creating a US-based support group. That organization came into being as the American Council for the International Promotion of Democracy under God (CIP). Early on, key AJC officers and lay supporters, among them Alan Stroock, Paul Warburg, Ralph Friedman, and David Danzig—all of them acting as individuals rather than formal representatives of the committee—began to serve on the CIP's board of directors.

According to a plan drawn up in 1961 for direct cooperation between the committee and the university, a three-year contract was signed under which the committee would endow a professorship of Interreligious Relations—the first such academic post to be created at any European institution of higher education. The plan also called for the committee to assist in devising an intergroup curriculum, establishing a reference library on intergroup relations, and establishing a sociology journal. The academic post would eventually be awarded to an eminent social psychologist, Dr. Otto Klineberg, formerly of Columbia University. The professor's lectures to graduate students in the social sciences and priests-in-training dealt with such important subjects as race, culture, ethnic stereotypes, causes of prejudice, and the nature of Nazi anti-Semitism.

The committee's relationship with Pro Deo was not limited to the furtherance of interreligious understanding through education. Even prior to the advent of academic cooperation, a valuable diplomatic bond had been established between AJC and Pro Deo. That association led to a breakthrough event, the granting of a papal audience to a delegation of ten American Jewish Committee representatives in June 1957. Led by Irving M. Engel, the AJC's president, the meeting was characterized by a highly placed cleric as "the opening of a new chapter in the Vatican's attitude toward Jewish problems."

The audience with Pope Pius XII had been arranged, ostensibly, to thank the pontiff for his aid to Jews during the Holocaust. But the committee's delegation used that occasion to advance a two-point agenda: First, to seek papal intervention with the Polish clergy, which, since the easing of restrictions by the Communist puppet regime of Władysław Gomułka, had increasingly expressed anti-Semitic sentiments. Second, to ask that the pope encourage Latin American nations, most notably Brazil, to grant asylum to Jewish refugees from Egypt in the wake of the 1956 Suez campaign. At that time, with only several days' notice, thousands of Jews were expelled after being forced to sign their property over to the government of Gamal Abdel Nasser.

In response, Pius XII presented the committee delegation with a formal statement—the first such document he would ever give to a Jewish organization—condemning anti-Semitism and calling upon all nations to welcome victims of religious persecution. The committee would learn later that anti-Semitic expression had been curbed in Poland. This landmark papal document was also likely to be the reason that Brazil would soon admit a considerable number of Jewish refugees from Egypt. Given the pope's condemnation of anti-Semitism, as well as Pro Deo's commitment to the opening of channels of communication with Church authorities, would the committee's concerns receive a fair hearing from the several thousand delegates to Vatican Council II?

The university's willingness to assist the committee in submitting various documents to Vatican Council II could prove to be crucial in advancing the agency's concerns. As Marc contemplated this question, he realized that the work of the Department of Interreligious Affairs would assume a far broader scope than the committee had earlier envisioned. Before Marc could turn his attention to the committee's response to events unfolding in Rome, there were two internal organizational priorities on his immediate agenda.

First, given the prospects of a Vatican Council focused on church doctrine, the ecumenically minded rabbi insisted that there would be no ban on "God-talk" at the committee. Spiritual and even theological language could be invoked in the effort to reverse two millennia of negative Church teachings and attitudes.

Second, and most important, for that to occur, the work of interreligious affairs—heretofore subsumed within the agency's Department of National Affairs, headed by Edwin J. Lukas—would require authority as a distinct department. Marc specified that as its director, he would be answerable only to the committee's executive director, John Slawson. Early on, Slawson had assured Marc that "Once you're clear about what you're doing and what is required, and we have approval to go ahead, I'll back you."

Soon, Marc, working out of the committee's Manhattan headquarters on East 56th Street, was putting his frustrating experience at the Synagogue Council behind him and coming to regard the committee as what he would call "a breath of fresh air." A major factor in Marc's newfound sense of well-being was the support and understanding of a major lay leader of the committee, the influential Baltimore industrialist Jacob Blaustein, founder of the American Oil Company. A legendary figure since Marc's childhood, Blaustein supported his efforts to foster interreligious understanding through dialogue with the Christian community.

The third major ingredient in Marc's optimism about his new role was his excellent staff. Among the most dedicated of them was Judith Banki, who had been hired in late 1959 by Marc's predecessor, Rabbi Morris Kertzer. Her main function, in addition to extracting the findings of the Protestant, Catholic, and Jewish textbooks, was as a researcher and writer. When Marc arrived at the agency, she had already begun work under the direction of David Danzig, the committee's director of Program, on a memorandum ultimately titled "The Image of the Jews in Catholic Teaching."

This memorandum was based on the findings of a Dominican nun who had studied Catholic textbooks. Sister Rose Thering, of Racine, Wisconsin, had compiled disturbing information about the way negative teaching and preaching traditions regarding Jews and Judaism infused Catholic textbooks and teaching manuals. This research was undertaken as part of the doctoral dissertation she had submitted to St. Louis University.

It was widely believed in the Christian world—and widely taught through the centuries—that the Jewish people were Christ killers. Because the Jews were supposedly responsible for Christ's death, it was said, they were accursed and cut off from God. That is why they were being punished by having to wander the face of the Earth for eternity. Thus, Christian theology and liturgy provided a rationale, indeed a respectable intellectual argument, in which anti-Semites could cloak their bigotry.

The Church's "official" liturgical justification for persecution of the Jews, as well as indifference to their fate, had been recognized by several Catholic theologians and scholars. As Father George H. Tavard wrote in 1959 in *The Church, the Layman and the Modern Man*, while "The idea that Jews are cursed because their ancestors crucified the Lord stands in contradiction to the Gospel . . . it is furthermore opposed to the Catholic doctrine on mankind's collective responsibility in sin." But he added:

> Nevertheless, the idea is still often met with among people who are counted good Catholics. To the mind of anti-Semitic bigots, it even explains a great deal of history. God would periodically "visit" the murderers of Christ and incite them to penance through persecution. All the anti-Semitic excesses of times past and present can thus be cheaply excused. They are freely granted the blessing of Providence.

Banki's paper would be the first-ever such document submitted by a

Jewish organization to the Secretariat for Promoting Christian Unity. This body was a Preparatory Commission of the Second Vatican Council headed by Cardinal Augustin Bea, a German-born prelate. The paper would be supplemented by material collected by the committee's offices in Paris, Buenos Aires, and Rio de Janeiro.

Among the problems disclosed in Banki's study were frequent accusations that the Jews were an accursed people, rejected by God; gratuitous use of the phrase "the Jews" only as enemies of Jesus; unjust and inaccurate comparisons between Christianity—described as a religion of love—and Judaism—characterized as a loveless religion of law; and invidious use of terminology such as "carnal" and "bloodthirsty" in describing Jews.

There was regular omission of mitigating facts and circumstances. For example, Jews were often employed as moneylenders during the Middle Ages not because of any inherent single-minded worship of money or greed, but because they were barred from membership in craft guilds and forbidden to own land.

The most pernicious slander of all was the characterization of the Jews as "deicides," even though, as Banki noted in the committee's document, the Church had officially denied that charge as early as the Council of Trent, which had taken place from 1545 to 1563. As that convocation declared, all human beings had been responsible for the Passion of Jesus.

Meanwhile, nowhere in the Church's teachings and texts were the Jewish roots of Christianity noted.

Banki concluded the committee's document, which was then reviewed by the agency's Catholic and Jewish advisory team, with a heartfelt exhortation that Pope John XXIII should:

> cause precise directives to be issued from the Vatican . . . for improving Catholic teaching about Jews and Judaism, by cleansing all Catholic educational and liturgical publications of inaccurate, distorted, slanderous or prejudiced statements about Jews as a group. . . . We believe that the improvement

of Catholic teaching about the Jews is an urgent task, of equal importance to the spiritual belief of America and that of the whole world.

The committee's initiative was partially inspired by Claire Huchet Bishop, a French-born writer and lecturer on Catholic issues who had relocated to New York. She had come to the committee and declared: "Now is the time; Vatican councils are few and far between. This is a unique opportunity to try to convince the Church to repudiate the theological roots of anti-Semitism, to open a new chapter in its relationship with the Jews."

Huchet Bishop was a disciple of the French scholar Jules Isaac. A secular Jewish historian later noted for his studies on anti-Semitic elements in Christian tradition, he had attained the highest civil service position ever achieved by a French Jew: in 1936, he had been appointed as his nation's inspector general of public instruction. In 1940, however, he would be dismissed from that post under the Vichy regime's discriminatory statute against Jews.

Such was the prevailing anti-Jewish sentiment that two years later, Abel Bonnard, a French poet, novelist, and politician who would become a minister in the Vichy regime, would declare: "It was not possible that France's history should be taught to young people by an Isaac." In 1943, Isaac's wife and daughter were arrested, deported to Auschwitz, and murdered there. The scholar's son was also arrested but escaped from a concentration camp in Germany and survived the war. Hidden for the duration of the war by Christian friends and colleagues, Isaac focused his considerable intellectual energy on discovering the roots of the anti-Semitism that had not only destroyed his family, but was destroying his civilization. He found his answer in the very negative and hostile Christian tradition of teaching about Jews and Judaism, which he characterized as "the teaching of contempt."

In June 1960, Isaac was granted an audience with Pope John XXIII, who was then trying to decide whether a special commission on Catholic-Jewish relations should be established. That meeting, which lasted for half an hour, would profoundly impact the pope's thinking regarding the need for change in Catholic teaching regarding the Jews.

Over the years, Isaac gathered together a group of Christian and Jewish disciples committed to his message, including Huchet Bishop. Banki believed that Huchet Bishop's exhortation, combined with David Danzig's personal relationship with the chancellor of Pro Deo University, contributed much to the success of the committee's activities regarding the Vatican.

The committee also consulted two other prominent Jews in its efforts vis-à-vis Vatican Council II: Dr. Elio R. Toaff and Dr. Jacob Kaplan, the chief rabbis of Rome and France, respectively. The AJC's American advisers were Dr. Salo Baron, professor of Jewish history at Columbia University, and the rabbi/scholar Louis Finkelstein, chancellor of the Jewish Theological Seminary of America. Marc also recruited his JTS mentor, Rabbi Abraham Joshua Heschel, who had been a professor of Jewish ethics and mysticism at the seminary, and he would come to play an important role on the committee's behalf in Rome.

After extensive consultations with the committee's advisers, the AJC decided that it would not seek to have unofficial delegates, or even observers, invited to Vatican Council II. The reasoning was that the Jewish community's interest would be best served by providing the appropriate Vatican body with research materials identifying Catholic teachings and practices in need of modification. But there was vociferous opposition to formal Jewish involvement with the Vatican Council as early as the winter of 1960. Led by important Orthodox figures, including Rabbis Joseph Soloveitchik and Toaff, their view was that Vatican II was an internal matter for the Church, and not open to outsiders. Rabbi Soloveitchik, a professor of Talmud at Yeshiva University, was esteemed as the spiritual leader of non-Hasidic Orthodox Jewry in the United States. The Conference of European Rabbis also weighed in at that stage, stating that it was not anticipating the granting of invitations to Jewish spiritual leaders.

At that point, the committee's leadership cautioned its colleagues at Pro Deo University that the Vatican should not be encouraged to single out a specific organization as representing the entire community. In the event that the Vatican did decide to invite Jewish observers to the Council, given that the delegates would be dealing with religious and moral issues, the committee argued that such a group should consist solely of rabbinical leaders. Any other form of representation, it was believed, would have undesirable political ramifications.

The committee also decided that in order to forestall opposition from within the Church's conservative wing, as well as anti-Semitic outbursts from the general population, the presentation to the Vatican of pertinent documentation had to be done without publicity. Furthermore, given the sensitivities of the issue, the committee's presentation was to be couched within the framework and language of human relations, rather than theology, so as to forestall any accusations that the agency's spokespeople would be requesting changes in Christian dogma.

On December 15, 1960, approximately six months after Jules Isaac's audience with John XXIII, and after reaching internal agreement on the AJC's approach to Vatican II, the committee's lay president, Herbert B. Ehrmann, wrote to the pontiff, offering the committee's assistance. In that letter, Ehrmann noted that recent papal initiatives had brought progress toward interreligious harmony, including the removal of anti-Jewish expressions from the Catholic liturgy. He then suggested that the pope's action could encourage additional improvements in the Catholic liturgy and teaching and added that "the Church may deem it useful to consult Jewish scholars and theologians."

Then, coupling an offer of assistance with implied criticism, Ehrmann added that the committee would be pleased to assist in establishing contacts with such learned individuals, as well as to provide "examples from religious educational texts and other sources that, in our view, constitute an obstacle to better apprehension between Catholics and Jews." Ending on a conciliatory note, Ehrmann expressed hope that the Church would encourage further inquiries into such teachings, with a view toward their eventual removal from both the Catholic liturgy and curriculum. Within the week, word would come from the Vatican that the pope had been impressed by the contents and tone of Ehrman's letter.

At the committee's headquarters, meanwhile, although there could be no publicity attached to their initiative, the rewards of silence would be great: it seemed likely that the issues that had dogged interreligious understanding for two millennia were going to be addressed during the Vatican Council II's deliberations. Over the next nine months, there was a flurry of committee activity, both in the United States and abroad. In Paris, *Évidences*, the committee's French-language magazine, published the minutes of a symposium in which leading European church officials and intellectuals—Protestant as well as Catholic—expressed their respective views on Christian teaching concerning Jews.

Marc established a close working relationship, as well as a personal friendship, with his European colleague Zach Shuster. The committee's Paris-based representative was erudite, wise, and spoke seven languages. (Marc was fond of mimicking the cultured Shuster's pronunciation: "But, Hainglish I'm speakin' best of all.") Despite his appreciation of the City of Light, Shuster used to quip, "The French, they are a sour people."

"Zach had authority and wisdom and a richness of experience; he was the European end of Marc's American initiative vis-à-vis the Vatican Council," Judith Banki recalled. "They went several times to Rome together. Marc could sometimes be impetuous, and Zach would either calm him down or say, 'You should do it *this* way,' and Marc deferred to him."

In the meantime, in New York, the committee, with Pro Deo's assistance, was establishing channels of communication with the Secretariat for Promoting Christian Unity, the body to which John XXIII had assigned study of the enormously complex issue of Christian-Jewish relations. The committee was fortunate to be dealing with the secretariat's scholarly head, Cardinal Bea. One of the Catholic world's leading authorities on the Hebrew Bible and the history of the people of Israel, he was regarded by his peers as the living embodiment of the ecumenical spirit that Marc eagerly sought.

That the "Jewish desk" came to rest in the secretariat, rather than in the seemingly more appropriate Pontifical Council for Interreligious Dialogue had everything to do with Cardinal Bea himself. Widely viewed as theologically enlightened, statesmanlike, and humane by nature, in Marc's opinion, the venerable cardinal was the ideal personality to entrust with the delicate role of mediator between Catholics and Jews. He found the prelate to be much more congenial and attuned to the interests of the Jewish community than were many of his colleagues in the Pontificate.

In Rome on July 4, 1961, during a meeting with Cardinal Bea, Zach Shuster and Ralph Friedman, chair of the agency's Foreign Affairs Committee, expressed their hope that the Ecumenical Council would take on the issue of the Church's anti-Semitic traditions, as well as affirm the bonds between Catholic and Jew and acknowledge Judaism's permanent value as a living religion. The committee representatives then offered to have their agency submit a paper on specific anti-Jewish elements in Catholic religious teaching.

The cardinal asked that such documentation be provided to him without delay, and he also requested evidence regarding anti-Jewish elements in the Catholic liturgy and in literature on Jesus's crucifixion. Cardinal Bea explained that recommendations agreed upon by the secretariat would be passed on to the Central Commission, the major planning agency for Vatican Council II, of which he was a member. In his report on this groundbreaking meeting, Shuster observed that "Cardinal Bea and the Secretariat are seriously engaged in the preparation of a declaration of the Ecumenical Council stating the position of the Church toward Jews." From the spirit in which Cardinal Bea spoke, Shuster added, "it might not be unwarranted to assume that this declaration might be of great significance."

At that point, "The Image of the Jew in Catholic Teaching" was once again fine-tuned and then sent to Cardinal Bea, who, on June 22, 1961, submitted the document to the secretariat. A second memorandum,

"Anti-Jewish Elements in Catholic Liturgy," was drafted by Dr. Eric Werner, a Jewish authority on sacred music and liturgy. Submitted on November 17, 1961, it called attention to certain passages in the Roman Catholic liturgy that expressed hostility toward Jews, as well as to even more negative statements in liturgical commentaries.

While acknowledging several modifications of offending passages published in 1947 and 1950, the memorandum noted that other offensive phraseology characterizing the Jews as "willfully blind" killers of Jesus remained in the sacred liturgy and texts, particularly in those read during Holy Week. "Most Jews are profoundly convinced that the charge of deicide, uttered through the centuries, has been a central figure in the persistent anti-Semitism of Western civilization," the memorandum said.

While the scholarly groundwork had been set out, Marc saw the need for a singular, authoritative, esteemed Jewish voice to offer suggestions for improved relations with the Jews. Thus, in an intriguing role reversal, he brought his mentor into the enormous effort—due, in his words, to Rabbi Heschel's "towering" presence in American spiritual and intellectual life. Given the importance and delicacy of the initiative, Marc asked Zach Shuster to confer with Rabbi Heschel. Following their meeting in Rome, Shuster wrote to Dr. Slawson on December 20, 1961, indicating that he and Marc believed that Rabbi Heschel was willing to be of service in the endeavor. Shuster added: "I do not think he would take the initiative of his own accord, but will respond quickly to an invitation from you."

Shuster also expressed his belief that Rabbi Heschel would gain much personal satisfaction "If he could be associated in some way with dynamic activities as projected by the AJC, and particularly with the long-range positive programs which will develop in connection with our activities in Rome"

Within a matter of weeks, Rabbi Heschel would agree to the committee's suggestion that he participate in its Vatican Council II initiatives. In November 1961, he began to draft the committee's third document, titled "On Improving Catholic-Jewish Relations," and prepared in cooperation with the committee's Interreligious Affairs Department. In that paper, the eminent scholar and theologian examined tensions between Catholics and Jews from the religious perspective and offered proposals for relieving them. As Rabbi Heschel wrote:

> In view of the past historical events which brought great sacrifice and suffering to Jews on account of their faith as Jews and their race, and particularly in view of the fact that anti-Semitism has in our time resulted in the greatest crime committed in the history of mankind, we consider it a matter of extreme importance that a strong declaration be issued by the Council stressing the grave nature of the sin of anti-Semitism. Anti-Semitism, one of the most grave and historically important sins of prejudice and contempt, is incompatible with Catholicism and in general with all morality.

That document, submitted to Cardinal Bea on May 22, 1962, contained a proposal for the establishment of a Vatican commission for the monitoring of Catholic-Jewish relations. Cardinal Bea had suggested that Rabbi Heschel should pursue this project following a meeting with him in Rome, attended also by Shuster and the AJC's consultant in Germany, Dr. Max Horkheimer, of the University of Frankfurt. That meeting, conducted in the German language, appeared to be more like a colloquy between fellow theologians than a diplomatic encounter. Reflecting their scholarly interests, the two men of God expressed their mutual interest in the "Song of Songs," as well as on issues bearing on the rift between Church and Synagogue.

Rabbi Heschel spoke candidly, expressing his hope for the Council's recognition of Jews as *Jews*, not merely as prospective converts to Christianity. The rabbi then proposed that he prepare a document offering positive steps toward Catholic-Jewish rapprochement—a step warmly endorsed by Cardinal Bea, who suggested that the two meet again. The cardinal then explained that any declaration made by the Council would be framed in *general* terms, with specifics of implementation to be worked out in the future. Toward the meeting's end, Cardinal Bea turned to the issue of rampant anti-Semitic unrest unfolding in Argentina. He pledged to his Jewish colleague that the Vatican would intercede against a certain priest known to be spreading anti-Jewish lies in that South American nation.

Rabbi Heschel's concerns, findings, and suggestions for concrete steps to be undertaken by the Church to redress these past injustices were presented to Cardinal Bea in March of the following year. That meeting occurred during Cardinal Bea's visit to the United States to attend a meeting that was arranged for him at the committee's Manhattan headquarters with leaders of the Orthodox, Conservative, and Reform movements.

Meanwhile, in October 1961, the committee had been informed by Msgr. Carlo Ferrero, the president of Pro Deo University, that the agency's memorandum had been received well in the Vatican. As Rabbi Heschel was writing his promised document, Cardinal Bea and his staff were preparing their recommendations to the Council's Central Preparatory Commission.

In June 1962, a draft of a declaration on Catholic-Jewish relations was being readied by an informal working group within the secretariat—a document that would reflect many of the American Jewish Committee's concerns. The Vatican's document acknowledged the close links between the Jewish Bible and the New Testament and emphasized the importance of the Old Testament to Christians. It also contained expressions of tribute and respect for contemporary Jews and condemned anti-Semitism. While it could not be determined at that time whether or not the draft document actually repudiated the "deicide" charge, on April 25 Cardinal Bea told the *New York Times* that the Council would likely discuss measures for removing that millennia-old stigma.

That issue was so crucial to the committee that Rabbi Heschel urged that it be dealt with explicitly. His demand was reiterated by the committee's president, A. M. Sonnabend, a financier and hotel industry leader, in a letter to Cardinal Bea. As discussions were underway between the committee in New York and the Vatican's representatives, parallel efforts were underway elsewhere. The agency's Latin American office, headed by Abraham Monk, was carrying out a survey of anti-Jewish material in textbooks used in Brazilian Catholic schools at the initiative of Father Bertrand de Margerie, executive director of the National Conference of Priests in Brazil and a close associate of Cardinal Bea. The survey's negative findings were transmitted to Cardinal Bea and published in the *Journal of the Conference of Catholic Priests*. As a result, a large-scale program of textbook revision was launched at the Catholic University of Rio de Janeiro.

It was now the late spring of 1962. The committee, having succeeded in establishing crucial channels to the Church, would at last have the unique opportunity to challenge two millennia of Church accusations and teachings. Marc, who had arrived at the American Jewish Committee in the hope of promoting "God Talk," was about to do so beyond his most vivid dreams. It would be his responsibility to marshal the committee's professional and lay resources, as well as to develop support within the wider Jewish communal world. Marc would also begin to meet with, and seek to mobilize, leading members of the Roman Catholic hierarchy, particularly in the United States.

His success in doing so would prove difficult to achieve. Four drama-filled years lay ahead—a period that would be marked by opposition both from within the Jewish community and from the vast gentile world beyond.

PART III
VATICAN COUNCIL II

CHAPTER 7

1,900 Years of Waiting

Vatican Council II, Session One:
October 13–December 8, 1962

"The Jews, too, have Immortal Souls and we must do something for them."

—Pope John XXIII, during his conversation with Cardinal Augustin Bea regarding a Declaration on the Jews

AMID THE HEADY PRE-VATICAN II atmosphere gripping Rome during that summer of 1962, Cardinal Bea went about making good on his intention to obtain a specific declaration on the Jews. During a visit with the cardinal in mid-September, Zach Shuster, accompanied by the AJC's Ralph Friedman, learned that Cardinal Bea had, indeed, taken up this crucial matter with the pope. While His Holiness had responded positively to the cardinal's entreaty, and Cardinal Bea himself believed this was the right course to follow, he warned his visitors that other, more conservative Church leaders would need additional persuasion. And he assured his guests that he would continue to determine the best way to bring such a document before the council.

During their stay in the Eternal City, Shuster and Friedman, accompanied by a high official of Pro Deo University, also sought out

Cardinal Eugène Tisserant, dean of the Sacred College of Cardinals, as well as a member of Vatican Council II's Preparatory Commission. The meeting was cordial, with Cardinal Tisserant seeking to make his guests feel at home by recalling childhood memories of Jewish neighbors and his later studies of Near Eastern culture. Cardinal Tisserant noted that the deicide charge was not enshrined in Catholic dogma and said that he had not been aware this issue might be placed on the Council's agenda. But, he promised Shuster and Friedman that he would look into the matter and asked for a written statement setting forth the committee's position.

As the Council's opening session approached, there were reports that the Secretariat for Christian Unity was working behind the scenes to obtain backing for a meaningful declaration. The source of that encouraging development was Abbot Leo Rudloff, a member of the secretariat's unofficial working group on Catholic-Jewish Relations. He informed Rabbi Heschel that Father Stephen Schmidt, a member of Cardinal Bea's staff, was seeking support from members of the Church hierarchy in the United States. Among the most important of the potential allies were Archbishop Cardinal Richard Cushing of Boston and Bishop John Joseph Wright of Pittsburgh.

Cardinal Cushing would emerge as the leading American churchman to champion interfaith rapprochement—a fact recognized by Jews and Protestants alike in sending him their good wishes for Vatican Council II's success. At Zach Shuster's suggestion, AJC president A. M. Sonnabend sent a message to Cardinal Cushing acknowledging his leadership and predicting the advent of a "new order of Christian-Jewish solidarity."

Optimism was in the air at the committee's Manhattan headquarters. After all, Shuster had just cabled the news that "Prospects for Council adopting declaration embodying all our major objectives excellent; caucus American cardinals including Spellman have promised support Bea's position." At the committee's suggestion, prayers for the success of Vatican Council II were being offered in synagogues throughout the United States. And in São Paolo, Brazil, Chief Rabbi

Fritz Pinkuss, in the presence of a Catholic prelate, preached a sermon about the coming Vatican conclave.

Meanwhile, in New York, Marc published an article in the *New York Herald Tribune* reviewing the long history of unhappy relations between Catholics and Jews. It concluded with the words: "Many Jews believe that the Ecumenical Council could literally start a new cycle in Christian-Jewish relationships by condemning vigorously all manifestations of anti-Semitism."

The committee's initial optimism would be short-lived: months of false hope, intrigue, drama, and frustration lay ahead. On Saturday, October 13, 1962—Marc's birthday— following formal opening ceremonies two days earlier, the deliberations of Vatican Council II began in earnest—and in protest—at St. Peter's Basilica. The Roman Curia, which along with the Preparatory Commissions had prepared the agenda and slate of 160 delegates to the Council's ten permanent commissions, was expecting a merely pro forma proceeding to take place. But when the slate was presented to the full complement of delegates, they rebelled.

They refused to function as a rubber-stamp council. As the names of those on the list were being read out, the angry cardinals and bishops who had traveled to the Vatican from Belgium, France, Germany, the Netherlands, Spain, and elsewhere began to lob notes, like paper airplanes, back and forth among themselves. Then, as the reading of the slate concluded, Cardinal Achille Liénart, of the French city of Lille, strode to the microphone and, addressing the animated gathering in Latin, observed that because the delegates had neither been provided with adequate information about the candidates nor time to consult with one another, the session should be adjourned.

At that moment, the day's presiding council president, Cardinal Josef Frings, of the Federal Republic of Germany, known as a progressive thinker, accepted the French cardinal's proposal, and the meeting was duly adjourned. The initial session had lasted for approximately thirty minutes. The outcome of that session surprised many of the delegates, as well as Pope John XXIII, who was observing the proceedings on closed-circuit television in the privacy of the nearby papal apartments.

The press was exhilarated by the drama, with one publication even headlining its report on the abbreviated session "The Revolt of the Bishops." Readers throughout the world were learning that this council would not be a sedate conclave and the Church was not a monolithic institution. The pontiff, himself, while surprised at first by the delegates' behavior, would come to regard that Saturday "revolt" as a positive omen for the renewal of the Church.

The council's next session would be postponed until the following Tuesday, October 16. As all those assembled bided their time, Pope John XXIII knew that he must act to eliminate stalemates in the voting process. So he took decisive action, mandating that delegates could now be elected by a mere plurality, rather than by an absolute majority.

As the Council progressed, the pope, realizing that chaos could again descend on the proceedings, would make additional changes in procedure. They included appointing an odd number of delegates to the Commission, thus avoiding any deadlocking tie votes. On October 18, one week after the Council's opening session, Shuster, who, along with representatives of Protestant organizations and two from the Greek Orthodox Church, had attended that memorable event as an invited official observer, offered his impressions to John Slawson, Marc, and other committee officials, in an eight-page, single-spaced memorandum. In that richly detailed report, the committee's European Affairs director described the Council's inaugural ceremonies as "most unusual in solemnity, splendor and profound dignity."

Shuster concentrated on "developments during the first week of the Council's proceedings with regard to the subjects which are relevant to matters of our concern"—namely, introduction of a resolution repudiating the false allegation of deicide against the Jewish people. Noting Pope John XXIII's "desire to find a way toward understanding non-Catholic groups," Shuster quoted what he characterized as His Holiness's "striking passages," adding his own italics. Following the pontiff's declaration that "Divine providence is leading us to a new order of human relations," the pope stated that "The Catholic Church, raising the torch of religious truth by means of the Ecumenical Council, desires to show herself the *loving mother of all*, benign, patient, full of mercy towards the *children* separated from her."

Turning to pre-Vatican Council II preparations, Shuster wrote that while "official Vatican sources—except for Cardinal Bea—have not referred to Christian/Jewish relations as a subject to be dealt with by the Council, references to the Jewish subject were made in some Italian publications, and they were obviously inspired by the Vatican." Shuster added, "In the various statements made by the arriving Church dignitaries, there were a great many references to the subject of Christian unity, but nothing about Jews."

He noted "a singular exception:" Cardinal Cushing's statement on arriving at a Rome airport on October 10, 1962, the day before the Council's opening session. He was welcomed by Vatican officials, and in remarks widely reported in the Italian press, the cardinal said:

> In the United States there is a plurality of Protestant confessions, and all look with interest to this Council. No one expects the unity of the churches on this occasion, but all expect that an atmosphere favorable to reaching this unity will be created. In a more or less near future, there will be one flock, and only one pastor. When I speak of a favorable atmosphere, I mean that this is the session for Catholics, Protestants, and Jews to better know each other. There are many differences, but even more things in common.

According to one of Cardinal Bea's associates, Cardinal Cushing was so adamant that his American colleagues support efforts on behalf of action on the declaration that he was heard to exclaim: "If it is necessary that I go to the Council in a *yarmulkah* in order to support Bea's plan in favor of the Jews, I shall be glad to do it!" There was, of course, irony in his assertion in that all cardinals, as well as bishops, wear skullcaps.

But by early November 1962, with only one month remaining in the Council's opening session, it was obvious to all concerned that the hoped-for introduction of a resolution on the Jews was not in the immediate offing. It was at that moment that Cardinal Bea, acting on the assumption that the issue *would* be dealt with in the Council's second session, intensified his efforts to gain support for the resolution among his colleagues throughout the world. He was confident that much could be gained by seeking his peers out privately. And he believed the assistance of Latin American prelates to be essential in achieving his, and the committee's, goal.

As that momentous year was ending, Cardinal Bea predicted to the committee that the council would ultimately act on the issue, most likely in the context of both ecumenism and religious liberty. At the same time, Cardinal Bea reiterated his warnings against rash moves or ill-considered publicity by the Jewish community. Within a matter of months, in March 1963, Father Schmidt, a member of the secretariat staff, indicated to Shuster that a strong, comprehensive draft resolution was in the works—a document in which the positive ties between Judaism and Christianity would be emphasized and contemporary as well as ancient Jewry would be discussed.

The committee believed that Cardinal Bea's caution would not preclude an innovative, homegrown enterprise focused on strengthening interreligious relations and deepening Catholic-Jewish dialogue. Thus, even before the Council's opening session, the AJC had begun to conceptualize such an event—one that would necessitate the cardinal's presence in the United States. This would lead to the creation of a meeting, known as an *agapé*—the Greek word for "love," often translated as a "love fest," which in this instance would be a fraternal gathering of clerics and laypeople.

The committee would soon learn that Pro Deo University—which was experienced in arranging *agapés*—was already planning such a gathering in the United States, during which representatives of various religious and racial groups would express their solidarity based on the principles of human dignity and equality. And the American Jewish Committee was likely to be asked to assist with the arrangements and advise on which Jewish and Protestant groups should be invited to participate.

Meanwhile, on December 28, Cardinal Bea hosted a formal delegation comprised of committee leaders, including A. M. Sonnabend, Morris Abram, and Professor Otto Klineberg, whose research on race and psychology Cardinal Bea had cited in his own writings. This audience led to the development of plans for Cardinal Bea to participate in the American *agapé*: in March 1963, the prelate would lecture at a Catholic-Protestant colloquy at Harvard University and then visit New York. A. M. Sonnabend formally offered the committee's assistance in arranging the *agapé*, and the AJC president also invited Cardinal Bea to address several of the agency's own meetings, either in New York or Boston. The cardinal seemed receptive to the committee's suggestions and encouraged it to proceed according to its judgment. Most important for the committee, however, Cardinal Bea offered assurances regarding the introduction of the Declaration on the Jews during the Council's next session.

In the coming months, Father Schmidt worked closely with David Danzig, the AJC's director of programs, on the arrangements for the cardinal's visit to the United States, which would take place for two days during the following spring: March 31 and April 1, 1963.

As a by-product of the collaboration between Father Schmidt and David Danzig, they arranged a meeting between Cardinal Cushing, who would be serving as Cardinal Bea's host in Boston, and Marc. During that meeting, the first of many fruitful encounters the two clergymen would have over the years, Cardinal Cushing told Marc that he intended to assist in improving relations between Catholics and Jews, and to encourage other prelates to do likewise. Cardinal Cushing then raised the possibility of establishing a chapter of CIF, Pro Deo University's American support organization, in his own diocese.

On March 27, at Cardinal Cushing's invitation, Marc and Rabbi Heschel traveled to Boston to welcome Cardinal Bea, who greeted his Jewish colleagues warmly. Those who were present recall the cardinal speaking to Rabbi Heschel as if to a dear friend of long standing.

During their private meeting, held at Cardinal Cushing's chancery on Commonwealth Avenue in Brighton, the Jewish leaders were stunned when Cardinal Bea stated that Pope John XXIII was exploring the possibility of establishing diplomatic relations with the State of Israel.

(The pontiff's gesture of goodwill toward the Jewish people would not be realized during his lifetime: Pope John XXIII died on June 4, 1963, and thirty years would pass before diplomatic accords between the Holy See and the State of Israel would be formalized.)

After Rabbi Heschel presented the cardinal with his book *The Sabbath*, the two men went into the chancery library. There they had a long, wide-ranging conversation. Cardinal Bea, speaking of a recent conversation with John XXIII, told his American colleague, "The Pope and I are completely agreed on these matters; I saw him last Friday before I left on this trip, and he had this problem on his mind." Based on the cardinal's news, Rabbi Heschel believed that the issuance of a strong papal statement condemning the notion of the Jews as a deicide people would now be possible.

And there was more good news: Cardinal Bea hinted that Jewish observers might be invited as guests of his secretariat to attend the second session of Vatican Council II—that is, provided they could be chosen without any contretemps. Before he and Rabbi Heschel rejoined Cardinal Cushing and Marc, Cardinal Bea suggested that a permanent subcommittee be established for the express purpose of improving relations between the Catholic and Jewish communities. He believed this could be accomplished through joint ventures in such fields as Biblical scholarship—an idea that had been suggested by Rabbi Heschel ten months earlier in a memorandum.

Now it was time for the cardinal to travel to New York for the eagerly anticipated *agapé*. The theme of the event, hosted by Pro Deo University's CIP and held at the Plaza Hotel, was "Civic Unity and Freedom under God." In addition to Marc, there were participants from a number of religious communities including Rabbi Heschel, Cardinal Cushing, and Father Morlion; the Greek Orthodox prelate, Archbishop Iakovos; and such Protestant leaders as Reverend Henry

Pitney Van Dusen, president of Union Theological Seminary, and Bishop Stephen Gill Spottswood of the A.M.E. Zion Church. There were also many prominent lay attendees, including UN Secretary General U Thant; Sir Muhammad Zafrulla Khan, president of the UN General Assembly; Governor Nelson A. Rockefeller of New York; Mayor Robert F. Wagner of New York City; and the publisher of *Life* magazine, C. D. Jackson, a prominent American Catholic.

During Cardinal Bea's address to the gathering, he spoke passionately of his hope that mankind was heading toward fraternal unity—a unity he envisioned as being "not that of well-oiled wheels and parts of a machine," but, rather, something to be achieved through "the conscious, free decision of responsible persons to live together in peaceful harmony . . . the mutual exchange not merely of material goods but above all of spiritual riches." In Rabbi Heschel's response, he observed that "minds are sick, hearts are mad, and humanity is drunk with a sense of absolute sovereignty. . . . God and nuclear stockpiles cannot dwell together in one world."

Marc wrote several articles about the *agapé*. The event was also widely covered by the media, as was a news conference during which Cardinal Bea emphasized that Catholic doctrine recognized the right of every man to choose his own religion, or *no* religion. However, he acknowledged that in certain nations—it was thought that the cardinal was referring to Spain—the Church had failed to respect this freedom.

Cardinal Bea's public statements during the *agapé* and afterward were electrifying. But it was a meeting that had taken place a day earlier that would prove to be of greater significance to those concerned specifically with Jewish issues at the Council. This event brought together the cardinal and a select group of Jewish religious leaders assembled at Marc's invitation in the AJC office. The six rabbis chosen to attend that unprecedented private session, representing the three major branches of Judaism, participated not as spokespeople for their respective organizations, but as *individuals*. In addition to Rabbi Heschel, they were Louis Finkelstein plus Theodore Friedman, of the Rabbinical Assembly; Julius Mark, of the Synagogue Council of America; Albert Minda, of the Central Conference of American Rabbis; and Joseph Lookstein, of Bar Ilan University.

Marc had asked Rabbi Heschel to chair the gathering—one that the Jewish participants considered "perhaps of historic significance." Their assessment would prove to be accurate, as a significant portion of the ultimate Vatican II declaration on the Jews, to be known as *Nostra aetate*, would emerge from Cardinal Bea's responses to their questions. The meeting was held in private at Cardinal Bea's request. He feared that any publicity would play into the hands of the Arabs, as well as hostile churchmen in Rome.

What ensued in that intimate setting was an unprecedented frank exchange of views concerning divisive issues between Catholics and Jews. Among the issues put before the group were whether the council could:

- explicitly reject the idea that Jews are an accursed people, guilty of deicide, and acknowledge the integrity of Jews and Judaism;
- condemn unjust allegations and imputations about religious, racial, or other groups generally;
- translate dogmas and moral principles in this sphere into concrete regulations and actions; and
- encourage the creation of a center for interreligious and intergroup studies to stimulate communication and cooperation.

Cardinal Bea began his reply by reminding the group that he could not speak officially for the council but could only state *his* expectations. He then proceeded to outline a theological approach to eliminating the deicide charge. It was obvious, he stated, that only individual Jewish leaders, rather than the entire Jewish people, had been involved in Jesus's crucifixion, and that Jesus had forgiven those who were. Moreover, the cardinal noted, St. Paul had condemned as sheer blasphemy the notion that God had rejected the Jews. And, he said, the advent of the

Jewish Diaspora was not evidence of divine punishment, as was widely believed in some circles. Indeed, that dispersion had a positive impact in serving to spread monotheism throughout the world. Cardinal Bea predicted that the deicide charge might be refuted without undermining belief in Jesus's divinity or the credibility of the Gospels.

In responding to the formal questions that had been proposed in advance by the Jewish religious leaders, the cardinal also emphasized that his secretariat had focused its attention on the deicide issue, as well as the roots of Christianity found in the Old Testament (as the Hebrew Scriptures are called by the Catholic Church and other Christian denominations).

As for combating unjust generalizations against groups such as the Jews, the prelate said that the council could produce guidelines stressing the responsibilities of justice, truth, and love. Practical implementation, however, would have to be pursued through such traditional channels as teaching, preaching, and confessional practice. He noted that programs featuring intergroup collaboration were certainly desirable, and he said that some work of this nature was already underway in Catholic universities and other institutions, but that a more robust effort was in order. As Cardinal Bea ended this milestone colloquy, he again expressed his optimism—a sentiment based on Pope John Paul XXIII's own positive outlook.

Within two months, on June 3, however, His Holiness would succumb to the ravages of cancer. Now Vatican watchers could only wonder: will John Paul XXIII's liberal-minded successor, Paul VI, né Giovanni Battista Montini, elected to the papacy on June 21, adopt the late, revered pontiff's enlightened views regarding Jews and Judaism?

CHAPTER 8

Regarding the Arabs:

A Political Tug-of-War

Vatican Council II, Session Two:
September 29–December 4, 1963

"Reported proposed declaration on Catholic Jewish relations to be introduced at second session Vatican Council has been received with great appreciation and universal expectancy on the part of the Jewish people here and abroad."
—Telegram sent by New York Judge Joseph Proskauer to his friend Cardinal Spellman, then staying at the Grand Hotel in Rome:

DURING THE WEEKS FOLLOWING THE New York *agapé*, there was a sense of optimism among progressive Catholics and Jews regarding the introduction of the long-hoped-for Resolution on the Jews. That climate of hope would be short-lived. As Cardinal Bea returned to Rome, portents of trouble were emerging. In June 1963, the first of several reports surfaced suggesting that because of intense pressure from the governments of Arab nations, the issue of anti-Semitism had been dropped from the council's agenda. The source of this disturbing information was Father Gustave Weigel, SJ, a consultant to Cardinal

Bea's Secretariat for Promoting Christian Unity and a friend of the American Jewish Committee.

On hearing this disturbing news, Zach Shuster investigated the matter. Using his excellent contacts in the Vatican, he discovered that the report from Father Weigel was mere rumor. But this incident was indicative of the continuing flurry of rumors surrounding what was, and wasn't, under consideration at Vatican II.

In the run-up to the council's second session, the AJC took several actions to keep the Jewish issue in front of all concerned: committee lay leaders, as well as Marc and other professional staff, met often with Cardinal Bea, as well as with influential American prelates. In addition, Shuster wrote an article, "Removing the Stain of Guilt," which appeared in the British newspaper *The Observer*, on August 11, 1963, and was discussed extensively in Catholic journals. In it, he not only called for a new approach to the crucifixion, but also for affirmation by the council of the common roots of Judaism and Christianity.

That article, and an essay by the eminent Catholic journalist and economist Lady Barbara Ward Jackson titled "Rooting out the Fatal Myths," published on August 18, were reprinted in booklet form, and copies were distributed to the entire American episcopate. However, in a letter dated September 18, Msgr. Johannes Willebrands, the secretary of Cardinal Bea's Secretariat for Christian Unity, offered "a few frank remarks" about Shuster's article in *The Observer*:

> I appreciate very much your clear distinction between the political question of the State of Israel and the religious question of Judaism and Christianity. You acknowledge the analysis made by Catholic scholars on the origins of anti-Semitism. . . . May I express the hope that there will be a more careful analysis and investigation by Jewish experts on the factors, flowing from their side, which have helped to create and continue anti-Semitism among Christians. Anti-Semitism has so many aspects, so many roots; it is surely not limited to theological factors.

Earlier in September, despite all the negative rumors swirling about the Vatican, Pope Paul VI was said to be approving of Cardinal Bea's efforts. Moreover, the committee had learned that a strong declaration on the Jews had already been drafted, and many felt this document would stand a good chance of being adopted toward the middle of the second session of Vatican Council II. This view was underscored in a memo Marc received from the AJC office in Paris dated September 11: the outlook was very favorable, it said; Cardinal Bea was prepared to submit the declaration on the Jews, which was drafted and adopted by the secretariat under his leadership, and he was hopeful that the majority of the council would vote in favor of it.

According to information received from "reliable sources in Rome," the memo went on, the essential elements of the Declaration on the Jews would be:

> A solemn affirmation that Christianity has emerged from Judaism and originated from the Jewish religion and history; that the founders of Christianity were persons born in a Jewish environment and spirit; that the Church was always respectful to the Jewish people. It then says in clearest terms that the Church rejects the accusation of deicide made against the Jews; that it deplores anti-Semitism in past and present times; and concludes with a statement deploring the persecutions of Jews and declaring anathema any person who has contempt or persecutes the Jews.

The sources in Rome suggested that the declaration might come up in the middle of the coming session, following the council's discussion of the declarations on the nature of the Church and the relationship of the Catholic Church to other religious groups. That would be the proper moment, it was thought in the Vatican, for Cardinal Bea to propose the declaration on the Jews. However, great prudence would be required on the part of the document's Jewish advocates. Well-meaning sources were advising the committee to refrain from any actions that could be interpreted as Jewish pressure being exerted on the Vatican and, specifically, on members of the council. The message was clear: no public statements could be issued on the subject.

Despite the wide support among progressive delegates for a strong resolution on the Jews, there was concern in the Vatican regarding the remaining opposition, primarily within the conservative wing of the curia and among bishops from Arab nations. Thus, according to Cardinal Bea's trusted aide, Father Schmidt, it would be unwise for the committee to publish a pamphlet on the council at this delicate time—a view Marc endorsed. It was suggested, however, that such material be prepared in anticipation of the declaration's adoption.

Despite the news of promising developments in Rome, there would be many ups and downs regarding the Declaration on the Jews in the months to come. Within days of the convening of the council's second session on September 29, it was apparent that progress on the document would not be achieved anytime soon. In fact, as of mid-October, presentation of the issue to the delegates was not yet in the offing.

Thus, it seemed clear to the AJC that a media offensive was in order. On October 17, the *New York Times* published a front-page story by Milton Bracker, reporting from Rome, that spelled out the purported contents of the seven-point document known in its English-language translation as "The Declaration Concerning the Jews and Concerning Non-Christians." The article said that Cardinal Bea, in his role as president of the Secretariat for Promoting Christian Unity, would introduce the document to the delegates. According to the *Times* article, "many will judge the Council good or bad by its approval or disapproval of the Declaration." In subsequent paragraphs, the document expounded on the theological, moral, and political considerations associated with the proposed declaration.

Cardinal Bea emphasized that while "a profound and special relationship between the chosen people of the New Covenant, that is, the Church, and the chosen people of the Old Covenant is common to all Christians . . . the bond between Christians and the Jewish people is not so close as the relations among Christians." Consequently, he said, in order to satisfy all concerned, "The question of our relationship to the Jews is not dealt with in a *chapter* of the schema on ecumenism, but separately in a Declaration, which is instead added to the schema on ecumenism." The cardinal noted that the questions dealt with in the proposed brief schema "for the first time in the history of the church by any council are matters of the greatest importance for the church and the world today."

The cardinal concluded that Pope John XXIII's aspiration for the Church's renewal is of such importance that:

> We must pay the price of accepting the danger that some may perhaps misuse this Declaration for political purposes. For there is a question here of our obligation to truth, and to justice—of our duty to gratitude to God, of our duty to initiate faithfully and most closely Christ the Lord Himself and His Apostles Peter and Paul. In doing this the Church and this Council cannot in any way permit the consideration of any political authority or political reason.

In New York during the coming weeks, Marc and his staff would carefully analyze the contents of the lengthy decree. In a confidential memo from Shuster on October 8, the AJC learned that the long-awaited presentation to the council of the Declaration on the Jews was likely to occur shortly. In all likelihood, Shuster's memo said, the Document, which was being withheld for the moment so as not to arouse opposition within the Vatican's conservative element and from Arab countries, would be adopted during the council's third session, to be convened in the fall of 1964.

The first part of Shuster's prediction would come to pass on November 8, with the distribution of a forty-two-page-long chapter 4 to the council delegates. Following the brief mention of other monotheistic religions, the document's focus turned exclusively to "the Jews, who have particular relationships with the Church of Christ." Chapter 4 stated it was "exclusively religious in content" and had been inspired solely by spiritual considerations; hence, the secretariat was vigorously opposed to any attempt to give the document a "political interpretation."

In anticipation of the document's formal presentation to the council, in October, the committee's new director of public relations, Morton "Mort" Yarmon, had distributed a one-page press release crafted by Rabbi Tanenbaum. It said the committee hailed the decree as "a milestone in the continuing endeavor for understanding and mutual esteem among men of all faiths." The release added, "We prayerfully hope that the Ecumenical Council, this historic gathering of the Church's fathers, will take affirmative action on this Decree, and that the Church will find means of implementing it in the minds and hearts of Catholic faithful all over the world." Yarmon had not scheduled a press briefing, however. "We are, understandably, concerned not to take any steps that would provide ammunition to the opposition," he explained.

On October 17, A. M. Sonnabend, in a confidential memo addressed to Members of Key Leadership Groups, stressed that "our work has just begun." Noting that "the positive views on Jewish–Catholic relations expressed by Pope John XXIII, and more recently by his successor, Paul VI, along with the sympathy of Cardinal Bea give us reason to be hopeful," Sonnabend nevertheless expressed caution about the future. If and when this decree was introduced and passed, Sonnabend warned, it would be followed by "the historic responsibility—and historic opportunity—of implementing a decree through creation of a special body. This work will engage our staff for many years and in many parts of the world."

On Monday, October 21, the Religious News Service reported from Rome: "The Vatican Secretariat for promoting Christian Unity issued a statement here confirming that it has completed the draft of a document on 'the purely religious relations between Catholics and Jews' and submitted it to authorities of the Second Vatican Council." The secretariat explained that its statement had been issued "in answer to questions which have been raised because of certain articles appearing in the daily newspapers." According to the report, a member of the U.S. Bishops' press panel that had reviewed the secretariat's statement deplored "unhelpful gossip and guesswork in connection with the statement on Jewish-Catholic relations."

The following day, John Slawson received a cable from Shuster—couched in the brief and unpunctuated style of the telegraph era—that reported:

> Situations still fluctuating and maybe no decision for week/ Action U.S. Protestants and observers with Bea most desirable. Also urge AJC inspire intervention persons close Cushing Spellman O'Boyle and Grace . . . to have these prelates express to highest sources Rome their pressing concern Hope presentation occur this second session/Important all action without publicity

That day, Marc sent two confidential memos to his colleagues. In one, he informed them that cables of appreciation had been sent to Cardinal Bea the previous evening. The rabbi also noted that a week earlier, similar sentiments had been forwarded to the prelate by the World Council of Synagogues and the United Synagogue of America, the international and US voices of the Conservative movement, respectively. The committee had not asked other Jewish groups to do likewise, however, as "an explosion of such cables taking place at the same time would appear to be too obviously contrived."

But Marc said that should additional action by Jewish religious groups or scholars be required, the committee "will try to get them to operate in a similar fashion." Groups under consideration were the Union of American Hebrew Congregations and the Synagogue Council of America, as well as leading rabbis, including Julius Mark, Joseph Lookstein, and Albert Minda.

It was also agreed that Shuster would be asked to encourage the sending of similar cables by European and Latin American Jewish religious leaders, and that copies of such wires should be forwarded to the committee's New York office.

Among those messages from prominent American Jews to delegates from their home cities was the one sent from New York by Judge Joseph Proskauer to his friend, Cardinal Spellman, then staying at the Grand Hotel in Rome:

> Your Eminence: Reported proposed declaration on Catholic Jewish relations to be introduced at second session Vatican Council has been received with great appreciation and universal expectancy on the part of the Jewish people here and abroad. Earnestly ask you support this historic report to strengthen brotherhood and solidarity between the great Catholic Church and members of our ancient faith. Entreat you vigorously to press for some steps be taken this session. Affectionate regards.

In Marc's second confidential memo on October 22, he circulated a letter that Rabbi Heschel had received that morning from "a Catholic friend in Rome" whom Heschel described as "an intimate friend of Cardinal Bea." In that memo, the friend had mentioned the damage that could very well ensue from too much publicity too soon:

> At present, all is well, very well indeed. The *New York Times* story by Milton Bracker went too far and was premature. But we hope and are confident that nothing pejorative will result from this story. It would take a lot, a mighty lot, to stop the march of events during the next ten days or so, I am confident that action will take place before the end of October.

That confident prediction would not be realized for several weeks. On Friday, November 8, in anticipation of the introduction of the draft document, the committee issued a background paper, "Vatican Council II and the Jews: Activities of the American Jewish Committee." While that document described the agency's many and varied efforts over the years in promotion of the issuance of the long-awaited Decree, it could be seen as an attempt to propel action forward. Indeed, the paper said, "Unquestionably, the adoption of the decree by the assembled Church

Fathers would be hailed by Jews the world over as a significant turning point in Catholic-Jewish relations."

That afternoon, moreover, the committee issued a press release in which it stated the Catholic Church could be "a powerful force for rooting out attitudes and beliefs that have caused hostility against the Jews through the decree put before the Ecumenical Council today by Augustin Cardinal Bea, president of the Secretariat for the Promotion of Christian Unity." Hailing the cardinal's action as "an historic event," A. M. Sonnabend declared that the decree had been put forward "in a spirit that recognizes the historic values of Judaism as a living religion and creed." He predicted that "acceptance of this decree will make it impossible for anyone to instigate hatred for Jews and claim sanction or support in Church teaching or dogma."

Later that day, in Rome the proposed "Declaration on the Attitude of Catholics toward Non-Christians, and Particularly toward the Jews" would finally be submitted to the council delegates, thus becoming an official council document. The declaration consisted of chapter 4 of a schema on ecumenical relations, followed by a chapter on religious freedom.

While the draft document was not made public, a detailed communiqué was issued by the secretariat describing its substance. The document emphasized the Church's appreciation of the Jews as the Chosen People of the Old Testament; recognized the Jews as the forebears of Jesus, Mary, and the Apostles; and affirmed that all mankind shared responsibility for the death of Jesus. Bowing to increasingly vocal opposition forces, however, the published statement also included an emphatic disavowal of any political intent. It was stated that "use of the text to support partisan discussions or particular political claims . . . would be completely unjustified and contrary to [our] intention."

Immediate reaction, particularly in the United States, was overwhelmingly positive. Surprisingly, despite the customary divisions among the Orthodox, Conservative, and Reform branches of Judaism, the document's submission to the council was widely hailed as a historic event in the annals of interreligious understanding.

The points contained in the communiqué were well received at the committee. While the idea of holding joint theological studies and fraternal dialogue between Catholics and Jews was not mentioned, there was reason to believe that this step was also recommended.

The American delegates to the conclave were also declaring their support for the draft document. They sensed that the council was beginning to distance itself from discussing only the internal structure of the Church and was now prepared to address broader social issues.

Many observers were elated that the council was blazing a new path in human relations, and the world media offered praise for this important event. Daily newspapers and Catholic publications alike were featuring the draft document's introduction to the council. Many mentioned the AJC's role in the document's preparation and dissemination as prominently as the day's other breaking news: the clash between the Conservative Ottaviani and reformist elements, with the latter group thought to be expressing the sentiments of the majority of the delegates.

But the full text of the declaration would remain secret for the moment. The media communiqué that was issued would convey much less of the solemnity and positive spirit that imbued the actual document. Moreover, the handout was tweaked to minimize misunderstandings in the Arab world. In fact, the communiqué spoke more to what the declaration was *not* than to what it actually was, namely, the endgame of the well-orchestrated collaboration between Arab nations and their backers within the Catholic Church hierarchy.

The Vatican, obviously uneasy regarding anticipated negative reaction to the declaration in the Arab nations, had prepared and distributed to those countries' accredited diplomats and media a specially tailored handout containing the following paragraphs, which were *not* included in the general communiqué:

It is clear, therefore, that both the contents and purpose of the document are purely religious. In proposing it, its authors are confident that it reflects the opinion of many Islamic leaders who are well aware of the value of a statement on the religious heritage of which is shared by all those who revere Abraham and the prophets of the Old Testament

There is no foundation in the document for any consideration of relations between the Vatican and the State of Israel. In fact, it does not consider any political groups which exist among Jews. The draft cannot be called pro-Zionist or anti-Zionist since it considers these questions as entirely outside its scope.

The communiqué's final paragraph dealt with repercussions in the Arab world following Nahum Goldmann's announcement in 1962 of the intended appointment of a former official of an Israeli government ministry as an official observer at Vatican Council II. That widely denounced power play by the head of the World Jewish Congress had infuriated Cardinal Bea and his close associates, all of whom believed that it was responsible for inciting a chain of hostile events among Arab nations and bedeviling Vatican progress on the Jewish issue.

The prelate and his associates were also angered by Goldmann's declaration—made amid the uproar over his previous indiscretion—that the submission of the Document on the Jews to the council had been due to *his* two-year-long effort, rather than to the actions of the American Jewish Committee and other agencies. Taking the high road, during a press briefing, Zack Shuster simply characterized the document's submission to the council as "one of the greatest moments of Jewish history," and in Latin America, interreligious leaders hailed what they regarded to be a milestone achievement.

Despite the efforts to mollify the Arab world, within days, voices of dissent were being heard in the Vatican. On November 18, the day the schema on ecumenism came up for debate, three Middle Eastern patriarchs erupted in fury, bitterly attacking the proposed chapter 4, in which Jews were referred to in an ecumenical Christian context and threatening anti-Church reprisals in Arab lands.

Objections to the controversial schema chapter were hardly

confined to delegates from Arab nations, however. Even sharper criticism was expressed by Cardinal Ernesto Ruffini, the archbishop of
Palermo. The conservative-minded churchman took issue with what
he described as "giving honorable mention" to Jews, in preference to
other, unnamed, faiths—those who, allegedly, were less hostile to the
Catholic religion. A theological tug-of-war was now underway with
conservative, anti-Jewish prelates on one side of a great divide buoyed
by two millennia of Church practice; while on the other side, there
were more reform-minded brethren, particularly an army of American
Bishops, including, for example, Cardinal Joseph Ritter, the archbishop of St. Louis.

The next day, Cardinal Bea reminded the council, to great
applause, that Pope John XXIII had explicitly ordered—and approved
in draft form—the Declaration on the Jews. Furthermore, the cardinal stated, one of the compelling reasons for the declaration's issuance
was the persistence among certain Catholics of Nazi-style, hard-core
anti-Semitism. The cardinal then reiterated that the declaration was of
no *political* significance—a fact of which the Arab nations had already
been informed.

On Saturday, November 16, following the Vatican's announcement
of the draft declaration's distribution to the delegates, but before the
beginning of the council's official debate, Marc and his colleagues
received an interim report from Rome. In a five-page, single-spaced
confidential memorandum, they learned that Cardinal Bea's intention
to deliver a major address before the council and to immediately publish its full text had been derailed due to mounting opposition by "the
conservative element to the entire schema on ecumenism." As a result,
he had decided to postpone distribution of the document until a more
propitious moment.

In addition to this unsettling development, other problems were
emerging. Opposition to the declaration by the Arab states, which
had been dormant since the end of the first Council session, was
being revived in early November via a campaign on radio stations
in Arab countries. On November 4, Pope Paul VI had received a

confidential message from one of the Arab world's most influential political leaders, who offered a veiled threat in the form of an expression of hope that the council would not take any action "to disturb relations between the Vatican and the Arab states in the Middle East." In his reply the next day, the pontiff insisted that no such step was intended and that the declaration on the Jews was solely of "a religious and spiritual nature, with no political implications." In support of that assurance, Pope Paul set out the parameters of the proposed Declaration on the Jews.

The Arab leaders would not be mollified, however. Upping the ante, on Thursday, November 7, radio stations in Cairo and other Middle Eastern capitals began to broadcast damning material on the Jewish issue. They went so far as to attempt to undermine existing positive Catholic-Jewish relations by citing Rolf Hochhuth's controversial new play, *The Deputy,* as evidence of the Church's traditionally negative attitude toward the Jews. On learning of this development, Pope Paul called an emergency meeting with high Church authorities, including Cardinal Bea, to consider the next step to be taken by the Vatican.

Those present agreed that the matter had reached a critical point— that the Church could not allow itself to be intimidated. The time had come to make the contents of the declaration public and official. As a result, the document was submitted to the council the very next morning, November 8. The Vatican's damage-control mechanism swung into urgent mode: a media communiqué was drafted, translated into many languages, and prepared for distribution.

On November 16, Marc received an internal memo that noted that in light of the vociferous opposition to the entire schema on ecumenism, high Vatican authorities had advised that "intervention by various Jewish bodies and individuals throughout the world would be of great help." Prompt and coordinated action by the Alliance Israélite Universelle in France, the Consistoire Central Israélite de Belgique, and American bishops had already yielded results. Cardinal Bea immediately transmitted the ensuing cables to Paul VI, "establishing in the mind of the pope himself and his closest advisers the fact that Jewish people throughout the world were impatiently expecting the council's action on this declaration during this session."

Discussion of the entire schema began on November 18, as scheduled. On the following day, Cardinal Bea read a four-page document to the delegates, in which he clarified its content, significance, and scope. During the ensuing tense debate, several delegates argued that any mention of the Jews would be inappropriate. Others insisted that if the Jews were to be mentioned, then other non-Christians, most notably Muslims, must be addressed, as well. Not surprisingly, delegates from the Arab-dominated Middle East were especially adamant about this issue.

Approximately six weeks following Cardinal Bea's presentation, the American Jewish Committee issued a press release written under Marc's supervision that said, "The introduction by Augustin Cardinal Bea at Vatican Council II of the decree on Catholic attitudes toward Jews and Judaism is regarded as an historic event by Jews everywhere." In anticipation of dissension within the organized American Jewish community regarding some of the decree's more controversial points, the press release added, "This memorandum highlights what we consider the significant aspects of the decree, and sets forth the historical background against which we think its importance should be assessed. Accordingly, we concentrate for the most part on those elements in the decree which deals with deicide and anti-Semitism."

The release noted that the Church had previously expressed its abhorrence of anti-Semitism. For example, in 1928, a decree of the Holy Office, confirmed by Pope Pius XI, condemned "in an especial manner the hatred against the people, once chosen by God, that hatred, namely, which nowadays is called anti-Semitism." Ten years later, as German Jews were being persecuted by the Nazis, Pius XI would declare to visiting Belgian pilgrims, "Anti-Semitism is a repugnant movement in which we Christians can have no part. . . . Spiritually we are all Semites." The next pope, Pius XII, would express that sentiment two decades later, following the Holocaust, to an American Jewish Committee delegation.

What was regarded as being particularly significant about the 1963 declaration, however, was that it struck "directly at the heart of a concept that has served to sanction hatred and persecution across the centuries: the invidious charge that the Jews are a deicide people—'Christ killers'—rejected and punished by God, and burdened with the same guilt in each successive generation."

The committee now took the initiative, embarking on a media counteroffensive to forestall pronouncements that might be interpreted in the Vatican as pressuring for passage of the Resolution on the Jews or, more damaging, providing additional provocation for the opposition forces. Rabbi Tanenbaum and other committee officials sought out private meetings with various journalists to emphasize the need for their discretion at this pivotal time in the history of Christian-Jewish relations.

That evening, a flurry of activity was underway at the committee's offices in New York, Paris, Buenos Aires, and Rio de Janeiro. Within hours, carefully worded cablegrams from Jewish religious and communal leaders in the Americas and Europe were on their way to the pontiff in an effort to strengthen Cardinal Bea's hand. At the same time, committee spokespeople, having learned that the American bishops present in the Vatican were about to hold a caucus, began to deluge those prelates with similar messages.

On November 20 and 21, delegates arrayed on both sides of the issue made speeches. For example, Cardinal Albert Gregory Meyer, the archbishop of Chicago, offered a spirited defense of the declaration. It was clear from reactions in the council chamber that the majority of the delegates were in favor of chapter 4, as well as of chapter 5, which dealt with religious freedom. But the conservative opposition was unmoved, and a filibuster was now in the offing. As a result, the council delegates voted to defer action on the two controversial chapters while adopting the remainder of the schema for debate.

On November 21, by an overwhelming vote of 1,966 in favor and 86 against, the delegates approved the schema's first three chapters, but not the chapter regarding the Jews. Seven sessions later, during the seventy-ninth and final General Congregation of that year's meeting, Cardinal Bea assured the delegates that, while that controversial chapter had not been part of the discussion, the debate's postponement was merely temporary and the chapter's contents would be carefully reworked.

A week later, the end of this session of Vatican Council II was approaching, and discussion of chapters 4 and 5 was still tabled, generating deep concern in the prodeclaration camp. On November 28, Rabbi Heschel cabled Cardinal Meyer, pointing out that there was great anxiety in the United States that the problematic chapters might never be voted on. The very next day, Bishop Charles H. Helmsing of Kansas City urged that at least a *preliminary* vote, which, he noted, "was expected by everybody," take place.

It was too late, however. The second session of Vatican Council II would recess on December 4, 1963, without having acted on the two chapters that meant so much to many churchmen and their Jewish "elder brothers." During Cardinal Bea's address to the delegates on that session's last day, he acknowledged that the two final chapters of the draft declaration remained to be considered by the delegates, and he added, "It is fitting to meditate and ponder everything carefully over and over again without haste and with a serene and tranquil spirit so that in the next session of the Council they may be treated and judged with mature consideration."

Would that debate be taken up when the council reconvened in December 1964? If so, would Cardinal Bea, who had said he would welcome amendments to the resolution, retain his control of the secretariat? Given the atmosphere of the just-concluded session, the answers to these questions were decidedly unclear.

CHAPTER 9

The Conservative Backlash

"What is put off is not put away."
—Cardinal Augustin Bea, speaking optimistically
at the end of the second session of Vatican Council II,
regarding the Declaration on the Jews

CARDINAL BEA'S OPTIMISM IN THE face of the challenges that lay ahead was a testament to his character and belief in justice for the Jewish people. On December 3, only one day before the end of the council's second session, a well-organized group of anti-Semites opposed to action by the delegates on the Resolution on the Jews mounted another attack. On that day, an innocuously titled pamphlet, "Gli Ebrei e il Concilio—Alla Luce della Sacra Scrittura e della Tradizione" (The Jews and the Council—in the light of the Holy Scriptures and Tradizione), written under the pseudonym "Bernardus," was sent to each Council delegate at his private quarters. "*Gli Ebrei e il Concilio*" was not the first anti-Jewish diatribe to be distributed to the prelates. In 1962, a negative, six-hundred-page book, *Il Complotto Contro La Chiesa* ("The Plot Against the Church), widely assumed to have been financed by Arab propagandists, was circulated among the council delegates.

While the 1962 tome was crudely written, and failed to produce its desired effect, *Gli Ebrei e il Consilio* was more sophisticated. At first glance seemingly harmless, it was in reality a viciously anti-Semitic diatribe invoking selective, long-standing Church traditions. And given the pamphlet's theological sophistication and its brevity, which encouraged easy reading, its impact on the delegates could be enormous. Rumors circulated that the slickly produced document had been prepared with the tacit approval of certain conservative prelates in the curia.

At the end of the council's second session, Cardinal Bea, smarting from critics' allegations concerning the council's failure to have taken up the contents of chapter 4, the Declaration on the Jews, insisted that it was simply a lack of time that had prevented the delegates from getting to this chapter. Indeed, only a fraction of the second session's agenda items were ever voted on. But the more liberal of the delegates, including most of the Americans, felt that they had been outmaneuvered by the opposition coalition of ultraconservative Italian bishops working in concert with colleagues from Arab nations.

Several other issues were also complicating the situation. For example, there were delegates who agreed with the sentiments expressed in the proposed declaration but did not believe it should be presented within the context of a discussion of ecumenism. There were also those who opposed chapter 5, which placed the Church on record as upholding religious liberty. The many dissenting voices were not confined to the Vatican. There was also pressure being exerted by reactionary elements within the Italian business community who feared that ecumenism might encourage socialist tendencies, as well as by Arab diplomats who opposed any action by the council on behalf of world Jewry.

Given these seemingly intractable difficulties, the American Jewish Committee welcomed analyses from friends within the Vatican. One of these allies was Father Gustave Weigel. On January 2, 1964, mere days before his untimely death in New York, he suggested to Rabbi Heschel that the committee work quietly with prelates who might be willing to intervene with the Vatican at the highest level. On December 9, five days following Cardinal Bea's message of hope concerning the draft Declaration on the Jews, Marc and his colleagues received Zach Shuster's seven-page, single-spaced analysis of the reasons for the declaration's deferment, as well as his insights regarding prospects for action during a future council session.

Shuster said it would be counterproductive to dwell on the delegates' failure to have acted during the second session. He also observed that Pope Paul's coming visit to Israel, to take place in January, could have been timed so as to put Vatican Council II on the back burner in the hope that irritations would subside.

Until the final two weeks of the second session, many had thought that no serious opposition would arise regarding the substance of the draft declaration, and thus it would be reasonable to expect that the council would at least consider it as a basis for further discussion. Despite Cardinal Bea's insistence that procedural issues alone had prevented deliberation on the declaration, other and much weightier factors—namely, the renewed and invigorated opposition of the Arab states—had surfaced early in November, thus precluding action on the issue.

Another, perhaps even more distressing, factor was the escalating intransigence of conservative elements both within and outside the curia. Among those who sought the ear of His Holiness were Cardinals Ottaviani, Ruffini, and Siri. They attacked Cardinal Bea personally, insisting that adoption of the schema on ecumenism would lead to "heresy, atheism, and communism." These divisions were heightened because the still-inexperienced pope was finding himself at the center of clashing forces, and some felt he was failing to demonstrate the strong leadership required at this critical juncture.

Marc felt it was increasingly clear that new strategies must be developed. Some felt the committee must intensify its efforts in Rome with the goal of impressing upon Vatican authorities that the Church must take a strong position regarding its view of the Jewish people. Church authorities would have to be convinced that the aspirations of forces in the Western world awaiting a historic stand on this issue would, in the long run, be of greater weight than would be the opposition of the Arab leaders.

AJC officials also concluded that there would be value in keeping the issue before the public. Doing so would require an aggressive media campaign, as well as intensifying contacts with Catholic lay and religious leaders at the local level to instill greater determination and make them realize their own potential.

Much of this message resonated with Marc, but for the time being, he concluded, the best policy would be to remain silent regarding the failures of the council's second session and to concentrate on developing an effective strategy for the third session.

In early 1964, Marc and his colleagues remained confident that the critical issues arising from the second session of Vatican Council II would soon be resolved, but the committee would now be beset by new crises, both at home and abroad.

In the United States, Rabbi Joseph Soloveitchik, who was troubled by aspects of the Jewish involvement in Vatican Council II, was about to spark a firestorm of fury and protest in the American Jewish community. Speaking during the midwinter conference of the Orthodox umbrella group, the Rabbinical Council of America, on February 7, 1964, he denounced the proposed Vatican document on the Jews as "Nothing more or less than evangelical propaganda."

Stating his view that "The schema does not recognize Jews as people with the right to live their own lives and worship in their own way," the Orthodox leader charged that the Church was actually just awaiting the day when "we see the light and embrace Christianity." The rabbi went on to anger many of his coreligionists by criticizing Jewish efforts to revise Catholic texts.

The news from Rome was also becoming increasingly ominous. On February 20, it was learned that Paul VI had ordered Cardinal Bea to eliminate the chapter on the Jews from his schema and to mention the Jewish issue merely in a general declaration on non-Christian religions—an action many thought would denude the hoped-for decree of its true significance. While Cardinal Bea was reportedly resisting Paul VI's order, in mid-March there were press accounts suggesting that many of the delegates were in favor of the pope's approach. There was worse to come for Cardinal Bea: it was likely that jurisdiction over this matter could be transferred to an as-yet-to-be-established Secretariat for Non-Christian Religions, a body that would come into being on May 17.

Bishop Helmsing of Kansas City stated publicly that on March 7, Pope Paul had informed him of his hope for "a good statement" on the Church's attitude toward Jews, Muslims, and "the whole world"—which could be interpreted to mean that Judaism would no longer be dealt with in the desired special context.

At this critical juncture, Cardinal Richard Cushing once again demonstrated his status as the leading American champion of a strong declaration on the Jews. On the very day of Pope Paul's implication that Judaism's position would not be dealt with in the desired special context, Rabbi Tanenbaum and Dr. Slawson encountered the archbishop of Boston at a funeral and voiced their anxieties. In response, he said he would communicate with the Vatican at the highest level. In fact, Cardinal Cushing said, he was in the process of drafting a statement to be signed by several American cardinals and sent to His Holiness.

That evening, Cardinal Cushing told a meeting of the National Conference of Christians and Jews that the whole world was awaiting the Church's condemnation of anti-Semitism. And later that month, Cardinal Cushing reassured the committee of his support. Then, responding to the agency's concerns, the prelate published a Lenten message in the *Boston Evening Traveller* in which he said, "Anti-Semitism is a profoundly un-Christian attitude," adding, "The spiritual ancestry of Christian is Jewish," "The Golden Rule that Christ preached was taught in the temple," and "When Jews do not accept Christ as the Promised One, they do not reject the ideals that Christ preached." Moreover, during a media interview, Cardinal Cushing stated that the proposed decree was at the heart of the Church's ecumenical concern and that the delegates' failure to act on this tradition-altering document would appear to sanction persecution of the Jews.

Meanwhile, the AJC's leadership was working privately to galvanize other American prelates into action. For example, Marc's fellow

Baltimorean, Jacob Blaustein, acting in his role as an honorary president of the AJC, discussed the declaration with his city's archbishop, Lawrence J. Shehan. In early April, the archbishop not only predicted that both of the controversial declarations would pass, he also promised to consider issuing a public statement of support for these documents.

Marc was also talking to other influential Church figures. Approaching Cardinals Ritter and Meyer, both of whom had fought bravely in the face of severe opposition during the council's tumultuous second session, he found they were convinced that the decree would be enacted during the third session. Marc also learned from Cardinal Ritter that he had spoken with Cardinal Cicognani, who was believed to have been responsible for the derailing of chapters 4 and 5 during the last council session, and that the Italian prelate assured his colleague that the chapters would be acted upon. Cardinal Cicognani even promised to join Cardinal Cushing in presenting the American bishops' position to Pope Paul VI.

But neither Cardinal Ritter nor Cicognani believed it was appropriate to go public just yet. Their view was shared by Bishop Patrick A. O'Boyle of Washington, who had recently written to Cardinal Bea at the urging of the prelate from St. Louis.

Meanwhile, Cardinal Francis Spellman would be persuaded to take a more public stance following a meeting with another prominent New Yorker, Judge Joseph M. Proskauer, who had consulted with Marc. A former AJC president and a close friend of Cardinal Spellman, the jurist observed that the Catholic clergy seemed to be unaware of how important action on the declaration would be in advancing interreligious understanding. The judge also pointed out that the Holy See had heard much more from the declaration's vociferous opponents than from its supporters. He insisted Cardinal Spellman could help spur its inclusion on the council's agenda by endorsing the document's contents. In order to provide Cardinal Spellman with a platform for publicly stating his support for the declaration, Judge Proskauer invited his friend to address the committee's Annual Dinner on April 30.

On that early spring evening, Cardinal Spellman, who shared the dais with other distinguished Americans, including Secretary of State Dean Rusk, the son of a Protestant clergyman, declared to thunderous applause from the 1,100 guests: "Anti-Semitism can never find a basis in the Catholic religion." While the cardinal did not refer specifically to the declaration in his stirring address, he said that he was appalled by a recent report that persecution of Jews was still being viewed by many of his coreligionists as punishment for their collective "guilt" in the crucifixion of Christ.

The cardinal then turned to an issue deeply troubling to many Jews and Christians alike: the wartime behavior of the late Pope Pius XII regarding the rescue of European Jewry. In an attempt to clarify that pontiff's position and actions, Cardinal Spellman, likely mindful of the coming opening in New York of Rolf Hochhuth's play *The Deputy*, argued that during the Holocaust Pius had, in fact, condemned both Nazism and anti-Semitism.

Cardinal Spellman's words were applauded in several highly regarded mass-circulation publications. For example, the *Saturday Evening Post* paid tribute to the prelate's "contribution to religious amity." *Look*, another popular weekly magazine of the era, published an article titled "The Christian War on Anti-Semitism" in its June 2 issue. Written by Arlene and Howard Eisenberg in consultation with the committee, it described several initiatives led by Marc and included memoranda on Catholic teaching and Catholic liturgy, as well as Rabbi Heschel's paper, "On Improving Catholic-Jewish Relations."

Earlier that spring, with many prominent churchmen already sensitized to uneasiness in the Jewish community regarding the impasse over the future of the declaration, Bishop James A. McNulty of Buffalo addressed the local AJC chapter, marking the first appearance of a Catholic prelate before a Jewish group in that upstate New York city's history. Other prominent churchmen who spoke under Jewish communal auspices at that time included John J. Krol and William E. Cousins, the archbishops of Philadelphia and Milwaukee, respectively, and Msgr. George Higgins.

Meanwhile, a global effort was being launched. In Europe, Zach

Shuster was working with the Alliance Israélite Universelle in garnering clerical support for action on the declaration. Their joint efforts would soon bear fruit: immediately prior to a critically important convocation of cardinals and bishops in February, the alliance would be granted a hearing with Cardinal Augustin Achille Liénart, the bishop of Lille, and other influential European prelates.

And in Latin America, sympathetic laymen and rank-and-file clergy, working toward their common goal, would succeed in reaching out to nearly all of their respective nations' cardinals. These meetings were cordial, yet frank, with most of the prelates agreeing to immediately draft urgent messages to Cardinal Cicognani. The most memorable of these meetings took place at the rustic summer residence of the eighty-eight-year-old Cardinal Augusto de Silva, the archbishop of Bahia, Brazil.

Alfred Hirschberg, the American Jewish Committee's representative in São Paolo, said of his visit to the Brazilian bishop's remote retreat:

> It is more than three hours' drive from the city, partially by dirt road, crossing swollen rivers on makeshift wooded bridges without railings. To be presentable, we changed into dark suits near the house, hiding behind bushes. . . . We sat on an open terrace, with a view of the ocean. The cardinal invited us for luncheon; we roamed through the fields of religion, science, and the current situation in Brazil. Only after three hours he reluctantly let us go, accompanying us to the car.

Back in the Vatican, Pope Paul VI referred obliquely to the long-sought Declaration in an apostolic letter in May, when he said he would "not neglect any means" to have the council adopt a decree committing the Church to the defense of all non-Catholics' natural rights. Then, on May 17, the pontiff announced the long-expected establishment of the Vatican Secretariat for Non-Christian Religions, to be headed by a relatively unknown prelate, Cardinal Paolo Marella.

Since little was known about where this churchman stood on inter-religious issues, the Jewish community was more uncertain than ever regarding the Decree's fate. Would the Jewish issue now be dealt with through this new secretariat, as a Vatican spokesman suggested to the press? Had the Declaration on the Jews been removed from the con-text of Christian unity and expanded to cover general relations with non-Christians?

These matters were further confused when the Vatican organ, *L'Osservatore Romano*, reported that the new secretariat was being "set up outside the Council" and that its establishment would not alter plans for clarifying relationships with Jews and non-Christians during the third session of Vatican Council II. Was the implication that the Jewish issue would remain under Cardinal Bea's control? Or not? Wherever the truth now lay, there were ominous signs that the declaration might be watered down or even sidelined.

Based on the American Jewish Committee's consultations with Pro Deo University officials, the agency's leadership believed that the time had come to seek reassurance at the highest level that the declaration would be on the agenda on the council's reconvening on September 14.

To that end, the committee requested a papal audience, which took place on May 30. The pontiff received a delegation comprised of the agency's president, Morris Abram, and several lay leaders—Ralph Friedman, Philip Hoffman, and Rose Adler Sperry—as well as John Slawson. Cardinal Eugène Tisserant, who earlier that month had met with Jewish and other non-Catholic spokespeople at the committee's Manhattan headquarters, was also present.

Marc was not there, but a briefing paper prepared under his super-vision for the meeting suggested that a dialogue, rather than a mere ceremonial exchange of prepared statements, might be appropriate. During Morris Abram's opening remarks, he emphasized that the American Jewish Committee had always stood for the rights of all reli-gious groups.

The pope then read a message of commendation regarding the committee's resolve "to safeguard the religious and cultural freedom of all people" and to condemn any curtailment of human rights on racial grounds. Paul VI also acknowledged "particular consideration for the Jewish tradition with which Christianity is so intimately linked, and from which it derives hope for trusting relations," deplored the Jews' ordeals, and wished them every favor from God.

Abram then steered the conversation to the deicide issue—a subject that Pope Paul had failed to mention in his remarks. The committee's president expressed his hope that this pivotally important issue would be dealt with in the coming session—a hope, he noted, that was shared by such American notables as Secretary of State Rusk and Cardinal Spellman.

In reply, His Holiness expressed his hope that "the Council will adopt the substance of what I have just read to you," and he added, "I have seen Cardinal Spellman's speech, and he speaks my sentiments." Among the issues of concern to the committee's delegation was whether during the council's third session the delegates might "diminish the clarity" of the two controversial chapters.

At that point, Abram announced that Mrs. Sperry, a niece of Julius Rosenwald, who had built Sears, Roebuck & Co. into a leading national retailer and became a major Jewish philanthropist, would endow a Center for Interreligious Relations at Pro Deo University in memory of her late husband, Leonard M. Sperry. Abram said her intention was "to help carry out the spirit of the Council's work in the field of intergroup relations" through analyzing and combating prejudice in the teachings of the various faiths, as well as via psychological and sociological research.

Abram later said that the pontiff might be thinking of allowing the proposed Center to evolve into an embryonic administrative venue for relations with non-Christian faiths. The pope expressed his appreciation to Pro Deo's benefactor and blessed objects she had brought to the audience on behalf of Catholic friends in the United States. While the central issue prompting the committee delegation's audience with the pope had not been resolved, the meeting did end on a cordial note.

The following day, May 31, much to the delegation's surprise,

L'Osservatore Romano featured the pontiff's prepared statement. No mention was made either of the conversation regarding the deicide charge or of Abram's reference to Cardinal Spellman. Could these omissions be portents of a disastrous third council session concerning the issue of primary importance to world Jewry? Or were they merely reflective of Pope Paul's caution in not appearing to prejudge the council's deliberations? Both questions would be answered within a matter of days.

On June 3, the committee was informed that per the order of the Coordinating Commission under Cardinal Cicognani's control, and with the pope's agreement, the deicide clause had indeed been deleted from the Resolution to be distributed to the Church Fathers between the fifteenth and thirtieth of the month. Furthermore, the revised document would not be formulated as a "constitution," as originally intended, but, rather, as a declaration—a document of diminished legal force.

While Cardinal Bea and members of his staff were reported to have objected strongly to this obstructionist maneuvering, their response would have no effect in the Vatican. Two days later, June 5, Father Morlion, the Pro Deo founder, acting on Cardinal Bea's behalf, formally notified the committee of the latest developments. As the cardinal put it, the declaration "had been brought to a higher plane" and had been broadened to condemn hatred for humankind, as well as the concept of the Jews as a cursed people.

Father Morlion contended that although the word *deicide,* which he characterized as a theological absurdity, was being stricken from the document, its substance had actually been strengthened. On June 12, during a radio interview, he predicted that Catholic-Jewish relations would, in fact, remain under Cardinal Bea's jurisdiction. Later, speaking off the record, he let it be known that for the time being only the pope's innermost circle would have knowledge of the revised document's text.

He also cautioned that Cardinal Bea would not welcome any attempt to obtain such information from him at this point in time.

Father Morlion explained that the pope had acted against Cardinal Bea's advice by granting an audience to the American Jewish Committee delegation. Cardinal Bea opposed this audience, according to Father Morlion, because the cardinal wanted to confront the opposition with an irreversible commitment.

Any doubts about Father Morlion's explanation would vanish within a matter of days. During a visit to the United States, the uncharacteristically piqued Cardinal Bea refused to meet with Rabbi Heschel. What was his reason for doing so? The text of the decree was supposed to have remained confidential.

On the very day of Cardinal Bea's rebuff of his rabbinic colleague, the Catholic churchman's aide, Father Stephen Schmidt, told Marc that things had not gone very well. But he expressed hope that once the third session of the council was underway, the draft would be amended from the floor. After further examination of this distressing turn of events, Marc began to sense the purpose of Cardinal Bea's impending visit to the United States: it was to lay the groundwork for action on the council floor, and Cardinals Spellman and Cushing were intending to play prominent roles in achieving their shared goal of enacting the Resolution on the Jews.

Marc's impression would be reinforced when another member of Cardinal Bea's staff, Father Thomas J. Stransky, said he was confident that the pontiff had received the revised text and that Cardinals Cushing, Meyer, Ritter, and Spellman had already urged the pontiff to restore the document's crucial point regarding deicide.

To complicate the situation further, on June 12, the day of Father Morlion's disturbing off-the-record statement, the *New York Times* published a front-page article by Robert C. Doty—who had succeeded Milton Bracker as the paper's Vatican correspondent in March—in which he reported that political as well as theological considerations were responsible for this unwelcome development. Doty claimed it was unlikely that the Decree would be amended from the council floor.

Upon reading the *Times* article, Morris Abram cabled Paul VI. After thanking the pope for the May 30 audience, the committee's president pointed out that any new statement would inevitably be measured against the previous year's strong draft. Meanwhile, the media jousts continued. The press service of *L'Osservatore Romano* countered the *New York Times* story with an oblique thrust. The text, it was stated, had not been distributed, the implication being that it could still be altered. According to Father Morlion, Doty's story in the *Times* had provoked consternation in the Vatican; Church officials suspected it was based on a leak by an individual who was not, in fact, fully informed about the text.

But Father Morlion also supplied the committee with what was purportedly a confidential summary of the proposed text. This useful document denied that Cardinal Bea's efforts had been defeated and the declaration had not been weakened, although "for reasons of terminology," the deicide charge would no longer be specifically condemned. Three weeks later, Don Carlo Ferrero of Pro Deo University appeared to confirm that a reasonably strong Document might be in process.

If Marc and the committee's lay leaders thought that there could be a positive outcome regarding action on the Document, however, worse was to come. In early July, Rabbi Heschel would be informed that the conservative European prelates, led by Cardinal Cicognani, would not allow a vote on either the Document on the Jews or the one on religious freedom during the council's third session. And as time passed, Cardinal Bea would no longer be in charge, so he would not be able to intervene. Confirming the committee's intelligence, Zach Shuster said that he had learned that although the relevant drafts might be submitted to the council, they would be stymied via a procedural pretext. At this point, he warned, only direct intervention by Cardinal Cicognani or by the pope himself could stave off disaster.

Amid this seemingly devastating development, during the summer of 1964, the American Jewish Committee intensified its efforts to make common cause with progressive-minded clerics whose voices, it was hoped, would eventually be heard at the highest level within the walls of the Vatican. To this end, John Slawson traveled to Boston, where he met with Cardinal Cushing to review the Council of Trent's rejection of the deicide charge four centuries earlier.

And at the committee's Manhattan headquarters, a twofold plan of action was underway: a draft statement was prepared by the Department of Interreligious Affairs to assist Cardinal Cushing in formulating his strategy for keeping the document on the council's agenda, and Slawson contacted Msgr. Higgins, a staunch ally who was working behind the scenes against any watering down of the Decree's contents.

In Baltimore, meanwhile, Jacob Blaustein yet again called on Archbishop Shehan. He, in turn, promised to consult with Cardinal Spellman regarding a possible appeal to Pope Paul VI. In addition, the Baltimore prelate would subsequently correspond with Cardinal Cicognani on that issue. From Kansas City, Bishop Helmsing voiced his concerns in an exchange of letters with Marc. From San Antonio, Archbishop Robert E. Lucey corresponded with Ralph Friedman, expressing his opinion that letters to Rome were of little use. He suggested instead that if there were no action during the coming council session, the American Church hierarchy should issue its own statement.

With the situation now so grave, and with time running out, the committee was convinced that any approach to the Holy See could only be accomplished outside the customary Church infrastructure. To that end, Zach Shuster sought assistance from Karl Barth, the famed Basel-based Protestant theologian. But he could not convince Barth of the deicide issue's importance. Shuster would be more successful in his appeal to Vittorino Veronese, a prominent Italian businessman and former director general of UNESCO, who was a close friend of Paul VI. Shuster had met Signor Veronese through the Alliance Israélite Universelle, which had prepared a document outlining the importance of the issue and which the Italian presented to the pope.

Across the Atlantic, in the wake of the recent rapprochement between the Roman Catholic and Eastern churches, Abram and Slawson turned for support to Archbishop Iakovos, the head of the

Greek Orthodox Church in North and South America, who had participated a year earlier in the New York *agapé*. The Greek Orthodox prelate was both cordial and sympathetic regarding the committee leaders' cause. He promised to speak with Patriarch Athenagoras, with whom the pope had met on January 4, during the pope's visit to the Holy Land. So intent was Archbishop Iakovos on resolving the deicide issue that he intimated he might approach the pope directly.

Meanwhile, the committee was pursuing an even more crucial diplomatic effort: seeking intervention from the highest levels of the US government. The push for such an intervention had begun in May, when the committee delegation that had been received by the pope went on to Washington to meet with Dean Rusk. The secretary of state had found it hard to believe that the Vatican Council would reverse itself, but he promised to keep the issue in mind. Moreover, in late June, Morris Abram appealed to Sargent Shriver, the late President Kennedy's brother-in-law. Shriver was a former director of the Peace Corps, while Abram had once been its legal counsel. However, Shriver said he thought the White House would not care to intervene, and in any case, action by high-ranking Church officials would be more effective.

Refusing to be deterred, the committee leaders accepted the offer of Sidney R. Rabb, a prominent Democrat and a major AJC supporter in the Boston region, to arrange a meeting for them with a fellow Massachusetts resident, Speaker of the US House of Representatives John W. McCormack. On hearing the committee leaders' presentation, the speaker appeared to be moved, and within twenty-four hours, he telephoned Abram and Slawson with the news that during a breakfast meeting that morning with President Lyndon Johnson, the president had said that he was thinking of sending a private emissary to Rome to meet with the pope.

The president did not follow through on his idea, but the committee's spirits were buoyed: the cause of world Jewry now had the attention of one of the most powerful men in the world. On July 2, Marc followed up on the lay leaders' conversation with Speaker McCormack by meeting in Washington with two key White House aides—Ralph Dungan, the President's special assistant, and Myer Feldman, the president's adviser on Jewish affairs.

In his remarks, Marc stressed that the Vatican ought to be made aware of "a genuine concern here at the highest levels" about the declaration on the Jews. Marc's immediate objective, however, was to arrange for Abram to meet with President Johnson—a request shot down by Dungan, who did not see a reason for the committee's sense of urgency. Despite entreaties during the next three weeks, the president's special assistant remained adamant: there would be no meeting with the president.

On July 23, Father Morlion was at last able to inform Slawson of a *positive* development: he had just met with Dungan, who informed him that while President Johnson was not inclined toward sending an envoy to meet with the pope before the 1964 presidential election, he had expressed the White House's concern "for unofficial transmission to the pope." Similarly, Sidney Rabb, who was often in contact with White House staff, reported that although the President would not be sending an envoy to the Vatican, he was considering forwarding a letter to His Holiness on the opening day of the council's third session. He would do so via the US ambassador to Italy, G. Frederick Reinhardt. Rabb also noted that Cardinal Cicognani had been replaced as leader of the opposition to the Decree by Cardinal Ottaviani.

Five days later, on July 28, Father Morlion, calling from Rome, reported that he had verbally transmitted to the pope what he described as "the message from the President . . . confirming the political necessity in America that the new Decree should be stronger than the old one." The priest noted that what he dubbed "the political explanation" had been received with particular interest and that it would be useful in forestalling a conservative-backed filibuster. Father Morlion also suggested that the future of the declaration was looking brighter, and no further action by the United States would be required.

Nonetheless, Marc intensified his effort to keep the need for a strongly worded Decree elevated in the consciousness of both the

Church and the Catholic public. He embarked on a vigorous campaign via speeches to diverse groups and the publication of numerous articles. His efforts would almost immediately bear fruit. His challenging address to the Catholic Press Association, for example, would be the subject of favorable comment in numerous religious journals. For example, in an article published on July 17 by the *St. Louis Review* and reprinted in other diocesan journals, the rabbi reviewed the proposed Decree in the context of Catholic-Jewish friction through the centuries.

In that article, he traced the history of Catholic theological anti-Semitism, beginning with the early Church fathers, particularly St. John Chrysostom, who in the year 387 A.D. had declared that the synagogue "is a place of prostitution, a den of thieves, and a hiding-place of wild animals." Marc also called attention to the Fourth Lateran Council. In the year 1215, that body had inaugurated ecclesiastical legislation relating to the Jews, which, according to the rabbi, "reduced them virtually to the status of pariahs throughout the whole Catholic world."

Then he brought the issue back to the present, quoting from the St. Louis University study of Catholic secondary-school religious textbooks. It included such hostile teachings as "The Jews as a nation refuse to accept Christ and since that time they have been wandering on the earth without a temple or a sacrifice and without the Messiah."

The general public was also being reached through a variety of publications. For example, a column distributed nationally in May by the Chicago Daily News Service explained the issues associated with the declaration and incorporated Pope Paul VI's positive March 7 statement to Bishop Helmsing. In late June, Bob Considine, a prominent Catholic layman and widely read syndicated columnist, wrote a piece that appeared in hundreds of newspapers, noting that the AJC "had campaigned with great tact" for a strong Declaration.

The stage was now set for action on that document in less than three months' time. A major issue had arisen, however—one that would sow doubt in the minds of many sympathetic Christians as to the Jewish community's true intention regarding the outcome of Vatican Council II.

CHAPTER 10

Can't You Jews Agree on Anything?

"It would be a mistake on the part of the responsible Jewish leadership to look upon 'the Jewish chapter' before the Ecumenical Council as a matter of do or die . . . the revolution has now begun and it would take a counter-revolution to stop it."
—Rabbi Marc H. Tanenbaum, as quoted in the British publication, the *Jewish Chronicle*, August 29, 1964

WHILE MARC TANENBAUM CONTINUALLY EXPRESSED an abiding faith in the efforts to prod the Catholic church into action, there were strongly negative views coursing through major branches of Judaism. As Judith Banki recalled,

There was a lot of resistance, particularly from the Orthodox, who said that it was demeaning, humiliating, to go begging to the Vatican. That's not what we were doing, but that's the way they saw it, and they maintained that posture for a long, long time, until they saw that there was really pay dirt there—that there was real progress in terms of opportunity to change things once the Vatican Council adopted the declaration on the Jewish people.

Rabbi Heschel's participation in the preparatory effort and endorsement of the council's aims was especially galling to leaders of the Orthodox movement. According to his daughter, Dr. Susannah Heschel, her father was "the target of much criticism for his involvement in Vatican Council II."

Among the negative reactions to Rabbi Heschel's stance, for example, there were strident letters to the editors of several Jewish newspapers. The rabbi took them in his stride, however. He and his wife would sometimes have a cup of tea in their dining room before retiring for the evening and would read these journalistic attacks aloud. While Susannah Heschel was upset by the tone of many of the letters, she said her parents thought they were "absurd, ridiculous and foolish and funny." In one of them, the writer demanded: "Why should Rabbi Heschel—why should any rabbi—go the Vatican or to Rome to see the pope? Let the pope come to *him*!"

In June 1964, Rabbi Soloveitchik not only reiterated his views in an article published by the *National Jewish Post*, but announced that the Rabbinical Council of America might publicly ask during its coming convention that the proposed Council Decree not be passed—a move believed by some to have been encouraged by Dr. Nahum Goldmann, the head of the World Jewish Congress (WJC).

Fearing that such a move by Rabbi Soleveitchik would play directly into the conservative Catholic opposition's hands, Marc wrote to his Orthodox colleague to inform him of recent changes in the draft decree, revisions that Marc hoped would temper the Orthodox leader's objections, and he expressed dismay regarding the many misconceptions within the Orthodox community regarding the document. On several occasions, Marc went to great lengths to meet with Rabbi Soloveitchik to discuss developments relating to the council. It is likely that because of Rabbi Tanenbaum's intervention, Rabbi Soloveitchik did not attack the decree at the Rabbinical Council's convention, as threatened.

Other delegates *did*, however. During a session that took place on June 22, Rabbi Israel Klavan attacked secular Jewish groups for becoming involved "in areas of theology in which they have no competence." Another delegate stated that the American Jewish Committee had offended Orthodox Jewry by allowing a delegation of Jews to visit Pope Paul VI on the Jewish Sabbath.

Rabbi Soloveitchik's pronouncements had angered more progressive-minded Jewish leaders who bridled at his insistence that any discussion between Catholics and Jews should be limited to strictly nonreligious matters, and that the council should merely ask for a condemnation of anti-Semitism rather than any assertion of brotherhood between the two groups.

As the Orthodox continued their attacks on the committee, a similar effort was, surprisingly, underway within the Reform rabbinate. During a convention of the Central Conference of American Rabbis (CCAR), that organization's president, Rabbi Leon L. Feuer, derided what he termed "obsequious appeals" being made to the council concerning the Resolution on the Jews and described the committee's efforts as "insulting to the Jewish spirit." Many CCAR delegates thought it was inappropriate for Jews to press for a statement regarding the crucifixion—that it was solely a *Christian* issue. A cartoon published in a Yiddish newspaper widely read in the Orthodox community showed Pope Paul VI holding Marc at the end of a leash.

Marc and Rabbi Heschel were deeply concerned with the harm these rifts within the Jewish community could cause during the next session of the council. Seeking to temper the divisiveness, Rabbi Heschel discussed the matter with one of Cardinal Bea's trusted assistants, thirty-year-old Father Thomas Stransky, a Paulist priest from Milwaukee, Wisconsin. Rabbi Heschel was surprised to learn that representatives from the Orthodox group had made great efforts to meet with Cardinal Bea during the prelate's visit to Boston but had been rebuffed by him.

The meeting with Father Stransky confirmed Rabbi Heschel's fear that the Orthodox and Reform rabbis' negative statements were of concern to high Church officials in Rome. How would the dissenting rabbis' behavior influence the Vatican? That would depend on the extent to which the Church's conservative forces decided to publicize that dissent, the priest suggested. Given Father Stransky's response, the committee decided that a public reply to the Orthodox and Reform rabbis' accusations was required as soon as possible.

Marc's public relations skills would be put to work in crafting a carefully calibrated campaign of damage control. A press release was issued in which charges of amateurish dabbling by the AJC in theology were vigorously refuted. In fact, the release said, the committee had formulated its strategy in dealing with the council in consultation with scholars representing the three major branches of Judaism.

Meanwhile, the Reform rabbis' specific objections were answered in a letter written by Morris Abram, then-chairman of the committee's executive board, to Rabbi Feuer. In that letter, which was afforded limited publicity so as not to prolong the public controversy, Abram observed that the notion of collective Jewish guilt had always been a cause of anti-Semitism and no more important step could be taken for the welfare of world Jewry than to eradicate it.

But dissension within the American Jewish community regarding the Vatican Council paled in comparison to a situation that several years earlier had already caused dismay at the AJC: this was a power play, in the eyes of the AJC, that, had it succeeded, would have probably derailed the Church's refutation of the "Deicide" charge against world Jewry. On November 4, 1960, the urbane Nahum Goldmann, president of both the Conference of Jewish Organizations (COJO) and the World Jewish Congress (WJC), had been quoted in the *London Jewish Chronicle* as claiming that Cardinal Augustin Bea had told him that Pope John XXIII, during an audience, stated that he might invite Jewish representatives to attend Vatican Council II as observers, and that certain unnamed American Jews, though not yet invited, were thinking of attending the conclave.

As expected, Cardinal Bea quickly disavowed Goldmann's claim, adding that he did not believe the Jewish organizational leader to be "representative of the entire Jewish people." Within days, as if to further rebuke Goldmann, the Vatican issued a statement indicating that only leading *religious* experts would be considered as partners in any Church-related dialogue.

Following these statements, it was assumed that the WJC had accepted the consensus that Jewish representation at Vatican Council II should not and would not be sought. But Goldmann told the Conference of Jewish Organizations in August 1961 that it was Rabbi Soloveitchik who had convinced him of the wisdom of backtracking.

Ten months later, on June 12, 1962, in a complete and startling about-face, the WJC announced that an Israeli official, Dr. Chaim Wardi, would attend the council as an unofficial observer and that he had been granted leave from his position as counselor on Christian Affairs to his nation's ministry of religion to represent the WJC. That announcement played directly into the hands of Arab accusations that Israel was manipulating the council for political gain. Marc perceived that the announcement would galvanize Arab opposition and that the agency's carefully calibrated relations with Cardinal Bea could be jeopardized. Thus, the committee's leadership decided to voice its serious objections to Israeli officials regarding the designation of Wardi, a secular public servant, as the representative of world Jewry at Vatican Council II.

The committee's consternation would pale in comparison to the fury of Church officials in the Vatican. Goldmann's announcement produced a sense of calamity and shock within the Vatican hierarchy, causing officials there to become much more reticent with regard to the subject of Jews and the Ecumenical Council.

As soon as they became aware of Goldmann's attempted power grab, Arab diplomats posted to the Vatican began to protest against what they regarded as "giving Israel access to the Council" when no other nation was being granted such a privilege. To compound the matter, certain Church officials believed that a plot was afoot between the Israeli government and the World Jewish Congress to obtain representative status for the Jewish state. Those officials went so far as to blame this so-called cabal for restrictive measures then being taken against the Church in Arab nations.

Anger within the Church hierarchy in Rome was escalating to the point where a highly placed monsignor would reportedly say to an American Jewish leader, "We have worked hard trying to help you, and will continue to do so. But why are you Jews making our task so difficult?" In a more personal blow to the committee, on July 7, Cardinal Bea expressed his abject outrage and embarrassment. He said that he had been "thunderstruck" on seeing Goldmann's statement in the press when, during their recent visit, the Jewish leader had not uttered a word about the impending announcement. Moreover, thanks to the Goldmann episode, the cardinal's position of influence with the Church's powerful conservative wing, which vehemently opposed any liberalization of the Church's traditional attitude toward the Jewish people, had been seriously weakened. If Cardinal Bea was furious at having been blindsided, his chief aide, Msgr. Johannes Willebrands, was even more so, declaring: "We shall not admit Mr. Wardi to any session of the Council. If he is in Rome, he is there as just another tourist!"

Despite Cardinal Bea's fury, nonetheless, he indicated that several Jewish as well as other non-Christian observers might yet be invited to attend Council sessions as guests of his secretariat; he also pledged that in order to assist in smoothing the way toward the much-sought-after declaration repudiating the charge of "Deicide" against the Jewish people, he would write an essay opposing the Jews' collective guilt.

The cardinal said that he would send proofs of that document to Rabbi Heschel—as well as to Pro Deo officials—for any suggested modifications. The essay would then be published in the influential Jesuit journal *La Civiltà Cattolica*. Cardinal Bea also said that he would attempt to meet with the pope concerning the issuance of a strong statement regarding anti-Semitism, incorporating a specific reference to the Nazi era. Both the cardinal and Msgr. Willebrands made it abundantly clear, however, that the Jewish issue would be put aside until tempers had cooled.

But the harm done by Nahum Goldmann in attempting to inject an Israeli official into council proceedings would be more severe than the cardinal could have predicted. Publication of his essay would be postponed indefinitely. And because of pressure exerted by the conservative Vatican Secretariat of State, the council's Preparatory Commission abruptly tabled the proposals of the Secretariat for Christian Unity for discussion of Jews and Judaism.

The committee did its best to calm the troubled waters. On July 25, A. M Sonnabend, in a letter to Israel's ambassador to the United States, Avraham Harmon, made it clear that Dr. Wardi's presence in Rome would serve no purpose. Thus, he wrote, the Israeli government ought to clarify its stand without delay. Four days later, the *New York Times* reported that in deference to Jewish public opinion, Wardi's appointment had been rescinded. At that point, in yet another about-face, Goldmann claimed that the WJC had never been in favor of having Jewish observers attend Vatican Council II. Ironically, the session of the commission at which the issue of Jews and Judaism was to have been discussed had begun on June 12, 1962, the very day of Nahum Goldmann's announcement regarding an Israeli presence at Vatican Council II.

While Wardi's removal from the process ostensibly put an end to this controversy, the episode had done much to stiffen and consolidate opposition to the adoption of any action by Vatican Council II seen as being favorable to the Jewish people. Moreover, anti-Jewish elements, both Christian and non-Christian, were feeling newly empowered in their determination to thwart the heartfelt Jewish desire for justice following nearly two millennia of being falsely accused of deicide.

Now, on the eve of the hoped-for hearing on the Declaration on the Jews, the outcome of the council's third session was uncertain.

CHAPTER 11

How Can a Gospel of Love Be Such a Gospel of Hate When It Comes to the Jews?

**Vatican Council II, Session Three:
September 14–November 21, 1964**

"The term deicide must be torn out of the vocabulary of Christendom. The term is absurd and an insult to the human intelligence—as if man can kill God. . . ."

> —Archbishop John C. Heenan of Great Britain, during the historic September 1964 debate in St. Peter's Basilica on the Decree on the Jews

"We must tear this word out of the Christian vocabulary so that it may never again be used against the Jews."

> —Bishop Stephen A. Leven of Texas

POPE PAUL VI INAUGURATED THE third session of Vatican Council II on September 14 by celebrating Mass with a small group of twenty-four priests. Eleven days earlier, on September 3, a revised version of the

Declaration on the Jews had been made public in a newspaper article. That considerably weakened text replaced the previous forthright denial of the Jews' collective responsibility for the death of Jesus with what Marc considered merely a vague warning not to impute to contemporary Jews "that which was perpetrated in the Passion of Christ."

Marc was also disappointed by the new draft's failure to touch upon the special nature of anti-Semitism and the persecution of Jews through the centuries. More egregious still was the hope expressed for an "eventual union of the Jewish people with the Church"—an aspiration, as he noted, that was not mentioned with regard to Muslims or to non-Catholic Christians.

Responding to the draft's wording regarding conversion, Marc issued a strong, widely quoted statement, which acknowledged the Church's right to hope for the eventual Christianization of mankind but took exception to the document's conversionary implications. As he observed: "Any declaration, no matter how well-intended, whose effect would mean . . . the elimination of Judaism as a religion would be received with resentment."

Rabbi Heschel also issued a statement strongly condemning the revised draft. In it he declared:

A message that regards the Jew as a candidate for conversion and proclaims that the destiny of Judaism is to disappear will be abhorred by Jews all over the world and is bound to foster reciprocal distrust as well as bitterness and resentment. . . . As I have repeatedly stated to leading personalities of the Vatican, I am ready to go to Auschwitz any time, if faced with the alternative of conversion or death.

In order to express the deep Jewish concern over the new text, the committee arranged an audience for Rabbi Heschel with Pope Paul VI. The two would meet on September 14, not only the opening day of the council's third session, but the eve of Yom Kippur. Rabbi Heschel would report to Marc that their conversation had been "very friendly and cordial," notwithstanding the pontiff's claim that he considered the new formulation to be friendly to the Jews. As the audience ended, the pope told Rabbi Heschel that it would be up to the council to decide the matter.

It was now apparent that those prelates supporting a stronger declaration would need to insist on getting onto the council floor to make their case. Debate on the various schemata being brought before the conclave began on September 16. Marc, who was witnessing the proceedings from the observers' section, would later characterize the ensuing discussion as "the greatest seminar in Catholic-Jewish relations."

Within a week, on September 23, consideration of the schema on religious liberty was underway, followed on the 25th by heated discussion on the most controversial of the schemata to be brought before the council—the Catholic Church's Relationship with the Jews.

Nearly seven months earlier, beginning on February 27, a ten-day-long plenary meeting of the Secretariat for Christian Unity had taken place at which proposals suggested for inclusion in the chapter on the Jews came to seventy-two pages. Following intense debate, the delegates reached four conclusions: that the schema on ecumenism would deal solely with the issue of "unity among Christians"; that the revised chapter on the Jews would be retained for "internal reasons" due to its "importance and because of the universal expectations which it has aroused"; that because of the special bonds that "united the people of the Old Covenant with the Church, the document on the Jews will be an appendix to the text on ecumenism, but not a chapter, because, strictly speaking, ecumenism deals only with the relationships between Christians"; and, finally, that, they agreed that this appendix "will touch on the relations of the Christians with non-Christian religions, with special emphasis on Islamism."

Marc was not comfortable with the use of the word *ecumenism* in reference to Jewish-Christian relations. As he would note during an October 1964 address to the Second Annual Interreligious Institute at Loyola University: "It is a misnomer and a misapplication of the term 'ecumenism' to apply it to relations between Christians and Jews. One can apply it, of course, to Christian-Jewish relations in its broadest, most generic sense; but in its authentic theological meaning, it is a term applicable to relations within Christendom." In his view, "for reasons of clarity, it is probably wise and prudential that we use the term 'interreligious relationships' to describe the relations between Christianity and Judaism and between Christians and the Jewish people."

On March 26, Morris Abram, who had succeeded to the committee's presidency on the death of A. M. Sonnabend, reported in a confidential memo to the staff that "the atmosphere in Rome and throughout the Catholic world generally seems more favorable now for passage of a schema which incorporates a chapter on Catholic-Jewish relations than it did when the second session of the Ecumenical Council adjourned last December."

Abram's optimistic tone was based on Zach Shuster's increasingly positive reports from Rome, in which the agency's director of European Affairs stated that the decree had been redrafted and strengthened after hundreds of amendments had been submitted by Council Fathers to Cardinal Bea.

Throughout this redrafting process, Marc and his staff continued to work closely with Catholic officials in the United States, Europe, and Latin America to promote action on the decree. Their efforts were bearing fruit. Prelates in France and Belgium, as well as in Rio de Janeiro, São Paolo, and Buenos Aires, were reported to be fully supportive of the need for passage of the long-awaited decree during Vatican Council II's coming session. Meanwhile, in the United States, Marc and his staff were meeting with Cardinals Cushing, Ritter, and Spellman, as well as conferring with Cardinals Meyer and McIntyre and with influential archbishops, bishops, and *periti*, or Council experts. According to information gleaned during these communications with the churchman, American Catholic clergy were overwhelmingly in favor of enacting the Declaration on the Jews during the third session of Vatican Council II.

The committee was also working closely with the National Council of Catholic Men; the Sister Formation Conference, which served

180,000 teaching nuns; the entire network of Catholic colleges and seminaries; and the Pius XII Religious Education Resource Center. The center, to which Marc was a consultant, had recently produced its first textbooks on religion intended for use in diocesan parochial schools, and these contained revised views on Jews and Judaism. It was evident by mid-March 1964 that Church leaders from France, Belgium, and Britain, as well as the majority of American prelates, would support the declaration.

Yet it was still not absolutely clear that the declaration would be adopted. It would not be sufficient for Western Church leaders to express their positive views; they would also have to make known to the Vatican their belief that the position of the Church in the Western nations would deteriorate radically should the council fail to act in a positive way.

Prior to the reconvening of the council in September, it was clear that opponents of the declaration would be marshaling their forces and developing new strategies for blocking the entire schema on ecumenism. If Marc and his staff were optimistic about the eventual outcome of the council's coming deliberations, they could not now let down their guard.

The committee was also continuing to deal with dissension within various Jewish communities regarding the propriety of supporting the concept of a Vatican Council. For example, on March 18, the Religious News Service quoted Rabbi Chaim Denburg, a highly regarded Orthodox rabbi and scholar from Montreal, as having said during a joint appearance with a Roman Catholic priest, Father Jean Martucci, a professor of the Old Testament at both the University of Montreal and the Grand Seminary: "We Jews do not owe the Church one iota of gratitude if we are cleared [of the charge of deicide]. On the contrary, it is the Church that owes us the apology for the centuries of their dark record towards us. Anti-Semitism," the rabbi continued, "is not a Jewish problem; it is the Christians' problem. The charge of deicide is a blot on the Christians' conscience. If this charge is removed, it will cleanse the Church's soul, not ours."

For his part, Father Martucci said that if the Christian churches were to be reunited, they must go back to the source of their beliefs—Judaism. He added that the ecumenical movement was not one to make Christians more powerful against the Jews. Rather, this movement "cannot but have positive effects with regard to Jews."

As the late, chilly winter of 1964 turned to an early, promising spring, on April 16 the Jewish Telegraphic Agency quoted Cardinal Bea as saying with regard to the deferment of action on chapters 4 and 5:

> Much was fancied about the presumed maneuvers, pressures and underhand dealings in this respect. Even admitting that many were puzzled by those two chapters, the reasons for the developments were not those whispered and bandied about. The facts were as follows: It was acknowledged that a bloc vote on all five chapters risked creating much perplexity among the Council Fathers, and much difficulty in interpreting the eventual results.

Injecting a note of optimism, Cardinal Bea intimated that a positive outcome regarding the declaration could be in the offing during the coming session of the council: "In view of the importance of these chapters for the life of the Church today and for its positioning the world, it is of the utmost necessity that their acceptance reflect really the widest and deepest conviction of the Council Fathers," he said.

New York Times correspondents reporting from Rome in mid-April were confirming Cardinal Bea's optimism. In a story filed on April 15, the prelate was quoted as having expressed hope that the council would approve the controversial chapters in votes reflecting "broad and profound convictions." In a dispatch filed two days later, headlined "Pontiff Expects Text on Liberty," Paul Hoffman of the *Times* wrote that Paul VI had affirmed that "The Roman Catholic Church's Ecumenical Council may be 'legitimately expected' to approve a text on religious liberty."

Nearly three weeks later, on May 5, Cardinal Bea described

provisions of the revised text of the proposed Document on the Jews and reiterated that the late Pope John XXIII had endorsed his own views on the larger issue of Catholic-Jewish relations. Regarding the charge of deicide, the prelate observed that "Even in Christ's time the whole people did not cooperate in His condemnation. The less so is it permitted today to consider those of the Jewish faith responsible."

The cardinal made it clear that the document to be put before the council in September "deduces the warning to avoid all that may cause contempt and provoke hatred against them [the Jewish People] in religious teaching, in sermons, in catechism, and, in particular, in explaining Christ's life and passion and the doctrine of His redeeming death, and in contact with the Jews." The document's second section, the prelate added, will enumerate "All the good that the Church received from God through the Jewish people, and everything that is common to both religions is mentioned."

Most important for future interreligious harmony, Cardinal Bea stated, "The text before the council recommends to Catholics that they work together with adherents of the Jewish faith for ever-improving, mutual esteem and knowledge, particularly by theological studies and fraternal conversation." To achieve these lofty goals, Cardinal Bea insisted on an unprecedented, powerful acknowledgement of Catholic complicity during the Holocaust: "The Council must consider the long, sad history of Christian-Jewish relations and, most of all, the tragic fruits of anti-Semitism, so laden with consequences in which we assisted with terror not longer than two decades ago," he argued.

Six days later, Paul VI told Archbishop Helmsing that in the upcoming council session, "We need a good declaration on religious liberty and on our relations with the Jews." As excitement mounted over the hoped-for outcome of the council's third session, the committee's leadership decided to send Marc to Rome as the organization's official representative.

He arrived in Rome early in September 1964 for a three-week stint and immediately began implementing his carefully crafted strategy of reaching out to the more liberal-minded delegates, namely, the

American bishops. Constantly traversing the Vatican's corridors, and holding a seemingly endless array of breakfasts, lunches, and dinners, the AJC's official representative adamantly, yet diplomatically, argued for the adoption of the document that would become known as *Nostra aetate*.

On Friday, September 25, Marc witnessed Cardinal Bea's stirring introduction of the proposed Declaration on the Jews. The cardinal told the council:

> I can only begin with the fact that this Declaration certainly must be counted among the matters in which public opinion has shown the greatest concern. Scarcely any other schema has been written up so much and so widely in periodicals. . . . Many will judge this Council good or bad by its approval or disapproval of the Declaration.

For the delegates—and for the committee's observer—the moment of truth would occur on the following Monday and Tuesday, September 28 and 29, when debate would take place on the decree.

As that debate unfolded, Marc, with his customary literary flair, recalled,

> Thirty-five cardinals and bishops of the Church from 22 countries arose on the floor of St. Peter's Basilica and one after another, in terms more powerful and more committed than had ever been heard before, called upon the Catholic Church to condemn anti-Semitism as a sin against the conscience of the Church.

The Church would, he observed, be required "to reconcile her teachings of love and charity and fraternity with the practices of her faithful, which have far too long been marked by contempt and animosity for the Jew." As the debate progressed, Marc recalled, "One after another, the Council Fathers called for the Church to reject the ancient and false charges of 'deicide' against the Jews." At debate's end, thirty-one of the thirty-five Council Fathers would declare their support for a strong declaration, one in which the onerous "Christ-killer" charge that had severely marred Catholic/Jewish relations for nearly two millennia would finally be laid to rest.

On Tuesday, September 29, following the debate's conclusion, Marc attended the Bishops' Briefing Panel. At one point, he was approached by an official of the American Church hierarchy, who, with tears in his eyes, exclaimed, "Marc, this was the greatest moment in the history of the Ecumenical Council, for on no other issue had so many cardinals of such great prominence spoken out." Despite what the Church official characterized as "pro forma opposition," on no other issue, including religious liberty, "had there been such unanimity of feeling as on this question."

Even Cardinal Ruffini stated his acceptance, in principle, of the Church's need to condemn anti-Semitism, although, this American church leader added, "he went on to say some other things which were not as acceptable to many around the Council." More surprising than Cardinal Ruffini's about-face, however, was the response of patriarchs from Arab nations, who agreed that the Church should condemn anti-Semitism. They did, however, raise the possibility of political repercussions.

For Marc, the events of those two days in late September represented the turning point in a historical cycle. That cycle of history, he observed,

> was for far too long malignant, but has begun to turn, and may yet become benign, may yet allow Christians and Jews to approach each other, not through the myths, the superstitions and the hostilities of a polemical past, but as human beings, sons of Abraham, to share a common patrimony in their love of God and, therefore, their love of one another.

On returning to New York, Marc reassumed his day-to-day responsibilities at the committee. But, reflecting on Cardinal Bea's oratory as he introduced the Declaration on the Jews, the rabbi could not help but marvel at the "concern and attention of 2,300 Council Fathers in Rome over a period of three years" regarding the issue, as well as the interest of the Protestant and Eastern Orthodox observers at Vatican Council II.

In October, shortly after Marc's return from Rome, he addressed the Second Annual Interreligious Institute at Loyola University, in Los Angeles, where he posed two rhetorical questions: "Why is the issue of the relationship of Christianity to Judaism and the practical relations between Christians and Jews on a daily level of such central significance?" And "Why has it attracted such attention?"

Responding to his own questions, Marc introduced one of the most crucial domestic issues that would engage his passionate interest in the months to come: "It is my thesis," he stated, "that the issue of relations between Christians and Jews has reached the point of ripeness, a point of maturation in a way that can be seen analogously in terms of the ripeness and the fullness which relations between the Negro and white societies have reached."

During that address, Marc, never one to mince words, administered a dose of hard reality, arguing that:

The Nazi Holocaust and all that has meant for the Christian conscience, as well as the tremendous needs of a new world of the twentieth century in which Christians and Jews together find themselves increasingly a minority in relation to a non-white, non-Judeo-Christian world, are compelling us to confront the deep realities of the contact between Christians and Jews. Fundamentally, Christianity has never made up its mind as to where it stands in terms of its common patrimony with Judaism and its daily attitudes and relationships and behavior toward Jews.

Then, injecting a characteristic note of optimism to offset his criticism of the Church, the rabbi stated: "We find as we look into the history of the Christian-Jewish encounter for the greater part of the past two millennia that there have been teachings and episodes betokening the greatest of mutual respect and esteem between Christians and Jews."

Returning again to his experience as an invited guest at the third session of Vatican Council II, Marc said, "If nothing else comes out of the Ecumenical Council other than what took place this past Monday and Tuesday (the delegates' debate on the Decree on the Jews), the Council has more than justified its existence in terms of Jewish interests."

Meanwhile, in Rome, delegates to the council's third session were considering other schemata. Some, including those on the apostolate of the laity, bishops, ecumenism, the Eastern Church, and priests, were found wanting and referred back to the commission for amending. Action on other schemata, including ones on divine revelation and religious freedom, were tabled for review during the final session.

By November 14, with only seven days remaining in the council's third session, action on the schemata was so uncertain and further progress before adjournment so unpromising that delegates were referring to that period as "Black Week."

Four days later, Cardinal Tisserant announced the deferment of the vote on religious freedom. The Decree on Ecumenism was issued on the session's closing day, November 21. But the decree of most concern to world Jewry and progressively inclined churchmen alike, the council's long-awaited Declaration on the Jews, would not be acted upon during this session of Vatican Council II. At that point, Marc, like Jews everywhere, could only hope that two millennia of persecution would be addressed during the council's upcoming final session.

CHAPTER 12

Ending Two Millenia of Contempt toward the Jews

The Decisive Fourth Session:
September 14–December 8, 1965

"In the final text that was promulgated by Pope Paul VI on October 28, 1965, the Catholic church took a great and historic leap forward. . . ."

—Rabbi Marc Tanenbaum, in March 1966,
addressing the International Conference of
Theological Issues of Vatican II, University of Notre Dame

"Marc was an extraordinary person which, of course, is why he was invited, among other things, to the Second Vatican Council. . . . He had a very significant impact and influence during the Council, for which I, and all Catholics, are very grateful."

—Dr. Leonard Swidler, Professor of Religion, Temple University

ON SEPTEMBER 15, 1965, ONE day after the reconvening of the council's final session, discussion was underway on the tabled schema on religious freedom. Within a week of the council's reconvening, Marc was back in Rome as the guest of Cardinal Lawrence Shehan, of Baltimore, who was chairing the American Bishops Commission on Ecumenism.

As he watched the council's crucial deliberations one Thursday morning in September, the rabbi stood before the magnificent Bernini canopy, where the pope had just celebrated Mass with several cardinals. Gazing out at the vast congregation of 2,300 colorfully clad delegates from all over the world flanking the center aisle of St. Peter's Basilica, Marc was deeply moved by the significance of events that were under-way in Rome affecting relations between the Catholic Church and world Jewry.

He recalled that five hundred years earlier, at approximately the same time of year, a delegation of Roman Jews, led by their chief rabbi, had emerged from their ghetto and marched through the streets of the city to fulfill their annual fourteenth-century obligation of coming in humiliation before the pope and presenting him with their sacred Torah scroll. In this ritual, the pontiff would hand the scroll back to the Jews while uttering derogatory words. One of the popes, Boniface VIII, who served for nine years, from 1294 to 1303, while acknowl-edging the Jews' reverence to the law, condemned their "misrepresenta-tion" of it. Thus further debased and humiliated, the Jews would return to their quarter to endure yet another year as the pariahs of Christian Europe.

As Marc pondered the ordeals of his ancestors at the hands of Christendom, his thoughts also turned to a much more recent occur-rence—one that had taken place only a year earlier, during the Jewish festival of Simchat Torah, marking the Jewish people's rejoicing over the divine revelation communicated to Israel through the Torah. For two days, September 28 and 29, the debate on the draft Declaration on the Jews had taken place. In that debate, which Marc had witnessed, he recalled that "Thirty-one of the cardinals and bishops from every major continent of the world" took positive positions regarding "Catholic attitudes in relation to the Jewish people, to Judaism, to the role of Israel in salvation history, toward the synagogue and its continued rel-evance, to conversion, and to anti-Semitism." They were positions that had never been heard before in 1,900 years of Catholic-Jewish history. "They were positions articulated with such friendship, indeed, fraternal love, as to make clear that a profound turning point had taken place in our lifetime," Marc observed.

While a total of sixteen declarations would be promulgated during Vatican Council II, much of the debate of the final session would focus on the document titled "The Church in the Modern World."

As October 1965 was unfolding, Marc, who had returned to New York, was eagerly awaiting news from Rome. On October 14, 1965, the delegates to the conclave formally approved *Nostra aetate* ("in our time"), the Declaration on the relation of the Church to Non-Christian Religions. It was a landslide vote of 1,763 in favor and 250 opposed. That five-paragraph, forty-one-sentence-long document, whose fourth paragraph consisted of the seventeen-sentence-long Declaration on the Jews, would become the shortest of the sixteen resolutions to be enacted by the council. *Nostra aetate* would represent one of Vatican II's three declarations. The other documents consisted of nine decrees and four constitutions.

Pope Paul VI, speaking from the long nave of St. Peter's Basilica, would formally issue the long-awaited document's proclamation two weeks later, on October 28, an unseasonably warm autumn day in Rome.

On this momentous day in the advancement of Catholic-Jewish relations, Marc was aware that exactly twenty-four years earlier, on October 28, 1941, two calamities had befallen the Jewish people: the massacre of more than nine thousand Jews crammed into the ghetto in Kaunas, Lithuania; and the deportation of two thousand children and six thousand adults from Kraków, Poland, to the Belzec death camp. The rabbi knew also that three years earlier to the day, on October 28, 1938, in a portent of much worse to befall European Jewry, thousands of Polish-born Jews, among them Dr. Abraham Joshua Heschel, as well as native German Jews, had been rounded up and expelled to the Polish border.

When Paul VI promulgated *Nostra aetate*, the ceremony was solemn, yet colorful. The pontiff uttered words of hope for a better world—a world in which there could never be another Holocaust. More than two thousand delegates to Vatican Council II, clad in white miters and conical hats, stood on a green platform as Archbishop Pericle Felici, secretary general of Vatican Council II, intoned in Latin the opening and closing portions of the declaration that had just been voted on—2,221 in favor and 288 opposed—by the bishops in the pope's presence.

In a bow to modernity, the delegates had voted using special magnetized pencils to mark ballots that were then fed into terminals installed in the basilica specifically for that occasion. In the prepersonal computer age, those devices would be described by the *New York Times* correspondent on the scene, Robert C. Doty, as "business machines."

As the bishops' votes were being counted, Pope Paul VI, now seated on the throne under the Bernini Canopy, offered a homily in Latin. In it, he referred to the Jewish people as "Israelites" worthy of "respect, love, and hope."

Marc Tanenbaum, the American Jewish community's organizational leader, who had been so intimately involved in the years-long process leading to the world-changing promulgation of *Nostra aetate*, viewed the document's passage as signaling "an historic turning point." The rabbi stated that "for the first time in the history of the twenty-one Ecumenical Councils, the highest ecclesiastical authorities have committed the Catholic Church throughout the world to uprooting the charge of collective guilt against the Jews, eliminating anti-Semitism and fostering mutual knowledge and respect between Catholics and Jews."

But Marc knew that promulgating *Nostra aetate* did not mean the battle was over; in fact, it was just beginning. As he said, "deepened understanding" between Jews and Catholics "will not spring up quickly or spontaneously. The antagonism of centuries will not be swept away overnight. For people of good will on both sides, decades of massive work would lie ahead."

That continual vigilance would be required quickly became all too apparent only a month following *Nostra aetate*'s promulgation, in something Cardinal Bea wrote. As quoted by John Connelly in his book *From Enemy to Brother*, Cardinal Bea said that Jerusalem had once been destroyed because of the "guilt" of its inhabitants "since they directly witnessed the preaching, the miracles, the solemn entrance of Jesus." According to the prelate, the Jewish people were "no longer the people of God in the sense of being the instrument of salvation for humanity."

Connelly also noted that in 2008, no less a theological authority than Pope Benedict XVI, a supporter of the premise of Vatican Council II, would amend the 1962 Good Friday prayer for the Jews in the Roman Missal from "Let us pray for the Jewish people, the first to hear the word of God, that they may continue to grow in the love of his name and in faithfulness to his covenant" to "Let us also pray for the Jews, that God our Lord should illuminate their hearts, so that they will recognize Jesus Christ, the savior of men."

In the wake of the council's vote on October 14 indicating their approval of *Nostra aetate*, Jewish and Catholic leaders throughout the world had already begun to react. On Sunday, October 17, the *New York Herald Tribune* published side-by-side pieces by Rabbi Tanenbaum and James O'Gara, the managing editor of *Commonweal*, a weekly journal of opinion edited by Catholic laymen, under the headline "The Catholics and the Jews: Two Views."

Within the American Jewish community, Marc wrote, "there exist roughly three sets of views regarding the declaration, held in common among Jews here and abroad." He said, "there are those who resent it," "those who are indifferent to it," and "those who welcome it, but with regrets." He added, "there is no question but that the number of Jews, either leaders or informed laymen, who are 'happy' with the document in its present form, is small." But Marc added, "Nevertheless, one is aware that there is a widespread desire on the part of many Jews to acknowledge those genuinely positive assertions in the document, in the expectation that liberal Catholics will seize upon them as guidelines for future relations between Catholics and Jews."

In his companion piece, O'Gara emphasized Hitler's role in conversations regarding the VC's declaration:

Under Hitler, 6 million Jews died in concentration camps and gas chambers in the heart of Christian Europe. . . . How could the pagan perversity of Hitler take root among Christian people? It could happen, I am convinced, for only one reason: the Nazis' attack was carried out in a climate of opinion prepared by centuries of hostility toward the Jewish people.

O'Gara pondered whether the original Declaration has "now been emasculated" and "watered down out of all recognition," and he concluded that it had not. Nonetheless, he said, "For some reason not completely clear, the declaration now 'deplores' rather than 'condemns' prejudice." More ominously, he explained, the word "deicide" was cut out of the text, which some theologians saw as a lack of perception of Christ as the son of God. That concern, coupled with mounting pressure from Christians in Arab countries, prompted the demands for a revised version.

"If I had my choice," O'Gara stated, "last year's version would be this year's. But this does not mean that the revised document is not worthy of enthusiastic support."

The Catholic editor's views were in harmony with those of his Jewish colleague-in-print. Marc also wrote that "much has been made of the fact that this latest version has added that the Church 'deplores anti-Semitism.'" He quoted an editorial recently published in a Jewish newspaper that said: "After the murder of six million Jews by the Nazis, the church can only 'deplore' anti-Semitism. How many more millions of Jewish lives will have to be lost before she can bring herself to 'condemn' anti-Semitism?" Rabbi Tanenbaum said,

In this view, with which I strongly associate myself, the adoption of the declaration is of historic significance because for the first time in the history of 21 Ecumenical Councils, the Catholic Church has committed herself to rejecting the invidious tradition of attributing corporate guilt to the Jewish people for the Crucifixion and to repudiating anti-Semitism.

As the impact of *Nostra aetate* was first being assessed, Marc insisted, "No person of good will can fail to be moved" by the document's content. He was very taken with its message of tolerance of, and respect for "those who think or act differently than we do in social, political, and even religious matters."

The negative reactions of certain (some?) Jews to the decree would be intensified following its official papal promulgation on October 28. A substantial segment of the Jewish community reacted "not to the content of the declaration," he said, "as much as to the headlines which reported about the Declaration." He was referring to ones such as VATICAN COUNCIL EXONERATES JEWS FOR DEATH of CHRIST and CATHOLIC CHURCH ABSOLVES JEWS OF CRUCIFIXION.

In fact, the rabbi pointed out, "No Jew in my acquaintance has ever felt guilty for the death of Jesus. Therefore, no Jew ever felt the need for absolution." Noting that it was print and broadcast commentators, not the writers of the council documents, who had used this inaccurate terminology, Marc pointed out that the words *absolve* and *exonerate* did not appear in the Document on the Jews.

While Marc understood the reasons for much of the negative sentiment regarding the decree, he said that having worked closely with members of the Catholic community both in the United States and abroad, especially in the fields of religious history and education, he was persuaded that "a vast and irreversible tide of self-purification and self-correction with regard to the portrayal of Jews and Judaism in the teaching process of the Catholic Church—nor should the Protestants be slighted—is underway and that the fruits of this process are already in evidence."

Expressing his view that in the wake of the promulgation of *Nostra aetate*, the Jewish and Catholic communities alike were facing a period of transition, Marc predicted that both groups would find themselves "fumbling and stumbling as they seek to find appropriate new modes of relating to each other in a growing climate of mutual tolerance and esteem."

Indeed, there would be a vast range of initiatives launched over the years to put the ideas in *Nostra aetate* into practice. AJC worked diligently throughout the 1960s organizing seminars, colloquia, and institutes for Catholics and Jews to better understand each other. In 1966, AJC published its first "Guide to Interreligious Dialogue" to help lay leaders conduct interreligious encounters. And in 1988, AJC launched the Catholic/Jewish Education Enrichment Program (C/JEEP) in six cities, underwritten by funding from the Steven Spielberg Righteous Persons Foundation. The program brought rabbis into Catholic high schools to teach Judaism and Catholic priests and educators into Jewish schools to teach Christianity. Through C/JEEP, Catholic and Jewish students learned about the religion of others from authentic sources.

A host of other Jewish and Catholic institutions were equally active in creating vehicles to take the lofty ideals in *Nostra aetate* to change ideas and practices in the relationship between Catholics and Jews.

In an essay published online at *First Things* to mark the fiftieth anniversary of *Nostra aetate*, Jonathan Sacks, the Chief Rabbi of the United Hebrew Congregations of the Commonwealth from 1991 to 2013, wrote:

> It was on the face of it, a minor theological gesture, yet it brought about one of the greatest revolutions in religious history. Nostra Aetate, the Catholic Church's 1965 statement of relationships with non-Christian faith, declared that "the Jews should not be spoken of as rejected or accursed as if this followed from Holy Scripture." Today, as a result, Jews and Catholics meet not as enemies but as cherished and respected friends.

In 2015, to commemorate the fiftieth anniversary of *Nostra aetate*, AJC published a report titled "In Our Time, AJC and Nostra Aetate: A Reflection After 50 Years." That document noted,

> The Catholic Church expanded upon Nostra Aetate with pronouncements, guidelines, and the establishment of departments

and human resources to expand the sentiments of Nostra Aetate into a living reality. AJC, other Jewish organizations, and the Jewish people readily responded to the extended hand of the Catholic Church and created vehicles for guaranteeing the accomplishments of Nostra Aetate. . . .

It added,

Catholic Jewish relations have reached a previously unimaginable Golden Age that could not possibly have happened without the follow-up of successive post-Nostra Aetate generations.

And, the AJC noted, the impact continues to the present day in many ways:

[Pope] Francis is truly a product of the Nostra Aetate spirit. Francis lived out Nostra Aetate in his close relationship with the Argentinian Jewish community, and has elevated his comfort level with Jews and Judaism to the world stage.

The Church's emergence from what Marc characterized as "something of a Maginot Line" and its increased willingness to join in dialogue with the modern world would be codified by Paul VI in his address in late 1965 before the United Nations General Assembly. On that occasion, after renouncing any pretense of maintaining temporal power for the Catholic Church, the pontiff had declared: "We make our own voice of the poor, the disinherited, the suffering, to those who hunger and thirst for justice, for the dignity of life, for freedom, for well-being and progress."

During Marc's March 1966 speech at the University of Notre Dame, he said of the pope's remarks:

If this mentality had been normative for the popes, the Vatican, and the Catholic and Protestant masses over the past 100 years, the incredible phenomenon of hundreds of thousands of so-called devout Christians becoming accomplices or passive spectators to the cruel slaughter of millions of men, women, and children who happened to be born Jews—or Gypsies— would not have been possible.

Although the Orthodox Jewish community was wary, at best, regarding the Vatican II deliberations, in an article published in the *Jerusalem Post* on November 27, 2015, reporting on the fiftieth anniversary of *Nostra aetate*, Rabbi Avi Shafran, an official at a major Orthodox group, Agudath Israel of America, was quoted as saying that the document and its disavowal of anti-Semitism were "deeply significant." He said they had "contributed much to the good relations shared by Catholics and Jews today," and the rabbi added, "It should serve as an example to follow, fifty years later, for some other Christian groups, and some other religions, to likewise disown the perennial scourge of mindless Jew-hatred."

But there were limits to the impact of *Nostra aetate*. To mark the fiftieth anniversary of *Nostra aetate*, Boston's Cardinal Seán O'Malley addressed an audience of hundreds at a synagogue in Newton, a heavily Jewish Boston suburb. According to a report by WBUR, the public television station in Boston, Cardinal O'Malley said, "I would urgently urge our Catholics to have a deeper awareness of the Jewish roots of our Catholic faith." The next day, the basketball team of Newton North, a high school with a number of Jewish students, played Catholic Memorial, an all-boys school. The Newton North students started cheering, "Where are your girls?" to the Catholic Memorial students. Typical high school stuff, perhaps. But then, according to an article in the March 12, 2016, edition of the *Boston Globe*, fifty to seventy-five Catholic Memorial students launched their cheer: "You killed Jesus." The Newton students fell silent, and the next day, the president of Catholic Memorial issued a statement condemning the "abhorrent behavior" of the students and promising to work to end it.

These events made the remarks offered by AJC President A. M.

Sonnabend in 1963 seem prophetic: If and when this decree were introduced and passed, Sonnabend had warned, it would be followed by "the historic responsibility—and historic opportunity—of implementing a decree through creation of a special body. This work will engage our staff for many years and in many parts of the world."

Indeed, the efforts by all concerned would have to continue for decades. A half century after *Nostra aetate*, a Reuters report dated December 10, 2015, said,

> The Vatican is taking steps toward fixing its long-troubled history with the Jewish faith with the Thursday release of a 10,000-word document that instructs Catholics to help Jews fight anti-Semitism instead of trying to convert them. The Commission for Religious Relations With the Jews explained that Catholicism and Judaism shared the same origins and that "the Church is therefore obliged to view evangelization . . . to Jews . . . in a different manner from that to people of other religions and world views." The document continues that "while affirming salvation through an explicit or even implicit faith in Christ, the Church does not question the continued love of God for the chosen people of Israel."

The report also noted "the Jewish roots of Christianity." Thus, the good news was that the Church stood by what it had said fifty years earlier. The bad news was that it needed to restate its position.

As for Rabbi Tanenbaum, even while contemplating the challenges presented by *Nostra aetate*, he was also already turning his attention to another major faith group in the United States: evangelical Christians.

PART IV
A PROPHET FOR OUR TIME

CHAPTER 13

Mr. Graham Comes to Visit

"In 1965, who would talk to Billy Graham? The Jewish community would be run out of town; they would be regarded as selling out the Jewish people."

—Rabbi Marc Tanenbaum, reminiscing in 1980

"People at the committee learned about a different kind of Billy Graham, as it were, because of Marc. He didn't just put them [evangelicals] down, which is the tendency of people on the moderate left to do"

—Howard I. Friedman, president,
the American Jewish Committee, 1983–1986

THE VAST NUMBER OF SEPARATE Protestant denominations in the US presented a substantial challenge to those interested in interfaith relations. Jews had substantial concerns about the views of many Protestants regarding Jews and the State of Israel, and in contrast to the hierarchical Catholic Church, the Protestants were a sea of autonomous and highly varied groupings. For many Jews, the major source of concern has long been evangelical Christians, because they have often been the most zealous in seeking to impose Christian values in the public sphere and in attempting to convince Jews to abandon their faith and become Christians.

Despite the anti-evangelical animus that pervaded much of the American Jewish community during the mid-1960s, Marc had the courage and vision to reach out to evangelical groups, and specifically to Rev. Billy Graham. In June 1969, Rev. Graham, the leading figure in evangelical Christianity, would make a historic visit to the AJC's headquarters in response to an invitation from Marc Tanenbaum.

In spearheading the effort to arrange this visit, Marc would incur the wrath of many of his associates in the Jewish community. Many Jews deeply resented the often fervent evangelical efforts to proselytize among the Jews and the constant pressure on them to embrace Jesus as their savior. They often suspected that the pro-Israel stance of many evangelicals was insincere—that the expressions of support for the Jewish state were based solely on the evangelicals' messianic goal of mass conversion.

Billy Graham, with his highly publicized crusades, massive following, and friends in the White House, was widely regarded as the most important of the evangelicals. And he would forge a close relationship with Marc Tanenbaum. This relationship would endure until Marc's death—although later revelations would call into question Billy Graham's sincerity.

What was it about Billy Graham and Marc Tanenbaum that drew them to trust and befriend each other? Given their differing religious persuasions, the two men of God would appear to have had little in common. Yet there were striking parallels in the background and experience of each man. While coming of age in rural North Carolina, Billy Graham had shed the racism, religious provincialism, and anti-Semitism of his forebears. As a college student, he was open to the broadening of his worldview. Then, as he developed his ministry, he became inclusive of people of color throughout the world, as well as an ardent champion of the Jewish people, Soviet Jewry, and the State of Israel.

As a youngster growing up in Baltimore, the future rabbi, influenced by his broad-minded parents, also abhorred and rejected the rampant racism and sectarian strife of his native city. During his student days at Yeshiva University, he began to question the strict Orthodox Judaism of his forebears. Then, going against the grain of that tight-knit academic community, he embraced the more moderate Conservative—indeed, Reconstructionist—form of observance. As a Jewish community professional, he participated in the nascent civil rights movement at a time when it was dangerous to do so. And he would never waiver in his fervent Zionism or defense of the rights of Jews to live in freedom everywhere.

Both men were intellectually gifted, physically imposing, and highly articulate. Marc Tanenbaum and Billy Graham were consummate communicators. Thus, their bonding would appear to have been inevitable. The paths of the rabbi and the evangelist would converge in New York City during the late 1960s, in an unprecedented and frank give-and-take regarding their respective religious and political agendas.

The genesis of their first encounter was a four-paragraph memo sent to Marc on May 13, 1969, by Gerald Strober, an AJC staff member. Noting that "Dr. Billy Graham will be in New York City from June 13–23 to hold a major crusade at Madison Square Garden," Strober suggested that the committee "explore the possibility of holding a private luncheon for Dr. Graham." Its purpose, Strober observed "could be to establish an interreligious relationship with Dr. Graham, to meet with key members of his staff . . . and to explore issues such as the Middle East and Jewish-Evangelical relations in the U.S."

Marc immediately invited Billy Graham to meet with him and his associates at the committee's Manhattan headquarters at 10 a.m. on the morning of Monday, June 23, 1969. Thus began Marc's decades-long relationship with *Mr.* Graham, as the Reverend Doctor Billy Graham preferred to be called.

The evangelist's associates had been in touch with the committee as early as January 31. On that day, Strober had spoken by telephone with T. W. Wilson, one of the reverend's closest aides, concerning the fate of Iraq's beleaguered Jewish community. Many Iraqi Jews were then being subjected to show trials and execution by that nation's repressive regime, and Strober, the Interreligious Affairs Department's consultant, raised the possibility of Rev. Graham issuing a statement condemning those atrocities.

According to Dr. Robert Ferm, another associate of Mr. Graham, the reverend's sympathies were with the Iraqi Jews, and he was not opposed *in principle* to speaking out, but he would need concrete proof of the persecutions. In order to facilitate that process, on February 4, Dr. Ferm met Strober, Judith Banki, and Rabbi James Rudin at the committee's New York office.

They provided Dr. Ferm with various, pertinent documents, including a fact sheet, copies of the grand rabbi of Iraq's petition to his government, and a book, *Jews in Arab Lands*. At meeting's end, as Dr. Ferm was being escorted to the building's lobby, he let it be known that certain people in the Christian community would be "quite concerned to know that Billy had sent him to the American Jewish Committee for a briefing." But, Dr. Ferm said, his attendance "evidences a willingness on the part of Dr. Graham to seek out information on vital contemporary issues."

Following up on that meeting, on February 12, Judith Banki drafted a letter for the signature of the committee's president, Justice Arthur Goldberg, in which he vouched for the accuracy of the documents provided to Dr. Ferm, and wrote,

> We would very much appreciate your adding voice to that of other eminent Christian spokesmen who have protested the barbarity of the Iraqi actions. Perhaps even more important in order to save the lives of the remaining members of the harassed and terrorized remnants of the Jewish community in Iraq would be a statement urging the Iraqi government to allow the remaining Jews to leave the country. Your stature as a religious leader and your personal reputation for outstanding integrity would do much to further such an appeal.

Several months later, on June 4, when Dr. Ferm telephoned Strober to say that Dr. Graham would like to accept the committee's invitation to meet later that month, he added that Rev. Graham was especially interested in having the participants attend a session of his Madison Square Garden Crusade. Strober and Judith Banki sensed that the reverend's invitation was more than a gesture. They concluded that Rev. Graham was concerned that the participants in the committee's meeting would, as Strober put it, "have a stereotyped view of his activities," and Billy must be thinking that if the Jewish leaders could observe him in the Crusade setting, they would have a more balanced view of his intentions and work.

Unfortunately, several of the Jewish participants in the meeting scheduled for June 23 said they would not be in New York during the period in which the Madison Square Garden event was to be held. But Billy's meeting with Marc and his colleagues would proceed as planned.

The committee's starting point was simply to establish a relationship with Billy. They not only wanted to discuss American Jewish concerns for Israel and Iraq's Jewish community, they sought to bring his attention to a planned Colloquium with Southern Baptists and other aspects of the agency's activities involving evangelical Protestants.

On June 10, Philip E. Hoffman, who had succeeded Justice Goldberg as the committee's president, wrote to a carefully selected group, inviting them to this milestone event, which he described as an "informal, off the record meeting between Dr. Graham and Jewish academic and communal leaders." He also expressed hope "that in such a session, a frank exchange of views will take place."

The rabbis responding to the committee's invitation represented the leadership of the Orthodox, Conservative, and Reform movements. Other attendees included AJC lay leaders, including Theodore Ellenoff, as well as AJC staff members Judith Banki, Morris Fine, Selma Hirsh, Rabbi James Rudin, Simon Segal, Gerald Strober, and Mort Yarmon.

On the appointed day, Hoffman, and the ACJ's executive vice president, Bertram Gold, welcomed Billy and the Jewish attendees to the committee's eighth-floor conference room. Hoffman began the meeting by noting, "It is fitting, that this morning we meet in the same room which was the site in 1963 of the historic meeting between American Jewish leaders and the Vatican official, of blessed memory, Cardinal Bea." On that occasion, Hoffman said, "a frank discussion ensued, which was to become the basis of the beginning of a new relationship between the Roman Catholic and Jewish communities." Six years later, Hoffman said, "It is in such a spirit that we meet today."

Marc, the session's moderator, introduced the issues to be discussed during this unprecedented coming together of American Jewish leaders with the famed evangelist. They included Israel and the Middle East; the relationship between American Jews and the Protestant evangelical community; Christian teaching and anti-Semitism; proselytism; conversion; and relations between church and state. In his introductory remarks, Marc said that he was "greatly impressed by the sensitivity and concern that Billy had expressed for social justice and for commitment to confront such basic issues as racial injustice, poverty, war, and the generation gap."

Mr. Graham began his remarks by stressing the need for communication between America's Jewish and Christian communities. Speaking of the historic persecution by Christians of Jews, he asked forgiveness. The evangelist, in describing his own ideology, characterized himself as being theologically conservative, yet liberal concerning many of the social issues of concern to Americans of all religions

He also spoke at length concerning his positive feelings for Israel. He attributed this to several factors, including his personal identification through extensive Bible study, as well as the Jewish heritage of Jesus and his disciples. He noted that one of his sons was working in Israel and that a daughter and son-in-law were planning to work on a moshav, a cooperative agricultural community, in the coming months. He also recalled that during a recent visit to the Jewish state, his wife, Ruth, had gazed down on Jerusalem from her vantage point on the Mount of Olives and described the holy city as "a Biblical Smorgasbord."

Regarding Israel's security, the evangelist noted his two-hour-long meeting held two months earlier with Golda Meir, Israel's new prime minister. At that time, Mr. Graham had explained his difficulty in speaking out on behalf of Israel: he was being pressured not to do so by Christians living in Arab nations. However, he pledged to continue speaking privately with US government officials concerning Israel's difficulties. And should a crisis arise that would threaten the Jewish state's existence—one requiring his public statement of support—he told the prime minister that she should inform him of that need via Israel's ambassador to the United States. He assured his Jewish colleagues that President Richard Nixon, with whom he had spoken three weeks earlier, was not only personally pro-Israel, but had become more sympathetic to that nation than he had been a year earlier.

In evaluating the meeting, Marc noted that a number of people had "carried around an image that certain versions of the Baptist tradition were rather insensitive to social or group concerns." But he said, "Mr. Graham, during his recent sermons, has helped to remove that caricature, and has demonstrated that personal religion can express itself in a very genuine concern for group morality and group justice." Marc said he felt a "genuine feeling of rapport" between the evangelist and his Jewish interlocutors. The rabbi also noted that the participants had "faced frankly" the differences in their respective traditions. But in doing so, they had also examined their strong bonds "as people who share a common reverence for the Bible and Biblical inheritance."

As for the attendees' responses, Rabbi Ronald Kronish, representing the Union of American Hebrew Congregations, the Reform umbrella organization, offered his own assessment of Mr. Graham's impact on his Jewish interlocutors: "To say the least, hearing Billy Graham talk in this small group meeting was a fantastic learning experience for me." Acknowledging that he had harbored a negative image of the committee's guest as "a wild, raving fanatic fundamentalist," the UAHC official said that that image "was severely shattered" as Mr. Graham had "talked softly and succinctly, and his position vis-à-vis Israel was very impressive."

Rabbi Kronish's original image of Mr. Graham was likely to have been informed by a view shared by many Jews of an evangelical desire to proselytize and convert non-evangelicals. Defusing this fear, Mr. Graham pointed out that the purpose of his recent visit to the Jewish state had been solely to visit the holy places and to interact on a nonreligious basis with Israelis. He also noted his sponsorship of two-week visits to the Jewish State of Israel for Christians—excursions guided by his "Staff expert on Israel."

At meeting's end, Marc presented Mr. Graham with a gift inscribed with the date in both Hebrew and English and the words: "To commemorate the first visit of the Reverend Doctor Billy Graham to the Institute of Human Relations, the American Jewish Committee is honored to present this unique volume of Sacred Scripture and commentary, the spiritual bond of God's word which links Christians and Jews." And that afternoon, Marc wrote to Mr. Graham expressing the agency's appreciation for his visit and noting that Mr. Graham's candor "helped overcome a number of misconceptions and strengthened the hands of fellowship between our peoples."

Marc also sent along a draft copy of the program for an event to be cosponsored by the committee and the Southern Baptist Convention on August 18–20 at the Louisville Theological Seminary. He invited Mr. Graham to attend. Responding nine days later, on July 2, 1969, Mr. Graham thanked the committee and said, "I certainly hope we can have a repetition of this meeting at some future date."

These two letters were the first of many that would be exchanged between Mr. Graham from his home in Montreat, North Carolina, and Marc Tanenbaum from his offices on Manhattan's East 56th Street over the next two decades. In the intervening years, Billy Graham would join with Marc in efforts to advance interreligious harmony while obliterating bigotry, injustice, and anti-Semitism, and he would voice unequivocal support of the State of Israel.

Mr. Graham's affinity for the Jewish state was evident in the production of a fifty-four-minute-long film shot on location in Israel by World Wide Pictures, the Minneapolis, Minnesota-based subsidiary of the Billy Graham Evangelistic Association. Entitled *His Land*, that film was released in 1969 in two versions: one intended for viewing by

Christians and ending with an evangelical message; the other, somewhat shorter, with Jewish audiences in mind, absent a Christological conclusion.

The committee learned of the film's existence early in 1970. On March 13, Marc and several colleagues met in New York with World Wide Pictures' director of distribution, Kenneth Bliss, and they agreed that *His Land* would be screened on May 13, during the committee's annual meeting. They also agreed that the AJC, in cooperation with World Wide Pictures, would show the film to "major Protestant denominational and interdenominational leadership," as well as Roman Catholic leaders and representatives of the religious press. The initial screening, held on May 1, at the Johnny Victor Theater on West 49th Street, was attended by more than sixty people. It would be followed by additional showings in May and June for motion picture distributors and theater owners.

Screenings would also be held for interfaith audiences in major cities, with AJC staff members in attendance. In order to facilitate understanding of the film's message, the committee also prepared a study guide. The committee worked closely with the Graham organization to stimulate media interest in the film.

There were a number of positive responses to *His Land*, including a piece by George Dugan published in the *New York Times*. The Associated Press religion correspondent, George Cornell, also wrote a widely circulated article. Israel's ambassador to the United States, Yitzhak Rabin, viewed the film as bearing a message of "love for the land of Israel and its people and the deep historic ties of the people of Israel and the land of the Bible."

On March 23, Marc wrote to the evangelist:

I find it hard to come by words adequate to express our appreciation for the tremendous contribution that you and your associates have made in helping the Christian community understand the deep spiritual and historical importance of the land and the State of Israel, both to Judaism and Christianity.

While we differ, obviously, about certain fundamentals, there is no question in my mind that the love and deep emotional empathy that is contained in this film for the Jewish people and Israel will contribute to strengthening profoundly the bonds between Jews and Christians.

Marc devoted one of his radio commentaries in early June to Billy Graham, noting that the evangelist regarded the rebirth of the city of Jerusalem "as the work of God acting in history in fulfillment of the Biblical prophecies." He added that Mr. Graham's pro-Israel stance "is reflected in the fact that under his spiritual influence, his own daughter and son-in-law have gone to Israel where they are now working on a kibbutz, helping to till the soil of the Holy Land as their way of serving God and humanity."

Later that month, during Mr. Graham's New York Crusade, just prior to that evening's service at Shea Stadium in Queens, home of the New York Mets, the evangelist and several of his closest aides met in his dressing room with Marc, his wife Helga, Gerald Strober, and Roger Hull, president of the New York Life Insurance Company. During this June 25 meeting, Mr. Graham thanked Marc for the committee's support for *His Land*, adding that he had "never gotten such a good press in the Jewish and secular publications."

The rabbi was pleasantly surprised when the reverend raised an issue very much on the Jewish community's mind: on that very day in 1970, Secretary of State William P. Rogers had seemingly waffled on promises previously made to Israel concerning the Nixon administration's willingness to supply jet aircraft to Israel. Mr. Graham said that he, too, was very disturbed by Rogers's refusal to commit to making the planes available to Israel. "Our friends [meaning the Israelis] have been in touch with and talked to me," Mr. Graham said, "and I have, in turn, been in touch with Washington. I was told that everything was going to be all right and now I just don't understand what has happened." Referring to the Nixon administration, the evangelist added, "They have not kept their word with me, and I intend to find out very shortly what is going on." Following Mr. Graham's frank talk with his guests, the committee group would observe the Crusade service from the vantage point of the baseball team's press box.

On September 1, *His Land* would be the topic of discussion between Marc and Irving Bernstein, the executive vice president of the United Jewish Appeal (UJA). Bernstein told the rabbi that the UJA's cabinet was about to decide whether to launch a $50 million fund-raising campaign among Christians. Bernstein said that the film would play a prominent role in the proposed effort. According to Marc, Bernstein then "raised the question of my possible availability, on a year's leave of absence basis, to help them think through their campaign with the Christian community."

While Marc suggested to Bernstein that he *could* be interested in joining that advisory effort, in a memorandum the next day, he told the AJC's Bert Gold, "I kept my reply deliberately vague, indicating that I would want to talk with you about the general question." Marc decided to remain in his position as the committee's Director of Interreligious Affairs and to seek $50,000 in funding to assist the AJC in implementing "our activities in interpreting Israel around the showing of *His Land* and building institutes and dialogues using a proposed study guide."

Later that month, Marc wrote to Philip Bernstein in response to a recent Associated Press article that had noted that some five thousand requests for screening the film had poured in from Christian churches of all denominations across the country. In his letter, Marc noted that World Wide Pictures lacked the resources to meet this "unexpected flood of requests" and asked for funds to purchase one hundred copies of the film, at $600 per print, as well as additional money to cover administrative costs. Marc also continued to urge AJC area directors, as well as local city Jewish Community Relations Council staffs, to utilize the film in their respective interreligious programming.

One year later, on September 2, 1971, after Mort Yarmon learned how widely viewed *His Land* had been, he suggested that there be "another go-around with the Billy Graham film." *His Land* would eventually be seen by tens of thousands of Christians throughout the non-Communist world.

Early in the spring of 1972, Marc and Billy would exchange letters demonstrating their growing collegiality and mutual trust. On April 14, the rabbi indicated that he had just read an account of Mr. Graham's remarks at his recent Crusade in Charlotte, North Carolina, in which he had commented on the still-sensitive issue of the Jewish people's role in Christ's crucifixion. Marc acknowledged the brevity of the account that he read, but he said, "Nevertheless, it gave me a sense of your continued contribution to educating and sensitizing the consciences of the Christian people to turn away from the ancient and unhistoric collective indictment of the Jews and rather to affirm the true spiritual character of the Crucifixion event." The rabbi expressed "appreciation of your invaluable efforts in seeking to overcome the negative aspects of our historic past and to lay the foundation for a more positive and mutually respectful approach to relations between Christians and Jews."

Marc also mentioned having read about plans for EXPLO '72, an evangelistic effort aimed at young people and scheduled to take place in Dallas in June. "I only hope," he wrote, "that something of this sensitivity with regard to the negative teaching about the Jewish people, as well as a respect for the living reality of Judaism, will be present in the spirit as well as in the program of these evangelical efforts." On April 18, Mr. Graham responded: "I shall most certainly see that this emphasis is made in the forthcoming EXPLO '72."

Meanwhile, Mr. Graham wrote to Marc proposing that the rabbi offer a prayer at the upcoming Republican National Convention. Marc responded that he could not accept that "great honor." As the rabbi explained, "I am seeking appropriate ways to advance our common cause without compromising my nonpolitical standing."

At the end of the summer of 1972, Billy Graham was deeply moved by the tragedy at the Olympic Games in Munich, when eleven Israeli athletes were killed by terrorists in the Olympic Village. The *San Francisco Examiner* reported that on September 8, Mr. Graham unexpectedly joined worshippers at a San Francisco temple to commemorate the Israeli victims' massacre.

Marc sent Mr. Graham the draft of an article by Leonard Yaseen, the national chair of the committee's Interreligious Affairs Commission, reflecting the lay leader's "deep concern over the prejudice and hatred, now climaxed so brutally by the Olympic massacres." Noting that Yaseen had written the article "with a view towards its possible publication in the *Readers Digest* or some similar publication," the rabbi said its author "would regard it as a personal favor if he could have the benefit of your reaction to it."

Responding on September 20, Mr. Graham offered a "top-of-the-head" reaction to the Yaseen article: "By and large, it is excellent. I agree with about ninety-five percent of it." But, he added, "I think it would have a far greater impact if such an article were written by a Christian leader rather than a Jewish leader." Mr. Graham added that certain paragraphs making light of the words of John, Mark, Matthew, and Luke "would be almost completely rejected by all evangelicals—and most other Christian groups, including the vast majority of Catholics, who were considered by both Catholics and Protestants alike to be inspired in their writings." The evangelist pointed out that this paragraph "would greatly detract from the rest of the article and blunt the message the writer is trying to get over to the Christians."

Three weeks later, Marc replied that Mr. Yaseen had agreed to revise his article. The rabbi then expressed his appreciation for the reverend's "personal involvement in the memorial service for the Israelis who were killed in Munich," noting that his act was "characteristic of your entire spirit of empathy and identification with our people in their hour of need."

The relationship between the rabbi and the evangelist would soon be tested as they disagreed for a time regarding the deeply fraught issue of proselytization. During the fall of 1972, a coalition of Christian organizations, led by the strident Campus Crusade for Christ, announced plans to launch Key '73, a year-long campaign of "calling our continent to Christ." Their effort was endorsed by the National Council of

Churches, several individual Protestant denominations, the National Conference of Catholic Bishops, numerous Roman Catholic dioceses and, surprisingly, given assurances made to Marc, by the Billy Graham Evangelistic Association.

Billy Graham had indeed been involved in the program's initial planning sessions, along with his close friend and adviser, the theologian Carl F. H. Henry, editor of *Christianity Today*. Those meetings were held at the Key Bridge Marriott Hotel in Arlington, Virginia, hence the word "Key" in the campaign's name. Jewish concerns were heightened when the Key '73 organizers declared their intention to "confront every person in North America more fully and more forcibly with the Gospel of Jesus Christ."

On January 23, 1973, Marc wrote to Mr. Graham, noting:

> It has been on my mind for some time to be in touch with you about the possibility of our having a conversation regarding Key '73. The problems of proselytization and respect for conscience require some basic clarification between the evangelical and Jewish communities. From my recent travels around the country, I am persuaded that the earliest it could be done the better for everybody concerned. Is there some chance we could meet in the near future?

A month later, Marc and the AJC's Gerald Strober traveled to Montreat for a three-hour lunch and discussion with the evangelist and his wife, Ruth, at the Grahams's rustic mountaintop home.

In his thank-you note, sent on March 1, Marc said, "you have the capacity to make a historic contribution to the clarification of relationships between Christians and Jews in our century." The rabbi said he was particularly moved by his host's words concerning God's Covenant with Israel. He suggested that if the evangelist's comments were to be made public "in an appropriate forum, I can assure you from the perspective of 20 years in this field that your declarations will literally help change the entire frame of reference within which Jews and Christians relate to each other. Your word will become a source of great healing and reconciliation that both our people desperately need."

Marc also mentioned his discussion with several of the committee's leaders about "extending to you an invitation to address one of our major national leadership conventions." The response to this idea, he wrote, "has been heartwarming and enthusiastic."

Enclosed with Marc's letter was a copy of the press release that Mort Yarmon would issue the next morning during the committee's press briefing on the rabbi's visit to Montreat. It included Mr. Graham's strong statement on God's special relationship with the Jews.

Two days later, Sunday, March 4, Marc devoted his radio commentary on WINS radio in New York and on the Westinghouse Broadcasting network of stations to the subject of "Billy Graham and Judaism." He began that day's broadcast by quoting from Mr. Graham's statement of reassurance to the Jewish community.

Marc also reported on Mr. Graham's disquieting experience a week earlier while traveling throughout the United States. During that trip, Mr. Graham said, he heard what the rabbi described as "reports over growing acts of psychological harassment, deception, and intimidation carried out by fervid young evangelists against Jewish young people on public high school and college campuses."

In his WINS radio commentary, the rabbi assured his listeners that Mr. Graham was "troubled about the deteriorating effect of such incidents on Christian-Jewish relations." Marc predicted that the evangelical leader was "destined to make a fundamental and lasting contribution to the improvement of Christian-Jewish understanding that may well become a historic turning point in relations between evangelical Christians and Jews."

Three days after their meeting in Montreat, the evangelist had written to Marc enclosing a press release "relative to the concerns over KEY '73." Mr. Graham expressed hope that the statement would help to "clarify in part the problems that have arisen." In his Key '73 press release, Mr. Graham stated that "just as Judaism frowns on proselytizing that is coercive, or that seeks to commit men against their will, so do I." Marc issued his own statement, in which he called Mr. Graham's clarification of his views on Key '73 and the Jewish people of "timely significance." He said it was an "important and constructive contribution to helping overcome the misunderstanding and stress that have developed between Christians and Jews in the absence of any policy statement by Key '73 leadership regarding proselytizing efforts aimed at the Jewish community."

Seizing on Mr. Graham's observations concerning God's relationship to the Jewish people, Marc stated: "To our knowledge this is the first time that Dr. Graham has publicly affirmed his belief that 'God has always had a special relationship with the Jewish people.'"

But in a letter to Mr. Graham dated April 3, Marc said of the evangelist's statement regarding Key '73 and Jewish-Christian relations, "there had been some critical reaction in Jewish circles, which felt that your statement falls short of clarifying your attitudes toward Judaism and the Jewish people in a clear-cut way."

The rabbi asked for an opportunity to "pick up our conversation and ascertain whether you feel ready to proceed with the further clarification on biblical and theological grounds of the views that you expressed to me during our last meeting." In Mr. Graham's reply, dated April 12, the evangelist said, "Naturally, I expected there would be some negative reaction. I seriously doubt if a statement could be devised that would please everyone." He added that his schedule was full for the next few months, and he asked that any further deliberations on this matter be postponed "until I have more time to think and pray it through—and consult people in both the Jewish and Christian community."

Mr. Graham had two weeks earlier informed *Newsweek*'s religion editor, Kenneth L Woodward, that he was "giving a lot of thought" to that special relationship "between God and Israel." He added that "The fact that in God's providence 16 million Jews have survived as Jews, despite scattering throughout the world, is a very mysterious thing to me."

In Marc's Interim Report on Key '73, he said, "To the degree that Key '73 concentrates its objectives and programs on deepening the commitment of Christians, and of transforming their lives as instruments of love, justice, and reconciliation," he added, "many Jews will not only not want to hinder their efforts, but indeed will bless their understanding and pray for its success." Indeed, he said Key '73 might offer a lesson for the Jews. He argued that the program

> has compelled the Jewish community to face dramatically what it has known all along—that you can't fight something with nothing. Key '73 has performed a positive service for the Jewish community by helping to raise the consciousness-levels of many Jews over the urgent need to pay more adequate attention and take more effective action in making living connections for young people between the spiritual richness of their traditions and their life situation. The energizing of current discussions within the Jewish community over enriching Jewish identity, strengthening Jewish education and the Jewish family and religious life in the wake of the Key '73 dialogue is the latest installment of a long story of Jewish creative response to the unending challenges of living in the Diaspora for the past 2,000 years.

Despite Mr. Graham's unequivocal stance on the issue of proselytizing, as well as his steadfast support of the Jewish state, Marc sought to dissuade some Jewish leaders who wanted to involve the evangelical leader in Jewish organizational programs. Writing on March 26, 1972, to Mel Bloom, the UJA's director of public relations, Marc said, "It is our considered judgment that it would be a mistake from the point of view of Israel's best interests to involve him in a UJA program." The rabbi's view was that "It would expose him instantly to further attack and harassment from pro-Arab elements in the Protestant community, and conceivably could limit his influence in Washington, where it is really needed."

The rabbi and the evangelist would remain in close touch throughout the 1970s. On September 22, 1974, Mr. Graham told Marc, "I wish everyone in the whole world were as broad, tolerant, and loving as you." And on February 9, 1976, following Mr. Graham's trip to Israel, which included a visit to Hadassah–Hebrew University Medical Center, where he met with wounded victims of a terrorist attack in Jerusalem's Zion Square, Mr. Graham concluded a letter to Marc with the words: "I hope you will always consider me a friend on whom you can call at any time to be of any service I possibly can. Shalom, Billy." That June, in yet another letter to the rabbi, the evangelist reminisced about their previous meetings. "Ruth and I will never forget your visit to our home, nor shall I ever forget the meeting with Jewish leaders in New York that you arranged several years ago, in which I had a wonderful opportunity of dialogue. Be assured, beloved friend, I have not changed my mind!"

On August 9, 1977, Marc wrote to Mr. Graham, inviting him to accept the American Jewish Committee's invitation to address its policy-making National Executive Council in Atlanta on October 28. During that event, the rabbi said, the evangelist would be presented with the committee's National Interreligious Award "in appreciation of the historic contributions that you have made in support of Israel, human rights, combatting anti-Semitism, and in strengthening friendship and understanding between members of the Evangelical and Jewish communities."

On that eagerly anticipated day, Marc broke with a long-held practice: although he was one of the ablest extemporaneous orators of his day, usually speaking from notes and documents retrieved from his bulging black leather briefcase, on this occasion, he had carefully written out his presentation speech in block letters. Addressing the attendees in an uncharacteristically intimate manner, he began:

This is a special moment for me in both my professional and personal life. If you will allow this personal reflection: for the past 25 years, I have tried to devote my life to seeking to uproot the poisonous weeds of misunderstanding, prejudice, and bigotry between Christians and Jews, and to try to plant seeds that might flower in time into mutual respect, friendship, and even love and caring for one another. It has not always been an easy or a smooth course to follow.

Then, after mentioning Vatican Council II, the rabbi spoke of "a new history of understanding, mutual respect, and reciprocal caring between the 50 million Evangelical Christians—the fastest growing Christian group in America—and the Jewish people in this country."

On the basis of "personal experience," the rabbi attributed this new understanding "in very large measure to the attitudes, convictions, and personal influence of the distinguished guest whom we honor today, the Reverend Billy Graham." The rabbi said that "Dr. Graham has been present to the Jewish people in virtually every moment of trial, threat, and testing, as well as in celebration." Marc added, "Dr. Billy Graham has been and continues to be one of the greatest friends of the Jewish people and of Israel in the entire Christian world in the 20th century."

Billy Graham, also speaking from a written text, recounted the distance he had traveled in his understanding of the Jewish community's role in American life. The evangelist recalled that as a young man, "as soon as I began to study the Bible in earnest I discovered the debt I owe to Israel, to Judaism, and to the Jewish people." Evangelical Christians in particular "have an affinity for the Jews because the Bible is essentially a Jewish book written under the influence of God's spirit," he said. Noting that "there are theological differences that we may never agree on," Mr. Graham suggested several areas where Jews and evangelicals could join together for a better America, including praying for the peace of Jerusalem, continuing to foster better race relations, and working together for a national spiritual and moral awakening. The evangelist then offered a stirring conclusion:

In the ancient synagogues of Israel upon the completion of any of the Books of Moses, it was the custom of the congregation to exclaim 'Be strong, be strong, and let us strengthen one another!' In like manner, when we see each other under the enemies' attack, let us encourage and strengthen one another. I would say to both Christian and Jew today: Be strong. Be strong. And let us strengthen one another.

That appearance, marking Mr. Graham's first address to a major national Jewish organization during an open meeting, would be widely reported in the press. The following January, Marc received an edited version of Mr. Graham's Atlanta speech, which would appear in *Decision*, a magazine published by the Graham organization. On January 12, 1978, the rabbi, in a memorandum to Bertram Gold, proposed that the committee publish the full text of Mr. Graham's address in a pamphlet. "I believe," he wrote,

> that a number of things that Graham said continue to be of importance for a large number of evangelical Christians in this country and abroad. Since it is not likely that he will make another talk like this for a long time to come, I think there are special values in preserving it in this form and seeing that it gets to major centers of Evangelical and other Christian public opinion.

Meanwhile, on July 4, 1979, Marc, as he had done on July 4, 1970, would join Billy Graham in Washington, D.C., to participate in a program to "Honor America." The rabbi, in his introduction to a reading from Leviticus 19, stated: "On this Independence Day celebration it is fitting to read from the Hebrew Scriptures, which historians have called 'the intellectual arsenal of the American Revolution' and the 'mortar which cemented the foundations of American democracy.'"

Less than two years later, during the winter of 1982, Marc spoke at a luncheon held at the Church Center for the United Nations marking Mr. Graham's designation as winner of the Templeton Foundation Prize for Progress in Religion. In his remarks, the *New York Times* reported on March 11, 1982, Marc "paid tribute to Pope John XXIII, but reserved his highest praise for Mr. Graham, calling him, 'the greatest friend of the Jewish people in the entire Christian community in the 20th century.'"

The next meeting between Marc and Mr. Graham would occur on April 2, in Boston, when the committee's regional office organized a meeting for the evangelist with New England Jewish leaders prior to the evangelist's Crusade in the state's capital. Dr. Marvin Wilson had suggested, through a friend, that Billy Graham meet prior to his Crusade not only with Boston's Christian leadership, but with the heads of the city's Jewish organizations. While the professor said that he "was not in regular contact with anybody about that," he had "planted the seed." And so, on the evangelist's arrival in the city, he sat down with the heads of the New England region's Jewish organizations, synagogues, and leading rabbis.

Dr. Wilson, who had asked Marc to permit him to be a silent observer in the room, called the session "one of the most dramatic things I've ever observed in my life in Christian-Jewish relations." The meeting, which took place in a Jewish lawyer's office on the twentieth floor of what was then the E.F. Hutton financial building, involved about twenty-five representative Jewish leaders from New England. Dr. Wilson wrote:

Marc Tanenbaum walked in with Billy Graham. When he got up to introduce Billy Graham, he said, "This man and his organization have made the best, most loving film on Israel out there today, "His Land.'" The next thing Marc said was something I had never heard of, and I am sure none of the Jewish leaders were aware of. Marc said that Billy Graham had a significant role in helping Israel at the time of the Yom Kippur War of October 1973. Marc said that Dr. Henry Kissinger, who at the time of the war was secretary of state, was not responding to the phone calls of Prime Minister Golda Meir, who was requesting aid for Israel, which was under siege in the war.

According to Marc Tanenbaum, Golda Meir called Billy Graham, who had established some kind of a relationship with her. Billy Graham, who was chaplain to eight presidents, then called President Nixon and told him about the dire situation in Israel. Within forty-eight hours, transport planes were loaded with medical supplies and other goods and flown to Israel.

Basically, Dr. Wilson recalled, "what Marc Tanenbaum was saying to these Jewish leaders was: here's a man who is a friend of Israel, who had that connection with the president, and because of his urging, things were able to get expedited. Then he introduced Billy Graham." As for Mr. Graham's remarks, Dr. Wilson recalled:

> Billy Graham said a few very memorable things. He used the exact words "The guilty silence of the Church" in recalling the Holocaust years. He spoke of the importance of a strong Israel; of the importance of Christian-Jewish relations; and some things on anti-Semitism. When he was done, he took questions, explaining what he meant by a Crusade; that he did not target Jewish people in his meetings.
>
> When he was done—it was very moving—the lawyer in whose office the meeting was held got up. I've got to confess I've never seen a lawyer cry before—I don't hang out with lawyers a lot—but there were tears in his eyes. And he said, "Dr. Graham, it has been a catharsis for my psyche to hear a Christian speak of the guilty silence of the Church." Those words were very moving to the people in that room.

Writing to Mr. Graham on April 21, Marc said, "It's extraordinary how these personal meetings contribute almost instantly to destroying stereotypes and caricatures that are uncritically picked up in the general culture."

In 1984, Mr. Graham, normally very cautious in lending his name to causes outside the purview of his organization, would, at Marc's suggestion, join the honorary board of the Campaign to Remember for the United States Holocaust Memorial Museum. The evangelist, who had visited the Auschwitz and Treblinka death camps, wrote in his letter of acceptance to Miles Lerman, chairman of the International Relations Committee of the United States Holocaust Memorial Council: "The Holocaust is something that we should remember so that it will never happen again. I promised a long time ago that if anti-Semitism raised its head in the United States I would be glad to make speeches or to use whatever influence I may have to help stamp it out. God has given me a great love for the Jewish people."

In the spring of 1985, Mr. Graham got Marc involved in advising the White House concerning President Ronald Reagan's scheduled visit to a cemetery in Bitburg, Germany, which turned out to contain the graves of Nazi Waffen SS troops. From his home in Montreat, Graham called Marc to discuss what he called "the terrible situation" that President Reagan was facing in his forthcoming visit to Germany. Billy added that he had "a long talk with Nancy Reagan" and she was "more upset than at almost any time I have known her over the past 30 years."

In a memo to the AJC's executive vice president David Gordis, as well as lay leaders, Marc explained that "Graham said that the President was bewildered over the difficulty and does not know how to get out of it." Marc noted that Billy had told the president "that this was far more a moral issue than a political one, and that unless he finds a way to straighten this out, it will undermine his moral authority in the country and overseas."

Michael Deaver, the White House deputy chief of staff, contacted Marc—some say at the behest of Nancy Reagan—seeking advice. The presidential aide told the rabbi that Helmut Kohl, West Germany's chancellor, did not understand the furor over the Bitburg visit. He said that Herr Kohl was insistent that the American president follow through on his pledge to visit the cemetery. And Reagan felt indebted to Kohl for standing united with him in deploying Pershing II missiles within West Germany, despite overwhelming opposition within Germany.

Marc was brought to the White House and agreed to draft a speech for the president. He also suggested the president could help to offset some of the controversy and shift the focus by visiting the grave of Konrad Adenauer, West Germany's first post–World War II leader, who was also buried in the Bitburg cemetery. This handling of the cemetery visit, along with the president's visit to the Bergen-Belsen concentration camp, would serve to defuse some of the controversy over Bitburg. On May 1, Marc's draft of the presidential speech was delivered to the White House. And four days later, Mr. Reagan would deliver the rabbi's words as the president and Chancellor Kohl stood together at Konrad Adenauer's grave.

The Reagan White House was "a little nonplussed by all the controversy," the AJC's Howard Friedman said: "I don't think that Michael Deaver ever really understood why there was such a fuss about this thing. Ultimately, I think, the president did get a sense of it, although at first he was nonplussed, as well."

Friedman added, "The Committee was responsible for negotiating directly with the Germans and with Chancellor Kohl" to reshape the President's visit to Bitburg by such measures as adding the visit to Adenauer's grave." Following all this, a German weekly magazine published a photograph of the president shaking hands with Marc, accompanied by the caption "Power and Voices of the Jews."

During the fall of 1989, Marc would be invited to participate in a tribute to Billy Graham on the fortieth anniversary of the evangelist's milestone Los Angeles Crusade. Incorporated in the rabbi's tribute would be his letter of October 2:

> I am particularly grateful, to you, Billy for the heartwarming and inspired leadership that you have given over decades in building bridges of reconciliation and friendship between Evangelical Christians and the Jewish people. I will never forget your generous acts of kindness and solidarity. It has been one of the great privileges of my life to know you as trusted friend and warmhearted colleague.

The professional paths of the rabbi and the evangelist would cross one last time. In August 1991, Marc Tanenbaum would introduce Billy

Graham during a luncheon and forum sponsored by the New York Board of Rabbis.

This lengthy love feast between two major religious leaders would come to an end when Marc passed away in 1992. But there would be a dramatic coda a decade later, when secret tape recordings from the Nixon presidency were released by the US National Archives in College Park, Maryland, and the Richard Nixon Presidential Library in Yorba Linda, California. The tapes included a February 1, 1972, meeting between President Nixon and Mr. Graham in which the evangelical leader joined the president in making what appeared to be anti-Semitic remarks.

According to a March 1, 2002, article in the *Chicago Tribune*, headlined "Nixon And Billy Graham Anti-Semitism Caught on Tape," President Nixon offered a stream of bigoted comments about Jews and their perceived influence in the media, and Mr. Graham expressed agreement: "This stranglehold has got to be broken or the country's going down the drain," Mr. Graham said. "You believe that?" Nixon said after the "stranglehold" comment. "Yes, sir," Graham said. "Oh, boy," replied Nixon. "So do I. I can't ever say that but I believe it." "No, but if you get elected a second time, then we might be able to do something," Graham replied.

Later, the conversation returned to the media, and Graham mentioned that he has friends in the media who are Jewish, saying they "swarm around me and are friendly to me." But, he confided to Nixon, "They don't know how I really feel about what they're doing to this country."

Nixon also commented on the news that Israel had mistakenly shot down a Libyan civilian airliner, killing all on board. The president then said, "What I really think is, deep down in this country, there is a lot of anti-Semitism, and all this is going to do is stir it up." Graham agreed that it will push anti-Semitism "right to the top." He then turned the conversation to a report he read that Israel supposedly wanted to "expel all the Christians." Graham also mentioned Jewish opposition to a Christian evangelical unified campaign, saying Jews are "going right after the church." Nixon mentioned an upcoming dinner with Israeli Prime Minister Golda Meir, and Mr. Graham said that Israelis were the best kind of Jews.

Mr. Graham also mentioned an upcoming meeting with Rabbi Marc Tanenbaum, and he described Marc as "probably the most outspoken and most listened-to rabbi in America" and as "one of the cleverest and most brilliant of the rabbis." Mr. Graham mentioned that the rabbi would be coming to see him soon at his home in Montreat, North Carolina. He told Mr. Nixon: "I'm going to have a real hair letting with Rabbi Tanenbaum," adding, "I think, basically [he] is our friend." The president responded, "I would be very, very tough with all of our Jewish friends in here, like Tanenbaum. You tell him he's making a terrible mistake and that they're going to get the damnedest wave of anti-Semitism here if they don't behave."

These taped remarks came during a ninety-minute session after a prayer breakfast the men attended on February 1, 1972. During the wide-ranging conversation, Graham heaped praise on the president, telling him, "Congratulations on everything," and "I believe the Lord is with you."

In the days after the release of these tape recordings, Jews reacted with a combination of outrage and bewilderment at Mr. Graham's apparent duplicity. Anti-Defamation League Director Abraham Foxman blasted both Nixon and Graham, saying that, "while never expressing these views in public, Rev. Graham unabashedly held forth with the president with age-old classical anti-Semitic canards." Michael Kotzin, a vice president at the Jewish United Fund in Chicago, told the *Chicago Tribune*, "One really did not associate him with this." He added, "Rather than try to direct Nixon in a different direction, he reinforces him and eggs him on when it came to these stereotypes, and that's troubling."

Larry Ross, a spokesman for Mr. Graham, who was then eighty-three and not in good health, said the reverend could not respond because he did not recall the conversation.

Others sought to comprehend what they had heard on the tapes. "I find this rather stunning," said William Martin, a professor of religion and sociology at Rice University in Houston and author of *A Prophet with Honor: The Billy Graham Story*. "This is out of character with anything else I have heard Billy Graham say or be quoted as saying. It is disappointing," Martin said. Martin Marty, a religious historian at the University of Chicago, noted the distinction some conservative evangelicals and Pentecostals have made between supporting Israel but not American Jews.

Marc would not live to learn of these remarks by the evangelical leader that he had so assiduously courted and whom he believed had come to be his close friend. In 1977, when the rabbi played a significant role in arranging for the AJC to honor Mr. Graham, Marc said, according to Graham biographer William Martin, that "most of the progress of Protestant-Jewish relations over the past quarter century was due to Billy Graham." Was Mr. Graham so two-faced as to flatter the Jews in public while disparaging them in private? Was this great communicator somehow making a clumsy argument that certain activities and demands on the part of some people in the Jewish community, particularly those associated with the mass media, would arouse anti-Semitism among parts of the public although he did not share this anti-Semitism? Or was he simply so obsequious in the presence of the president of the United States that he would go along with anti-Semitic comments rather than stand up for his putative friends? There would be no definitive answer to these questions. Many, however, would be reminded of a Jewish saying: "Even in the warmest of hearts, there's a cold spot for the Jews."

CHAPTER 14

The Jews' Foremost Apostle to the Gentiles

"Marc Tanenbaum was a centrist in the best sense of the word. . . . He wanted to speak for the Jewish community at large, and he wanted to pay respect to the differences in that community, but also respect to the differences between Christian organizations and Jewish. He was, in the best sense of the word, a peace-maker."
—Reverend Donald W. Shriver, president emeritus, Union Theological Seminary, New York

MARC TANENBAUM'S GROUNDBREAKING INTERRELIGIOUS WORK extended beyond historic and high-profile initiatives with the Catholic Church and Billy Graham and his evangelical organization. Equally important, he helped advance relations between faith groups on the local level.

He was able to accomplish this by developing an organization that was focused on enhancing harmony with a wide range of Christian denominations and organizations. Under Marc's leadership, the Department of Interreligious Affairs was constantly carrying on a substantial number of different projects and initiatives.

When Marc came to the AJC, he was well aware that as early as the 1920s, the committee had filed an amicus brief in Oregon in support of Catholic parochial schools. He knew also that Cardinal James McIntyre of Los Angeles had established ties with the committee's lay leadership dating back to Al Smith's failed presidential bid of 1928, when the prominent New York attorney Joseph Proskauer had served as the first Catholic presidential candidate's campaign manager.

In the post–Vatican II era, during meetings with the pope or with leaders of the Catholic Church or major Protestant denominations in the United States, Marc was constantly seeking to build a process and an agenda that would move relations between Christians and Jews from centuries-old conflicts to mutual respect, conciliation, and appreciation. Under his leadership, the AJC, and in particular Marc's department, were at the center of a vast range of initiatives across the United States.

As Marc focused on pursuing his interreligious agenda, he emphasized recruiting highly qualified specialists with ties to both the Jewish and gentile worlds. In 1968, he increased his staff to include a Reform rabbi with congregational experience as well as a lay consultant who would carry out a highly regarded research project for which Marc had raised the funds.

The rabbi, Virginia-born A. James Rudin, was a graduate of Hebrew Union College in Cincinnati. He had also completed history studies at the University of Illinois. Following two years of military service as an Air Force chaplain stationed in Japan and Korea, he served as an assistant rabbi at Congregation B'nai B'rith in Kansas City, Missouri, and then as senior rabbi at Sinai Temple in Champaign-Urbana, Illinois.

After his first, "transformative," visit to Israel in July 1967, immediately following the Six-Day War, the young rabbi realized that there was a larger stage than a synagogue bimah on which he could play a role in Jewish life. On returning to the United States that fall, Rabbi Rudin concluded that his professional fulfillment lay in Jewish communal service. To that end, he sent his résumé to the leaders of three national agencies—the American Jewish Committee, the American

Jewish Congress, and the Anti-Defamation League (ADL). Marc would be the only one to respond.

In early 1968, the young job applicant learned that Marc would be speaking at the University of Wisconsin, in Madison, about the Six-Day War, and Rabbi Rudin drove there from Champaign-Urbana to meet him. Their ensuing conversation was "very, very good," according to Rabbi Rudin. But Marc was not prepared to commit himself further at that point; he said he wished to formally interview Rudin in New York. That interview went well, and in 1968, A. James Rudin became the Department of Interreligious Affairs' assistant director. Fifteen years later, in 1983, he would succeed Marc as its director.

Meanwhile, Brooklyn-born Gerald Strober had fulfilled his two-year military obligation in 1958. Stationed in Germany during the heart of the Cold War, he made a point during furloughs to query local civilians as to what they believed had been the fate of their Jewish neighbors during World War II. In the early 1960s, Strober pursued graduate work in Jewish Studies at New York University under the tutelage of the highly regarded Dr. Abraham Katsh, the head of NYU's Institute of Hebrew Studies. In 1967, Strober joined the staff of the National Conference of Christians and Jews (NCCJ) as director of a research project aimed, in his words, "at analyzing the image of Jews and Judaism in Protestant Church school curricula."

The following year, Marc recruited him as a consultant to the Interreligious Affairs Department. Strober reported for work on December 2, 1968, and during the six years he would spend at the AJC, he and Rabbi Rudin would travel the nation, often in Marc's company, in pursuit of the committee's interreligious objectives.

Judith Banki, a key member of Marc's staff who had played such a major research role in the run-up to Vatican Council II, originally had some second thoughts about continuing her work with the Department of Interreligious Affairs. She had two concerns: First, she was uneasy about Marc continually looking over her shoulder. Second, although the human rights agency was at that time relatively progressive regarding feminist issues, Banki was aware that "some people there didn't think that a *woman* could do the work in the interreligious sphere." As she noted, "There were no female rabbis then," and she was "representing one patriarchal religion to another patriarchal religion."

Banki never discussed her concerns with Marc. But, given traditional male attitudes of that era, she believed that "If he had come to the committee *before* me, there would have been a very good chance that he wouldn't have hired me, not out of antagonism, because we got along very well." On the other hand, he would eventually hire another influential woman, Inge Lederer Gibel. Moreover, as Banki noted, "The committee was the first organization in the Jewish community relations field to establish a department to deal with feminist issues. So Marc was not antifeminist."

Despite Banki's unease, she realized that Marc appreciated her skills in writing and evaluating research materials. She also knew that the rabbi required her services as "an interlocutor between him and the committee's other departments." While each department "was going its own way," according to Banki, "we had weekly or biweekly cabinet meetings, where all the departments reported on what they were doing."

Thus, Jerry Goodman, as head of the Department of European Affairs, maintained frequent contact with Zach Shuster in the committee's Paris office, and later with his successor, Abe Karlikow. Goodman was also in the advance party of a European mission whose Rome meetings Marc would arrange.

Given the rabbi's position at the forefront of the agency's efforts on such crucial issues as human rights and relations between Jews and the Catholic Church, "There were certain overlaps between the functions of our departments," Goodman observed. "Marc could facilitate contacts and meetings, and help us to understand what the Church was going through from the Jewish community's point of view." Later, as Goodman became more focused on Soviet Jewry, Marc's contacts with the Church in Rome would prove to be very helpful in Goodman's efforts to get American Church leaders "to become outspoken in regard to the official Jewish minority in the Soviet Union."

In addition to working closely with AJC colleagues in New York, among Marc's many organizational responsibilities were his frequent visits to committee offices throughout the country. On those occasions, he would work closely with the agency's regional directors. At that time, they included Eugene DuBow, who had moved on to Chicago to head the Midwest Region; Philip Perlmutter, in Boston; Irving Levine, the longtime director of the Cleveland Field Office; and Dr. Neil Sandberg in Los Angeles.

Perlmutter had first observed Marc at close range during a dialogue with officials of St. Louis University, a Catholic institution. According to Perlmutter, the rabbi was so focused on his outreach that he was "a one-issue person, an intellectual and spiritual leader." One of the Boston personalities with whom both Perlmutter and Marc interacted at that time was Father Robert Drinan, a Catholic priest and member of the US House of Representatives who would one day be forced by the Vatican to relinquish his seat. According to Perlmutter, Father Drinan "was a player, but he wasn't a leader in a sense that Marc was; he wasn't in Marc's league." Perlmutter added, "Of all the organizations—the Anti-Defamation League, and the American Jewish Congress—the committee was the pioneer in dialogue."

To be sure, there remained considerable controversy in the Jewish community concerning Marc's outreach to the Catholic Church. The AJC's Howard Friedman, although a self-described "neophyte" in interreligious affairs, was well aware of the lingering tension concerning involvement with the Church. As he observed, in hindsight, "There were—and are—a number of Orthodox rabbis who believe as a matter of faith that you don't deal with the Catholic Church and you don't have dialogue with them; you just get away from them."

Irving Levine, who would later move from the AJC's Cleveland office to New York to serve as the organization's Director of Education and Urban Planning, as well as head of its Institute for American Pluralism, acknowledged that the Interreligious Affairs Department played a major role in the committee's larger program. "It was *big*," he recalled. "Later, of course, the ethnic stuff became pretty well known in many circles. But we were known for Interreligious Affairs; it was a major factor, especially coming out of the Ecumenical Council." Acknowledging the existence of what Levine describes as "a lot of romantic stuff about what Tanenbaum did," the former Cleveland director said that there was continuing "controversy over who did it; and who did *not* do it." But, as he observed, "It was heavily publicized—all the newspaper and magazine articles."

Looking back on Tanenbaum's leadership in interreligious affairs, Levine viewed the rabbi as having been "a great publicist about what the American Jewish *Committee* did. Everybody talked about the fact that we had a man in the Vatican for many years working with Cardinal Augustin Bea and preparing the way. There was a lot of hype about the committee's role." Levine added, "I have to be honest; I always thought that he was gifted, but that he had a great staff—Jim Rudin, Judy Banki—a great group of people working for him." Levine added, "I could not always distinguish who was doing the work.

Marc's influence was continually being felt in the agency's offices throughout the nation.

As soon as Marc arrived at the committee in 1961, he began to visit the Western Region regularly. There, he would assist Sandberg in the various western offices under his supervision, as well as in communities where the committee did not maintain chapters.

For example, during the late 1970s, Marc developed contacts in Las Vegas with the Mormon Church, which had many adherents in Nevada. A by-product of his efforts would be "Jewish Week." A series of events that also involved Mormons, the program featured an exhibit of Jewish artifacts. "While the Mormons wanted to call it 'Hebrew Week,' through Marc's efforts, we were able to call it 'Jewish Week,'" Sandberg said.

The regional director recalled that Marc's appearance at the opening day's festivities "was the highlight of the program," in which the governor of Utah, Scott Matheson, spoke of the warmth of relations between his state's Mormon and Jewish citizens. In fact, one of Matheson's earliest predecessors, Simon Bamberger, was a Jew. He had been elected governor in 1916, only ten years after Utah's admission to the Union as its forty-fifth state.

Under Sandberg's supervision, the committee's Los Angeles staff would utilize what he characterized as "Marc's enormous skills and his ability to communicate. We relied on him very heavily over the years, and we would call on him to develop outreach and dialogue. And Marc was always available."

During visits to LA, Marc would also cultivate relations with its archdiocese, particularly with Cardinal Timothy Manning. "They were crucial for the committee," Sandberg observed. "They had actually begun before Marc's tenure there, even before my own." When Sandberg arrived in Los Angeles in 1962, he carried with him a message from the committee's president, Joseph Proskauer, to Cardinal James McIntyre. The cardinal received Sandberg immediately, Sandberg said.

With Marc's encouragement, the agency's Los Angeles chapter would continue to expand its interfaith relationships during the 1960s, reaching out to local organizations and institutions, including Loyola University, a Jesuit school later known as Loyola Marymount University. That institution would develop research in Catholic-Jewish relations and invite Marc as a featured speaker. But tension would develop within the Catholic community, according to Sandberg: "Loyola's outreach was accomplished over the objections of the archdiocese, which wanted to have a primary role in dialogue. Thus Loyola decided to act independently."

Cardinal McIntyre would frequently call Father Raymond D'Souza, an official of the Jesuit order, and berate him for conducting that outreach. While the committee found itself in the middle of the dispute, the agency would succeed in maintaining its relationship with Loyola, as well as with the archdiocese.

Another individual with whom Marc and the AJC worked closely was Monsignor Royale Vadakin, the archdiocese's ecumenical officer, who also enjoyed close ties to the LA Jewish community. According to Howard Friedman, "Vadakin became almost Jewish because of Marc." Sandberg believed that their affinity, deemed "excessive" within the diocese's hierarchy, would in part be responsible for preventing the monsignor from being named a bishop.

Monsignor Vadakin would demonstrate his loyalty to the American Jewish community during the Egyptian attack on Israel in the Yom Kippur War of 1973, and on the imposition the following year of an oil embargo. "Royale was willing to go public and become a Catholic face of the public mobilization that the committee was developing at the time," Sandberg said.

During Pope John Paul II's visit to Los Angeles in the 1980s, the monsignor would be instrumental in involving other faith groups, but once again, he would be perceived as being too close to the Jews. This time, the main target of the diocese's disapproval would be a Reform rabbi, Alfred Wolf, of the Wilshire Boulevard Temple, who served that congregation under its senior rabbi, Edgar Magnin. But Rabbi Wolf and Monsignor Vadakin—with Marc's assistance—persevered, and they would be instrumental in creating the Interreligious Council of Southern California.

"That was particularly important," Sandberg said. "Marc was really inspirational. For the first time we moved beyond Catholic-Jewish or Protestant-Jewish dialogue, into trifaith discussion. And we brought in Hindus, Baha'is, and adherents of Islam. It became the largest, multi-faced interreligious group in the country."

Indeed, during the Dalai Lama's visit to Los Angeles some years following the council's establishment, more than seventy-five religious leaders, including a number of Jews, would meet with him at a Buddhist temple. The exiled Tibetan spiritual leader commended the council on its impressive interfaith outreach

In the question period following the Dalai Lama's prepared remarks, Sandberg asked whether the kind of dialogue the two religious groups had just concluded would be welcomed in Asia. "He thought about it for a moment," Sandberg recalls, "and then responded, 'Very difficult, very difficult.'"

During the rabbi's many visits to Los Angeles in those years, Sandberg said, "He would do virtually everything we asked of him.

For example, when we developed our outreach to the film industry, banks, and other enterprises, he would come out to speak at major fund-raising events. He would inspire an audience of three hundred or one thousand. And we increased those capabilities, which had been almost nonexistent prior to the 1960s."

On those occasions, the Los Angeles office would also tie the rabbi's presence in the city to an interfaith meeting at Loyola University, where the participants would discuss specific issues.

"With the Catholics it might be *Nostra aetate*; with the mainline Protestant denominations, the position of the World Council of Churches on Israel, which was not always favorable," Sandberg observed. "The Presbyterians, in particular, had interests in the Middle East that made it impossible for them to be supportive of Israel, and so were often negative and hostile."

While dissension concerning the Jewish state remained a sticking point, many agreed there was a marked improvement in general interfaith dialogue over the years. Rabbi Joseph Potasnik, the host of the *Religion on the Line* broadcast every Sunday on WABC Radio in New York, would attest to that. During each program, the rabbi would talk with a representative of the Catholic Church. "Whether it's belief in Christ or the pro-life/pro-choice argument, I can talk to him about my beliefs and he can share his, and we still walk away with mutual respect," the host said. "Those of us who grew up pre-1965 remember that we would talk *about* each other but not *to* each other. These kinds of exchanges are remarkable."

During the early years of Marc's tenure at the committee, he was the main purveyor of religious thought, speaking eloquently on such issues as proselytizing. Marc's oratorical gifts were such that when he addressed a gathering at the Fuller Theological Seminary, a conservative Protestant institution, its president exclaimed in amazement: "He had five words on a piece of paper, and he spoke for an hour and a half!" Rabbi Tanenbaum would be the keynote speaker at a subsequent, three-day meeting at the seminary, where the committee would bring together the leadership of the Southern California Board of Rabbis and the National Association of Evangelicals.

"Marc's role was central to its success," Sandberg maintained. He recounts an exchange that took place during a session in which ties between evangelicals and Jews, very much stimulated by the rabbi's relationship to Billy Graham, were discussed. "A Protestant minister stood up and said something about God having to sacrifice his only son, Jesus. Marc responded that with Abraham, God chose *not* to sacrifice a son, Isaac. It was that kind of stimulation that Marc would encourage and cause to happen."

The Catholic Church's most prominent theologians were also impressed with Rabbi Tanenbaum's interreligious outreach. The Reverend Theodore M. Hesburgh, at that time president of the University of Notre Dame, observed that the rabbi "never came through as being selfish or one-sided. He was always broadminded and open to everybody. That was his great glory."

In the early 1970s, Marc had begun to reach out to the American evangelical community beyond Billy Graham. Among those with whom he would interact was an academician named Marvin Wilson, who was a close associate of Billy Graham. One of Wilson's classmates at Brandeis University, Dr. G. Douglas Young, who would later become the president of the Institute for Holy Land Studies in Jerusalem, suggested that Wilson convene a conference of evangelicals and Jews. Wilson knew that Marc's participation would be crucial to the success of such a conference. Thus he arranged to meet in New York with the rabbi and members of his staff, including Judith Banki, Julius Briller, Rabbi Rudin, and Marc's longtime personal assistant, Florence Mordhurst. "The rabbi was very focused and very intense, with great passion for interfaith relations, and tremendous energy for social justice issues," Wilson recalled. More important, Young's idea, as presented by Wilson, immediately appealed to Marc, who envisioned a three-day meeting expressly to discuss issues of theology and history from both the Jewish and evangelical Christian perspectives.

It was decided that the gathering would be cochaired by Marc and Young, and coordinated by Wilson and Rabbi Rudin. While Wilson and Rudin were given a free hand in planning the meeting and recruiting participants, "Marc was the visionary," according to Wilson. During one of the planning sessions, Wilson asked if Billy Graham might come to the conference. Deeming that unlikely, Wilson suggested that Mr. Graham's brother-in-law, Leighton Ford, an official of the Billy Graham Association, might wish to participate. Ford, who was a trustee of Gordon College, agreed, and there followed what Professor Wilson recalled as "a wonderful nine months of helping Ford with his address, as he had never spoken to a Jewish audience and knew very few Jewish people."

The first-ever national conference bringing together the two groups, titled "Evangelicals and Jews in Conversation on Scripture, Theology and History," was convened in Manhattan on December 8, 1975. So that the participants could deliberate in both Jewish and Christian settings, the group met for two days at the committee's headquarters and on the final day, December 10, at the Calvary Baptist Church, on West 57th Street.

Dr. Young and Rabbi Tanenbaum opened the meeting by presenting papers that were published in 1978 in a book that would be awarded a prize by *Christianity Today*.

Because of the success of that seminal conference, its sponsors decided to convene a follow-up meeting in 1980. That event, held at the Trinity Evangelical Divinity School, north of Chicago, was cochaired by Rabbi Tanenbaum, who addressed moral, spiritual, and ethical themes; and Kenneth Kantzer, the editor of *Christianity Today*. Once again, Dr. Wilson and Rabbi Rudin served as the conference coordinators. Building on the accomplishments of the first conference five years earlier, the participants in the Chicago event achieved "a greater sense of camaraderie, openness, and candor," according to Wilson.

In 1984, Marc's presentation, as well as other conference papers, would be edited by Rabbi Rudin and Wilson for publication under Rabbi Tanenbaum's name. The book's title, *Evangelicals and Jews in an Age of Pluralism*, reflected Marc's goal, as defined by Wilson, "of developing a theology of pluralism, presupposing that any religious person, or group, sitting at the dialogue table wanted to define itself in its own terms, as well as to respectfully listen to the others."

Marc and Professor Wilson had coauthored two books during the 1970s. In 1978, a month after the release of their first effort, *Evangelicals and Jews in Conversation*, Wilson invited Marc to address the students at Gordon College, approximately 40 percent of whom had Baptist backgrounds.

"Marc was quite a media celebrity," Wilson recalled: "A crew from CBS television came out to cover his appearance." Wilson also recalled Marc's first words to the students: "How many of you are Baptists?" On seeing many hands shoot up, the rabbi exclaimed, "You ought to be so proud that you are Baptists!" "A lot of students were scratching their heads, wondering *why* they were among the elite," Wilson recalled. Marc launched into a conversation with the students about Roger Williams's significance. Many Americans believe the Puritans introduced the concept of religious liberty to the colonies. In fact, Marc said, they had quickly set up a theocracy. It was Roger Williams and the Baptists who put forward the idea of religious freedom.

A year later, Marc invited Wilson to New York, where they participated in a half-hour-long *Religion in the News* program on CBS to discuss evangelical-Jewish relations with Jimmy Allen, the then-president of the Southern Baptist Convention.

At about that time, Wilson received what he describes as "two unsolicited telephone calls" from Marc. During one, the rabbi asked him, "Do you know Jimmy Carter?" "No," Wilson replied. "Well, he's a Baptist," the rabbi responded—according to Wilson, the rabbi probably assumed that many evangelicals were Baptists. "Someone needs to inform the president that it's a Baptist position to support Israel!" the staunchly Zionist rabbi exclaimed.

During Marc's second call, he expressed his strongly held views on the importance of maintaining common ground between evangelicals and Jews. Then he asked: "Why can't evangelical Christians and Jews come together to declare the authority and eternal validity of the Ten Commandments in a world that's becoming increasingly secular?"

Marc was at that time also very involved in forging relationships with mainline Protestant personalities, among them Reverend Donald W. Shriver and his wife, Peggy.

The reverend said that he regarded the rabbi as having been "an important catalyst for the connections that we, as Christians, needed to have in this city with the Jews—and with their schools and synagogues and other institutions."

Marc generally achieved cordial relationships with many of his Protestant colleagues, but one major source of tension would mar their otherwise positive dealings: the sovereignty of the Jewish state and the relationship between Israelis and Palestinians.

One of Shriver's predecessors at Union Theological Seminary, Henry P. Van Dusen, the institution's head from the 1950s to 1969, had written a letter to the *New York Times* in 1967, in which he had expressed considerable friendliness toward the Palestinian side during the Six-Day War. Reverend Shriver said, "I know for a fact that this complicated our school's relationship to the Jewish Theological Seminary across the street."

"He had to have a forgiving spirit," Peggy Shriver observed, "because not everything we said was appreciated; not everything that we understood was understood in the same way by our different faith groups." The National Council of Churches consisted of more than forty Christian denominations whose points of view varied considerably, and while some of them may have enjoyed positive relationships with the Jewish community, from Peggy Shiver's perspective, "others really had very little contact, consisting, maybe, of the missionaries that they had worked with in Palestine, so we had a broad gamut of points of view to try to work with within the National Council of Churches. So some patience was required."

During the 1980s, Marc was not only dealing with the diverse issues bedeviling his goal of achieving lasting interreligious harmony at home, he was playing a major role in the committee's meetings with Pope John Paul II in the Vatican. In 1985, the rabbi facilitated, and participated in, the agency's eight-member mission commemorating two events of major historic significance to world Jewry: The fortieth anniversary of the end of World War II, which vanquished Hitler's genocidal regime; and the twentieth anniversary of Paul VI's promulgation on October 28, 1965, of *Nostra aetate*, repudiating the charge of deicide against the Jews.

The committee had encountered some difficulty getting the meeting on John Paul II's schedule, but because of Marc's efforts, the agency's delegation, led by AJC president Howard Friedman, met with the pope on Thursday, February 14, in the Apostolic Palace in Vatican City. According to Friedman, the pontiff "was very, very cordial and very warm toward Marc and to all of us. He was aware of some of the things the committee had been doing. And he certainly was aware of our role in the Vatican conclave."

Marc drafted Friedman's opening remarks. After extending the delegates' "heartfelt greetings of Shalom, of peace and well-being to you," the committee's president stated:

> We regard this audience with your Holiness as a particularly auspicious occasion in the history of the Catholic Church and the Jewish people. We meet with you to acknowledge the anniversaries of two climactic events: First, 1985 marks the 40th anniversary of the end of World War II and the defeat of the demonic ideology on Nazism, whose core was racial and religious anti-Semitism. Second, 1985 commemorates the 20th anniversary of the ending of Vatican Council II and its adoption of the historic declaration of *Nostra Aetate*.

Friedman went on to say that "As the Nazi trauma has appalled us with despair over human evil, so the 20th anniversary of the close of Vatican Council II has inspired all of us with hope and promise for a more humane future." In his remarks, Friedman also paid tribute to the late Cardinal Augustin Bea and his secretariat, with whom "We [the committee] were privileged to be intimately involved" throughout Vatican Council II. Friedman reported on the progress of the committee's efforts "in close cooperation with Catholic Relief Services and other relief agencies in seeking to relieve the suffering, hunger, and deprivation of millions of fellow human beings in Ethiopia and Africa generally"—a vital collaboration that he said testified "to the new spirit made possible by Vatican Council II."

Noting that the committee delegation had come to this papal audience immediately following a ten-day mission to Israel, where the American Jewish leaders had met with a broad representation of Israeli society—from Jews to Muslims to Christians—Friedman told the pope, "Everywhere we have found a great yearning for peace, for coexistence, for an end to conflict, violence and terrorism." These goals, the committee's president said, reinforced the agency's belief that "Without formal recognition of sovereign legitimacy of other states, Israel's continued existence can be undermined."

Thus, while acknowledging "the complexity of the problems involved" in granting formal Vatican recognition of Israel, Friedman said, "We dare to hope that the spirit that inspired your Apostolic Letter will lead to steps that will formalize the diplomatic ties between the Holy See and the State of Israel and her people."

Friedman's reference was to *Redemptionis Anno*, issued by John Paul II on April 20, 1984. In that precedent-shattering letter, recognizing the deep ties of the Jewish people with Jerusalem, the term "State of Israel" was uttered for the first time within the walls of the Vatican. Such a historic act on the Vatican's part would be, Friedman declared, "a watershed event in Catholic-Jewish relations. It would help create a sense of reality that is indispensable to peace, and would be a fitting culmination of Vatican Council II. Above all," he concluded, "it would be an act of profound spiritual and ethical significance in advancing the cause of world peace."

In response, John Paul II told the mission members that the teachings proclaimed in *Nostra aetate* "have radically improved in these years" and that ignorance, prejudice, and stereotypes were giving way to "growing mutual knowledge, appreciation, and respect."

Afterward, Friedman recalled, "It was a very successful meeting. It couldn't have happened without Marc; he really knew how to deal with that sort of thing."

But despite the warm sentiments expressed during the committee's commemorative audience, Marc would find it necessary in the coming years to confront tensions stemming from the Vatican actions perceived by the Jewish community as missteps. In 1986, one such papal gaffe would not only offend Jewish sensibilities, but generate sensational headlines. The controversy erupted over an audience granted by John Paul II to Kurt Waldheim, who was Austria's president at that time. It had been revealed that he had engaged in pro-Nazi activities while stationed in occupied Greece during World War II. The ensuing media firestorm reflected the Jewish community's outrage that the pope would receive a reputed war criminal. The Vatican was insisting that the charges against Waldheim had not been proven, that while he had served in the German Army during the war, there was no indication that he had been *personally* complicit at that time in the deportation of Greek Jews. To the Jewish leaders, papal explanation and reconciliation were clearly indicated. To that end, a delegation consisting of Marc and nine other Jewish leaders met with John Paul II at Castel Gandolfo, the pontiff's summer residence.

The Castel Gandolfo meeting was occurring at a time of very fertile dialogue between American Jewish leaders and the Vatican. According to Joe Berger, the *New York Times* correspondent who covered that event, "Marc understood the limits of what they were going to get out of this, and was able to communicate that. He understood that the pope was not going to apologize." After the meeting, the *Times* correspondent noted, "Marc was able to say that during this meeting at Castel Gandolfo, basically, the Jews would express their pain at what had happened with Waldheim, and the pope would express his sorrow at the Holocaust. But, nobody would apologize."

Ken Briggs, who by that time was covering religion for the *New York Times*, believed that "a lot of the loose ends and unexplored dilemmas that the Christians were taking, including the Catholic Church, were not being explored closely enough. There were a whole group of issues that really needed bearing down on, where pockets of anti-Semitism still were; where holes in the Vatican II documents were."

At that time, Briggs often felt that "both the Vatican and other Christian groups knew quite well how to court the Jewish leaders, and vice versa. They sometimes had the illusion that having 'solved' these questions among themselves, they *had* been solved." Briggs believed that "a layer of critique was needed. The pioneering group had formed a bond and wouldn't disturb that in any way. It's probably human nature. I think some things got neglected."

But in light of John Paul II's upcoming ten-day trip to the United States, his first US visit as pontiff, it was important to clear the air prior to the pontiff's trip. Thus, Berger believed. "The Vatican was interested that there be a good result. And so was the Jewish community, because they were also interested in maintaining this dialogue."

As Marc continued to pursue dialogue in his quest for interreligious reconciliation, he would also be broadening his mandate to grapple with the growing civil rights movement in America, anti-Semitism, Soviet Jewry, and ensuring the status of Israel.

CHAPTER 15

Civil Rights:
To Truly Overcome

"Unless we face up to and do something radically constructive about overcoming our conventional misperceptions and distortions of each other's essential nature and integrity as human beings . . . unless we learn out of this experience to understand, to appreciate in depth, to love unconditionally each other in our full humanity, we will not have come very far from those pre–Civil War days which found religious leadership so wanting and, indeed, bankrupt."

—Rabbi Marc Tanenbaum in a press release issued
on January 11, 1963, by the National Catholic Conference
for Interracial Justice, the Secretariat for the First National Conference
on Religion and Race, exhorting delegates to action

DURING THE FALL OF 1962, with Vatican Council II underway in Rome, Marc also became increasingly engaged in another endeavor of great magnitude, the growing struggle to obtain equal rights for America's black population. This was a natural segue for him, an organic outgrowth of being alive at a particular moment in American history. Shortly, Marc would find himself at the forefront of a coalition, an often uneasy coalition, between Jews and blacks in the civil rights movement.

His role symbolized and reflected much of what the nation's Jewish leaders sought to achieve in order to help the nation fulfill its commitment to the belief that all men are created equal.

A little more than five weeks following the end of the Vatican Council's first session, the rabbi was deeply involved in planning the milestone first National Conference on Religion and Race, which was designed to commemorate the hundredth anniversary of the Emancipation Proclamation. He would serve as program chair and member of the conference steering committee.

The four-day meeting was convened at the Edgewater Beach Hotel on January 14, 1963. On that historic day, Marc introduced two great religious icons and civil rights champions to each other: his mentor, Rabbi Abraham Joshua Heschel, and the Reverend Martin Luther King Jr., the eloquent president of the Southern Christian Leadership Conference (SCLC).

Three days earlier, in a statement released by the National Catholic Conference for Interracial Justice on January 11, Marc had observed that the Conference was "already an historic event, it is yet to be determined whether it will be an event that will make history." Marc added: "Had this confrontation between Catholics, Protestants, Orthodox, and Jews taken place 130 years ago, the course of our nation's history, the character of our present society, could have been radically altered for the better." The failure of religious leaders to have confronted the evils of slavery as early as the fourth decade of the nineteenth century was, the rabbi argued, "among the primary factors leading to the tragic sundering of the nation through the Civil War."

Despite the positive heritage of the Emancipation Proclamation, the preservation of the Union, and the progress in achieving civil and human rights for the descendants of America's slaves, Marc insisted that "far too much of the legacy of bitterness, social distance, and inequality is still with us." He noted that "beneath the courtesies and rhetoric of much of present-day interrelationships between Negroes and whites there surge deep feelings of frustration, animosity, and resentment." He cited "The violent attacks against the white man, epitomized in the writings of James Baldwin, and the broad acceptance of the Black Muslim movement's racist ideology," as well as "the nativist, white supremacist demagoguery of the White Citizen's Councils, abetted by the indifference and inaction of silent, 'respectable' allies in the white community."

The rabbi warned that such conflicting sentiments could prove to be "the ingredients for a recipe that can only lead to a social explosion and national disunity—neither of which can we long endure and still remain an effective leader of the Western democratic community." He added that it is "the devout hope" of its conveners—the Department of Racial and Cultural Relations of the National Council of Churches, the Social Action Department of the National Catholic Welfare Conference, and the Social Action Commission of the Synagogue Council of America—that "the delegates to the Conference will seek out in a profound and searching way the sources of our present inter-racial dilemma."

The opening plenum, which took place on the afternoon of January 14, began with a message from President John F. Kennedy, America's first Catholic president. During that session, and in the days to come, the 657 delegates from thirty-four states and the District of Columbia, representing sixty-seven American Jewish, Catholic, and Protestant organizations, as well as approximately four hundred observers from the Chicago area, would share in a unique, threefold experience.

In plenary sessions, they would hear trenchant addresses by leading figures from American religious and political life. During breaks in the formal program, they would have informal encounters with delegates of differing religious and racial backgrounds. Third, they could join one of thirty-two working groups, each composed of between fifteen and twenty-five participants, each mandated to examine various aspects of the complex racial problems convulsing the country. Many believed these workshop sessions would prove to be most valuable in enhancing the participants' understanding of the issues before them.

During the first plenum on January 14, Rabbi Abraham Joshua Heschel, whom Marc had encouraged to become active in the civil rights movement, addressed the delegates on "The Religious Basis of Equality of Opportunity." Characterizing racism as "universal and evil," Rabbi Heschel stated that the phenomenon was "Man's gravest threat to man, the maximum of hatred for a minimum of reason, the maximum of cruelty for a minimum of thinking."

Marc also invited Dr. Martin Luther King Jr., a member of the Conference Steering Committee, to address the opening plenum. Dr. King described the convocation as the means by which to "rectify past moments of apathy" and hailed the event as "the most significant and historic" gathering ever held for attacking racial injustice. "Through American scientific genius," he observed, "we have made of our nation—and even the world—a neighborhood, but we have failed to employ our moral and spiritual genius to make of it a brotherhood. The problem of race and color prejudice remains America's chief moral dilemma."

Dr. King then put forward five challenges to America's religious institutions and communities: "To enhance the dignity of the human person," "To uproot prejudice," "To support social justice," "To encourage nonviolent direct action," and "To promote universal love."

After several days of deliberations, at the Conference's conclusion, the conveners issued a Declaration of Conscience, in which Marc's literary skills were evident. The Declaration began, "We have met as members of the great Jewish and Christian faiths held by the majority of the American people, to counsel together concerning the tragic fact of racial prejudice, discrimination, and segregation in our society." Racism was characterized as "our most serious domestic evil. We desire to eradicate it with all diligence and speed. For this purpose we have assembled. For this purpose we make our appeal to the conscience of the American people."

The Declaration of Conscience clearly evinced Marc's historical sense, arguing that:

While the Declaration of 1776 did declare that "All men are created equal," and "are endowed by their Creator with certain unalienable rights," the Constitution of 1789 did not specifically guarantee all men their unalienable rights. Human slavery was permitted for almost a century, and, when it finally ended, compulsory racial segregation, with its degrading badge of racial inequality, found constitutional sanction even into our own time.

Despite the landmark Supreme Court decision that separate educational facilities for the black and white races could no longer be considered equal, the declaration noted that "entrenched patterns of segregation" were still deeply embedded throughout the United States and "no one can pretend in the face of them that the spirit or the letter of our laws are practiced and upheld."

The conference declaration continued:

> But our concern is for the laws of God. We are grieved that Americans of all religious faiths have been slow to recognize that racial discrimination and segregation constitute a practical denial of belief in God, who is the Giver of human dignity and human rights. . . . And worse still, even our houses of worship, our religious schools, hospitals, welfare institutions, and fraternal organizations have failed our own religious commitments. We have plainly not lived by the teachings and promises of the faiths we represent.

The framers of this declaration said they sought the forgiveness of God, "whose supreme law we have broken," and of "all human beings, our brothers, whose rights we have ignored and whose dignity we have offended." In the declaration's concluding paragraph, there was a call to the American people "to pray perseveringly and act courageously in the cause of human equality and dignity while there is still time, to eliminate racism permanently and decisively, to seize the historic opportunity the Lord has given us for healing an ancient rupture in the human family."

The delegates put forward a long list of recommendations. They also offered materials for use in Catholic sermons and effective ways of assisting Protestant ministers with teaching and sermon materials. Meanwhile, in the wake of the resignation of the organization's chairman, S. Garry Onniki, Marc agreed to serve in that post temporarily.

The National Conference on Religion and Race was only one element of Marc's deep involvement in the civil rights movement in the 1960s.

In October 1964, following Rabbi Tanenbaum's return from the third session of Vatican Council II in Rome, he would lose no time in continuing to speak out forcefully in the escalating struggle to achieve full civil rights for America's black population.

During the Second Annual Interreligious Institute at Loyola University in Los Angeles, Marc observed that "We have been dealing with Negroes in the main as abstractions, as mythic perceptions, but not as real people; not as persons who have human dignity, which demands a certain response from us as brothers."

Underlying the struggle for equal rights in education, employment, housing, and public accommodations was the enduring prejudice that black Americans were inferior to whites in a variety of ways. As Marc pointed out, white American society had refused to acknowledge the fact that "By the year 1830, every state in the South had passed a law proscribing, prohibiting Negroes from learning to read or write because of the fear that a literate, educated Negro would rise up in rebellion against his white master, the plantation baron." Thus, white America continued to justify southern segregation policies by belittling black intelligence and behavior. Driving home his point, Marc quoted Swedish economist, sociologist, and politician Gunnar Myrdal, an expert on race relations, author of *An American Dilemma*, and future Nobel laureate: "This has never prevented us from using Negroes as porters or as people who run our houses for us as maids."

Marc was pleased to be invited to participate in a National Conference on Human Rights, which took place from August 17 to 21, 1964, on the Princeton University campus. During that meeting, sponsored by the New York–based National Social Welfare Assembly, the rabbi served as one of three resource consultants to a workshop session on Religion and Race, along with representatives of two other New York groups: Msgr. Gregory L. Mooney, director of the John F. Kennedy Cultural Center, and the Reverend Robert L. Polk, the Riverside Church's minister to youth. In accepting the assembly's invitation to participate in the conference, Marc enclosed a copy of one of his recent articles, "The American Negro's Myths and Realities."

Marc's civil rights advocacy would hardly be confined to speechmaking and writing articles during the 1960s. He would travel to the South at crucial moments in civil rights history to participate in desegregation attempts. On one such occasion, as the rabbi sat with Christian clergymen from New York at an all-white lunch counter in Florida, they were arrested and briefly jailed.

In early 1965, the rabbi encouraged Rabbi Heschel to express his own abhorrence of racism by participating, along with Dr. Martin Luther King Jr. and other civil rights leaders, in an event that would go down in history as "the March on Selma." That event would consist of a series of demonstrations, the first one taking place on Sunday, March 7, and the final one two weeks later, on March 21.

On the Friday afternoon preceding the last demonstration, mere hours before the onset of the Jewish Sabbath, Rabbi Heschel's wife received a telegram from Dr. King. He was requesting that her husband take part in that Sunday's march. There was no hesitation on the rabbi's part in doing so. In anticipation of his leaving for Alabama immediately following Sabbath's end, the Heschels canceled their plans to dine at a friend's home that evening. Likewise, Marc sent a telegram to Detroit indicating that he would have to cancel a scheduled speech because he was flying to Selma, Alabama:

SISTERS MARY JOHNICE AND MARY ELIZABETH,
PIOUS XII
RELIGIOUS EDUCATION CENTER 610 ELM AVE
MONROE MICH

DEEPLY REGARET [*SIC*] EMERGENCY RELATING
TO SELMA PREVENTS MY COMING TO
DETROIT THIS MONDAY WILL
ARNAGE SUBSTITUTE APPOINTMENT VERY
SHORTLY. REGARDS
MARC TANENBAUM.

Given the violence of that era, there was a strong possibility that Rabbi Heschel and Dr. King could be injured. Thus, the march's organizers decided to petition the authorities in Washington for the intervention of federal troops. Approval would only come through at the last minute.

The danger inherent in Rabbi Heschel's participation was not lost on the rabbi's daughter, Susannah, then a child. "There had been so much violence, not only in Selma, but everywhere," she observed more than fifty years later. "At the same time, I knew that this was the most important thing a person could *do* on that day. My father gave me that feeling. Yes, it was lonely. No one at my school talked about it. But my father came back, and I was relieved and happy."

But "It was a nervous Shabbat," the rabbi's daughter recalled. "After *Havdalah*, my father got his things together for the trip. Then we went outside. When the taxi taking him to the airport pulled up, my father kissed me good-bye. Then he turned and got into the taxi. As he did so, I thought: I may never see him again!" The next day, Drs. Heschel and King would be seen walking side by side, their solidarity documented in one of the iconic photographs of the civil rights movement.

Following the March on Selma, in late September 1965, as the AJC was regrouping after the exhilaration generated by Pope Paul VI's promulgation of *Nostra aetate*, Marc spoke at the North American College in Rome, where he warned, "In an age in which there is instantaneous global communication, rapid transportation and mobility, it is no longer possible to keep under wraps for long, or to withhold from the judgment of a restive contempt for the human person or which deny him his natural rights." Thus, he observed, "An attack on a Negro in Birmingham is condemned the next day in an editorial in a Ghana newspaper."

Birmingham, Alabama, had been racked by racial strife. A Ku Klux Klan stronghold for some years, the city had become the focus of nonviolent resistance by Dr. King and other black civil rights leaders by 1963. Because of live television coverage, millions of viewers throughout the world witnessed the terrible excesses of Bull Connor, the city's segregationist police chief, against the Freedom Riders. And viewers also learned of the firebombing of the 16th Street Baptist Church on September 15, 1963, in which four young black girls were incinerated.

In the coming years, Marc would maintain, and strengthen, his relationships with the civil rights movement's major black leaders, chief among them Dr. King. But in the late 1960s, despite the alliance that had been forged between the Jewish and black communities, tensions were beginning to surface. For example, in the late summer of 1967, the committee's leadership was so concerned over the Southern Christian Leadership Conference's purported negative position on combating anti-Semitism that Morris Abram, the agency's president, felt compelled to correspond with Dr. King.

Responding to Abram's letter on September 27, Dr. King explained, "Serious distortions by the press have created an impression that SCLC was part of a group at the Chicago Conference of New Politics which introduced a resolution condemning Israel and unqualifiedly endorsing all the policies of the Arab powers." The reverend then reviewed "the facts." The staff members of SCLC who attended the conference (not as official delegates) were, he said, "the most vigorous and articulate opponents of the simplistic resolution on the Middle East question." As a result of this opposition," he added, "the Black Caucus modified its stance and the convention voted to eliminate references to Zionism and referred to the executive board the matter of final wording."

Dr. King, who left immediately after addressing the meeting's opening session, said that had he been present during the ensuing discussion, he would have "made it crystal clear" that he would have regarded "any resolution calling for black separatism or calling for a condemnation of Israel" as "an unqualified endorsement of the policy of the Arab powers." He would subsequently make that point to the press. But, as he noted ruefully, "a disclaimer seldom gets the attention that an original, sensational attack receives."

While assuring Abram of the SCLC's position that "Israel's right to exist as a state in security is incontestable," Dr. King clarified the organization's position in a manner with which Marc was in agreement:

At the same time, the great powers have the obligation to recognize that the Arab world is in a state of imposed poverty and backwardness that must threaten peace and harmony. Until a concerted and democratic program of assistance is affected, tensions cannot be relieved. Neither Israel nor its neighbors can live in peace without an underlying basis of economic and social development.

In his conclusion, Dr. King stated:

SCLC has expressly, frequently and vigorously denounced anti-Semitism and will continue to do so. It is not only that anti-Semitism is immoral—though that alone is enough. It is used to divide Negro and Jew, who have effectively collaborated in the struggle for justice. It injures Negroes because it upholds the doctrine of racism which they have the greatest stake in destroying.

Unfortunately, Dr. King's message would fail to resonate among certain civil rights advocates within the religious communities—both black and white—with whom Marc sought to make common cause. Worse still, that resonant voice of moral authority would soon be silenced forever. On April 4, 1968, Dr. King was in Memphis, Tennessee, to support local sanitation workers who had gone on strike. At dusk, as he stood on the balcony of his motel room in the company of colleagues, including a young pastor named Jesse Jackson, shots rang out. The reverend, whose espousal of nonviolence despite provocation had been at the core of his philosophy in overcoming the injustices and brutality of his segregationist adversaries, was mortally wounded.

Civil rights advocates throughout the nation were shocked and dismayed. Marc mourned not only the passing of a public figure of great moral courage, but a dear friend, as well. Years later, the rabbi was invited by Coretta Scott King to preach at Ebenezer Baptist Church on January 15, 1980, on what would have been Dr. King's fifty-first birthday. Addressing that gathering on "The Moral Legacy of Martin Luther King, Jr.," Marc observed: "The same sense of justice that motivated Dr. King to speak out against Soviet anti-Semitism led him to speak out in support of Israel, and to urge his country to work for peace in the Middle East."

As part of Marc's effort to join forces with civil rights advocates within the religious communities, he would serve as president of the Interreligious Foundation for Community Organizations (IFCO), established in 1966 by Protestant leaders. The group's black executive director was the Reverend Lucius Walker Jr.

On May 11, 1969, one of the more notable instances of interracial tensions erupted—several students at the Union Theological Seminary in New York City presented the prestigious Protestant institution's president, John C. Bennett, with an inflammatory document that maintained, among other allegations, that "The white religious institutions of this country have contributed to the systematic efforts to keep black people from exercising control over their own destinies. We believe black people must have complete control over economic and political institutions which determine their development."

The students made three demands based on their commitment to the Black Manifesto that had been adopted by the IFCO-sponsored National Black Economic Development Conference at its recent meeting in Detroit. They called on the Seminary to:

- Commit to support of the Black Manifesto;
- Immediately convene an open meeting of the Seminary's

Board of Directors to enact the following: A commitment of $100,000 to IFCO for the next fiscal year, and a commitment of $1,000,000 to be contributed by the members of the Board of Directors to the seminary, payable to IFCO;
- Conduct an all-day teach-in on May 12 to discuss the Black Manifesto.

Responding to the students' demands, President Bennett stated that he could not act on the first two demands and he would not take the initiative on the third one. Their demands refused, the students prevailed on others to join them in taking over the Seminary's administration and classroom buildings. They then pledged to occupy the structures until their demands were met.

Foreshadowing what would transpire on May 11, two weeks earlier, on April 26, the Black Caucus at the Union Theological Seminary, citing the Church's "Divine imperative to respond dramatically to the crisis of those who suffer," had presented the National Black Economic Development Conference with its demand for $500,000,000. It argued that sum should be extracted from churches and synagogues as "reparations" for the perceived injustices endured by black Americans over the centuries.

The major black groups endorsing the allocation of the half-billion dollars in reparations included the National Committee of Black Churchmen and the Black Caucus of IFCO's Board of Directors. On May 7, the *New York Times* published a story about an IFCO-sponsored press conference endorsing the Black Manifesto, and the American Jewish Committee reacted instantly. In a brief, curt letter addressed to Reverend Walker, the agency's executive vice president, Bertram Gold, stated: "I am writing to inform you that the matter of our relationship to IFCO is being brought for review to our governing board. As you must know, we cannot support the ideological principles and the specific tactics contained in the 'black manifesto.'"

Nine days later, Reverend Walker, in a somewhat conciliatory but ultimately chastising response, wrote: "In preparation for your governing board's review of its relationship with IFCO in light of the May 7, 1969, *New York Times* report of a telephone conversation with me, I am available for a more accurate and detailed discussion of both IFCO's and my point of view than was carried in that article."

After requesting an appointment with Gold "at the earliest possible date," the reverend lambasted "religious institutions for their lack of appropriate and adequate retribution for their participation in the ravages of racism. For example, over a two-year period the American Jewish Committee has seen fit to contribute only $3,000 to IFCO."

The letter ends with an implied threat: "To withdraw from IFCO because we pledge our meager help to people who have a case against the inhuman indifference to their fellow man would only add to the proof that others don't care and mitigate against IFCO's efforts to win viable change without violence."

Meanwhile, Marc weighed in with an impassioned response. In a draft of a "Dear Lu" letter discovered among his papers housed at the Jacob Marcus Center of the American Jewish Archives in Cincinnati, he wrote to his IFCO colleague,

> The events that have taken place since the convening of the National Black Economic Development Conference in Detroit, the issuance of the Black Manifesto by Mr. Forman at that conference, the public association of IFCO with "the principles and programs" of that manifesto, and the tactics designed to intimidate churches and synagogues have created a serious crisis of conscience for me in my role as President of IFCO.

When Marc accepted IFCO's invitation to serve as its president, he did so in agreement with its ideology and program. He also believed then that "IFCO represented a unique opportunity to serve on an interfaith basis the cause of effective social change through reforms of our system by democratic means." But he could not abide the organization's evolution to the point of endorsing the Black Manifesto's "clear call for the use of force and power of the gun to bring this government down;

for armed confrontation and long years of sustained guerrilla warfare inside this country; for an armed, well-disciplined, black-controlled government; for a revolutionary seizure of state power by violence and terror."

Given that "the turn of events around the Black Manifesto has changed the situation drastically for IFCO, as I see it, and therefore for me," on May 6, the rabbi submitted a memo to the White Caucus of IFCO's Board. In it, he wrote, "I cannot in conscience stand by in silence and appear as President of IFCO to give assent to the revolutionary ideology and racist rhetoric of the Black Manifesto, nor to Mr. [James] Forman's programs for disruption of churches and synagogues." Thus, "under the circumstances," the rabbi said, "I have no alternative but to submit my resignation as President of IFCO, and ask that it become effective immediately." He added that he would "continue to be committed to the original purpose of IFCO, and hope to find appropriate ways to help advance those objectives."

In the next few years, Marc would diligently honor that commitment. A major opportunity to do so would arise in the early 1970s. Professor C. Eric Lincoln, an eminent black sociologist and chairman of the Department of Religious and Philosophical Studies at Fisk University, in Nashville, Tennessee, believed that it was necessary to convene an interreligious, interracial national conference on Black-Jewish Relations to discuss what he characterized as "misunderstandings and misconceptions" that had arisen between the two communities.

The professor suggested that the meeting be held on the Fisk campus. Marc heartily endorsed this proposal, and on November 14, 1972, the two met at the Union Theological Seminary in New York to discuss plans for convening the conference the following spring.

It was decided that the conference would encompass an intensive review of black-Jewish relations from the Biblical era through the American historic experience as well as present specific proposals for the future. Marc was accompanied to that planning session by Rabbi James Rudin and Gerald Strober, both of whom would serve with him on the Conference Planning Committee, along with prominent members of the black community appointed by Professor Lincoln.

The intergroup conference, cochaired by Rabbi Tanenbaum and Professor Lincoln, would take place on the Fisk campus June 9–12, 1974. The contentious issues of concern to the black community in its relations with American Jewry included affirmative action, employment opportunities, overcoming Islam's "romantic" impact on some blacks, Israel's significance, affirmative action and equal opportunity quotas, and the implications of the growing interest in the developing nations that had come to be known as the third world.

More than fifty black and Jewish academicians, graduate students, seminarians, theologians, and others participated in the wide-ranging discussions. They included the Jewish scholars Dr. William Braude, of Providence, Rhode Island, Dr. Lou Silberman of Vanderbilt University, Dr. James Cone of Union Theological Seminary; and such eminent black community leaders as Vernon Jordan, Bayard Rustin, and Roy Wilkins.

On June 15, 1974, Professor Lincoln was quoted in the Harlem-based *Amsterdam News* as saying, "The interest of destinies of Jews and blacks have touched and at times run together for thousands of years. . . . Jews are going to continue being Jews and blacks will remain black. But when this conference is over, each should have a better understanding of what is involved in the self-perception of the other."

Two days later, on June 17, Marc utilized one of his major media platforms, his weekly radio commentary broadcast on WINS in New York and its affiliated Westinghouse stations around the nation, to inform listeners that "The most significant fact about the National Consultation on black-Jewish relations that was held at Fisk University on June 9 through 12 in Nashville, Tennessee, was that it was the first meeting of its kind since the close of the civil rights struggle at the end of the 1960s."

He noted that while there had been discussions of specific issues, such as housing and job opportunities, during previous meetings between blacks and Jews, the uniqueness of the Fisk gathering resided in its desire "to bring together a broad representation of black and Jewish academic figures and institutional leaders in an effort to explore systematically and with the equipment of scholarship virtually every aspect of black-Jewish relations."

The rabbi reported that "On some levels, new ground was broken," in which positive insights were provided "for future understanding." On another troubling yet instructive level, he lamented, "stale and ugly stereotypes surfaced, including an erratic expression of anti-Semitism that demonstrated how far both communities have still to go and to grow together."

Regarding historical studies on the respective roles of blacks and Jews during the era of slavery, Marc noted that the discussion became "very sticky and demonstrated how great is the need for both black and Jewish historians in writing together a history of that period." Demonstrating the existing divide between the two groups, one Jewish historian implied that Jews had not played any role in facilitating slavery, while a black scholar suggested, in what Marc characterized as "a kind of black version of *The Protocols of the Elders of Zion*," that Jews were almost completely responsible for the slave trade. Since both views were "obvious distortions" of the facts, the rabbi said that "after lengthy discussion, both black and Jewish scholars agreed on the need for more serious, balanced, and fair-minded writing of that period."

The rabbi noted, "Both blacks and Jews realized that no two groups have had their humanity attacked as violently as they had." He then pointed out that in order to survive the oil crisis then engulfing the world, the black nations of Africa and the Jewish state alike were desperately in need of American aid.

The rabbi added that "blacks and Jews have important work to do together in this country." As Marc explained to his listeners, "Enough sorting out of distortions and fears on both sides had taken place allowing for the close [of the conference] to be upbeat, with both blacks and Jews searching for new ways to find common ground and to build a consensus to their mutual advantage."

In the coming years, Marc would remain a forceful advocate for civil rights. But at the same time, additional strains would emerge between the black and Jewish communities—ones that would jeopardize the cooperation that had existed during the era of civil rights advocacy. On those occasions, Marc would regularly speak out on these issues.

In 1984, for example, Marc expressed outrage over a report published in the *Washington Post* in which Reverend Jesse Jackson told *Post* reporter Milton Coleman: "All Hymie [i.e., Jews] wants to talk about is Israel; every time I go to Hymie Town [New York City], that's all they want to talk about." The black civil rights activist Jesse Jackson, then a candidate for the Democratic Party's presidential nomination, used this term during his January 20 conversation with Milton Coleman. The *Post* had not immediately published this epithet, but on February 13, it ran a story in which another *Post* reporter, Rick Atkinson, would quote Rev. Jackson's remark, albeit secondhand.

Marc wasted no time in calling Jackson on the carpet. Later that month, the chastened reverend, during a meeting of national Jewish leaders in Manchester, New Hampshire, not only acknowledged having uttered those disparaging, racist words, but sought the community's forgiveness.

The issues threatening the historic alliance of blacks and Jews would be clarified little more than three years later. On the evening of March 11, 1987, Reverend Jackson would visit "Hymie Town" to join Marc in a no-holds-barred dialogue held at the Colden Auditorium at Queens College, New York City. The program was titled "The Religious Leader as Political Activist," and the remarks by the two speakers would offer important insights into the forces that sometimes linked and sometimes separated Jews and blacks. Presented under the aegis of the Queens Black-Jewish People to People Project, the forum was moderated by Alan Hevesi, the assistant majority leader of the New York State Senate and a professor of political science at Queens College.

As several dozen members of Kach, an extremist Jewish defense organization founded by Meir Kahane, demonstrated outside the auditorium and ended up in a melee with campus police, Marc began his prepared remarks by saying, "This is not an easy evening either for the Reverend Jesse Jackson or myself. If the bigots and extremists in our society had their way, this evening would not take place." The rabbi noted that he and Rev. Jackson had decided to participate in this forum "in the face of threats, slanders, and intimidations." Their decision to dialogue, Marc observed, was testimony to "our determination to reject hatred, bigotry, and verbal violence." The purpose of the evening's discussion would be "to try to find a better way, a more civil and constructive way for blacks and Jews to live and work together."

Following a richly detailed historical review of the nation's accomplishments and failures in the field of civil rights, including "far too much of racism, anti-Semitism, lynchings, and verbal violence," the rabbi turned specifically to the contentious issue of black-Jewish relations. Regarding the American Jewish community's support of the civil rights movement, Marc invoked the memory of the late Dr. Martin Luther King Jr.: "No other person could have evoked such an instantaneous and uncritical response from us . . . there was implicit trust, a profound bond of mutual respect, and a deep sense of solidarity with his mission." The rabbi added,

> I can only hope and pray that this shared evening with the Reverend Jesse Jackson will mark a turning away from abstractions and deviations in black-Jewish relations of the past, and will return us to the highway of justice and mutual respect, for the sake of the black and Jewish peoples of our nation, and for the well-being of all Americans.

Rev. Jesse Jackson began his remarks by noting that the tradition of the religious figure as a political leader dated back to the time of Moses, when the enslaved Jew had possessed the courage to speak his mind to Pharaoh before leading his people across the Red Sea on the way to the Promised Land. Rev. Jackson reminded his audience that during the Jews' forty years of wandering in the desert, Moses had come down from Mt. Sinai bearing the Ten Commandments only to discover that people were worshipping the Golden Calf. Moses chastised his people for this transgression.

"This is the finest tradition of religious leaders," Rev. Jackson observed, "to speak the truth, to stand up to authority when necessary, and to speak out to one's own congregation when appropriate, but always to be prepared in God's name to speak the truth as you know it."

While observing that "American history begins with religious figures serving as political leaders," Jackson observed that "what they valued for themselves they denied to others, forbidding dissension, persecuting Quakers, demanding adherence to a strict sectarian line." However, some early religious figures, Roger Williams among them, "preached and practiced tolerance," Jackson said, "and religious figures stepped to the frontlines of leadership in the fight to abolish slavery." He cited two historical figures, John Brown and Frederick Douglass, both of whom, Jackson noted, were deeply religious and "used their talent, public platforms, pulpits, and their moral authority to speak out against the evil of slavery, to insist that this nation live up to its own best principles of freedom and equality."

Then, in reference to the common destiny of Jews and blacks in having overcome slavery, Reverend Jackson pointed out that "in fields and cabins, slaves told each other the story of the Exodus secretly at night." The reverend also pointed out the "similarities between these black communities in the 19th and early 20th century and the Jewish communities of Eastern Europe during the same time." He noted commonalities in the oppression of Jews and blacks, including the Holocaust in Nazi-occupied Europe and racial segregation in America, "carried out in the name of the law, carried out by people even wearing the uniform of the law."

The reverend also talked about the "walls of ignorance and fear, which breed insecurity and hatred, that manifests itself in acts of blind and mean violence. Caught in the prism of racism, we see natural allies kept apart." He went on: "It is because I believe so strongly in that which we have in common that I came here tonight to talk about our common future—our cooperation—for the common good."

Jackson acknowledged the existence of ongoing, divisive, issues between blacks and Jews, referring to them as "real problems and real concerns." But, he cautioned, "Let us also be aware that some of these problems are exaggerated—that some of these conflicts have been exacerbated, that some of the so-called issues are better exposed as modern-day myths."

One of these myths, according to Rev. Jackson, was "that the biggest problems facing blacks and Jews are those posed by extremists within each group; that black/Jewish relationships are so fragile, in such bad shape that they are somehow worse than relations between other ethnic groups"; and "potentially the most dangerous myth—that the positive relationship is over; that divisions between blacks and Jews have split the old Roosevelt coalition."

While the reverend debunked these myths, he suggested that "it is also time to say that we can express our differences aloud and still be friends." For example, Jackson noted that "blacks and Jews have very different reactions to the word 'quotas.'" For blacks, he observed, "a quota can be a door to opportunity. For Jews, the quota system has meant a ceiling on success." According to the reverend, those differing definitions of the Q word should not preclude agreement on "affirmative action, opening the way for minorities and women to participate in every phase of American life."

Jackson pointed out the differences in the Jewish and black experience of reaching America's shores: For the Jews, "leaving Europe to come to the United States was to leave oppression and arrive at freedom." For *his* people, Jackson said, "the experience was reversed, leaving Africa to come to the United States meant leaving independence and being forced into slavery."

Despite these experiential differences, Jackson said that he and Marc "can agree that that political refugees deserve the right to immigrate, and both of us will fight for these rights." Exhorting the audience to "Look around this room; look at the person sitting next to you; look at the people sitting in your row and in front of you." Jackson said: "We are the people who care—the people who make the effort to come out tonight to share with each other our feelings and commitment—the people who want to reach out and work together."

Noting that a heated demonstration was taking place outside the auditorium between Jewish militants and campus police, he said, "The enemy is not within this room but outside, among those people who would deny our young people the chance for a better life." When "we understand that the enemy is outside," the reverend said, "then we understand too that our allies are inside. For us inside this room let there be no question that the alliance is real, the goals are shared, and that our directions will be forward."

During the ensuing question-and-answer session, Marc and Reverend Jackson repeatedly clashed over several divisive issues. They included Israel's sale of arms to the apartheid government of South Africa and Jackson's continuing support for Louis Farrakhan, the black Muslim leader who persisted in referring to Judaism as "a gutter religion."

Regarding Rev. Jackson's refusal to disavow Farrakhan's Nazi-like anti-Semitism, Marc warned Rev. Jackson: "I think you're fooling yourself if you think the issue of Louis Farrakhan is marginal altogether."

Noting that "in Madison Square Garden 23,000 people give him a standing ovation when he utters the most vile anti-Semitic bigotry," the rabbi asserted that "we are not dealing with a minor phenomenon." Instead, the rabbi declared support for the bigoted black Muslim leader to be "an ideological problem of a very profound nature"—one that must be dealt with "almost as a pathology." Invoking the milestone achievement of *Nostra aetate*, Marc said, "If the Vatican and the Catholic Church after 1,900 years of preaching that kind of stuff has the courage to face it and say it is wrong, we have the right to ask that it be rejected with no ands, ifs, or buts."

As the rabbi continued to press the reverend to repudiate Farrakhan's anti-Semitism, Jackson insisted that that should not be the "litmus test" for improved black-Jewish relations. While Rev. Jackson continued, paradoxically, to maintain that "almost nobody black" took Farrakhan's rants seriously, he refused to repudiate the black Muslim leader.

Speaking with reporters after the event, Marc said diplomatically, "We're determined the time has come to make a breakthrough in black-Jewish relations." But the event at Queens College symbolized both the continuing efforts to maintain and strengthen the coalition of blacks and Jews and the differences in opinions and interests between the two groups.

During the quarter century of Rabbi Tanenbaum's unrelenting post–Vatican II advocacy on behalf of America's black citizens, he was also focusing substantial attention on expressions of anti-Semitism both at home and abroad.

CHAPTER 16

Redeeming Soviet Jewry

"Marc was gracious enough to involve me, and he and I would visit congressional offices together. He arranged for me to give testimony to congressional committees about religious life in the Soviet Union and, particularly, about the plight of Soviet Jews."
—Dr. Thomas Bird, professor of Slavic languages, Queens College, New York City, an early Christian activist on behalf of Soviet Jewry

"There was a meeting out of which grew the National Interreligious Task Force on Soviet Jewry. And, of course, Marc Tanenbaum played a key role in that."
—Eugene DuBow, director of the American Jewish Committee's Midwest regional office, 1970–1980

MARC HAD BEEN DEEPLY AFFECTED as a small boy by his father's descriptions of their family's persecution during Tsarist-era pogroms, so the plight of the Jews in the USSR was always very much on his mind. As an avid student of history, the future rabbi had been horrified to learn of Joseph Stalin's purges of Jews from his regime and to hear about the dictator's blatantly anti-Semitic perpetration of the Doctors' Plot of the early 1950s.

Following a succession of power struggles in the Soviet Union in the wake of Stalin's death in March 1953, Soviet Jews hoped that such persecutions would cease. Instead, during the early 1960s, the regime of Nikita Khrushchev would intensify persecution of the Jewish minority living within the vast borders of the USSR and in the Warsaw Pact nations of Eastern Europe that had come under Soviet hegemony following Germany's defeat in World War II.

Amid the Soviet Union's mounting Cold War–era hostility to the United States, Marc was determined to achieve full human rights, including freedom of religious observance and freedom to emigrate, for the USSR's three million Jews whose unique suffering was becoming known.

But the organized Jewish community was deeply divided on how to come to grips with the issue of Soviet Jewry. As Rabbi Joseph Potasnik observed, "There are always people who say 'shush, don't make noise.' There are—and have been over the years—people in the Jewish world who are always afraid that by saying something we are going to somehow antagonize the other side."

Marc was definitely not one of those people: in fact, he would never let up in pressing for community-wide action on behalf of Soviet Jewry. As Rabbi Potasnik recalled, "He did it because he respected the best of Jewish tradition, the tenets of Jewish faith, and he wanted to make sure that others knew that. He respected others, but he wasn't going to stand back and compromise on what was essential."

One of Marc's key insights was recognizing that those seeking freedom for Soviet Jewry had to be perceived as a broad-based coalition representing a wide range of people, a range that extended well beyond the Jewish community.

Not surprisingly, one of those he sought to enlist in the cause of Soviet Jewry was Billy Graham. On April 25, 1972, Rabbi Tanenbaum forwarded what he characterized as "a warm and friendly" exchange of correspondence between the rabbi and Billy Graham to Max Fisher, the Detroit-based industrialist who then served as chairman of the American Jewish Committee's National Executive Committee. "As you can see," the rabbi told Fisher, "I dealt solely with some of our concerns about the growing Evangelical campaign and its implications for Jews. I have not as yet raised the question of Soviet Jewry with Billy."

But recognizing that the question of religious freedom in the Soviet Union would resonate mightily with Mr. Graham, the rabbi soon brought up the issue with his colleague. In fact, he called upon the evangelical leader to intervene at the highest level of the United States government on behalf of those Soviet Jews who were being persecuted by the anti-Semitic successor state to Tsarist Russia.

Dr. Martin Luther King Jr. was another of Marc's prominent Christian colleagues who was enlisted in the struggle against Soviet anti-Semitism. On December 11, 1966, speaking from Atlanta on a nationwide telephone hookup sponsored by the New York-based American Jewish Conference on Soviet Jewry, Dr. King reaffirmed his advocacy for the endangered community.

Quoting from the sixteenth-century English poet and clergyman John Donne's verse regarding the interdependence and interrelatedness of mankind, Dr. King stated: "No man is an island entirely of itself." Now, four hundred years later, Dr. King insisted: "No person of good will can stand by as a silent auditor while there is a possibility of the complete spiritual and cultural destruction of a once-flourishing Jewish community. The denial of human rights anywhere," he maintained, "is a threat to the affirmation of human rights everywhere. Jewish communal life is deprived by the Soviet government of elementary needs to sustain even a modest level of existence and growth."

Even as Marc continued to be deeply engaged in consciousness-raising within the Jewish and non-Jewish communities, he was setting the stage for the coming phase of his interreligious outreach: the creation of the Interreligous Task Force on Soviet Jewry in 1971.

His actions would prove to be a major development in the development of the worldwide effort to secure human rights for Soviet Jewry. As chairman of the task force, the rabbi would bring together a broad coalition of Jews and gentiles. The genesis of the task force lay in a series of meetings organized by the AJC during 1970 in Chicago.

That year, Judah Graubart, a staff member in the committee's Chicago office, had read a newspaper article reporting that a Roman Catholic nun named Margaret Ellen Traxler had made a speech on Soviet Jewry. "Why don't we call her and take her to lunch?" his colleague Eugene DuBow suggested. He and Graubart did so, thus initiating their long and productive relationship with the dedicated sister. At that crucial moment in the struggle on behalf of Soviet Jewry, Sister Traxler was on loan from her order as director of the Chicago-based National Catholic Conference for Interracial Justice. According to DuBow, that agency was composed of "the very liberal Catholics who were involved in the civil rights movement."

The AJC's Chicago staff members asked Sister Traxler whether she would be willing to call together additional people and, with the committee's assistance, convene a meeting of Christians on the Soviet Jewry issue. Sister Traxler readily agreed to do so. Following that seminal meeting, it was understood that Marc and the committee would quietly obtain funding for the establishment of dedicated professional quarters. The task force was soon up and running in an office building south of the Loop that also housed numerous Catholic organizations. Sister Traxler then recruited one of her close friends, a nun from Texas named Ann Gillen, to direct the task force. "She was another one of these dynamic nuns; they are some of the most terrific, dedicated people in the world," Eugene DuBow recalled.

While the task force and the committee were not formally connected—and did not wish to appear to be—DuBow recalled that "all of the task force's work, including printing, was done in our office, and Sister Gillen's secretary was back and forth all the time." One day, Sister Traxler, who was planning to attend an international meeting in Brussels, called the committee's office to ask whether Eugene DuBow would also be doing so.

"You know, I'm not that important," DuBow replied. "I'm a regional director and I'm important in Chicago, but I'm not so important in New York. So I think your national people will be going, not *me*." "I think you should go," the determined nun replied. "Well, thank you," DuBow responded, "but I don't think I'm going to be invited."

About a week or two later, Bert Gold was calling from New York, and DuBow recalled that the committee's national director was demanding of DuBow, in rather unflattering language, "Did you engineer that?" "What are you talking about?" the surprised Chicago director wanted to know. "I got a letter from Sister Traxler and a check for $100 toward your going to the meeting in Belgium," Gold replied. "Well, I guess I'll have to send you!"

While the nuns proved to be vigorous leaders, DuBow believed that they regarded Marc Tanenbaum as "the great leader of the Jewish people in terms of the Catholic Church—the great leader in the interreligious affairs league." Thus, DuBow said, "he was almost above doing any of the scut work. Jim Rudin did most of it, and I did some of it."

Another early gentile advocate for Soviet Jewry was Dr. Thomas Bird, an activist from his student days at Queens College, in New York City. In September 1963, following a year of graduate work toward his doctorate at Princeton, Bird happened to read an article in *Foreign Affairs* magazine by Moshe Decter titled "The Status of Jews in the Soviet Union." The PhD candidate was mesmerized. By 1965, the young man, now *Dr.* Bird, had obtained his advanced degree, relocated to New York City with his wife and two young children, and was beginning what would turn out to be a lengthy academic career at Queens College.

Once Bird's family was settled in its new surroundings, he "made a beeline" to Moshe Decter's office to discuss the Soviet Jewry issue with the Jewish writer and activist. It wasn't long before Marc was on the telephone with the young professor, telling him that Moshe Decter had suggested they meet. Bird said, "We had a two-hour conversation, and from then on he and I were in regular conversation by phone, or over coffee, or in his office, or out of his office."

Marc also brought the professor face-to-face with a number of beleaguered Soviet Jews. "He involved me generously from the beginning," Bird said. "Through his good offices, and through David

Harris's, I went with him or Rabbi Jim Rudin, Sister Ann Gillen, and Rabbi Alan Mittleman to Russia, Belarus, and Ukraine to visit Soviet Jewish refuseniks being denied their civil right to emigrate." In preparation for those visits, Bird said, Marc "clearly did his homework. He had data at his fingertips and he had an itinerary of people he wanted to see."

Reflecting on that era, Bird says: "The movement was a very exciting phenomenon. Rabbi Avi Weiss, Glenn Richter, and others were all very active, very involved." To the professor, as well as to his travel companions, the rabbi was larger than life. "He understood that that was the perception people had of him at the World Council of Churches and in the Vatican and in the various Episcopal residences where he was a frequent visitor and guest." Bird remembers an international conference in Brussels that he and the rabbi attended in the company of "a stellar cast of political figures and East Coast illuminati." There, Bird recalled, "Marc Tanenbaum played a very important role as spokesman, and advocate and information briefer, as he was almost incredibly au courant with data, figures, and personal information."

To the rabbi, Soviet Jewish refuseniks were *his* family, relatives in whom he took a special interest. "That, obviously, had an enormous impact when they met face-to-face," Bird observed. "He was aware of where they had been and what they had gone through. It was that up-close and personal part of his character—professional and, on the other hand, very personal, very human. It was striking about him and gave authority to what he did."

Several additional meetings would be convened in Chicago, and because of their increasing importance to the cause of Soviet Jewry, Marc would participate in all of them, as would Rabbi Rudin and Gerald Strober. "Marc was a person of great standing. The local people, mostly from the University of Chicago and from the various seminaries, all came to help *him*," DuBow recalled.

Those early sessions led to the development of plans for an even larger gathering, at which Marc delivered what DuBow recalled as "a great speech at a tremendous meeting." As he saw it, "What Marc really did was to move the Soviet Jewry movement from being just a *Jewish* one to being an international human rights movement. Of course, all of those non-Jews really saw it in terms of its being a major human rights problem, so they were all glad to be participating."

At the core of the task force's efforts was the fate of refuseniks—Jews denied exit visas—and the steadily increasing numbers of Prisoners of Zion who had been incarcerated for alleged crimes against the Soviet regime. Those "crimes" included the observance and promotion of Judaism. Even the possession of materials printed in the Hebrew language was deemed by the authorities to be an offense punishable by long incarceration in the gulag. As those restrictions severely impacted the psychic health of the Soviet Jewish community, members of the task force sought to visit the refuseniks in the hope of offering comfort, and, in some cases, medicine and Hebrew-language reading materials. Father John Pawlikowski, a professor of ethics at the Catholic Theological Union in Chicago, was among those non-Jews who joined Marc in his task force. "I got very involved," he recalled, adding, "Marc wanted to involve me."

As for Sister Ann Gillen's efforts, he noted: "There was a certain amount of tension down the pike because Ann wanted to expand the program to include persecuted people in other situations while the committee wanted to stay focused on Soviet Jewry." Despite the inclusive nature of the task force, Marc was dealing with not inconsiderable tension and competition within the organized American Jewish community. As Father Pawlikowski recalled, "Marc's group tried to take—I wouldn't call it a softer tone. Others, like the Union of Councils for Soviet Jews, were quite aggressive toward the Russian government."

A major goal of the task force was to mobilize non-Jewish efforts in order to maximize the pressure brought to bear on the repressive Soviet regime because of such measures as Jewish quotas in institutions of higher education. Thus, while Jewish communities throughout the free world were becoming galvanized to action, so were freedom-loving gentiles—academics, clergy, and members of Congress, notably Senator Henry M. "Scoop" Jackson, a Democrat from the state of Washington.

Jerry Goodman, the committee's director of European Affairs at that time, would go on to become the founding executive director of the National Conference on Soviet Jewry (NCSJ). While still at the committee, Goodman had worked with Sisters Traxler and Gillen, whose advocacy would be crucial to the task force's effectiveness. The NCSJ's executive director would have Marc's "full blessing" when he met with the committee's professional staff, especially Rabbi Rudin and Judith Banki. "The NCSJ wouldn't have gotten launched without Marc Tanenbaum," Goodman insisted.

Despite criticism within the organized American Jewish community regarding Marc's efforts to join forces with Billy Graham, a constant ally on behalf of Soviet Jewry, the rabbi would continue to do so. In fact, the evangelical leader would quickly respond when asked to intervene with officials at high levels of the US government on behalf of numerous longtime refuseniks and Prisoners of Zion. For example, in 1971, the two Soviet Jewry advocates, working together, managed to secure the freedom of a refusenik named Ruth Alexandrovitch. On her behalf, Mr. Graham met with her mother, Rivka Alexandrovitch, on short notice at the Conrad Hilton Hotel, in Chicago. Moved by her daughter's plight, the reverend wasted no time in intervening on her behalf with Secretary of State Henry Kissinger.

The development of a national, indeed international, organization advocating for the rights of Soviet Jews had a powerful impact in Washington, where it helped lead the US government to put pressure on the Kremlin to change its ways with regard to Soviet Jews. Those advocating on behalf of Soviet Jewry not only sought to generate public attention to their cause, they also focused on elected officials. Their efforts led to the enactment of the Jackson-Vanik amendment to the Trade Act of 1974. This amendment dealt with trade relations with Communist bloc countries that restricted freedom of emigration and other human rights. The amendment, named after its major cosponsors, Henry M. "Scoop" Jackson of Washington in the Senate and Charles Vanik of Ohio in the House of Representatives, both Democrats, denied "most favored nation" status to countries with nonmarket economies that restricted emigration—which the legislation considered a human right. Permanent normal trade relations could be extended to a country subject to the law only if the president determined that it was in compliance with the freedom of emigration requirements of the amendment. The troubled Soviet economy was eager for trade with the United States, and it reluctantly decided it had to offer freedom for Soviet Jews.

The sparks that Marc Tanenbaum helped to ignite would lead to a massive exodus of Soviet Jews. Many long-term refuseniks and Prisoners of Zion would be allowed to leave their birthland, either to join relatives in Western nations or to move to Israel. Hundreds of thousands of other Soviet Jews, less vocal than the activists but no less eager for religious freedom, would also take advantage of the opportunity to move to Israel or the United States. And the ferment created helped pave the way for the phenomena of glasnost and perestroika initiated by Mikhail Gorbachev following his rise to power in 1985.

CHAPTER 17

Defender of the Faith

"You are to portray persons who hated and persecuted the beloved
and most holy. You must portray these people in all their evil, hate-
fulness and hypocrisy in order to evoke disgust at such shameful
behavior in the mind of the spectator."
—Father Alois Daisenberger, author of the Oberammergau Passion
Play text, as staged from 1850 through 1960, instructing the actors
portraying Jews on the eve of his version's first performance

"Kill him he says he's God—a blasphemer
He'll conquer you and us and even Caesar
Crucify him!
Crucify him!"
—A lyric from the Broadway hit *Jesus Christ Superstar*

WHILE *NOSTRA AETATE* REPRESENTED A giant step forward in the battle
against anti-Semitism, a variety of abuses and instances of ill-treatment
continued to plague Jewish communities around the world. Rabbi
Marc Tanenbaum and the American Jewish Committee remained
focused on combating these abuses wherever they occurred. And they
did not want for work: seemingly every day, there were new expressions

of anti-Semitism somewhere in the world. Some were cases of blatant bigotry, while some were simply ignorant assertions that did harm to the standing of Jews. But Marc Tanenbaum and his AJC colleagues aggressively sought to respond to or forestall expressions of anti-Semitism.

In addition to focusing on the standing of Jews in the United States and around the world, Marc was also a tireless advocate for the State of Israel. While Israel was cheered on by many as the underdog when it was initially created in the late 1940s, it became increasingly embattled, facing a coalition of those who supported the Arab cause, those who expected it to live up to its promise as a light onto the nations, and those who were classic anti-Semites masquerading as proponents of global justice.

Advocating for the Jewish State

As part of Marc Tanenbaum's ongoing efforts on behalf of Israel, he was a highly visible and articulate public advocate for the interests of the Jewish state. In addition, he was deeply involved in the AJC's often behind-the-scenes efforts to support and advance Israel's standing in the eyes of the world. Toward this end, he helped undertake research to probe the thinking of gentiles regarding Israel and also to design statements and activities to advance that nation's interests. And he was also involved in efforts to cajole and lobby public officials to be supportive of Israel.

Marc's abiding interest in the State of Israel's survival amid a sea of hostile neighbors was often integrated with the work he was doing on a number of other issues. For example, in his dealings with the Vatican, an issue of continuing concern was the Vatican's failure to recognize Israel as the legitimate Jewish state. While diplomacy existed on a basic level, formal relations were not on the horizon in the mid-1980s. In fact, the Jewish community's long-sought diplomatic breakthrough would not come about until June 15, 1994, more than a decade after the pope's use of the phrase "State of Israel" in a precedent-shattering Apostolic Letter.

Prior to that, a continuing dialogue with the Vatican would be essential, and many believed that the Jewish community possessed no better an interlocutor than Marc Tanenbaum. As journalist Joe Berger, who covered these kinds of issues as a reporter for the *New York Times*, observed, "Marc understood the dynamics, the politics, and the sensitivities involved on both sides; he was not a true believer in the way that more than one or two of the other Jewish leaders at that time were."

During the fall of 1984, the Vatican would launch what Marc described as "a serious trial balloon" regarding Israel's *potential* recognition. In an article published on October 26 in the *New York Jewish Week*, he suggested that possibility "despite subsequent denials by a Vatican spokesman." Earlier that week, Andrzej Maria Deskur, a Polish archbishop serving in Vatican City, had said as much in what the rabbi characterized as "a carefully constructed scenario."

Meanwhile, Marc and the AJC were an integral part of what critics would call "the Jewish lobby," seeking to influence political decisions regarding Israel. In 1970, for example, Marc and the AJC were active in expressing "disappointment" at the US government's decision to hold in abeyance Israel's request for more fighter jets. The views of the Conference of Presidents of Major Jewish Organizations were expressed in a March 23, 1970, telegram to Secretary of State William P. Rogers, who had announced the Nixon administration's decision earlier in the day.

On another occasion, Marc would call on Billy Graham to come to the aid of Israel. At the darkest point of the 1973 Yom Kippur War, as Israel's survival hung in the balance, Marc called upon the evangelist to intervene with President Richard Nixon and request that the commander in chief authorize a resupply of weaponry to the beleaguered nation. Nixon would soon be airlifting supplies to Israel.

Later on, Marc would find it necessary to challenge what he and other Jewish leaders perceived as anti-Zionist behavior on the part of Andrew Young, a major black civil rights pioneer who had been appointed by President Jimmy Carter to serve as the United States' ambassador to the United Nations. On July 26, 1979, Ambassador

Young would engage in an unsanctioned meeting with Zuhdi L. Terzi, the Palestine Liberation Organization's (PLO's) United Nations observer, at the Manhattan apartment of Abdullah Bishara, Kuwait's permanent representative to the UN. By conferring with Terzi, the American envoy was clearly in violation of President Jimmy Carter's assurance to the government of Israel that no representative of his administration would meet with the PLO until that entity recognized the Jewish state's right to exist.

Although Ambassador Young claimed that his meeting with Terzi had been inadvertent, he was on record as having made statements in favor of the PLO—utterances loaded with potential for damaging black-Jewish relations. Jewish community leaders were troubled that the black civil rights activists with whom they had marched hand in hand in the cause of racial justice appeared to be expressing sympathy with the murderous organization, which had been founded in 1964 by Yasser Arafat. But they were also troubled by the prospect of exacerbating black-Jewish relations by criticizing a respected black leader.

After a cacophony of criticism from a range of voices—including a number of black leaders—Andrew Young resigned his post in August, 1979. On Friday, August 31, 1979, Marc, writing in the New York–based *Jewish Press*, characterized the prompt issuance of a declaration by certain national black leaders during "an otherwise confused and deeply upsetting episode" as "an act of genuine moral courage and authentic statesmanship." He noted that black and Jewish leaders alike had identified the source of the ambassador's unauthorized meeting as "elements within the State Department who with clumsy stealth have sought to legitimize the PLO in clear violation of American policy not to deal with a group that continues to preach and practice terrorism and massacre of innocent human beings in Israel and elsewhere." Marc added:

> The nation at large owes a debt of gratitude to Vernon Jordan of the Urban league, Benjamin Hooks of the NAACP [National Association for the Advancement of Colored People], Mrs.

Coretta Scott King [the widow of Martin Luther King Jr.] and Bayard Rustin [president of the A. Phillip Randolph Institute] among others for their refusal to allow demagogues and PLO representatives to distort a complex Middle East political issue into a confrontation between the black and Jewish communities.

It needs to be made clear that no Jewish group or leader held Andy Young personally responsible for this policy, but rather demanded that President [Jimmy] Carter and the State Department adhere faithfully to their commitments made at Camp David [in September 1978; the Camp David Accords were signed on March 26, 1979] not to baptize the PLO. In the present situation, a PLO state will inevitably become a Soviet satellite, and a Soviet-dominated state will threaten every single oil supply to the Middle East on which the United States and other nations depend. That's the central issue, and nothing should be allowed to divert us from that critical understanding.

But some of the black leaders who stood with Israel on this issue were concerned about what would happen next. For example, on September 5, Benjamin Hooks wrote to Marc, noting, "Those of us who appreciate the contribution which Ambassador Young made in his capacity as United States Permanent Representative to the United Nations are hopeful that his departure will not mean a de-emphasizing of America's commitment to human rights and peace around the world."

Meanwhile, Marc was confronting another urgent issue: a spate of horrific acts of terrorism directed against Israel, most notably murder at the site of the Summer Olympic Games in Munich, Germany. On September 5, 1972, PLO terrorists infiltrated the Olympic Village. First, they murdered several members of the Jewish state's wrestling team. Then, following a tense standoff in the early evening, the killers forced the eleven survivors into a bus and drove them to the airport. The abductors' intent was to fly their hostages to an Arab country, where a ransom would be extracted in exchange for their freedom.

Rabbi Marc Tanenbaum with Rabbi Abraham Joshua Heschel and Cardinal Augustin Bea during Vatican Council II in 1964. *Courtesy of the American Jewish Committee Archives*

Rabbi Tanenbaum with Hugh Downs on the Today Show, ca. 1960s, demonstrating the seder table for Passover. *Courtesy of the Jacob Rader Marcus Center of the American Jewish Archives, Cincinnati, Ohio at americanjewisharchives.org*

Rabbi Marc Tanenbaum speaking at the Honor America Day rally in Washington DC, at which he spoke in 1970 and 1979. The Rev. Billy Graham sits to his left.

The Rev. Billy Graham receiving AJC's National Interreligious Award from Rabbi Marc Tanenbaum in 1977. *Courtesy of the Jacob Rader Marcus Center of the American Jewish Archives, Cincinnati, Ohio at americanjewisharchives.org*

Marc Tanenbaum in Cambodia, surrounded by Vietnamese Boat People, 1978.

Marc Tanenbaum with the newly published book he co-edited, Evangelicals and Jews in Conversation, 1978. *Courtesy of the American Jewish Committee Archives*

Rabbi Tanenbaum at the "State of the Nation" summit meeting at Camp David with President Jimmy Carter, 1979. *Courtesy of the Jacob Rader Marcus Center of the American Jewish Archives, Cincinnati, Ohio at americanjewisharchives. org*

Marc Tanenbaum being sworn into the National Holocaust Museum Committee by Elie Wiesel and House Speaker "Tip" O'Neill, 1979. *Courtesy of the Jacob Rader Marcus Center of the American Jewish Archives, Cincinnati, Ohio at americanjewisharchives.org*

Rabbi Tanenbaum with Rev. Jerry Falwell, undated. *Courtesy of the Jacob Rader Marcus Center of the American Jewish Archives, Cincinnati, Ohio at americanjewisharchives.org*

Marc Tanenbaum with Coretta Scott King and Rosalind Carter at Ebenezer Baptist Church, where Martin Luther King, Jr.'s widow invited him to preach on what would have been King's 51st birthday, 1980. The Kansas City Jewish Chronicle *60th Anniversary Edition, an RNS photo*

Liv Ullman and Marc Tanenbaum at an American Jewish Committee dinner at which she was honored in 1981. *Courtesy of the Jacob Rader Marcus Center of the American Jewish Archives, Cincinnati, Ohio at americanjewisharchives.org*

Georgette Bennett and Marc Tanenbaum's wedding day in New York City, 1982. *Photo by Valache*

Rabbi Tanenbaum holding a delegate's baby at the World Council of Churches meeting in Vancouver, 1983. He was the first Jewish leader to address the WCC. *Courtesy of the Jacob Rader Marcus Center of the American Jewish Archives, Cincinnati, Ohio at americanjewisharchives.org*

Marc Tanenbaum with President Ronald Reagan, following the Bitburg controversy, 1985. *Courtesy of the Jacob Rader Marcus Center of the American Jewish Archives, Cincinnati, Ohio at americanjewisharchives.org*

Marc Tanenbaum at his surprise 60th birthday party, at home in New York, with civil rights leader, Bayard Rustin and friends, Linda Jacobson and Peter Arthur-Smith.

Marc Tanenbaum with Pope John Paul II in Rome, ca. 1985. *Courtesy of the American Jewish Committee Archives*

Marc Tanenbaum at a White House meeting with George H.W. Bush, 1987. *Courtesy of the Jacob Rader Marcus Center of the American Jewish Archives, Cincinnati, Ohio at americanjewisharchives. org*

Marc Tanenbaum and the Reverend Jesse Jackson at the Queens College CUNY People-to-People program in New York City, following Jackson's controversial "Hymietown" comments, 1987. *Courtesy of the Jacob Rader Marcus Center of the American Jewish Archives, Cincinnati, Ohio at americanjewisharchives.org*

Georgette Bennett, Marc Tanenbaum's widow, with their son, Joshua-Marc Bennett Tanenbaum, at age one, at home in New York. Joshua-Marc was born seven weeks after his father died.

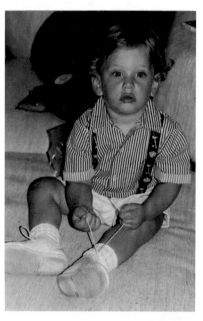

Joshua-Marc at age two, home in New York, 1994.

Joshua-Marc Tanenbaum moderating a panel at the Council of Young Jewish Presidents Meeting, UJA-Federation, New York City, 2017.

Joshua-Marc Tanenbaum at age 24 speaking at LAVAN Impact Investing Pitch Competition, New York City, 2016.

As the athletes were being transferred to the waiting aircraft, they were caught in a cross fire, leaving no survivors among them. All the world could watch this drama unfold on live television.

Much of Marc's work on behalf of Israel took the form of low-key, behind-the-scenes discussions with opinion leaders. He would be a vigorous advocate of Israeli needs and views. There were a number of Americans who once eagerly supported Israel as the underdog, but as Israel developed and prospered, they began transferring their support to the new underdog, the Palestinian cause. Hence:

- In 1967, Marc's department released a new publication, "Christian Reactions to the Middle East Crisis," prepared by Judith Banki. The document sought to provide an objective and balanced analysis of the various responses of Catholic and Protestant leaders and organizations to the Israeli-Arab crisis early in the year. In announcing the publication, Marc wrote, the AJC had:

    > undertaken to sponsor cooperatively with Catholic and Protestant groups' institutes, seminars and public meetings at which an opportunity is provided for examining in depth the respective Christian and Jewish understandings of Israel, the Holy Land, and the Arab refugee problems.

- In 1971, in response to proposals for the "internationalization" of Jerusalem, removing it from Israeli control, Marc's department undertook a survey of Christian public opinion. The survey found substantial opposition to these proposals. In releasing the survey results, Marc wrote:

    > Those who have charged with incredibly polemical language that Israel was engaged in the "Judaization of Jerusalem" and in "the suffocation of Christians and Muslims" in the Holy City have managed to attract the overwhelming attention

for their viewpoint in the general mass media and especially in the Christian journals and media.

He added, "To the uninformed, the impact of that Anti-Israel—and in some cases anti-Jewish—publicity has been to suggest that there is a monolithic, or at least a majority, Christian sentiment that opposes reunification of Jerusalem under Israeli sovereignty." A recent UN Security Council debate had "undoubtedly reinforced that impression," he wrote, because the Jordanian representative "cited a whole range of Christian spokesmen" who seemed to be agreeing with the Arab position.

Marc explained that "the frank intent" of the survey was "to demonstrate that there is a substantial and growing body of respected and responsible Christian leadership whose positive sympathies toward Israel deserve to be taken into serious account as those other Christian voices who have been more vocal and aggressive in advocating their anti-Israel positions."

- In 1982, Marc reported on his interactions with George W. Cornell, the religion writer for the Associated Press, the newsgathering cooperative that provides much of the news reported in newspapers across the country. On August 8, 1982, Cornell published a lengthy piece in which he wrote, "Many Christian leaders contend that the news media are presenting a biased, misleading picture of Israel's military action in Lebanon."

  These leaders, Cornell wrote, "say news reports have exaggerated casualties, misplaced blame and ignored broad Lebanese support for the efforts to root out terrorists in the region." Cornell went on to say, "While mainline denominational officials have sharply criticized Israel's operations, many other U.S. Christians say Israel's purposes are justified, its tactics carefully restrained and news reports often slanted against it."

- In 1985, the AJC sponsored a conference on "Perceptions of Israel in the American Media." As Joshua Muravchik explained in his summary of the proceedings, published in 1985, "The conference met in the aftermath of the disappointment among Israelis and American Jews in how the American Media reported Israel's 1982 war in Lebanon." Much of his report centers on discussions of how and why the press provides a distorted view of issues in the Middle East, and there are suggestions of ways to improve news coverage.

- In August 1988, Marc received a memo from colleagues in San Francisco discussing news coverage of a visit by Mubarak Awad, a Palestinian-American psychologist and an advocate of nonviolent resistance. The AJC goal would be to seek balance by presenting views that differed with those of Dr. Awad.

All of this was decidedly subtle, but also decidedly meaningful. The AJC had its own department charged with Israeli matters, but Marc Tanenbaum was often involved in shaping AJC policies and initiatives with regard to making the case for Israel.

For the AJC, and indeed, for many American Jews, relations with Israel were decidedly complex. On the one hand, most felt an obligation to support the Jewish homeland, but while some American Jews insisted on supporting any and all Israeli actions and policies, others were highly critical, arguing that Israel should be a light onto the world and meet higher standards than other countries. Moreover, some American Jews saw Israel as the future of Jewry in a world of increasing secularism and assimilation, while others emphasized a need to strengthen Jewish communities outside of Israel. The American Jewish Committee was always among the most conflicted groups. Its German-Jewish founders were often anti-Zionist and opposed to what they saw as excessive efforts to create and maintain a separate Jewish identity. And many were Reform Jews who often disliked the dictates emanating from the Orthodox rabbis who controlled many of Israel's policies on religious doctrines and practices. As Howard I. Friedman, the AJC president from 1983 to 1986, noted, "The committee had its own complexities in its approach to Israel, based on its own history and Jewish identification. We did have to go through a major reformulation, as it were, regarding our relations with Israel, and Marc was a major force in helping us do that."

Among the issues that became focal points for AJC efforts, there was the startlingly offensive, centuries-old portrayal of Jews in a hugely popular theatrical tourist attraction held every ten years in a quaint Bavarian town; the blatant anti-Semitism of a hit musical performed amid the glitter of Broadway—the cradle of the Jewish-inspired American musical theater—and the establishment of a Catholic convent on the site of a notorious Nazi extermination camp, where millions of Jewish men, women, and children were incinerated—without one word acknowledging this fact. These assaults on the Jewish psyche are illustrative of the scope of insensitivity and bigotry rampant in the world in the immediate post–Vatican II era.

Oberammergau

One of the most contentious issues Marc and his staff would confront was the overtly anti-Semitic nature of the Oberammergau Passion Play. There have been five versions of that spectacle since its inception in the Middle Ages. It had first been performed in 1634, during a conflict that began in 1618 and would go down in history as the Thirty Years' War. That war, initially religiously motivated, pitted Catholics and Protestants against each other. But it would evolve into an extended conflagration fought for hegemony among the great powers of Europe. The passion play's staging dates from a vow made by the residents of Oberammergau as they endured both the devastation of war and the ravages of bubonic plague, "The Black Death." Those who survived these traumas vowed that the pageant would be presented every ten years thereafter.

That pledge would be faithfully fulfilled, virtually every decade for more than three centuries in this heavily Catholic Bavarian town. In addition, in 1934, the play would be staged as Adolf Hitler was coming to power. He would attend and enormously enjoy a performance that year. And it would be performed in 1984 to mark the 350th anniversary of the play.

The American Jewish Committee had been at the forefront of efforts to change the anti-Semitic character of that theatrical tour de force since the 1950s. With the promulgation of *Nostra aetate* in 1965, the agency had every reason to expect that the play's text and staging would be revised to reflect changed attitudes toward Jews and Judaism. Indeed, a statement relating specifically to the passion play genre had been issued on February 28, 1968, by the Executive Committee of the Secretariat for Catholic-Jewish Relations of the National Conference of Catholic Bishops.

That committee noted that fidelity to the principles of *Nostra aetate* "is expected of all members of the Church. A particular responsibility, however, rests upon composers and producers of passion plays, preachers, catechists and educators, because it is easy to portray Jews, even inadvertently, in such a way as to misrepresent or exaggerate their role in the Passion."

As the committee was intensifying its efforts to achieve substantive changes in the play's content, Marc wrote to Cardinal Leo Jozef Suenens of Belgium and Cardinal Julius Döpfner, the Archbishop of Munich and Freising, on March 8, 1968, concerning the possibility of revisions being made in advance of the 1970 edition.

Responding to the rabbi's letter on April 2, the German cardinal stated that a contract had been concluded during the preceding year between "the responsible Board of Oberammergau" and the Ettal Monastery, under which Father Dr. Stephan Schaller, the principal of the Ettal academic high school, "would thoroughly revise the existing text." Cardinal Döpfner also promised that Father Schaller would submit a script written "in the spirit of the Second Vatican Council." Moreover, Cardinal Döpfner assured Marc, who had initiated a discussion with the prelate during Vatican Council II regarding the anti-Semitic nature of the passion play, that "as the Catholic bishop for Oberammergau I am endeavoring to see that the coming performance of 1970 will in no way give rise to misinterpretations and hostile sentiments among contemporaries of good will." But there was a deeply disturbing caveat: "However," the cardinal wrote, "I would find it basically regrettable if, because of unnecessary agitation, another piece of genuine folk art had to be sacrificed."

The committee's continuing efforts to achieve changes in time for the 1970 season would include meetings with Cardinal Suenens and Cardinal Franz König of Austria. Both prelates would write to Marc, describing their interventions with Cardinal Döpfner regarding revisions. In addition, AJC representatives would meet with major West German politicians, including the Bavarian leader Franz Josef Strauss, Chancellor Kurt Georg Kiesinger, associates of Willy Brandt, and members of the Munich city government.

The committee's concerns were not solely academic in nature. In both 1950 and 1960, nearly 100,000 people had attended the Oberammergau passion play. An additional 153,000 were expected to attend the 102 performances to be staged in 1970. In short, the play communicated its themes to a large audience.

During the latter part of 1969, after obtaining the proposed 1970 script, Marc asked his staff to prepare a detailed analysis of the texts of the two previous productions. Despite assurances to the contrary, the text of the coming production reflected the ingrained, highly negative attitudes toward Jews and Judaism. The 1970 production would once again essentially portray the Jewish priests as vicious, bloodthirsty, sadistic enemies of Jesus. And "the people" would be portrayed as a sadistic lynch mob. The money changers, mentioned but briefly in the New Testament when Jesus confronts them at the temple, become a gang of traders and usurers who play a major role in the arrest of Jesus.

Moreover, in perhaps most explicit contradiction of the letter and spirit of *Nostra aetate*, the so-called "blood curse" of previous productions is retained: the "priests and the people" invoke the verse in Matthew's Gospel: "His blood be upon us and our children."

Although failing to exert a meaningful impact on the 1970 production of the passion play, Oberammergau would remain a major issue of the committee's concern, and beginning in 1977, Marc would initiate a campaign to achieve changes in the 1980 production. During a three-year period of intense activity, he would take four trips to the Federal Republic of Germany. During the rabbi's first visit to Oberammergau, in August 1977, he headed a delegation including William Trosten, the committee's director of development who spoke fluent German, and Miles Jaffe of Detroit, the lay chairman of the agency's Department of Interreligious Affairs.

On August 15, the agency group attended a preview performance of the 1980 production. Rather than utilizing Father Daisenberger's text, this production would feature a revised version of the 1750 text written by a Benedictine priest, Father Ferdinand Rosner. Marc and his associates met following the preview with Alois Fink, editor of the revised text; Hans Schwaighofer, the townsperson who would direct the coming production; Helmut Fischer, who portrayed Jesus in the 1970 production; and several Oberammergau town officials, as well as representatives of the West German government.

While the committee's delegates informed the local officials that they welcomed the "forthright initiatives" being taken to do away with Daisenberger's text and praised "positive features" of the revised version, they also discovered what they characterized as "a number of problems." These included the suggestion that the Sanhedrin and Jewish people might be perceived as "instruments of Lucifer." Furthermore, Pontius Pilate is depicted as being a weakling manipulated by the Sanhedrin and a howling Jewish mob.

Nonetheless, the rabbi regarded his delegation's dialogue with the Oberammergau officials to be "serious and constructive," as reported by the *New York Times* on September 4, 1977. Prospects for resolution of these issues would be dimmed in early 1978, however, as Marc received confidential letters from Alois Fink and Hans Schwaighofer, both of whom expressed "growing concern on the part of 'ultra-conservative' forces in Oberammergau." There were efforts underway to prevent the adoption of Rosner's more balanced, undefamatory version of the passion play and to return to Daisenberger's anti-Semitic script.

In response, Marc and Messrs. Trosten and Jaffe, accompanied by the public relations director of Lufthansa Airlines, traveled to the picturesque Bavarian village yet again, staying there February 3–5. At the rabbi's suggestion, the AJC group met with the opposing forces. Their key session would be a four-and-a-half-hour meeting with Oberammergau's *Burgomeister*, Ernst Zwink, the apparent leader of the town's pro-Daisenberger forces.

As Marc would write in a February 9 memorandum to Bert Gold, "We made it clear to Zwink in forceful and unmistakable terms that we regarded the Daisenberger text as 'structurally anti-Semitic' and that no cosmetic changes could redeem its fundamental anti-Jewish nature." Only a day earlier, William Trosten had received a telephone call from Hans Schwaighofer, informing the committee that the Oberammergau town council had voted 9 to 6 in favor of Rosner's revised text. On February 16, during a news conference held at the committee's headquarters in New York, the agency applauded the vote. Jaffe praised the council for "taking upon itself the risk of the new, the untried," in voting in favor of the Rosner version.

His sentiments would be echoed by Dr. Eugene Fisher, executive secretary of the office of Catholic-Jewish Relations of the National Conference of Catholic Bishops, as well as by the Reverend Nathan H. VanderWerf, executive director of the Commission on Regional and Local Ecumenism of the National Council of Churches.

But in snowy Oberammergau, the Daisenberger die-hards were determined to stand their ground. On February 25, a group calling itself "Citizen's Initiative for the 1980 Passion Play" addressed an "Open Letter" to Rabbi Tanenbaum in which they noted, "During the years of the Third Reich, this very community aided many Jews"—an assertion likely inaccurate given the large number of suspected National Socialist Party members living in Oberammergau during the Nazi era. The group went on reject "any meddling in the internal affairs of the village."

Following a token request for points of criticism regarding the Daisenberger text, the Citizen's Initiative adopted a threatening tone: "It would be in our mutual interest if you were to accept this offer of cooperation, because we would have to explain to the world press that Jewish quarters declined to help *with the version preferred by Oberammergau.*"

The group then cited what it described as the committee's "boycott threat in the name of the American people and of the world's citizens." The disquieting letter ended with the words "we will be glad to cooperate with you, but only on an appropriate basis. The final and decisive word lies with Oberammergau and its citizens."

In a response that Marc is believed to have written in March, the committee said it had not sought to "meddle" in the internal affairs of Oberammergau. Nor was the agency advocating a boycott of the 1980 production. As the AJC response put it:

> The issue is not whether we would or would not boycott or participate in a boycott. The issue is what reaction in this country and elsewhere would be to performance of the Daisenbeger text in 1980 . . . it is the right of Oberammergau to nonetheless choose to perform Daisenberger. It would also be the right of both Christians and Jews to draw their own conclusions about such a decision.

Writing to Mayor Zwink on April 2, Marc articulated a similar view, albeit in a somewhat more conciliatory tone:

> because we have come to know you as a friend, we hope you will accept our desire simply to inform you of one of the implications of the choice before you. Your right to produce Daisenberger cannot be denied. The certainty and the strength of the result of such a choice in America and in other countries cannot be avoided.

Then on May 11, Marc wrote to Cardinal Joseph Ratzinger, Cardinal Döpfner's successor as the archbishop of Munich and Freising—and a future pope—to seek his assistance in the matter. In response, the future Pope Benedict XVI wrote:

> To get to the heart of the matter, in the total context of this complex problem, I cannot see it as my task as Archbishop of Munich to force adoption of the Rosner text. . . . On the other hand, as I have repeatedly stated, I will emphatically urge that, consonant with *Nostra Aetate*, no assertion of a collective guilt will be allowed to remain. On this matter, I will make contact with currently responsible agencies in Oberammergau.

Following that exchange of correspondence, an intra-Jewish organizational squabble would threaten to undermine the committee's insistence that the revised Rosner text be utilized in the passion play's 1980 production. On June 13, the Anti-Defamation League (ADL) of B'nai B'rith issued a press release proclaiming that as a result of an organizational delegation's visit to Oberammergau on May 5, "drastic changes would be made in the world-famous Oberammergau Passion Play to conform with the 1974 Vatican guidelines for Catholic-Jewish relations." According to the ADL, those changes, including an "expanded prologue explicitly stating that the Jews are not to be considered collectively guilty for Jesus' death," would result in "an important breakthrough on a vital issue which has disturbed the American and world Jewish communities for many years."

There was consternation at the committee regarding one sentence in the ADL release that the agency believed was undermining its own efforts to ensure the 1980 production used the revised Rosner text: "The ADL group made it clear to the Oberammergau officials that while we were aware of the current controversy in Oberammergau over two different Passion Play texts, we were not advocating one over the other."

On June 26, the committee's Bert Gold fired off a confidential, unusually harsh, memorandum to Benjamin Epstein, the ADL's national director. He said, "it would seem evident that the ADL has encouraged Mayor Zwink and his associates to believe that a major Jewish group has for the first time endorsed the Daisenberger text of the Passion Play, provided that certain 'changes' have been made." Gold also noted his telephone conversation with Epstein prior to the ADL group's visit to Oberammergau, in which he had stated that the Daisenberger text is "both theologically and dramaturgically structurally anti-Semitic."

In mid-July, Marc, accompanied by William Trosten and Karl Koepcke, the publicity director of Lufthansa Airlines, made his third Oberammergau-related visit to West Germany. Writing to Bert Gold and Miles Jaffe on July 21, the rabbi described that trip as "potentially far-reaching, (of) constructive importance on a number of levels."

The Tanenbaum group's meetings had not begun on a positive note. Hans Schwaighofer reported that 70 percent of Oberammergau's population was likely pro-Daisenberger, for both practical and ideological reasons. Furthermore, although Mayor Zwink had assigned the passion play's new director, Hans Meyer, to "revise Daisenberger so that it would conform as much as possible to Vatican Council II teaching," Marc reported that opponents of that text in the town thought that it would be "impossible to rectify (its) anti-Semitic structure."

At that point, Marc realized the larger implications of the debate over the competing texts. As he concluded: "The time had come to move from polemics to dialogue—deep and serious communication about the fundamental historic and theological issues that Oberammergau represents." To that end, the rabbi scheduled a meeting with the leaders of the Catholic Academy in Bavaria, in his words Bavaria's "Brookings Institution" to explore the possibility of their sponsoring—with the committee's cooperation—a seminar to explore those issues.

Following a high-level discussion lasting through lunch, the Academy's president, Dr. Franz Heinrich, immediately agreed to sponsor the seminar, whose theme would be "The Passion of Jesus: Yesterday and Today." After further refinements of the theme, on October 27, during the AJC's National Executive Board meeting in

Cambridge, Massachusetts, the committee announced plans for "a symposium of Catholic and Jewish scholars in Munich next month on the relationship of the Oberammergau Passion Play to the development of anti-Semitism in Germany and in German culture." Not only would Marc present one of the symposium's major papers, he would also be invited to speak in Oberammergau "on the religious and historical factors that have contributed to anti-Semitism in Germany and elsewhere."

In an obvious put-down of the ADL, the committee's release describing the upcoming event would state: "It is believed that never before has a Jewish spokesman been invited to address a public gathering in Oberammergau on anti-Semitism and Jewish-Christian relations."

The response of Oberammergau's pro-Daisenberger advocates was predictable. In a letter to Dr. Heinrich and Mayor Zwink, they charged that "this symposium was a conspiracy on the part of the American Jewish Committee and certain Oberammergau people." Not surprisingly, the Town Council refused to send official representatives to the gathering.

Yet by conceiving the symposium, as well as having a hand in its implementation, Marc would succeed in pitting learned Roman Catholic scholars aligned with the advances articulated in *Nostra aetate* against the Oberammergau traditionalists. As the rabbi would write in a memorandum widely distributed throughout the Jewish organizational world: "The scholars separately concluded with this consensus: In the portrayal of the Passion of Jesus, the Jews must now be portrayed with more honesty, with greater respect for their religious traditions, and with greater recognition of their rich traditions of scholarship."

Marc also wrote of "an unexpected surprise." The famed Italian film director Franco Zeffirelli—who had enlisted Marc as a consultant to the NBC-television network's production of *Jesus of Nazareth*—was also present at the symposium. Whether Zeffirelli's participation was actually a surprise or due to the rabbi's finely tuned PR sense, his presence added the perspective of an acclaimed director of dramatic productions to the debate. To "great applause" from the symposium's attendees, Zeffirelli appealed to the producers of the passion play "as a Christian and a son of Abraham not to use any further their production as a means to incite anti-Semitism, or to persecute Jews, or bring about further separation, and not to repeat the errors of the past."

On the evening following the symposium's conclusion, Marc—accompanied by AJC colleagues William Trosten, Zach Schuster, Miles Jaffe, and Richard Weis, a committee lay leader from Los Angeles—gave a speech to some two hundred townspeople, which was greeted with sustained applause.

On Marc's return to New York, he would lose no time in capitalizing on his experiences in Germany. On November 29, writing to Cardinal Ratzinger, the rabbi praised the prelate for "the high intellectual standards and moral inspiration which you most assuredly provide the academy." (Among Ratzinger's positions, he was the Episcopal Moderator of Heinrich's academy.) And then he got to the real point of his letter. Marc wrote:

> As you can undoubtedly know from the newspaper reports and possibly other accounts, the majority consensus of the Symposium was overwhelmingly opposed to the Daisenberger text of the Oberammergau Passion Play and its fundamentally anti-Jewish content and called for a passion play that was far truer to the authentic spirituality of the Passion of Jesus as formulated in the Council of Trent and the Second Vatican Council. I sincerely trust that under your spiritual guidance that such an ennobling result will finally be possible in 1980.

As the forces in Oberammergau continued to do battle over textual changes, in New York, the committee and the ADL clashed publicly over the issue. The issue, as reported by the National Catholic News Service (NCNS), remained "whether script changes for the 1980 Oberammergau Passion Play have gone far enough in eliminating anti-Semitism from the text."

The ADL had commissioned an analysis of the revised 1980 text from Marc's close friend Leonard Swidler, a professor of Catholic thought and interreligious dialogue at Temple University and the editor of the prestigious *Journal of Ecumenical Studies*. He would be joined in the project by Father Gerard S. Sloyan, an editor of the *New English Bible*. According to Professor Swidler, "All of the essential problems and trouble spots have been eliminated in recent revisions of the 1860 Weis-Daisenberger text." But Marc disputed this finding and told the NCNS, "The problem remains that the basic construct of the text portrays the Jews collectively guilty for the death of Christ. It also portrays the Jews as being ferocious in their determination to bring about the death of Jesus."

The committee's line-by-line analysis, "Oberammergau 1980: Progress and Problems," would be released in San Francisco on October 25, 1979, during the agency's National Executive Board meeting. In presenting its conclusions, Marc stated:

> Our systematic study of the 1980 text finds that a number of significant passages, scenes, and language changes have been made which correspond in detail to the German-language analysis which AJC delegations submitted to the Oberammergau Town Council. . . . Nevertheless the overriding conclusion of our analysis . . . as it stands . . . the drama retains an anti-Jewish impact despite the well-intentioned efforts of those who have revised it.

The disagreement between the committee and the ADL, while making for good copy in the religious and secular press, would have wider implications for the two agencies. As the best-known, most prolific fund-raiser on the committee's national staff, Marc was now at the center of the overall competition between the positions and programs of the two organizations. That was an unenviable position to occupy, because both agencies were not only engaged in competition for media attention, but for affluent and/or influential lay leaders, as well.

What was at stake was funding from individuals, foundations, and the Large City Budgeting Conference (LCBC), the monetary alloca- tions arm of the powerful Council of Jewish Federations and Welfare Funds. While the debate concerning Oberammergau may not have had resonance in the world at large, in the post-Holocaust world, the issue was of intense interest to the vast majority of Jews everywhere. Thus, the agency that could claim greater influence in bringing about changes in the offensive Oberammergau text, as well as in the play's production values, would be viewed as the more effective defender of Jewish honor and rights.

In late May of 1980, Marc, accompanied by William Trosten and several committee lay leaders, embarked on his fourth trip to Oberammergau. From May 23 to May 27, the group conducted a series of meetings and held a press conference. On the twenty-fifth, a Sunday, they attended a five-and-a-half-hour performance of the 1980 production.

As the audience gathered at nine o'clock that morning, church bells began to peal throughout the village. The scene, as Marc described it in a memorandum to Bert Gold the following day, "suggested that the people streaming in from all sides were attending a cross between going to church in a New England Puritan hamlet and scrambling for seats in Yankee Stadium."

The AJC visitors estimated the attendance of American visitors at approximately 20 to 30 percent of each day's audience—in monetary terms, about $100,000 of the daily gross receipts. Since all performances until September were sold out, they projected that a total of 500,000 people would attend the 1980 production.

The committee's initial analysis of the play's content would be confirmed by the group, which reported that "all the theological and historical issues that AJC identified were present in the actual per- formance, only intensified and exacerbated by the production—the staging, the costumes, and the acting." In order to counter the negativ- ity of the production, and to reach out to potential attendees, the com- mittee made available to interested parties, such as travel agencies and church groups, a twenty-page booklet written by Judy Banki and titled "What Viewers Should Know About the Oberammergau Passion Play, 1980."

Marc was clearly dismayed at the failure of efforts to implement significant change in the passion play's production values. Most upsetting to him was the continuing presentation of Jews as being collectively responsible for the death of Jesus. By June, the usually diplomatic rabbi had had enough. He would proclaim to the NCNS: "The fact that two million people will have been exposed to its emotion-laden anti-Jewish message since World War II suggests that Oberammergau has become the international capital of some of the worst forms of demonic anti-Semitism in the world today."

During the coming years, Oberammergau's cultural and political leadership would not only remain obdurate in its opposition to real change, but in the AJC's view, it would continue to engage in a pattern of double-talk. For example, on May 7, 1983, the Oberammergau Press Service would issue a release stating that "The Passion Play Village Oberammergau has still not forgotten the charges of anti-Semitism which in 1970 led to a temporary boycott with the result that in August/September often whole sections of the Passion Playhouse remained empty."

A mere eleven days later, the Press Service would make the outrageous assertion that "It was confirmed by a team of theological experts that the text [of the 1984 passion play] is in accord with the insights of [Vatican II] and is free of all anti-Judaism. . . . The Oberammergau people can now with assurance begin the auditions for the Jubilee Passion Play 1984 since the text has been unanimously approved by all experts."

Marc was not, of course, among those "experts" referred to in the release. Nor were Professor Swidler or any members of the team of Catholic and Jewish scholars from the United States that the committee had offered to assemble.

In 1984, a committee delegation would travel to Oberammergau to attend the May 22 performance of the passion play. The group included Rabbi James Rudin, Marc's successor as director of the Interreligious Affairs Department (at that point in time, Marc had recently moved over to head the committee's International Affairs Department); lay leader Mimi Alperin, making her first trip abroad as chair of the Interreligious Affairs Commission; Roman Catholic theologian Professor Eva Fleischner; and the Reverend William Harter, a Presbyterian leader.

Rabbi Rudin found the 1984 script to be "fundamentally flawed and still perpetuating the pernicious myth that the Jews are eternally guilty for Jesus' crucifixion," while Alperin found "the dramatization of the text to be more problematic than its actual words." Following the performance, the committee delegation would meet with village elders and religious leaders. But they would not come away with a pledge of substantive revisions to the play's script or production values.

While the agency's interest in this issue would continue under Rabbi Rudin's supervision, the committee was beginning to be criticized in some circles. As Mimi Alperin recalled, "They were saying, 'Why are you involved when so few people see it?' What people didn't realize," she observed, "is that lots of American tourists were going to see it. And it had an impact here. Also, that it was taking place in Germany was quite an experience."

The script for the passion play would remain problematic, to say the least. It was becoming increasingly obvious that only through continuing pressure emanating from progressive organizations and religious leaders of all faiths, as well as the advent of a more enlightened generation of town leaders in Oberammergau, would there be true change as had been enunciated in the principles of Vatican II.

Over the years, there would be additional tinkering with the production, as recounted in an article in *The Forward* in 2010 indicating the problems were never solved. The article by A. J. Goldmann, published in the May 26, 2010, edition of *The Forward*, was titled "New Kind of Passion in an 'Alpine Jerusalem,'" and it noted: "Otto Huber, the play's second director and dramatic adviser, and possibly the person most knowledgeable about its history, sought to persuade the ADL's national director, Abraham Foxman, before the 2000 production that the play's transcendent theme was about love and redemption." But according to James Shapiro's 2000 book *Oberammergau: The Troubling Story of the World's Most Famous Passion Play*, Foxman responded: "If you want to give me love and understanding, there are a lot of other Christian subjects. Give me another play; if it's about a Crucifixion in which the Jews kill Christ, you can never clean it up enough."

Marc Tanenbaum, along with other Jewish leaders, raised the issues about the play and doggedly insisted on changes. They presented a challenge to the town's unreconstructed elders and to church leaders in Germany. By bearing witness, Marc and others raised the consciousness of these issues, but they could never fully resolve the Jewish concerns.

Jesus Christ Superstar

In 1970, as longtime passion play aficionados and tourists alike were eagerly making their way to Oberammergau to revel in this latest, offensive production, a musical theater piece replete with age-old stereotypical images worthy of *Der Stürmer* during the Nazi era, was being readied for production in 1971, most surprisingly, on Broadway.

Marc was becoming actively involved in seeking to expose the blatant anti-Semitism of Andrew Lloyd Webber and Tim Rice's appealingly titled rock opera *Jesus Christ Superstar*, which would open on Broadway to mixed reviews.

The rabbi assigned Gerald Strober to compile a detailed analysis of the book, lyrics, and production values of the upcoming musical with its attention-getting name and catchy songs. Strober carefully read the musical's book and then attended two preview performances. He reported that he was "deeply troubled by the production's stereotypical images, including sexual innuendo, and by its negative implications for relationships between Christians and Jews." Strober was also offended by the production's theological implications, especially in the way the title character was depicted.

Writing to Billy Graham on October 19, 1971, Strober noted, "The

Jesus that is presented is rather different from the Jesus of the Gospels and the New Testament. He is weak, unsure of himself, uncertain concerning his role and future." In addition, and most disquieting in terms of the musical's historical integrity, he said, the Jesus character "appears to misstate or misunderstand key Christian teachings." For example, during the Last Supper, he is pessimistic, wondering "whether he will be remembered." In the garden, he bursts into song, asking "whether he is to die in vain, and in his questioning, he articulates an almost blasphemous view of the meaning of his life and death." Furthermore, Strober wrote in his critique, "The production never once mentions the Resurrection. Indeed, the play ends with Jesus crucified and dead." Because of the dubious theology and its portrayal of Jesus, many Christian groups would be as upset as Jewish organizations regarding the show.

Although the committee's analysis of *Jesus Christ Superstar* would be widely circulated, no action would be taken by the musical's creators to alter its inaccuracies and offensive content. The show opened on Broadway in 1971 and ran for nearly two years.

The filmed version, released by Universal Pictures in 1973, was characterized by Rabbi Tanenbaum as "a witches' brew of anti-black and anti-Semitic venom." When Universal announced its intention to make a movie out of the stage musical, the committee had offered its consultative services. In fact, the agency's president, Elmer Winter, called Lew Wasserman, the studio's chairman, and suggested ways in which the anti-Jewish imagery of the Broadway production could be avoided in the film. Rather than welcoming Winter's overture, however, the legendary Hollywood mogul was said to have treated Winter, a dynamic entrepreneur and founder of Manpower, Inc., as if he were a studio office boy, contemptuously dismissing the committee's concerns.

Nonetheless, the committee continued to take issue with the film's script. Mort Yarmon undertook an all-out media effort to expose the musical's bigotry, and this helped generate a widely distributed Associated Press story by George Cornell chronicling Jewish concern about the film. In any case, the film was a box-office failure. The play, however, would be revived periodically by theater groups across the country, in many cases by religious groups that had no idea of the play's bigotry and dubious theology.

Nuns at Auschwitz

As the "Hymie Town" incident was coming to a head in 1984, discord was erupting over the action of a small group of Polish Carmelite nuns—one that would come to involve the Polish Catholic hierarchy and the Vatican.

During 1984, unbeknownst to much of the world, the Carmelite order of Kraków had obtained permission from the Polish government to establish a Carmel—the technical term for a convent—in a two-story brick building located within the grounds of the Auschwitz death camp. During the Holocaust, that structure had served as the storage site for the Zyklon-B gas employed by the Nazis to murder approximately two million Jewish men, women, and children, as well as tens of thousands of Polish gentiles, Roma, and others.

Eight to twelve Carmelite nuns had initially moved into the convent. Their presence on the site of the notorious concentration camp would probably have gone unnoticed save for the fund-raising efforts of the Belgian branch of a little-known group called "Aid to the Church in Distress." Organizational literature distributed in 1985 described the nuns as "doing penance for us who are still alive. They build with their hands the sacred sign . . . which will witness the victorious power of the cross of Jesus. The convent will become a spiritual fortress, a token of the conversion of brothers from various countries who went astray."

However, not all Catholic churchmen favored the convent's establishment on the site of the death camp. On December 6, 1984, Cardinal Albert Decourtray, the Archbishop of Lyon, France, declared:

> For me, the Nazi barbarism that descended on Auschwitz descended first and foremost on the Jewish people, even if there were others than Jews at Auschwitz. . . . Such affliction and suffering has conferred on the Jewish people, through its

martyrs, a particular dignity that is quite properly its own. And to construct a convent at Auschwitz would, for me, impinge upon that dignity.

On January 8, 1986, the Christian members of the Amitié Judéo-Chrétienne (Jewish-Christian Friendship Society) of France issued a statement strongly criticizing the fund-raising publication. Noting that the word "Jew" does not appear in the text, that organization charged that the document reveals "a triumphalism of the Church that we thought Vatican Council II had ended."

The controversy deepened when Cardinal Franciszek Macharski, the archbishop of Kraków, in a letter to Dr. Victor Goldbloom, the president of the International Council of Christians and Jews, defended the establishment of the convent. The archbishop promised the Jewish leader that the number of nuns at the Auschwitz convent would not exceed twenty-two. According to a Religious News Service dispatch on May 14, 1986, he said: "This limitation serves well the care of imperceptibleness of the Christian presence in the largest place of extermination of the Jewish nation." And he pledged that the convent "will never overshadow that historic and emotional significance of the camp."

The archbishop's promises notwithstanding, the fact that the Polish Church would allow the nuns to maintain a presence within the Auschwitz perimeter was upsetting to numerous cardinals and leaders of Jewish organizations in both Western Europe and the United States. Thus, a plan to move the convent outside the camp was adopted during a meeting of Catholics and Jews held in Geneva in February 1987. A statement signed by the archbishops of Brussels, Kraków, Lyon, and Paris, as well as by the grand rabbi of France and the president of the European Jewish Congress, called for the establishment of a center for "information, education, meeting, and prayer . . . outside the Auschwitz-Birkenau camp grounds."

While the Carmelite sisters appeared to assent to the agreement that had been forged in Geneva, they would refuse to move until the establishment of their new center. Whether due to the nuns' innocence of worldly matters, or to the calculation of their superiors that significant funds would be required for the purchase of land for the center's construction, the sisters would be able to further their determination to remain within the camp well into the indefinite future.

On January 12, 1989, during an interview with Religious News Service, Marc would note the "unexpected resistance from the Carmelite nuns, who refused up until now to obey Cardinal Macharski and even the Vatican and the pope." While the rabbi was not opposed to the Carmelites' prayers and understood the appropriateness of their honoring Polish Catholic victims of Nazism, he adamantly opposed the Carmelites' conducting their spiritual activities at Auschwitz. With the passage of time, Marc would be increasingly concerned that the controversy could negatively impact Catholic-Jewish relations.

Many Jews believed that the issue could be resolved by the "snap of the [pope's] fingers" as the rabbi would write in a commentary published by Jewish Telegraphic Agency (JTA) on June 7, 1989. But he pointed out that while the Vatican could help in the convent's transfer, it could do so "only in the background." He explained, "By church law and discipline, only the Polish church has the power to remove the convent, which is under its jurisdiction. The pope and the Vatican have much influence, but not the decision-making power, and there is a basic difference between power and influence."

But the rabbi indicated that the issue was becoming an ongoing point of conflict between the Jewish community and Polish Church leaders and laity. That struggle would be exacerbated in July 1989 when Rabbi Avraham Weiss, the spiritual leader of the Hebrew Institute of Riverdale, New York, along with six others, scaled the Auschwitz convent wall.

Obviously upset over the failure of efforts to relocate the nuns to an interim site by January 22, as promised in the 1987 agreement, and concerned that the new date, July 22, would not be honored, Rabbi Weiss and his group, dressed in concentration camp stripes, blew a shofar—the ram's horn used in Jewish rituals—and shouted anti-Nazi slogans. Their demonstration prompted Polish workers laboring near the convent to douse them with paint and water while forcing them from the area.

That incident, while hardly representative of a strategy advocated by the Jewish organizational world, would only stiffen the Polish hierarchy's resistance to any demand for the nuns' relocation. In a statement issued by Cardinal Józef Glemp, the archbishop of Warsaw, the prelate advised the Jews "not to talk to us from the position of a superior nation" and to refrain from dictating "terms that cannot be fulfilled."

It took nearly three years of efforts by Jewish leaders, notably Marc and his close friend Sir Sigmund Sternberg, chairman of the International Council of Christians and Jews, to achieve a compromise under which, pending the construction of a planned information center, the Carmelite nuns would relocate to an interim site outside Auschwitz.

That would prove to be difficult to achieve. The Vatican had gone on record as calling for the removal of the nuns to a convent away from the grounds of Auschwitz and was even following the actual construction of their center. But, the sisters, supported by certain Polish Church officials, were refusing to budge. Only in April 1993, on the eve of the fiftieth anniversary of the Warsaw ghetto uprising, would Pope John Paul II order the fourteen Carmelite sisters remaining within the boundary of Auschwitz leave that site.

Marc Tanenbaum would not live to witness the positive outcome of his impassioned campaign to preserve the history of the Shoah. He would live long enough, however, to declare to the NCNS in 1989 that Auschwitz would never "be converted into a chapel . . . you cannot make a holy place out of a place of death and murder." Instead, he could rest assured, in the words of a statement published by NCNS on January 13, 1989, that Auschwitz would remain intact "as a lasting reminder of what barbarism and anti-Semitism have led to."

Producing *Holocaust*

In his efforts to protect and promote the interests of the Jewish people, Marc Tanenbaum would prove to be highly skilled in engaging with the mass media to ensure that Jewish life and Jewish views were illuminated. He wrote numerous articles for newspapers and magazines and was frequently quoted in the press. He was equally prominent in the broadcast media: he was frequently interviewed on radio and television, and he created broadcast content from his days writing scripts for *The Eternal Light* to his long stint as an award-winning, popular commentator on WINS radio and other Westinghouse Broadcasting stations around the country.

His interest in the media led him to become involved in several major television ventures that sought to combat anti-Semitism by disseminating stories of the Jewish experience.

In 1977, he was engaged by Robert Berger and Herbert Brodkin, the producers of NBC's proposed eight-hour-long prime-time dramatization, *Holocaust*, to serve as the American Jewish community's consultant to that monumental project. The rabbi prepared a detailed critique of the script, which had been written by the well-known author Gerald Green. His suggested revisions would be adopted in the shooting scenario of the landmark miniseries, which would be broadcast in four installments, beginning on the evening of April 16, 1978, and concluding on the nineteenth.

After viewing the "rushes" of *Holocaust* in late December 1977, Marc would praise the series in a memo to AJC area directors, Jewish Community Relations Councils (JCRCs), federations, national Jewish organizations, and rabbinic associations. He wrote:

> In ways that documentaries are not able to achieve, this dramatization translates the trauma, the unspeakable horrors, as well as the heroism of Jews in human terms that cannot but help reach the conscience of millions of Americans, non-Jews as well as Jews. Recent efforts to whitewash the Nazi massacre of Jews makes this program all the more necessary and compelling, in ways that documentaries are not able to achieve.

As the series airdate approached, the committee would facilitate the wide distribution of study guides and promotional materials. And in cooperation with NBC, it agreed to solicit testimonial blurbs from prominent Jews and gentiles.

Several weeks prior to the series' airing, early morning press screenings were offered in the basement screening room of the Rizzoli bookstore on Manhattan's Fifth Avenue. They were followed by discussions over lunch at a nearby hotel with Marc and NBC's producers and creative team. The latter included writer Gerald Green and several of the miniseries stars, including Meryl Streep, Fritz Weaver, and James Woods along with Blanche Baker (the daughter of film star Carroll Baker), who portrayed a young Jewish girl, and Michael Moriarty, cast as a vicious Nazi functionary in the "Final Solution."

The screening attendees, and ultimately the audience for the four two-hour-long segments, would have a mixed reaction. Holocaust survivor and scholar Elie Wiesel would weigh in, contending that the Hollywood-style production values, in which depictions of life in the Warsaw Ghetto and in a concentration camp were sanitized, served to trivialize the Nazi genocide of European Jewry. Meanwhile, Adam Simms, of the AJC's office in Chicago, reported that among ethnic Eastern European communities in Chicago there were "hurt expressions" regarding the depiction of non-Jewish Poles and Ukrainians as Nazi collaborators. As Simms put it:

> Several people commented specifically that it was unfortunate that the only positive portrayal of cooperation in resistance was the story of the Sobibor rebellion, in which captured Red Army soldiers [read: Communists] were the Jews' main ally. The question posed in this regard was: Why did the program not depict the aid that Polish partisans provided and attempted to provide to the Warsaw ghetto?

Simms went on to observe that "Such expressions were balanced by a general feeling that the program served a positive good by driving home the point that people cannot and should not remain silent when people are being persecuted."

Simms also observed another dynamic at work. He noted "the feeling that many Americans are not sufficiently aware of and concerned with the conditions of human rights violations that their 'landsmen' currently suffer overseas." He also said, "It is interesting to see how a Jewish story, which had particular overtones . . . was still interpreted to have universal meaning."

Between the airing of the third and fourth installments of *Holocaust*, Marc spoke by telephone with public officials in West Germany, as well as leaders of the Bavarian village of Oberammergau, regarding the impact of the series, which was being broadcast by Cologne-based Westdeutsche Rundfunk (WDR). In a report on those conversations, the rabbi wrote, "Nothing—no book, no TV documentary, no film, no lecture—has touched the soul of Modern Germany on the moral watershed tragedy of the Nazi Holocaust as has the NBC TV series, 'Holocaust.'"

Amid steadily increasing German viewing audiences for each of the first three episodes, Marc noted that "According to reports from West Germany in major American newspapers, an estimated 13 million people, or 39 percent of the 34 million people in the viewing audience, watched the third of the four installments last Thursday night," more than double the predicted number of 15 percent. In addition, Marc reported, "More than 20 million people called the WDR television offices following the Tuesday night showing, and two-thirds of the callers were in favor of 'Holocaust' being televised in Germany."

According to the rabbi, "Many of the viewers told the TV station authorities that they could not go on watching it, and some said they could not sleep and had to take valium or sleeping pills, so powerful was the program's impact." One West German official informed Marc that "The experience with the program already has been quite extraordinary. Nobody, even the most sympathetic in the TV industry, expected such an emotional reaction. It has staggered everybody." Meanwhile, residents of East Germany, most of them living beyond WDR's broadcasting range, were demanding that they be allowed to view the series.

The impact extended beyond Germany. Austria's advance poll revealed that 74 percent of respondents initially opposed broadcasting the series, while only 24 percent were in favor. But after the fact, only 5 percent objected. Moreover, Nazi hunter Simon Wiesenthal reported that his Vienna office was flooded with phone tips regarding the current whereabouts of former Nazis.

The rabbi also spoke with people in Oberammergau who were involved in preparations for the 1980 edition of that village's notoriously anti-Semitic passion play. They included Hans Schwaighofer, director of the version that had been written in 1750 by the Reverend Ferdinand Rosner, a Benedictine monk. He informed the rabbi that "Practically everybody in Oberammergau has watched the first two installments . . . the impact has been tremendous. There is a feeling of shock throughout much of Oberammergau. Many people are walking around the streets of the village saying: 'God's sake!' and shaking their heads in disbelief: 'How did we let that happen?'"

During his conversation with Herr Schwaighofer, Marc also learned that Oberammergau's town council had circulated a questionnaire among the village's residents inviting them to sign up to attend the following year's edition of the passion play. Given the impact of *Holocaust*, however, "many are refusing to answer the questionnaire, and it is now being extended for another eight days," Herr Schwaighofer said.

Prior to his work on *Holocaust*, Marc also worked with the Italian filmmaker Vincenzo Labella during the filming of the miniseries *Moses, the Lawgiver*, which was broadcast on CBS Television in 1975 and featured the American movie star Burt Lancaster. Labella said of his work with Marc: "He was a true teacher, a rabbi. I learned a lot from him and fell in love with one of his heroes, Maimonides." The two developed "a treatment" for a miniseries together about the Spanish rabbinic authority, philosopher, and royal physician, but later, Labella said, "Many things happened, and we had to postpone it."

However, Marc would be an adviser on several other Labella projects, including *Jesus of Nazareth*, directed by well-known filmmaker Franco Zeffirelli and broadcast in 1981 on NBC; and *A.D.*, a twelve-hour miniseries chronicling the life and adventures of Jesus's disciples, and events in Rome during the reigns of the Emperors Tiberius, Caligula, Claudius, and Nero. It was broadcast by NBC Television in the 1984–1985 season.

Labella recalled that he had benefited from the rabbi's "assistance and gravitas." In the preparation of *Jesus of Nazareth*, he credited Marc with the idea of seeking "to recover the image of Jesus, the Jew—the man who had come not to divert from the ancient Testament, but to revert to it." Labella described their collaboration as "a continuous debate," in which "we both moved from positions of understanding and a tendency to find the common ground."

Reverend Jerry Falwell Pays a Visit

During the 1980s, there was an upsurge in evangelical Christianity in America. This revival reflected the sweeping, sometimes traumatic, changes taking place in American life, particularly in the highly conservative old South. One result of this was the rise of the Moral Majority, which took issue with many of the changes it saw taking place in American values. Its leader was Rev. Jerry Falwell, a televangelist who created an empire that not only included his broadcasts, but also a megachurch, a university, and a nationwide movement.

Falwell's supporters often disparaged Jews and argued that G-d did not hear their prayers. Moreover, they aggressively sought to proselytize among the Jews. They were often fervent supporters of Israel, but many Jews worried that support was only a means to an end: a State of Israel was required in order to hasten the return of the Messiah, after which Israel, and the Jews, would no longer be needed.

Marc undertook what was called "a major counteroffensive," which led to Rev. Falwell visiting the AJC offices in New York. During their discussion of theology, Falwell noted that he did not share the view held by others, including Bailey Smith, the president of the Southern Baptist Convention, that G-d does not hear the prayers of a Jew. And Falwell also stated that he opposed the view that the United States should be a "Christian republic" or that evangelicals should only vote for "born-again Christians."

Marc told Falwell he was saying things "never attributed to you before," and he asked if the reverend was prepared to "make a statement." When Falwell agreed, Marc said he "pulled out a yellow pad" that he said he had "handy for such circumstances" and wrote out a page-and-a-half statement repudiating a number of views common among Moral Majority adherents.

The reverend and the rabbi then issued a joint press communiqué noting the points they had discussed—and agreed on. Later Marc would say that this meeting was "probably the first time" that Falwell had ever "talked to a Jew longer than ten minutes."

While keeping a close eye on the treatment of Jews in the United States and around the world, Marc would also remain deeply involved in issues of oppression and bigotry affecting individuals in a host of nations.

CHAPTER 18

Do Not Stand Idly By

"Marc Tanenbaum compared it [the plight of South Vietnamese boat people] to what happened to the Jewish people during the Second World War—that people knew about it but didn't care. But we could not allow this."

—Liv Ullmann, stage and screen star; author;
UNICEF Goodwill Ambassador; participant
with Rabbi Marc Tanenbaum in the International Rescue
Committee (IRC) Mission to Southeast Asia, February 1978

MARC TANENBAUM'S ACTIVISM ON BEHALF of the poor and oppressed was an integral part of his life mission. For him, addressing injustice was synonymous with being alive. Besides being active in the civil rights movement in the United States and the campaign to free Soviet Jewry, the rabbi spoke out in support of Cesar Chavez and his efforts to achieve a better life for Mexican farmworkers in the United States. Marc also became deeply involved in efforts to help the oppressed and downtrodden in Asia, Africa, South America, and Europe.

During the early 1960s, for example, Marc was appalled by the continuing existence of apartheid in South Africa. Thus, he continually spoke out against the injustices being perpetrated by South Africa's white minority government on its majority black population.

Nor would the rabbi ignore the plight of the people of war-torn Biafra later in that decade. Dismayed by their misery, in 1968 he would be instrumental in urging Jewish organizations to assist victims of that nation's conflict with Nigeria under the auspices of the American Jewish Emergency Effort for Biafran Relief. During an address at Marquette University, in Milwaukee, Wisconsin, on July 19, Marc announced the creation of a Jewish-sponsored ad hoc committee to prevent starvation there. He noted "The ghastly reports and photographs of men, women, and children reduced to skeletons or dying in the thousands" and said those images had evoked in the American Jewish community "a flood of nightmarish memories" of the Holocaust, stirring "such profound memories of identification of this community of suffering mankind that it has now become intolerable and immoral to remain silent spectators."

Indeed, the human rights rabbi was increasingly vocal about the parallels between the plights of the persecuted Jews during the Nazi era and the thousands of victims of a series of brutal conflicts in war-torn Southeast Asia in the 1970s. Thus, he did not hesitate to offer the American Jewish Committee's moral support, as well as practical life-saving assistance, to that region's endangered populations, most notably on behalf of Vietnamese boat people and Cambodian refugees then suffering from the ravages of famine and disease as the result of the callous behavior of ruthless dictators.

One notable example of his activism came in February 1978, when Marc accepted the invitation of Leo Cherne, the executive director of the International Rescue Committee (IRC), to join a two-week-long, IRC-sponsored, humanitarian mission to Asia as one of fourteen members of the U.S. Citizens Committee for Indochinese Refugees. Described by the IRC as a "March for Survival," that agency's pioneering initiative sought to enhance worldwide awareness of the crimes being perpetrated against 150,000 people then subsisting in fear for their very lives.

In February 1978, as the first of Marc's two visits to the region within a year got underway, he was joined by medical personnel and concerned notables. The delegation included folksinger Joan Baez; former Soviet refusenik and prisoner of Zion Alexander Ginzburg; black civil rights activist Bayard Rustin; stage and film star Liv Ullmann; and Holocaust survivor, scholar, and author Elie Wiesel.

The group visited many refugee camps in the region, offering humanitarian assistance and compassion to many victims of Pol Pot's brutality in Cambodia, as well as to Vietnamese boat people, whom Marc would come to regard as the "Jews of Asia."

Liv Ullmann was among the most emotionally affected and vocal of the mission's marchers. The genesis of her participation lay in an offer made to Leo Cherne that she could not refuse. The actress was then starring in famed composer Richard Rodgers's final Broadway musical, *I Remember Mama*, as the matriarch of a Norwegian immigrant family. Following a time-honored Broadway tradition, the play's cast was collecting money for donation to a worthy charity. As Ullmann recalled, "All of us agreed that it had to go to the International Rescue Committee because of what they were doing for refugees all over the world, specifically, for the boat refugees from Vietnam and from Cambodia."

The cast collected approximately $200,000, which the star presented to the IRC's director. Then, "being very well brought up," Ullmann said, "If you ever want something from me, just call on me." Within days, Cherne was on the phone with Ullmann. "We would like you to be part of our March for Survival toward the border of Cambodia," he said. "There will be doctors and nurses and politicians. You and Joan Baez would be the celebrities because we want that too." Ullmann who was quite busy professionally at that time but was also eager to accept Cherne's request, asked, "How long will that journey be?" "It will last for the rest of your life," he replied.

Cherne knew what he was talking about. As Ullmann confirmed in an interview some thirty-five years later, "That March for Survival really did change my life, very slowly, in my priorities, in my understanding of human rights, by meeting with people who were not statistics, but real people, like my mother and my sister and my grandmother."

On the evening of the group's arrival in Thailand, they sat outside. Amid the glow of a campfire, they sang songs and spoke of their motivations for having joined the March for Survival. Marc compared the likely destiny of the "boat people," if not rescued, to the fate that had befallen six million European Jews during the Holocaust. Liv Ullmann was heartened both by what she regarded as the rabbi's "incredible" manner of speaking and by his inclusiveness of the Christians among the marchers. She had until then "felt that if you were Jewish, you might feel a distance from Christians," she observed, "but this was a man who loved me *because* I am a Christian."

As Ullmann heard the rabbi's words that evening, she experienced a self-revelatory moment. "So many of the reasons why I was there had to do with *my* background, which I hadn't even thought about," she recalled. The actress had begun to think about the tragedy that had befallen her grandfather, Hultson Ullmann, during the Nazi occupation of her native Norway during World War II. "He was taken as a hostage as most of the Jewish people from the small town where he lived had managed to escape because people helped them. When the Germans couldn't take them, they took my grandfather, among others."

The Ullmann family would not learn of his fate for some years. In 1960, when Ullmann was twenty-one years old, she happened to be visiting Poland on a cultural exchange. One evening, as she sat in a restaurant, talking with her minders—this was during Poland's years as a Warsaw Pact nation under Soviet hegemony—an elderly man approached her table. Having obviously overheard their conversation, the man said to the actress, "I understand that you are Norwegian. Do you know a family named Ullmann?"

"My name is Ullmann, and there's only one Ullmann family in Norway," she replied. "I was in Dachau during the war," he said, "and I shared a bed with Hulston Ullmann for two years." Ullman said, "This stranger had shared a bed with my grandfather! He said that Hulston

Ullmann had died of a lung disease." Reflecting more than fifty years later on that providential encounter with a total stranger in a restaurant in Eastern Europe, Ullmann said: "I don't think God does those things by accident." Likewise, she said, "to meet someone like Marc Tanenbaum did not happen by accident."

Although Ullmann had never really gotten to know her grandfather, his fate would loom very large as she prepared to undertake her first major role in the theater—as Anne Frank in the Norwegian production of *The Diary of Anne Frank*. Ullmann was portraying the German-born teenager who had hidden for two years with her immediate family and other occupants of a "Secret Annex" in Amsterdam before being betrayed, seized by the Nazis, and deported to the Bergen-Belsen concentration camp, where she died in March 1945, only weeks before the war's end.

"Her words on one of the last days before the Germans took her from where she had been hiding for two years meant so much to me: 'I believe that deep down, all human beings are really good.' And my grandfather, in his destiny, and in the words of Anne Frank, always stayed with me. He is a part of me."

As Marc spoke of *his* family's ordeal many years earlier at the hands of Ukrainian anti-Semites, as well as of the refuge they were able to find in America, Ullmann knew that they "had a link." Now, Ullmann realized that "the words of a Jewish girl had really been with me all my life, without my knowing it. Here we are going to have an incredible march for freedom for *other* people—the boat people from Vietnam and the refugees from Cambodia in Hong Kong. To me it was destiny."

It was also her destiny that Elie Wiesel was among those marching for survival. The star would share with him her account of Grandfather Ullmann's fate. According to Ullmann, the noted Holocaust survivor was so moved by her account that he encouraged the women's organization Hadassah to send her to Israel on speaking engagements.

The Jewish faith and bravery of yet another participant, Alexander Ginzburg, would also exert a powerful impact on the actress. A founder of the Helsinki Monitoring Group, he served three sentences in a harsh Soviet labor camp before being deported and sent to New York in April 1970, along with four other dissidents, in exchange for two Soviets who had been jailed by the United States on espionage charges. Ginzburg had suffered so badly at the hands of his Soviet tormentors that he would barely be able to keep up with the mission's other participants in their March for Survival.

Looking back on her encounters with these survivors of terrible repression, Ullmann said, "This was my *destiny* and not the least because I talked on that first night with a man of God." While God "has always been part of my life," Ullmann maintained, "now he is really living *within* me. I know that my choices are always according to His will. And it was on this march that I also experienced that."

On their first full day in Thailand, the marchers, including the medical personnel carrying fifty truckloads of medicine, attempted in vain to enter Cambodia. At that point, Ullmann recalled, Alexander Ginzburg sounded an eerily prophetic note: "This is going to be one of the last marches. From now on, it's going to be in vain because soon the marches will be not for freedom; but for terrorism and death. So right now we are one of the last marchers only for humanity—with no weapons."

Leo Cherne, communicating via loudspeaker, implored the phalanx of impassive guards preventing the marchers from crossing the border: "Please let us in! We have no weapons. We have *medicine*." Then, in a moment Liv Ullmann said she won't "ever, *ever* forget," the thwarted but resolute marchers, led by Bayard Rustin, sang the civil rights anthem "We Shall Overcome."

That evening, Ullmann joined Marc, Leo Cherne, Alexander Ginzburg, Bayard Rustin, and Elie Wiesel in standing vigil for a time where they had been turned away by the callous officials. Later, the marchers retired for the night to a small, modest house near their border staging area. As there were not enough beds, or even mattresses there, to accommodate the group en masse, they were required to sleep in shifts.

Ullmann quipped that she and Marc literally "slept together," albeit in the company of other mission participants—"snoring old men," as the rabbi would describe their somnolent companions to his family. Despite the sparseness of their accommodations, the actress looked back on the mission as a time of great joy. "I have never, *never* in my life been so happy as when I was lying there, listening to the snoring of my brothers!" she declared decades after the event.

Early one morning, after Ullmann and the rabbi had relinquished their mattresses, they sat together on the front steps of the house. Then the rabbi, in his characteristically mentoring fashion, provided the actress with a lesson in recent Jewish history. The rabbi spoke of how the world had turned its collective back on European Jewry during the 1930s as Adolf Hitler literally tested the waters by sending 836 German Jews—men, women, and children—on an odyssey across the Atlantic Ocean on an ocean liner, the SS *St. Louis*, in search of a safe harbor.

As Marc would write in an article published by *Newsday* on December 1, 1978, the ship's Jewish human cargo had paid huge sums of money to purchase landing certificates guaranteeing their entry to Cuba. And 730 of them had even managed to secure American immigration quota numbers as a backup. When the *St. Louis* docked in Havana's harbor on May 27, 1939, however, the passengers were informed that their documents were invalid and they would only be permitted ashore on providing the Cuban government with $1 million within twenty-four hours. The Cuban government's demand for ransom could not be fulfilled. The ship's passengers were now so desperate that several of them committed suicide in the harbor before the authorities forced the liner out into the open sea.

The American Jewish Joint Distribution Committee pleaded with several South American nations to accept the refugees, but that relief agency's entreaties would be refused. Then, the US government, claiming that it could not interfere in Nazi Germany's internal affairs, refused the Jews entry into the land that had since 1903, per poet Emma Lazarus in "The New Colossus," beckoned: "Send these, the homeless, tempest-tost to me." And so the SS *St. Louis* returned to

Europe, with many of her Jewish passengers doomed to perish within a matter of years in the Nazi death camps.

In Marc's *Newsday* article, he would describe how "the *St. Louis* episode changed my life." Having attended a rally "for the 'boat people' of the *St. Louis in* Madison Square Garden" at that time, he had silently vowed to himself, paraphrasing from the book of Leviticus: "You shall not stand idly by while the blood of your brothers and sisters cries out to you from the earth." As Marc continued to speak with the actress that morning, she found him to be "everything I thought a rabbi would be: big, when it comes to the soul; serious, and daunting, but not in a *bad* way; and very special. Maybe I was a little bit afraid of him."

Less than ten months later, in early December 1978, Marc would return to the region on a two-week mission to Malaysia, Thailand, Indonesia, and Hong Kong. The trip was undertaken, he wrote in a *Newsday* article published on December 1, "in an effort to increase public knowledge and understanding of the refugee crisis." Marc was joined on this second mission by Leo Cherne; Bayard Rustin; Neal Ball, a Chicago executive at the American Hospital Supply Corp. who was active in refugee issues; William Casey, who would be appointed by President Reagan to head the Central Intelligence Agency; and the novelist James Michener.

Marc was accused by border guards of being "an Israeli spy" and was initially denied entry into Malaysia with the IRC group. Casey immediately stated emphatically that if the Jewish clergyman were to be turned away, then he, too, would remain behind. Only then would the officials relent.

As Neal Ball recalled their trek to one refugee camp in Thailand: "It was a long train trip up in the morning and back at night. A great deal of time in any of the camps was spent on foot, with someone who knew the situation there, seeing the numbers, getting statistics but also actually talking, through translators, with some of the refugees." As the group traveled from one emotionally devastating site to another, enduring "some pretty rough riding" in jeeps and other bare-bones vehicles, according to Ball, Marc proved to be not only indefatigable, but a delightful traveling companion—one who was "absolutely uncomplaining," said Ball. "And all of his remarks were on what we were seeing or about the work being done or what needed to be done."

Despite the group's hectic daytime pace, there was hardly any evening downtime. Following long hours spent in the field, the mission participants would spend hours discussing the next day's logistics and meetings. It was during those visits that Ball was "especially impressed by Marc's personal response to people and their response to *him*. Although they were talking through translators, his concern and his interest were remarkable."

Ball was not sure whether the refugees with whom he and Marc were interacting understood the role of their visitors. They did know, however, that they were from the West. "The help they asked for was mostly in delivering letters; they all had papers with addresses in Vietnam and were eager to have those forwarded to, I assume, family and friends there. There was no procedure in the camp for doing it, so we had these envelopes thrust into our hands at every stop. We had great amounts of them and we would have postage put on them, and they would be sent on." Marc and Neal Ball were moved by what Ball recalled as the refugees' "desperate need to connect with people outside. Sometimes there were questions about whether we knew of someone. Of course, the chance of our knowing the location of a refugee wasn't that great."

Prior to the mission, Ball had been in contact with Laotian refugees in Chicago, and he brought with him the names of three brothers, one married with one child. The refugee he had sponsored in Chicago had requested that he try to learn of their whereabouts as he hadn't heard from them in a very long time. "Two of them were thought to have been sent back to Laos after swimming across the Mekong River," Ball was told. Throughout his journey, Ball was struck by "the eagerness of these people to get word to family or friends, or try to make contact. They were pretty much cut off from communication."

As the rabbi and Ball made their way through the camps, they would ask questions concerning where the refugees were from, how long they had been in the camp, and how they had gotten there. "There was usually a harrowing story," Ball recalled. "They would pay money to someone who had a small fishing boat. Then that overloaded boat would be sent off. They didn't know where they were going." Marc also learned that refugees were often caught and returned to their chaotic homelands. Others would be besieged by pirates, who would raid their rescue ships and look for valuables of any kind. They would, on occasion, even throw the helpless passengers into the water. "Their stories were beyond belief," Ball recalled.

The mission participants' experiences rendered them physically exhausted, emotionally drained, and deeply frustrated, because, as Ball observed, "we knew that the refugees' needs went way beyond what we saw, and it showed no sign of being reduced."

During the mission, the American ambassador to Thailand, Morton Abramowitz, and his wife, both active in relieving the suffering of thousands of Vietnamese boat people, hosted a dinner at the US Embassy in Bangkok in honor of the mission participants. As the group was sitting down to dinner, an aide to the ambassador announced, "Billy Graham is opening a weeklong Crusade in Singapore tonight." "We need all the help we can get to persuade the Singapore authorities to change their policy and start taking in some of the boat people," the envoy replied.

"I know Billy Graham. We are good friends. I'll be glad to talk to him," Marc said.

"That's terrific!" Ambassador Abramowitz responded. An aide then called the US Embassy in Singapore, urgently requesting that an attempt be made to reach the evangelist by phone. Within the hour, Mr. Graham was on the line, pledging his assistance.

On the group's return to the United States during an interview with United Press International on December 18, Marc declared, "A world that stood by silently while Jewish lives became worthless is now a world that stands by silently while thousands of Boat People perish in the sea." And one year later to the day, on December 18, 1979, Marc testified before the US House of Representatives Foreign Affairs Committee's Subcommittee on Asian and Pacific Affairs, chaired by Representative Lester Wolff, a Democrat from New York.

While pointing out that he was not "an expert on refugee or rehabilitation programs," the rabbi stated that his experiences on those fact-finding missions "literally changed my life." Marc told the legislators of having walked through Aranyaprathet, among the first major camps in Thailand to have received Cambodian refugees. He testified to the subsistence in the facility's desolate medical clinic of 125 starving men, women, and children—youngsters who were "bags of bones, with bloated stomachs, hair turned orange by virtue of protein malnutrition." The rabbi told of a mother, "a starved wraith of a woman" who despite her condition was "going through the ritual of putting the flap of her breast into the mouth of a child, and she did not have enough nourishment to sustain her own life. Both of them collapsed and died."

To the rabbi, the sight of these emaciated corpses evoked memories of the bodies of the starved and otherwise brutalized Jewish inmates of the Nazi concentration camps of the Holocaust. "As an American Jew, I came away from the Nazi experience with an obsession that is an obsession for most Jewish people today," the rabbi told the Congressional committee, as epitomized in the paraphrase of a verse from the Book of Leviticus: "Tears cry out to you from the earth." The rabbi testified that he found it incredible that "we are here, calmly discussing statistics and conventional approaches as though this were just another social problem." He expressed his disbelief that

> forty years after the Nazi Holocaust, the international community can respond so blandly to the destruction of three million human beings in Cambodia, and then consider casually—as if it were a daily weather report—the horrendous fact that if this food is not gotten through in the next few months, some 200,000 people will die, and, by extrapolation, an estimated

two more million people will perish before our eyes within the period of the next six months or so.

The rabbi added that he could not grasp "how the international community can go on with its conventional affairs and not feel the urgent sense that the sanity of mankind is at stake here." The "cruel irony," he continued, "is that there is the capacity to provide that food *now*. It is on the borders of that country, and the whole issue of whether human beings will be kept alive or will die depends on politics and ideology— that is, the callous presumption that it is business as usual."

Contending that "the whole question of the value of life is at stake, and the whole meaning of human existence is at stake," the human rights rabbi then demanded of the legislators: "How many Nazi Holocausts, how many Cambodian genocides can the world endure and regard itself as worthwhile to continue?" Marc added:

> It seems to me that it is absolutely essential that in addition to the extraordinary contribution made by this committee and Congress—whose record has been, I think, one of the most glorious chapters in American history in terms of reflecting the generosity of American people and concern for this issue—an initiative must be taken *now*, not two months from now, to bring about an emergency conference through the United Nations, of the major nations of the world, including the United States, the Soviet Union, Vietnam, Cambodia, and China, before whom the issue of life and death survival is put.

Marc noted that there was a proposal "for organizing an international truck convoy," and he expressed his hope "that we can do everything possible to assure that that takes place within the coming weeks, and that we realize that the time factor is critical for the survival of a great many human beings."

Little more than three months later, on March 19, 1980, Marc would be among the representatives of American religious and secular agencies engaged in relief for Southeast Asian refugees to be thanked by Her Majesty Queen Sirikit of Thailand for their efforts. In an extraordinary departure from her nation's royal protocol, the monarch, who was visiting the United States to promote silk weaving and other Thai cottage industries, stood without aides at her side in her suite at the Waldorf Towers hotel in Manhattan. She then said to the attendees, "May I stand in a gesture to all of you. You are the people whom I have longed to meet and to whom I owe this tremendous sense of gratitude."

The queen, in her capacity as both honorary commander in chief of the Thai army regiment tasked with dealing with the refugees and president of her nation's Red Cross, was an advocate on behalf of the refugees. She had even spent the night in a crowded camp, where she witnessed "the compassion and care" shown by the American activists, who, she observed, "had fed and cleaned refugees too sick and too weak to care for themselves."

Now, amid the elegant trappings of the Waldorf Towers, Marc expressed his deep appreciation of the queen's efforts. Evoking the Jewish community's deeply painful memories of the trauma of the SS *St. Louis*, he said, "How different our history might have been had there been a Thailand in 1939." Then, speaking of the shared belief of Buddhists, Christians, and Jews in "the dignity of every human life created in the sacred image," the human rights rabbi said: "Thailand has become a symbol to the world of what a difference people can make."

The following year, in January, Liv Ullmann would open her mail one day to find an invitation from Marc to receive the American Jewish Committee's Distinguished Service Award during the agency's annual dinner in May. Responding to the rabbi on January 20, 1981, the actress said she would be both "honored" to accept the agency's accolade and "delighted to attend the Annual Banquet."

In 1981, Marc would return yet again to Asia. He would do so at a time of significant change in his personal life.

PART V

NEW PERSONAL AND PROFESSIONAL HORIZONS

CHAPTER 19

The Private Life
of a Public Man

"I was determined that I was going to connect him with Georgette.
It just hit me that this was the right man for her."
—Roz Goldberg, Jewish community activist,
retired financial services professional, and close friend of both
Dr. Georgette Bennett and Rabbi Tanenbaum

AS THE 1970S WERE COMING to an end, the human rights rabbi was
beset by exhaustion and personal loss.

The end of that tumultuous decade found him mourning the
death of his mother, Sadie, following a debilitating illness. When she
was hospitalized, Sadie summoned the strength to express her innate
optimism and love of Marc, Ernie, and Sima. At her funeral, Marc
eulogized his mother as a role model for tolerance and caring, his voice
trembling with emotion as he recalled his childhood with her. No
matter how bleak the family's financial circumstances, she had risen
early each morning and squeezed cups of fresh orange juice, which she
hand-delivered to her children while they were still in bed. He also
recalled Sadie's final days; her body ravaged, but her spirit intact.

The second loss was the sudden breakup of Marc's marriage to

Helga Weiss after twenty-two years. The couple had married in May 1955 and had three children: Adena, born in 1958; Michael, born in 1961; and Susan Johanna, born in 1964. Adena earned a PhD from Harvard, married an Oxford don, and spent several years in England. When she returned to the United States, as Adena Tanenbaum, she joined the faculty at Ohio State University as an associate professor of Near Eastern Languages and Cultures. Michael, quite the gentle soul, would end up living in Staten Island. Susan Johanna attended Vassar and Oberlin and became a social worker who now lives in Queens, New York.

The initial years of Marc's marriage to Helga Weiss seemed, by all outward appearances, to be harmonious. He took pride in her achievements—her PhD, her appointment by Mayor Koch to the New York City Commission on Human Rights. Yet, in the late 1970s, Helga asked Marc to move out of their home in Queens, and they went on to a bitter divorce. The children became estranged from their father. Years later, Marc would have some contact with Michael, but not with his daughters.

Although there are varying accounts, several things are clear. As Marc Tanenbaum became increasingly involved in his human rights and interreligious activities, there was little work/life balance. He brought his work home with him and was always preoccupied with it. He traveled widely and was often away from home. Even when he was in New York, he was often out, on weekdays and weekends, for breakfasts, lunches, and dinners, for daylong symposia and weekend-long conferences. Despite the rabbi's increasing professional obligations, in his view, he had remained a deeply involved, affectionate father to his children and a loving companion to his wife. The abrupt end to their marriage seems to indicate that Helga saw things very differently.

Observers noted that the relationship between Marc and Helga had become increasingly embittered. As his marriage was unraveling in the late 1970s, Marc would seek refuge with his sister Sima, her husband, and their children, Abby and Adam. The rabbi's niece and nephew understood that between all the traveling and all the problems within the family, their uncle was under an enormous amount of stress. As Adam recalled, "I would give him a wide berth and try not to be overbearing toward him, just to let him have his space, and let him have his peace and rest. He was always very tired and he would sleep for a long time."

Once revived, Adam recalled, the rabbi would regale the children with anecdotes "about some of his trips, and the personalities, and the egos involved—he was dealing with some pretty important people— and we would just listen in awe. We felt like we were privy to some information we wouldn't normally get."

Yet his own children missed that intimacy with their father.

Despite the trauma inherent in the impending dissolution of his marriage, as well as anxiety that his public image and moral authority would be compromised by divorce, Marc would confide to the AJC's Mimi Alperin in his 1980 oral history that he was yearning for a soul-mate with whom he could achieve personal harmony and further his work:

> I'm not a loner. I just hope someday I meet someone and we'll marry and rebuild some kind of personal life, 'cause it's not possible to continue living this kind of rich public life and not have the personal, emotional nurture that comes out of a relationship between two people who care for each other and depend on each other. I have not had too much of that.

Marc Tanenbaum could not have known that on that very day in 1980, unseen angels were at work. Noting that he longed for a life partner, Roz Goldberg, a lay leader at the AJC, had decided to introduce the iconic rabbi to her friend, Dr. Georgette Bennett.

Having served as a member of the AJC's board of directors, Roz Goldberg was personally acquainted with Marc Tanenbaum. She learned of his traumatic, "very painful, ugly, heartrending" divorce, which, she said, "had wounded him very deeply." At the suggestion of a mutual friend, the rabbi had initially asked Goldberg out on a date. The chemistry wasn't there, but the two would enjoy "a deep and abiding friendship." In that context, Goldberg came to know "that other, amazing, side of him—the kindness, the sweetness, the empathy."

Though she and Marc were not destined for romance, Roz Goldberg determined that Marc would be a good match for her friend.

Roz's pal Georgette Bennett had been born Francisca Gyorgyi Beitscher in Budapest to Holocaust survivors immediately following the war. She was acutely conscious of how terribly her parents had suffered under the Nazi occupation of Poland and Hungary. Scores of family members had been murdered, including her father's first family—a mother and two daughters who were shot in front of him during the selections in the Tarnow Ghetto.

In 1948, following the Moscow-imposed Communist coup, the Beitschers managed to escape from Hungary as stateless refugees. They fled first to France, where "Francisca Gyorgyi" became "Georgette Françoise," and then to the United States, where the family settled in Queens, New York. There she became Georgette Frances. Her father died one year after their arrival, when his daughter was only six years old. Georgette and her young, widowed mother were now left to fend for themselves. Nine years later, when Sidonie Beitscher sought US citizenship for herself and her teenaged daughter, she was offered the opportunity to change their name.

So traumatized was she by the war that she could not bear their Germanic surname. (The Beitschers had come by their name, as had other Central and Eastern European Jews, because of an edict imposed during the Austro-Hungarian Empire, requiring Jews to adopt German names, as a way for the emperor to deal with anti-Semitism.) Eager to rid herself of their German surname, she assigned Georgette the task of choosing their new name.

Georgette thought, "It should at least have the same number of syllables as our original name and should have the same first two letters." And so the resourceful girl thumbed through the Queens Telephone Directory to the "B's." There, she narrowed her choices to "Bentley,"

"Bennett," and "Bender." She recalled that Sylvia Bennett, a dress shop on Queens Boulevard, not far from where the Beitschers lived, always displayed very elegant clothes in its windows. "Bennett," she decided, was "the classiest of those three names." And thus, the Beitschers became the Bennetts.

Georgette would go on to graduate from Vassar and earn a doctorate in sociology from New York University, followed, later, by an advanced degree in banking. Her career included positions as a highly regarded criminologist, personal consultant to the New York City police commissioner, senior research associate at the Columbia University Center for Policy Research, executive in the New York City Office of Management and Budget, NBC News network correspondent, and founder of Bennett Associates, a consulting firm serving the insurance industry.

As she reached her early thirties, Dr. Bennett had accomplished much in her career, but her private life had not been fulfilling. In 1968, she had married her high school sweetheart, but they divorced in 1974. In contrast to Marc Tanenbaum's, Georgette's divorce was amicable, but she would go on to a series of unsatisfying relationships. Because of her rocky romantic life, she had become convinced that her "married days were over," and she became resigned "to living alone."

Meanwhile, following Roz's chance introduction to Georgette in 1977 at a holiday party, the two women became very close friends. As they confided in each other, Goldberg decided the time was ripe to introduce Georgette to the man whose intellectual curiosity and deeply caring nature, coupled with physical attractiveness, would cause Bennett to rethink her single lifestyle.

She decided to raise the matter with Georgette one evening early in March 1981. Yet, the more Goldberg extolled Marc Tanenbaum's virtues, the more the object of her attempted matchmaking was thinking: "What a turn-off!" A proud but secular Jew, Georgette simply could not envision dating a rabbi—even one so distinguished as Marc Tanenbaum. End of discussion.

But Roz Goldberg was determined to bring her reluctant friend face-to-face with the rabbi and then let nature take its course. To that end, she invited Georgette to join her on the evening of Monday, March 23, 1981, at St. Peter's Lutheran Church, in midtown Manhattan, where Marc was presiding over an American Jewish Committee–sponsored seminar on the Moral Majority, the controversial political movement founded by the Reverend Jerry Falwell.

The church was crowded that evening, but Georgette spotted an NBC cameraman with whom she had frequently worked while a reporter at the network. Making a beeline for him, she sat on the nearby steps as he recorded the event for airing the following Sunday. While she recalled that she "spent more time swapping war stories with him than I did sizing up the rabbi," Georgette acknowledged that Marc Tanenbaum's charisma did not escape her notice. But at program's end, the rabbi, looking at his watch, hurried off to the airport to catch a plane for California—a portent of what life with him would be like.

Wasting no time as they left the church, Roz demanded of Georgette, "How did you like him?" "He's very impressive and he's obviously very intelligent," she replied, "but I don't think I'm interested, Roz." Rabbi Tanenbaum, who was Georgette's senior by two decades, was "too old for me," she said.

Goldberg persisted, and Georgette finally agreed to meet the rabbi though she was beginning a relationship with a captivating man who was a supermarket mogul. The two men could not be more dissimilar. Days later, on Saturday, March 28, having just returned from California, Marc called Georgette. Their initial conversation was energetic, organic, intriguing. The formerly reluctant Georgette found herself responding to the rabbi in a new light. They decided to meet that very evening.

As the day wore on, the newly enthusiastic Georgette took the time to consider the impression she wished to make on the mature, serious rabbi. She opted for well-tailored gray slacks set off by a burgundy turtleneck sweater. Meanwhile, Marc was steeling himself for another "courtesy" blind date. Having never met Georgette, he was certain he was being set up with a sweet, yet unappealing middle-aged woman. As he arrived at Georgette's front door at the appointed hour, he was primed for what he assumed would be another wasted evening.

Then he rang the bell. As Dr. Bennett opened the door, he blurted out in surprise, "You're lovely!" "*You're* lovely, too!" she replied. But as her eye traveled from the celebrated rabbi's finely chiseled face to his well-proportioned torso, she experienced a momentary twinge. He, too, was clad in a turtleneck sweater. But his trousers and jacket were made from polyester—hardly suitable attire, his chic date thought, for one who was revered as "the Secretary of State for the Jews." Beguiled by the rabbi's warmth of personality, however, Georgette summoned her "better self" and decided to overlook the imperfections of his wardrobe.

Georgette and Marc would spend the remainder of the evening revealing themselves to each other, sharing memories both pleasurable and deeply painful. To Marc, Georgette was a person of seeming contradictions. On the one hand, she eschewed religious ritual and had dated gentile men. On the other hand, she had studied the writings of Martin Buber as well as Marc's own mentor, Rabbi Abraham Joshua Heschel, and other renowned Jewish scholars at Vassar. She had also studied the sociology of religion as a doctoral student at New York University. While her life seemed thin on observance, she was deeply immersed in Jewish values and scholarship.

During their memorable first date, the rabbi revealed his own story of having renounced the strictures of his Orthodox Judaism. Early on, Georgette characterized Marc as "a rabbinic maverick." His nondogmatic approach was what she credited for his ability to accept her own freethinking approach to Jewish identity and practice.

As the evening wore on, Georgette intuited that Marc was frightened by their obvious attraction to each other. Realizing that "this fragile new nectar needed to be sipped, not gulped," she steered him toward the door through which he had entered many hours earlier.

Before venturing out into the night, the rabbi made plans to see Georgette on the following weekend. In the interim, he would be off to

London to attend meetings of the International Council of Christians and Jews.

The next day, during brunch with a friend, Georgette confided: "I think I met the man I'm going to marry last night."

CHAPTER 20

More Oy Than Joy—A Year of Indecision and Turmoil

I walked along the rim of the world
Along the sun-blanched beach edging the great ocean
I walked with you along that rim of creation
Hugging it, feeling, tasting it fresh as if a first time
at the beginning of it all.
It was a walk of mystery, hand-in-clasped hand
Not the hand of flesh of your marvelous body self
But the grasped hand of your life-filling presence.

—An excerpt from "For Georgette,"
a poem written by Marc Tanenbaum in August 1981

GEORGETTE'S CONFIDENT BRUNCH DECLARATION NOTWITHSTANDING, in the coming months she would "do nothing but give Marc a hard time; it was amazing that he stuck with me because I was in a state of panic," she said. Within days of leaving for London, the rabbi was calling long distance—the beginning of his practice of touching base with Georgette by telephone from wherever in the world he happened to be on a given day. His sonorous voice, with its contrasting nuances of strength and yearning, never ceased to pierce her heart.

His call was followed by "an absolutely beautiful letter" addressed to "My Dear Lovely Francesca Georgette": "I think I perpetrated a fraud on TWA coming over the Atlantic. I paid for one air ticket and there were two of us all the way. It was such a high that when I stretched out across three empty seats to sleep the tumbling hours away, it felt cozier, more peaceful and reviving than ever before. Imagine the alchemy had you been actually present rather than the sensibilities that I embraced and would not let go." He went on to describe the substance of that first evening's 8 p.m. Jewish caucus strategy meeting. The seemingly staid rabbi expressed his hope that during his presentation the next morning, on "The Images of Christians and Christianity in Jewish Teaching and Culture," he would be able to "repress the temptation to blurt out" certain of Georgette's epigrams.

As Georgette read and reread the rabbi's enchanting prose, she thought to herself: This is a man of extraordinary depth, passion, and wit. Here is a man to whom I could make an ultimate commitment and who would make one to me—a man to trust, a man to love, a man with whom to feel safe, everything for which I have been searching. The perfect denouement to a turbulent personal journey. Yet Georgette—with her complex history—was thrown into an emotional tailspin. The supermarket mogul was still in her life, and she was torn between two extraordinary, albeit different, men.

The day following Marc's return, an old family friend, Randolph Braham, was being honored by the World Federation of Hungarian Jewry for his work in documenting the near-destruction of the Jews of Georgette's native land during the Holocaust. Marc accompanied Georgette to that gathering, where they were greeted by Georgette's close relatives, Olga and Gary "Pips" Phillips, who were Holocaust survivors. Soon Marc Tanenbaum's presence was broadcast throughout the room. Guests began to approach him, Georgette recalled, "to pay homage" to the celebrated rabbi. Georgette had dated a fair number of notables, but she had never before witnessed the kind of reverence that was now being shown to this man.

On Sunday, April 12, 1981, Georgette accompanied Marc to the stately Holy Trinity Cathedral on Manhattan's East 74th Street for the wedding of New York's widowed governor, Hugh Carey, to the dynamic Greek-born real estate magnate Evangeline Goulatis. The Greek Orthodox service was conducted by Archbishop Iakovos, the rabbi's close friend and comrade-in-arms in countless human rights struggles.

Following the religious ceremony, the rabbi and Georgette attended the celebrity-filled reception held at the rooftop ballroom of the St. Regis Hotel on Fifth Avenue. Later, as they were leaving, they were followed to the elevator by New York State Governor Mario Cuomo. The two men stopped to chat about Cuomo's coming gubernatorial race. Georgette was struck, yet again, by the fact that everybody seemed to know and admire the man she was dating.

Georgette and the rabbi continued to see each other, as their intense professional travel schedules allowed. He would fly to Baltimore, Boston, Cincinnati, Dallas, Maxwell Air Force Base, Mobile, and Pittsburgh. Her travels took her to Atlanta to consult with police chief Lee Brown and to Los Angeles to tape a segment of *Hour Magazine*. She was also working with HBO on a treatment for a crime-prevention series the cable network had asked her to develop for them.

The affable supermarket mogul was still on the scene, in hindsight as a security blanket of sorts. Georgette's lighthearted, platonic dates with him stood in sharp contrast to those with the rabbi—profound encounters that would leave her with a sense of emotional heaviness. Georgette and Marc, two accomplished, complicated individuals, nevertheless had a dating history with each other more fitting to celebrities. When Georgette and Marc spent time together, invariably, one or the other would become frightened and pull away. The fact that another man stood in the wings, vying for Georgette's affections, was irksome . . . no matter how many times Georgette assured him that their bond was not romantic. Yet Georgette just wasn't ready to commit.

In the months to come, as Georgette continued to date casually, Marc persisted in sending charming, romantically infused, notes. Some of them were accompanied by press clippings—photographs of himself with other celebrated newsmakers: Pope John Paul II, Billy Graham, and Bishop Fulton J. Sheen. In others, the rabbi recalled his childhood experiences, his motivations for building bridges among the religions, and his thoughts about recent missions to Southeast Asia on behalf of refugees.

These clippings served to increase Georgette's admiration for Marc but would also plunge her headlong into a cycle of paralyzing ambivalence. Adding to her turmoil was the rabbi's often gloomy frame of mind. As she recalled: "His moods were dark; his clothes were dark; even his *car* was dark."

Yet by May, despite their approach-avoid pattern, Georgette and Marc were seeing each other almost every day. On May 8, Georgette finally broke off her relationship with the supermarket executive, thus removing a major self-imposed emotional obstacle.

Georgette alternated between running from the rabbi's embrace and welcoming his reassuring presence. She was uncomfortable with the idea of making a new life with a man whose generational views, style, and world seemed so alien to her own. Yet Marc could amaze and delight her by continuing to reveal his more carefree side.

On Memorial Day weekend of 1981, Marc was in Omaha for the wedding of his brother's son. His sister, Sima, and niece, Abby, also attended the festivities. Abby recalled that she had never before seen her distinguished uncle "light up as much as he did when telling us that he'd met this great person, and that he just adored her." Nonetheless, within three days, this romance would be derailed again. Marc was still troubled by Georgette's friendships with other men. Enough, she insisted! She wanted no more of the rabbi's "wrathful God" judgments and refused to assure him about their future. Feeling rejected, the rabbi called it quits.

Marc's retreat had a cataclysmic effect on Georgette, shocking her into realizing that she had just pushed away the best man she would ever know. She was certain that she had to win him back. So, on the following Monday, despite being unsure about whether the rabbi would even take her call, she telephoned his office. They agreed to meet for lunch two days later. Marc was late. Georgette was anxious as she waited. When he finally did appear, he launched the romantic equivalent of a nuclear warhead: he informed Georgette that, having felt both angry and rejected, he had reached out to the woman he had been dating prior to embarking on their relationship.

That news was a huge shock to Georgette. But every instinct told her that this was a pivotal moment. Just before saying good-bye, she and Marc slipped into the restaurant's cloakroom for a long embrace. The woman who had seemingly been spurned moments earlier knew now that she had won back Marc's heart—if, indeed, she had ever really lost it.

Unsurprisingly, there were more bumps in the road in the months to come. These two extraordinary, self-made people sought to find that sweet spot between intimacy and independence. For Marc, there would be continuing unease over Georgette's wish to maintain relationships, however innocent, with male friends. For Georgette, Marc's failure to call at an appointed time after their reunion had devastating consequences.

Marc had gone off to his beloved beach house in Loveladies, New Jersey. Left on her own in her Greenwich Village apartment, Georgette spent time with neighbors who were organizing a trip to the Far East. When the expected call from Marc failed to materialize, in a fit of pique, she told her friends, "I'm in!" By the time Marc returned from the weekend and made his overdue call, he was greeted with the news that Georgette was soon to leave for Asia. But by the time of her departure, they had revived their fragile tendrils of trust. Immediately before Georgette left for the airport, Marc brought her a packet of yen for her arrival in Japan—a protective gesture that touched her deeply. She boarded the plane, regretting that she had ever agreed to make this trip. But, once in Tokyo, the quartet energetically followed their itinerary.

When the group arrived in Taipei, Georgette worked on an assignment for Merrill Lynch—a feasibility study regarding the Taipei World Trade Center, in which the company was considering an investment.

With Georgette's meetings in Taipei completed, the group was scheduled to fly to the other side of Taiwan to do some sightseeing. The friends raced to catch their flight but missed it. Barely two hours later, that plane crashed, and all of the passengers were killed.

Back in New York, Marc was listening to WINS, where he was a weekly commentator, and also a habitual listener. Suddenly, he heard the newscaster announce the crash of an airplane on the other side of the world. He knew Georgette was supposed to be on that flight. He frantically called the news desk at WINS. "Please," he begged, "you *must* get me a copy of the passenger manifest for that plane."

Hours passed. A distraught Marc assumed that Georgette was dead. Then he heard her voice, and the world righted itself again. And she, hearing of his valiant efforts to learn her fate, again felt embraced and protected by him.

After Georgette returned from the Far East, the couple realized that they needed some healing time together. That came along in the form of a long and magical weekend at Pebble Beach. While there were some anxious moments for Georgette en route from San Francisco, her tensions soon melted away as she and the rabbi experienced "four days of utter bliss and beauty." At the conclusion of their trip, Marc and Georgette parted company, he to spend ten days as a scholar-in-residence at the Brandeis-Bardin Institute, and she to return home to New York.

It didn't take long after Marc returned to New York for him to propose to Georgette. Shedding the last of her ambivalence about their age difference, Georgette said to herself: "Ten good years with this man are worth a lifetime with any other man." That insight would turn out to be prophetic.

The *New York Times* announcement of the engagement of "Georgette Bennett and Rabbi Marc Tanenbaum" prompted Marc's close friend, Rabbi Wolfe Kelman, to exclaim, "Marc: *Bennett*? *Bennett*? Aren't you taking this interreligious stuff too far"? "No," he responded. "She's *Jewish*!"

Marc and Georgette exchanged vows on June 6, 1982, at Manhattan's Park Avenue Synagogue, in a ceremony conducted by

Rabbi Judah Nadich, the synagogue's spiritual leader. He was assisted by Rabbis Israel Mowshowitz and James Rudin, the groom's close colleague at the American Jewish Committee, and the bride's colleague, Judge Luis Neco.

Their honeymoon would be a monthlong odyssey retracing millennia of Jewish history. They traveled first to Egypt, the land of the Jews' liberation by Moses from enslavement four thousand years earlier. And then it was on to Israel. At Cairo airport, the sight of the El Al plane's tail against the Egyptian sky took Georgette's breath away. But this exodus, she observed, "was 30 minutes by air instead of 40 years through the Sinai Desert." It would be Georgette's first visit to the Jewish state. Upon disembarking, she dropped to her knees and kissed the ground. Her presence in this hallowed place would be her family's triumphal answer to Hitler's Final Solution.

Setting out on a tour of the nation, the couple went to the usual Jewish historical sights. But in a manner typical of the rabbi's many previous visits there, they also spent time in Arab villages, meeting residents, along with Interns for Peace, an organization run by Rabbi Bruce Cohen.

For Georgette, there awaited an intensely personal experience in Israel. She would learn more about the father she had barely known and, much to her surprise, about other relatives she hadn't even known existed. She knew that her father, Ignace Beitscher, had had two sisters —one of whom, Maria, who had escaped from Poland with him and found refuge in Israel. Having received occasional letters and gifts from her aunt, she looked her up in Israel, only to learn that she had died. Neighbors directed her to a cousin of whose existence she had been completely unaware. From him, she learned that she had an uncle who had settled in Brooklyn. Having grown up with almost no family, this was a new and welcome link to her father.

Following their return from their Middle East honeymoon, the couple would live for a time in Georgette's apartment in Greenwich Village before moving to a new building located on Madison Avenue in Manhattan's elegant Carnegie Hill neighborhood.

In the years to come, Marc would show himself to be open to new, even highly controversial, ideas. For example, he came to know Norman Lear, who in the 1970s created barrier-breaking TV programs such as *All in the Family, Maude, Good Times*, and *The Jeffersons*. In 1981, Lear would found People For the American Way (PFAW) as a counterweight to the Religious Right, with Marc as a cofounder. Noting that "the ultrafundamentalist leadership has found a way to use their pulpits to literally terrorize political opponents—a tactic that smacked of 'moral McCarthyism'"—Lear told Marc, "I want you to know that—together—we will mount the most effective challenge the Religious Right has ever seen. And America will be a better place for it!"

As a criminologist, Georgette had become deeply interested in the link between religion and violence. At a time when religious zealots felt justified in blowing up abortion clinics and dehumanizing secular humanists, she was an avid believer in PFAW's mission. Meanwhile, Roz Goldberg described the rabbi's involvement with People For the American Way as "a perfect manifestation of Marc's commitment to the principles of human rights and dignity and tolerance."

However, tensions would soon arise in their marriage. Ever conscious of their age difference, the rabbi often interpreted his wife's outgoing personality as flirtatious. The couple eventually found their balance: for Marc, it was a greater sense of freedom; for Georgette, it was a bit more restraint. More difficult was the issue of time. The rabbi's work knew no boundaries. With his piles of papers growing ever higher, his home was as much of a work site as his AJC office. He would often forget the pledge he had made to Georgette to carve out private time with her.

Thus, there would be many frustrating weekends when they were supposed to go out. "I would be watching the clock very impatiently," she recalled. "Marc, it's two o'clock; Marc, it's three o'clock; Marc, it's four o'clock. Damn it, Marc, you *promised!*" That would happen frequently, according to Georgette, because "His work was the 'other woman' in our relationship."

Despite the rabbi's preoccupation with work, their time together was intense and passionate. Whether they were taking a long walk, a drive in the country, or holding hands at the movies, they shared "really wonderful times of togetherness." The rabbi not only introduced Georgette to his colleagues in the interreligious sphere over the years, but encouraged her in her own career. In 1987, when she was seeking jacket blurbs for her soon-to-be-published book, *Crime Warps: The Future of Crime in America*, the rabbi reached out to his boldface contacts. As a result, the book was published with endorsements from Justice Arthur Goldberg, Governor Mario Cuomo, Norman Lear, and Billy Graham, among others.

CHAPTER 21

Denouement:
A Decisive Personal Pivot

"It surprised me because he had become so well known in this field that it just seemed to me that 'interfaith' and Marc Tanenbaum were interchangeable. But Marc wanted new challenges and, of course, the interfaith work had been global; it had been international; it involved so much diplomacy. . . . So those skills were readily transferable."

—David Harris, executive director, American Jewish Committee

"He knew what he wanted; he was committed and sincere about many issues and, certainly, about those in which I was then involved, the whole range of European experiences following World War II— the remnants of Nazism, Eastern Germany, Israel, and, eventually, Soviet Jewry-related issues."

—Jerry Goodman, former director, the American Jewish Committee's Department of European Affairs, founding executive director, National Conference on Soviet Jewry (NCSJ)

IN 1983, A YEAR AFTER his marriage to Georgette, Marc decided that after two eventful decades as the AJC's groundbreaking director of Interreligious Affairs, it was time for a change. The Human Rights

Rabbi decided to employ his considerable skills, already honed in the corridors of the Vatican and throughout the world, in the increasingly challenging realm of international relations. Thus, he sought to become the head of the AJC's International Affairs Department.

In many ways, this move seemed like a natural transition. But Howard Friedman, the committee's president at that time, was quite surprised by the rabbi's proposal. At the same time, he said, "In some respects, it was an extension of what he had been doing in interreligious affairs." Marc's proposed portfolio change also took several of the committee's staff members by surprise, among them Jerry Goodman and Irving Levine. "I thought at first that it was a little unusual, and a mistake," Goodman recalled. In contrast to one of Marc's predecessors, Polish-born Dr. Simon Segal, who "had extensive European experience," Marc "was *American*." However, given the rabbi's extensive contacts in Rome and in the committee's Paris office, Goodman would come to believe that the rabbi "was qualified to head the American Jewish Committee's International Affairs program."

It was not until Marc assumed his new portfolio that David Harris, who later became the AJC's executive vice president, would become well acquainted with him. Harris was to be Marc's deputy, and he recalled, "My office was next to his. We were in each other's office many times a day when we were both in New York, and so I got to know Marc on a deeply personal level."

Almost immediately on assuming his new post in 1983, Marc embarked on a demanding schedule of high-profile meetings in the United States and abroad.

First came Mexico. Late in his first year as the committee's director of International Relations, a member of Mexico's House of Representatives disparaged Jewish residents of his nation during a legislative session. Marc immediately demanded that the Mexican government disavow the legislator's blatantly anti-Semitic remarks. Early the next year, on January 19, 1984, Marc, accompanied by committee lay leaders, conferred with local government officials and members of the Jewish community in Mexico City.

In May, an agency delegation met in New York with Mexico's president, Miguel de la Madrid. At that time, Marc urged the Mexican leader to intervene with Soviet officials on behalf of Russian dissidents Andrei Sakharov and his Jewish wife, Yelena Bonner. The rabbi noted that "Bonner faces imminent death unless the Soviet authorities allow her to obtain immediate medical treatment."

Marc and committee lay leaders also traveled to Paris to confer with President François Mitterrand prior to his visit to the United States. Their discussion also focused on Soviet Jewry as well as France's relations with Israel. Later that year, the rabbi arranged a meeting in New York with Foreign Minister Dante Caputo of Argentina to discuss that nation's intention to pass legislation banning anti-Semitism, racism, and all forms of discrimination.

There continued to be controversy within the American Jewish community regarding the AJC's cooperation with Reverend Billy Graham. Marc made it clear that the evangelical leader had strongly advocated for Soviet Jews during recent, private meetings with Soviet leaders.

The year 1985 would also be equally busy. In January, Marc met privately in New York with the Italian defense minister, Giovanni Spadolini, to discuss the issues of Middle East peace and terrorism. Early the following month, the rabbi and a committee delegation met with Minister Spadolini and other government officials in Rome. And on February 15, Marc and a committee delegation met with Pope John Paul II in the Vatican's Apostolic Palace.

In the coming days, Marc revealed that Jacobo Kovadloff, the committee's director of South American Affairs, had visited Cuba on three occasions in the past two years to express solidarity with the eight-hundred-member Cuban Jewish community.

Meanwhile, in the spring of 1985, as has been noted, Marc was summoned to Washington to help defuse the crisis created when President Reagan agreed to visit the Bitburg cemetery in Germany.

During another visit to Washington in 1985, Marc conferred with Spanish Embassy officials to discuss Spain's intention to establish diplomatic relations with Israel.

In 1986, Rabbi Tanenbaum traveled to Austria. There, an agreement was reached to establish a joint American Jewish Committee–Austrian government working group to implement a program designed to stem anti-Semitism in that nation. During that year, the rabbi also encouraged the Polish Roman Catholic Church to establish seminars "on the meaning of Auschwitz to Christians and Jews."

During 1987, he would continue to maintain his whirlwind, globe-trotting schedule.

Rabbi Tanenbaum, along with other Jewish leaders, met in New York with Cardinal Augostino Casaroli, the Vatican's secretary of state, and other Vatican officials. During that session, the participants engaged in what the rabbi characterized as a no-holds-barred discussion concerning Pope John Paul II's granting of an audience to the Austrian president Kurt Waldheim, whose pro-Nazi activities during World War II had recently been revealed.

In late August, Marc and other Jewish leaders participated in a nine-hour-long meeting with church officials in the Vatican. After an additional session the following day, the Jewish and Catholic conferees were driven to Castel Gandolfo, the pontiff's summer residence, where they met for more than an hour with John Paul II.

Later that year and into 1988, Marc, in his role as chairman of the International Jewish Committee on Interreligious Consultations, led numerous discussions with his Catholic counterparts on various issues. These issues included the Vatican's recognition of Israel, the controversy over the removal of the Carmelite convent from the grounds of Auschwitz, and changes in Catholic teaching on Jews and Judaism.

In his role as the director of international relations, Marc was also involved in China, Japan, Eastern Europe, Lebanon, Syria, South Africa, Tibet, and Turkey, as well as with the United Nations. And amid all his traveling, he continued to pursue his activities in black-Jewish relations, expressed keen interest in women's rights, and participated in the National Coalition Against Pornography.

After four years at this job, how was Marc faring? AJC's Jerry

Goodman said, "It turned out to be okay." Indeed, he added, "In hind-sight, it was excellent."

There were mixed reviews outside the AJC. For example, Father John Pawlikowski said, "I don't think it was the best move. I think he found it difficult. One would have to say he wasn't nearly as successful in that area as he was in Christian-Jewish relations." But many oth-ers found Marc to be an effective leader and spokesman focused on issues with which he had already become engaged during his decades as director of interreligious affairs.

In any case, in early 1987, as Marc continued to pursue his inter-national agenda, he was also contemplating a different journey in his professional life. He would soon be sixty-two years old, and he began taking steps that would lead to his retirement from the agency where for more than a quarter of a century he had held two major portfolios.

Bertram Gold announced that, following many years of service as the committee's executive vice president, he would be leaving. Rabbi David Gordis would be appointed to that position. But Gordis would soon be forced out, and Bert Gold would return to the agency until his second successor could be selected. Gold's initial decision to retire had engendered speculation that Marc hoped to assume his position. That was hardly the case, according to Georgette. "Marc always told me that he was *not* interested in doing so," she said, noting that the rabbi desired to retire so as to have more time to pursue other interests.

Despite Marc's determination to retire, several of his colleagues believe that he would have been eminently qualified to succeed Gold. As Irving Levine observed, "Marc was a substance guy and a pretty good reader. He kept things together. He knew how to orchestrate his different divas. We were divas. And Marc was the *biggest* diva!" For his part, Jerry Goodman believed that the rabbi "could have been a good person to head the American Jewish Committee: he had a broad range of interests, and he had many contacts in the Jewish and non-Jewish worlds, which would have been an asset." While Goodman noted that the rabbi did not possess the traditional American Jewish Committee staff person's background in social work and sociology, "he had *other* assets." Thus, "it would have been fine if he *had* become the agency's chief executive."

But Marc was determined to pursue his own personal agenda. Thus, in early 1987, he would begin a protracted, seven-month-long series of negotiations with the committee. Its in-house team would be headed by Bert Gold and Theodore "Ted" Ellenoff, the president of the agency. The negotiations were decidedly formal, with each side represented by legal counsel.

Marc was not planning to completely absent himself from the committee. He wanted to serve as a consultant to the agency for the immediate future, and on March 2, 1987, he outlined his hoped-for agenda in a confidential memorandum addressed to Ted Ellenoff.

In that four-page, single-spaced communication, titled "International Relations Program Priorities for 1987–88," the rabbi stated, "In keeping with our recent conversation, I see the following international relations projects/programs as major efforts that I would seek to undertake during 1987–88." Marc, who was hardly unfamiliar with organizational imperatives, added that his proposed program was "designed, among other reasons, to lend dramatic distinction to the Ted Ellenoff presidency."

Marc put forward a long list of nations with which he sought to interact. And in order to fulfill his complex agenda, he had one major caveat: he must be able "to function in relative freedom and with a reasonable measure of agency support; such as, the ability to inform AJC leadership adequately about these programs in order to elicit and sustain their moral and financial support." For all of these programs, the rabbi added, the committee "should find effective ways to tell our AJC membership about these programs and, also, seek where appropriate, maximum exposure for you and other AJC officers in the press, TV, and radio. I stand ready to help in every way."

On November 7, Rabbi Tanenbaum received a formal letter from Messrs. Gold and Ellenoff that noted that the rabbi had advised the agency of his plan to retire on October 13, 1990, on his sixty-fifth birthday. While indicating that he would continue to work as a full-time employee until that date, and following that time as a special consul-tant to the agency, in their letter, the committee's team specifically sought to inhibit the rabbi from working for two other agencies—the Anti-Defamation League and the American Jewish Congress, both of which could be seen as having similar briefs as the AJC. The protracted negotiations would culminate with the rabbi receiving a financial set-tlement upon relinquishing his post as director of international affairs and becoming a consultant to the agency.

Toward the end of an agency board meeting that fall, Bert Gold announced that the rabbi would be retiring at the end of the following year. The committee's voice on interreligious harmony and global out-reach would now have time to revisit his long-held ambition to write—he was working on two books for a major publisher. More important, he would now be able to travel and enjoy an abundance of cultural interests with Georgette.

And—unbeknownst to all but a few of the couple's closest friends—Georgette and Marc were thinking of having a child.

CHAPTER 22

Kimpitur!

"It was really magical! Marc was standing there, next to me, trying to keep me from falling apart because I had been a nervous wreck for days; the suspense was just killing me."

—Dr. Georgette Bennett, recalling the moment she and Rabbi Tanenbaum learned that she was pregnant

ON THE LATE AFTERNOON OF December 23, 1991, Georgette Bennett and Marc Tanenbaum were awaiting what they fervently hoped would be a life-altering telephone call from the in vitro fertilization clinic at New York Hospital–Cornell Medical Center. She had been assured that she would hear one way or the other by five o'clock.

When the call didn't come by the appointed hour, taking matters into her own hands, she dialed the clinic's telephone number. Her nerves taut with suspense, she said: "Hi, this is Georgette Bennett. I was supposed to get the results of my pregnancy test, and I haven't heard from anyone yet." The results were still being processed; someone would call her shortly, the disembodied voice replied.

Minutes later—it was now 5:07—the telephone finally rang. "Congratulations!" the caller exclaimed: "You're pregnant!" As Georgette, drained now from her ordeal of anticipation, collapsed in relief, her ecstatic soul mate hugged her. He then uttered a word she had never heard before. *"Kimpitur!"* he exclaimed, intoning the Yiddish-language endearment for an expectant mother.

It had been a tumultuous journey, mostly emotionally but partially physically, for the couple since the day several years earlier when they first debated the pros and cons of having a child at such advanced ages. The irrepressible Roz Goldberg had been urging her close friend on. But as reluctant to consider parenthood as she once was to date a rabbi, Georgette Bennett at first demurred. She would eventually overcome her profound ambivalence, to embark on what would turn out to be an uncertain, often painful, reproductive odyssey.

Marc was also hesitant. He already had three children, two of them estranged and one troubled, from his first marriage, and he was now discussing parenthood with a spouse who was twenty-one years younger than he. He would often declare, "I wish I had met you twenty years ago and had a family with you; what a different experience it would have been!"

Yet it would be comforting for Marc to know that his much younger wife would have the love and company of their child in the likelihood that he passed away before her. For Georgette, a child would be a way to memorialize the very special love she and Marc shared. In addition, as a child of the Holocaust, she yearned to deny Hitler a posthumous victory. "At the very least," she explained, "I wanted to give one Jew back for all the members of my family who perished in the fires of the Nazi ovens and the hail of their bullets."

On October 13, 1985, the couple had celebrated Marc's sixtieth birthday—albeit separated by thousands of miles. The rabbi's travel schedule had reached what Georgette regarded as "the apex of insanity"—flying trips to Brazil, Miami, Milwaukee, Rome, and, finally, South Africa, all undertaken within a single month.

Marc was in Johannesburg when he collapsed. He was hospitalized and diagnosed with pneumonia. Two weeks transpired before physicians determined that the virus had not lodged in his heart. But his heartbeats had become irregular, and he would undergo a cardioversion in which an electric current is sent through the heart to shock that organ into normal rhythm. Now Marc added a heart condition to his list of concerns about embarking on parenthood.

Another year went by. It was now 1987, and Georgette, at forty-one years of age, was embarking on a new career, this time as a vice president of the First Woman's Bank, a landmark financial institution founded by women. Working twelve-hour days, she advanced to the post of chief marketing officer and senior vice president for private banking within eighteen months.

At that point in Georgette's very busy life, motherhood faded as a priority. But the unresolved issue would surface from time to time. Georgette was hoping that her husband would make up her mind for her, and he was waiting for her to tell him that she was ready for motherhood.

Then, once again, *life* intervened. In 1988, while Marc was preparing to leave for Boston, he collapsed in their bathroom. Unable to maneuver him into a position in which she could administer CPR, Georgette tore down the hallway screaming for any neighbor to help her. His heart had stopped beating, but thanks to a next-door neighbor who heard her cries, Georgette was able to do CPR while waiting for the paramedics. By the time they arrived, Marc was, technically, dead. Miraculously, the paramedics were able to resuscitate the rabbi. But from that moment on, his heart rhythm would be regulated only by taking powerful drugs.

And life and death would become wed to each other—inseparable—in this final chapter of their marriage.

With Marc having stared death down and won—at least for the moment—was parenthood now out of the question? If not now, *when*? While Georgette was pulled away with business travel to Brazil and Mexico, Marc was spending more and more time working at home.

The couple went about debating the pros, as well as the considerable cons, of parenthood at this stage in their lives—they were now sixty-three and forty-three years of age, respectively.

On a friend's recommendation, Georgette made an appointment

with Dr. Richard Hausknecht, a fertility specialist. Four months later—it was now March 1990—Dr. Hausknecht performed a laparoscopy that revealed the need for major surgery, requiring a long recuperation. Given the huge odds against success, the specialist said that it would be unethical for him to put Georgette under the scalpel. Now in vitro fertilization would be Georgette's only chance—and a slim one at that—for conceiving a biological child.

But Georgette was nearly forty-four years old and the rabbi approaching his sixty-fifth birthday. At this stage in their lives, how would they be able to find the energy to care for a healthy, lively youngster?

As fate would have it, on Georgette's return from work one day in late 1990, the rabbi would press a slip of paper into her hand that could change their lives. On it was written a name: Dr. Ernst Bartsich. Marc Tanenbaum, like his father before him, was a self-confessed "news junkie." He had just watched a report by Earl Ubell, the local WCBS television science reporter—a close friend and mentor of Georgette's—about a doctor "who has a technique for doing fibroid surgery and still saving the uterus," the rabbi said, adding, "Maybe you ought to see him."

The couple's arrival in a most unusual medical office—a place strewn with oriental rugs and lovely antique furniture—would mark the next step in their parenting odyssey. Dr. Bartsich would refer Georgette to the Israeli-born fertility specialist Dr. Zev Rosenwaks. On March 22, 1991, following much hesitation and a series of tests to determine Georgette's eligibility for the IVF program, Dr. Bartsich performed the surgery that might enable her to carry a child to term. Even more important to Georgette, the surgeon promised to press Dr. Rosenwaks to admit her to his IVF program—and he would do so despite the fact that forty-two was the cutoff age for participation.

On July 1, despite Georgette's anticipation of being promoted to the post of executive vice president at her workplace, she would instead become a victim of "downsizing." The bank said it simply couldn't afford her any longer. One year later, the bank went under. Freed, for better or worse, from any immediate career-related pressures, Georgette would now go full steam ahead with her medical plans. Finally, in October, she and Marc obtained an appointment with the one specialist who could hold the key to their aspiration for parenthood.

Now, on the day of their long-awaited appointment, Georgette and Marc were ushered into an office. Soon, two male physicians entered the room. One of them had flowing blond hair, sea-blue eyes, fair skin, and the physique of a latter-day Adonis—an Aryan poster boy, Georgette Bennett thought. But, she wondered: where was Dr. Rosenwaks, the Sabra—the native-born Israeli she had waited so long to see?

As the doctor stood there, flipping through the pages of this patient's chart, he paused. Looking puzzled, he asked Georgette: "What is your *real* age"? Realizing that the specialist standing before her was, in fact, Zev Rosenwaks, Georgette sheepishly fessed up: "I'm forty-five. I lied about my age, and I hated doing that. But I thought it was the only way I could get into your program. I'm glad you caught me."

And thus began Georgette Bennett and Marc Tanenbaum's punishing, but ultimately rewarding, ordeal to achieve their daunting goal. Six of Georgette's ova would eventually be extracted from her body and placed in the petri dish for uniting with her husband's gametes. Following that procedure, the couple would receive wonderful news: three of the eggs had been fertilized! They were now embryos. The next step in the couple's quest for parenthood, the long-anticipated transfer of fertilized ova to Georgette's uterus, would have to be precisely timed. That momentous event would take place on a Friday evening, the Jewish Sabbath.

The procedure completed, a nurse handed Georgette a Polaroid photo of her three tiny embryos, taken through a microscope only moments earlier as they were literally growing before her eyes in the petri dish. Georgette's spirits soaring as she was wheeled out of the operating room, she spotted Marc waiting there. Thrusting the Polaroid pictures into his hands, she cried out: "Here are your children!"

Moments later, the couple, together now in the clinic's recovery room, gazed at the images of the three tiny beings they had created.

There would be one more hurdle to surmount: a pregnancy test. The couple would then have to wait ten days for the results. Georgette would be required to undergo yet another procedure a week later—a blood test confirming that her pregnancy was firmly established. As she was driving to the center on the morning of December 30—she was rushing in order get there before the 8:30 deadline for learning the results that day—her car was broadsided by a huge Mack truck. Badly shaken but not *physically* injured, she wondered: has the truck driver destroyed my fragile two-week-old pregnancy? Fortunately, he had not. And despite Georgette's late arrival at the clinic, the staff responded to her urgent plea to do the test and provide the results as scheduled.

By the end of that day, her pregnancy would be confirmed and her due date calculated. On hearing the news, the delighted father-to-be would post this entry in his diary for September 3, 1992: "MESSIAH EXPECTED." As the jubilant couple eagerly anticipated that day, they would often revisit the blurry Polaroids of their embryos.

But quite a different sort of shadowy image was now clouding their every waking moment. This was no fuzzy photographic depiction. Rather, a heavy dose of reality was intruding on their joy.

Marc Tanenbaum's health was failing.

CHAPTER 23

Trading a Life for a Life

"I was carrying a boy! Weeping as the technician spoke the word, I knew that my family's chain of doomed women had just been broken. . . . I knew this boy would be the start of a healthy new cycle in the life of my family."

—Georgette Bennett, sixteen weeks pregnant,
on learning the gender of her child-to-be

As Marc's health continued to decline at what should have been a joyous time in his life, he could hardly ignore the fact that cardiac ailments had already claimed the lives of his beloved father, Abraham, and his brother, Ernie. Given Abraham's medical history, his death in 1975 was not exactly unexpected. But Ernie's was. He collapsed and died instantly one day in 1985 while exiting a subway station in Philadelphia and running up a flight of stairs. He was sixty-four years old.

Georgette faced a worry of her own during her first trimester—the doctors needed to check the strength of the fetal heartbeat. And so another test would be ordered. As she lay in the hospital's ultrasound room four weeks following the first signs of life within her body, she would hear eight magical words: "A healthy single pregnancy with a good heartbeat." The unit's previously skeptical staff now shared in their patient's joy. As they looked on, the nurse who would soon discharge Georgette to Dr. Bartsich's care for the duration of her gestation revealed that "No one here believed for a minute that this was going to work."

Now, as Georgette and Marc went off to thank Dr. Rosenwaks for having undertaken this long shot, they understood that their path to parenthood could be strewn with pitfalls in the coming months. Rather than confirming the couple's fear, Dr. Rosenwaks, the champion of in vitro fertilization, declared reassuringly that Georgette had already beaten the odds. In light of that fact, he declared, he was raising the age limit for future IVF candidates—a decision that would benefit countless women.

On March 19, 1992, as a late-winter blizzard raged, blanketing much of the East Coast with mountains of snow, Georgette, now sixteen weeks' pregnant, would undergo "the final hurdle" of her gestation—amniocentesis. Gazing raptly at a monitor, she and the rabbi were amazed: every inch of their unborn child was being revealed—tiny, perfectly formed limbs, fingers, toes, and spinal cord. And to top it all off, a picture-perfect profile—a round head accentuated by a pug nose.

As the entranced couple continued to stare at the image before them, their eyes fastened on what Georgette would call the "most mind-blowing sight of all." An appendage not previously seen was now visible between their child's legs—incontrovertible evidence that Georgette Bennett was carrying a son. Overcome, Georgette turned to Marc and swore that she would raise their son in his father's footsteps.

There would be precious little time for the couple to continue to rejoice together that day. Despite a storm raging outside, as well as the rabbi feeling poorly, he was intent on keeping an engagement that evening in Wisconsin. He had promised Archbishop Rembert Weakland of Milwaukee, a colleague and friend of long standing, that he would participate that evening in a dialogue at St. Norbert's College in De Pere, near Green Bay, commemorating their groundbreaking work in Catholic-Jewish relations. That program was one of a series of Killeen

Lectures, named in honor of Sylvester Michael Killeen, a chancellor and abbot at St. Norbert's.

As the blizzard intensified, New York area airports were shutting down. When the rabbi's flight on American Airlines was canceled, he began to search for another way to reach his destination. He was determined to get to an airport that was still operating and would provide a flight that would get him to Milwaukee by late afternoon. From there, he would make his way by car to De Pere. After all, a promise was a promise, and he would not let his friend down.

Georgette was, understandably, deeply concerned about her increasingly frail husband traveling so far in such inclement weather. Brushing her anxiety aside and persevering in his quest, he managed to find a way—albeit circuitously: He would fly to Detroit via Northwest Airlines and then to Wisconsin.

On landing at Green Bay at 7:15 that evening, the rabbi raced directly to the auditorium at St. Norbert's, where the program was already underway. Playing for time, the master of ceremonies told the audience of six hundred that when he had awakened that morning, the weather in De Pere had been "simply gorgeous." But, as he would soon be informed, that was not the case in New York, where flights were being canceled. Now, he was relieved to report, "Marc has made it to Detroit." But as he would be a bit late in arriving at the auditorium, Archbishop Weakland, originally scheduled to be the second presenter, would speak first.

Thirty-five minutes into the archbishop's remarks, he proclaimed that the rabbi had arrived. Soon, a noticeably thinner and paler Marc Tanenbaum—he had recently lost twenty-five pounds—joined his colleagues on the platform.

Introduced to great applause, the evening's long-anticipated guest, rejuvenated by his warm reception, raised his arms and in a playful gesture and exclaimed, "If you knew the kind of day I've had! I'll take encouragement from wherever I can find it. Today I experienced a millennium, and a piece of the Exodus, as well."

Then, acknowledging why he had come to De Pere despite the

daunting weather, he said, "I came to pay reverence, respect, and homage to one of the genuine leaders of the Catholic religious community—a hero since Vatican Council II." The only rabbi to have attended sessions of that milestone conclave then proceeded to speak of his childhood trauma on having learned at his father's knee of the horrific details of the murder of his uncle at the hands of anti-Semitic Ukrainian Catholic zealots.

He characterized *Nostra aetate* as "The greatest creative seminar on Catholic-Jewish relations in two thousand years" and recalled the future Pope John XXIII's rescue of three thousand Turkish Jewish children as the Holocaust raged in Europe. He spoke of the birth of the Jewish state and of his hopes for Jewish-Palestinian rapprochement. He also addressed the plight of refugees throughout the world and spoke of his own role in trying to ease their trauma. Archbishop Weakland recalled that forum as having been "a wonderful, ground-breaking dialogue."

Following the program, the two men of faith were able to enjoy some private time together. Marc intimated that this could very well be their last visit. "He was realistic rather than depressed," the archbishop would recall many years later. The rabbi also spoke of his unborn son. "He was excited about it. It probably was one of the things that kept him going," the archbishop observed. "He was—what should I say—a very emotionally rich mensch."

On returning to New York the following day, the exhausted rabbi took to his bed. He and the sixteen-weeks-pregnant Georgette hoped he would then recuperate quickly from the effects of his strenuous journey. But that would not be. He would continue to spend much of every day in seclusion. While Georgette had initially assumed her husband's long sojourns in bed had been procrastination or worse, acute depression, she now understood how very ill he really was. But she could not have anticipated the terrible event that would transpire before their son was born.

CHAPTER 24

The Stilling of a Great Heart

"Our lives were becoming more and more circumscribed, with Marc rarely feeling fit enough to share in any social life. Plans would be made and broken, appointments arranged and cancelled. Our private outings were now confined to occasional drives, movies, and short walks."

—Dr. Georgette Bennett, describing Rabbi Tanenbaum's decline following his return from Wisconsin, March 1992

"Please tell the man in the bed next to mine that I'm sorry for all the trouble I caused today."

—Rabbi Tanenbaum's last words to Georgette on the evening of Thursday, July 2, 1992, six hours before his death

MARC'S ALL-TOO-EVIDENT MALAISE FOLLOWING HIS trip to Wisconsin would be attributed in great measure to the precipitous decline in his blood platelet count. On those increasingly rare occasions when he could still summon the strength to leave his bed and venture out-side, he and Georgette enjoyed exploring the streets to the east of their Madison Avenue apartment building. But the rabbi could no longer easily navigate the gentle rises of their Carnegie Hill neighborhood, so the only route he could follow was along the relatively level 89th Street. But even *that* route was becoming more and more challenging. Despite being supported every inch of the way by Georgette, he would be left not only winded, but utterly exhausted.

It wasn't long before the couple's excursions were taking their toll on Georgette, too—albeit emotionally. She couldn't help but be sad as she recalled the marvelous day during their courtship when her then-vigorous beau, exhilarated simply by being in her company, had vaulted over a fire hydrant. Georgette, unlike her husband, was the epitome of excellent health. Despite being in her midforties, she was having "the easiest pregnancy in the world"—no fatigue, no morning sickness.

On April 2, with the rigors of harsh winter finally giving way to the promise of a verdant spring, the parents-to-be would receive very welcome news. Based on the results of the amniocentesis Georgette had undergone the day of the rabbi's trek to Wisconsin, the male fetus within her body was both healthy and viable. She was now feeling her unborn son's movements and sharing those life-affirming sensations with Marc.

But on April 3, *life* would intervene yet again. Only a day after rejoicing over his unborn son's excellent health, the rabbi would undergo a blood marrow biopsy revealing that he was experiencing an autoimmune response: his increasingly frail system was literally killing off its own blood platelets. Procaine, his anti-arrhythmia medication, was the culprit.

Less than two weeks later, on April 16, Georgette's milestone twenty-week sonogram would reveal that she was carrying a perfectly formed fetus. Am I trading a life for a life, she now wondered? Is it true that the more established my pregnancy is, the more rapidly Marc's health is declining?

At that point, many of the rabbi's friends and colleagues had no inkling that he was in such a precipitous physical decline. "Where his health was concerned, he wasn't going to publicize it," Rabbi Joseph Potasnik recalled. Thus, as ill as he was, he would insist on responding to an urgent request from the Sutton Place Synagogue. For many years, he had conducted High Holy Day services there, and now the house of worship's spiritual leader, Rabbi David Kahane, lay dying of cancer. Marc readily agreed to officiate over its final Passover service in his close associate's stead.

His own Passover celebration had taken place on April 18. It had been in sharp contrast to previous holiday gatherings when they had invited gentile friends from many walks of life to join with them in reliving the Jewish people's Exodus from slavery in Egypt. Given the uncertainty this year concerning the rabbi's stamina, for the first time since their marriage, the couple strictly limited their guests to close family members. Georgette began the 1992 festivities by announcing that this would be their last all-adult Passover. Hereafter, their seder table would be graced by the presence of their son.

Within days of that intimate family seder, many of Marc Tanenbaum's friends and colleagues would realize just how precarious his health had become. That revelatory moment would occur on April 29. Despite the recent, dramatic decline in his health, he had been planning to be present at the Manhattan headquarters of the New York Board of Rabbis on that day to accept the organization's Rabbi Israel and Libby Mowshowitz Award, bestowed in recognition of his service to the Jewish people. But he would not be able to attend, prompting "some whispers that he was not well," Rabbi Joseph Potasnik recalled. "When you can't be there when you are being honored, that is a message."

On the day before the Board of Rabbis' ceremony, Marc's platelet count had fallen precipitously. When his cardiologist ordered him to be hospitalized immediately, the rabbi was devastated. His dear friend Israel Mowshowitz, also a close associate of Governor Mario Cuomo's and one of the officiators ten years earlier at the Bennett-Tanenbaum wedding, had for years fought valiantly against cancer. Now he was losing that battle, yet he cared so deeply for this year's recipient that he insisted on being present for the ceremony.

Georgette and Marc had pleaded with his heart specialist to allow him to postpone his hospitalization for just one day or, alternatively, to release him for two hours on the twenty-ninth so that he could honor Rabbi Mowshowitz by being present. But Marc's condition had grown so critical that he could not be permitted to leave Lenox Hill Hospital even for the time it would take to reach the nearby Board of Rabbis, greet his dear friend, and accept the agency's prestigious honor.

It was decided that the rabbi's soul mate—and, increasingly, his helpmate— would accept the award in his stead. And so they discussed the points Georgette would touch on in her remarks. Above all, the rabbi insisted, his surrogate was to minimize his health issues. He simply could not bear the thought that his colleagues could think he might be past his prime.

It was with a heavy heart that Georgette Bennett brought the rabbi to Lenox Hill Hospital on April 28 for what would turn out to be a stay of two and a half weeks. During the admissions process, the staff administered the rabbi's lengthy list of drugs designed to slow his heart, ease his breathing, lower his blood pressure, increase his potassium, boost his platelets, and reduce his blood sugar.

The next morning, she put on a red suit. Steeling herself emotionally, she made her way to the New York Board of Rabbis. There, with Olga and Pips providing moral support, she took a seat in the very auditorium where only a year earlier, Marc had shared the platform with the Reverend Billy Graham, whose precedent-shattering appearance he had orchestrated.

Although word had gotten around that this year's honoree would not be present to accept his award, Marc's colleagues had come, joining the standing-room-only assemblage. With his parents looking on, Dr. Simon Mowshowitz presented Georgette Bennett with the Rabbi Israel and Libby Mowshowitz Award. Then, recounting the many aspects of Marc's career for which he would wish to be remembered, Dr. Mowshowitz said Marc had struck "a crucial balance between public relations and real dialogue, between advocacy and substantive communication, between diplomacy and authenticity."

Dr. Mowshowitz recalled Marc's threefold motto, "Be effective, know the facts, and do it right." He then noted the honoree's ironic title:

"*Navi Lagoyim*," in Hebrew, "Prophet to the Gentiles" in English—a designation first awarded by God to the prophet Jeremiah. "Jeremiah spoke to the hearts of the Jewish people," he noted, adding, "Marc, in his capacity of *Navi Lagoyim* also speaks directly to the Jewish heart. . . . We are grateful for Rabbi Tanenbaum's diplomatic mastery, but even more enriched by his vision of ourselves, for the crucial balance that shows Jews how to be in the world."

Then, posing the question "How shall we communicate with Goyim in the post-Holocaust era?" Dr. Mowshowitz observed that "Our guides are Rabbi Tanenbaum's unwavering clarity and sense of balance—neither groveling *shtadlanut* nor angry, solipsistic rhetoric will serve, but only his formula of Truth with Grace." As Georgette absorbed what Dr. Mowshowitz was saying, she could only wonder: why do his words seem so like a eulogy?

Georgette then offered an acceptance speech—one that should have been Marc's to deliver, and that instead was recorded for him to hear—and she felt as if she, too, had just eulogized the man considered by many of her husband's friends and colleagues to be the Jewish community's Apostle to the Gentiles.

Following Georgette's remarks, the video of Marc's appearance six weeks earlier at the Killeen Lecture in Wisconsin was shown. At its conclusion, his friends and colleagues rose in a standing ovation. Who among them could possibly have known on that late April day in 1992 that the video they had viewed showed the globetrotting rabbi on his final out-of-town trip?

Certainly not Georgette Bennett, who was so elated that she could hardly contain her joy as she raced the few blocks to the hospital. There, she not only reported to the rabbi on the ceremony, but played an audiotape of the accolades that had just been bestowed upon him. His spirits buoyed as well due to visits from several colleagues, the bedridden rabbi wrote in his diary: "GB triumph."

Meanwhile, his platelet count had dropped even further, requiring restorative doses of steroids and gamma globulin. Although his count did rise by the following day, the steroids would eventually diminish his muscle mass. In fact, he had already lost so much weight that his once well-proportioned physique had become skeletal.

But the rabbi was hardly idle as he lay in his hospital bed. Weeks earlier, as he and Georgette had begun to feel their son's movements, they had realized that the time had come to choose the name he would bear. Ashkenazi Jewish parents traditionally don't name their children after anyone living; instead, they either memorialize a deceased relative or pay tribute to a great Biblical personage. Those opting for the latter approach often do so bearing in mind words from the Talmud, Ber. 7b, that a person's name can determine his or her destiny.

Prior to the rabbi's hospitalization, Georgette had begun to research Biblical names. On reading aloud passages from the book of Joshua, she decided he would be a great historic role model for her son. There would be another, equally compelling, reason to call their son Joshua. His Hebrew name, Yehoshua, and her father's, Yitzhak, begin with the same letter, a kind of similarity that many American Jews favored in giving their children English names. Thus, she wanted to memorialize both her father and the great Biblical leader who had brought the Jewish people into the Promised Land.

But then Marc wished to weigh the many factors implicit in their doing so. Donning his skullcap, he resumed his research, rereading the book of Joshua in both the Hebrew and English-language versions. While Moses had brought the Jews out of Egypt and led them for forty years through the desert, he had transgressed. And so God would not permit him to enter the Land of Israel. His sin-free minister, Joshua, who was beloved by God, would be given the honor of bringing the former slaves into the Promised Land. As He exhorted Joshua: "Be strong and of good courage; be not afraid, neither be thou dismayed; for the Lord thy God is with thee whithersoever thou goest."

A man of law, Joshua would revive the Hebrews' covenant with the Lord, define the boundaries of the Land of Israel, and apportion it among the Twelve Tribes. Under his command, they would conquer all of the additional lands that would become part of the Jewish nation.

Despite the glory of nationhood, the book of Joshua chronicles a bloody chapter in the history of the Jewish people. For Georgette, this chapter raised important moral questions about just war that she hoped their son would contemplate in his life. The rabbi would have the final word: their son would bear the name of the great leader and warrior— the man who had fought and won many battles.

On May 1, from his hospital bed, Marc penned a blessing to his unborn son: "May the angel who redeems us from everything bad protect and save our precious son, Yehoshua ben Mordechai ben Abish ben Frumetka bat Yitzak (the son of Mordechai, the son of Abraham, the son of Georgette the daughter of Ignace), and bring him to a life of blessings and good deeds." It was signed "Your mother and father."

Edwin Turner, a close friend, then carried this precious bit of paper with him on his trip to Jerusalem and slipped into one of the many crevices of the Western Wall—the retaining structure of the ancient temple that once stood on the site and a monument sacred to Jewish people throughout the world. Traditionally, Jews have inserted their hopes and prayers into these fissures, knowing they will be read by God. Turner carefully documented his gesture in a photograph.

Georgette was beginning to dream now of her scholarly husband, who felt so passionately about being a Jew, guiding their son in his own spiritual life, as well as in his broader intellectual growth. She was realistic, however, concerning another aspect of the rabbi's role. She knew that the rabbi's age and fragile health would prevent him from throwing curveballs and running bases with Joshua.

Meanwhile, Marc was increasingly troubled by the powerful drugs he had to take—so much so that the previously easygoing patient was feeling betrayed by his physicians. When the rabbi's doctors switched him from Procaine to Amiodarone, he demanded to know why they hadn't they placed him on that medication sooner. Georgette observed that this newly prescribed drug was turning her husband's skin gray. Worse still, it could damage his liver. Then she heard the physicians' ominous words: Amiodarone was their last hope of saving her husband's life.

Mother's Day 1992 would be observed in Marc's hospital room. An obliging nurse took a picture of him with Georgette, her mother, Sidonie, and her mother's companion, Tibor. In that commemorative snapshot, the patient's hair was slicked back and he was attired in a gray velour robe, a gift from Olga and Pips. No one present in Marc Tanenbaum's room on that day in May could have known that that photograph would be the last one ever to be taken of him.

On arriving home that evening, Georgette discovered a floral arrangement sent by her soul mate. On the accompanying card, he penned the words: "My sweetest love, the happiest Pre–Mother's Day to you. Soon Joshua will join in signing this with me. I love you, rain or shine, forever!" The rabbi's love note was signed "Marc, der kimpit"

Because of the rabbi's continuing hospitalization, he and Georgette were forced to cancel plans to attend Norman Lear's surprise birthday party for his wife, Lyn. But the couple did compose a poem to be read at the party, which would take place at Montrachet, a fashionable French restaurant, on the evening of May 14.

The following day would bring long-awaited news: Since Marc's vital signs were now stable and his platelet count improving, he was being discharged from Lenox Hill. Before leaving the hospital, the rabbi received a telephone call that warmed his fragile heart. Norman Lear was on the line to thank him and Georgette for having composed a poem in Lyn Lear's honor. Marc had assumed that his longtime friend was upset with him over events surrounding Lear's bruising battle with David Gordis at the American Jewish Committee. Now, as the two men chatted, the rabbi was cheered and reassured. He realized that the innovative television personality with whom he had fought so many battles against bigotry had *never* been miffed with him.

Despite being allowed to return home, Marc remained both weak and fatigued—so much so that his physicians forbade him to travel. Thus, he was forced to cancel a trip to Chicago, where he had been scheduled to give a speech on the Vatican, Israel, and the Jews. Thinking ahead to the fall, he was concerned that he would be too indisposed to conduct that year's High Holy Day services at the Sutton

Place Synagogue. His life's work was crumbling before his very eyes, and he was becoming severely depressed. The steroids surging through his system were causing him to believe that people were out to undermine his career—and had made him severely diabetic.

On Sunday, May 17, two days following the rabbi's homecoming, the couple hosted a small, subdued family lunch in honor of Georgette's mother's birthday. Given the rabbi's severe dietary restrictions, the menu had to be carefully planned. Following the meal, Georgette, knowing how much Sidonie enjoyed outings by car, drove the guests, including Sidonie's partner, Tibor, and Olga, and Pips, to Wave Hill, the lovely estate in the Riverdale section of the Bronx where the Italian maestro Arturo Toscanini had lived during his years in New York.

As the afternoon wore on, the idyllic mood would be shattered: the guest of honor and her companion would begin to bicker, and Olga and Pips would leave. The normally good-natured and stoic rabbi, enervated by the resulting stress, asked to be driven home immediately.

While the now-seven-months-pregnant mother-to-be was the picture of prenatal health, having gained a mere seventeen pounds, her husband had become frighteningly thin and had lost so much muscle mass, Georgette recalled that "he started looking almost like a concentration camp survivor." As the days went on, it was becoming increasingly clear to Georgette that the trajectories of their lives were moving in opposite directions.

Despite the rabbi's steadily deteriorating condition, the couple would return to Wave Hill once again. This time, they strolled slowly downhill through the estate's magnificent grounds before lunching on the mansion's patio overlooking the Hudson River. They then began to climb upward. The rabbi managed his ascent without incident. Cheering him on, Georgette hugged him and exclaimed: "That's terrific! You were able to climb the hills!" She was convinced that her husband was on the road to recovery.

But during a United Jewish Appeal fund-raising function at the Mountain Ridge Country Club, in Caldwell, New Jersey, on May 31, Marc appeared to be not simply exhausted, but utterly wasted physically.

Perspiring heavily, as he addressed the assemblage, he could only speak for twenty minutes. Later that afternoon, as Georgette drove her husband home, she could not have realized that she had just witnessed the rabbi's final public appearance. Nor could she have known that the rabbi's prerecorded WINS Radio broadcast, his voice grown hoarse and thin—a commentary on the reunification of Jerusalem—would be his last ever.

Within ten days, Marc would be bedridden. The rabbi who for twenty-seven years had dispensed insights and wisdom in meticulously written, minute-long radio segments could no longer muster the strength to record his widely acclaimed commentaries. Unwilling to publicly acknowledge the severity of his illness, Marc asked Georgette to call WINS's news director and inform him that their star commentator had laryngitis. Despite the rabbi's attempts to deny the seriousness of his condition, even to close friends and professional associates, his physical and emotional conditions were declining precipitously.

On Saturday, June 6, the couple's tenth wedding anniversary, Georgette presented her husband with a fine blue Dior kimono to replace the gray fleece robe he had worn during his protracted stay at Lenox Hill. A day earlier, as was the rabbi's custom, he had sent his beloved a floral arrangement—the lushest one he had ever ordered—along with an affectionately worded card. This year, however, that enclosure lacked his customary ardent prose. He had simply written: "Ten years and still going strong."

Georgette placed the rabbi's floral tribute in their bedroom so that it would be the first and last object she would glimpse each day. But she threw away the rabbi's card—the first time she had ever discarded one of his notes. How could she have known it would be his last?

The couple had planned to host a gala party in celebration of their milestone tenth anniversary. But that was not to be. Marc's glucose count dropped from 279 to a dangerously low 114—and they decided that they would enjoy an intimate dinner at the Hudson River Club as soon as the rabbi felt up to leaving their apartment for several hours. And so they spent June 6 at home. During the afternoon, they were visited by Judith Oringer, a childhood friend of Georgette's. As the hostess prepared refreshments in the kitchen, Oringer regaled the rabbi with anecdotes about her early years with Georgette. Even as a girl of seven or eight, she recalled, Georgette had been "a wonderful hostess, a little adult."

Marc would feel well enough the next day to attend a belated anniversary dinner, along with Olga and Pips, at the home of their friends Ethelee and Herb Hahn. But they would not be able to keep their appointment to go out to dinner with the Phillipses on the following evening. The rabbi's hematologist had called Georgette at her workplace during the day to inform her that while being examined, her husband had gone into insulin shock.

On arriving at the physician's office, she found the rabbi to be soaking wet, his skin blue. After rushing him to Lenox Hill's emergency room—his fourteenth hospitalization within four years—medical personnel hooked him up to various monitors. When Georgette was finally allowed to see her husband, finding it difficult to stand, she pulled a stool over to the side of his gurney and sat down, only to be harshly rebuked by the duty nurse for doing so. "Did she have to do that? Can't she see that I'm *pregnant?*" she cried out. Then the tears began to stream down her cheeks. The rabbi, observing Georgette's fatigue-induced distress, took her hand in his and urged her to go home and get some rest.

At that time, she was balancing the stresses inherent in being some seven months pregnant, while being solely responsible for preparing for the baby's arrival; and seeking to improve the family's financial situation by advancing her career, she was scheduled to leave for her graduate banking course in Delaware in three days. But, even more devastating to Georgette's sense of well-being and security, her beloved husband appeared to be fading rapidly.

The following days would be filled with anxiety as the rabbi's physicians determined what had caused his condition to deteriorate so alarmingly. Finally, the specialists delivered their verdict: their patient was suffering from a blood clot, perhaps infected, that had formed around the wires of his pacemaker and was now invading his heart's right atrial chamber. "It has to come out or else he's a dead man!" declared one of the cardiologists, Dr. Jeffrey Matos.

All that remained to be determined was whether to operate immediately or to wait until after the weekend—and the rabbi's medical team was not even sure that he would survive the surgery. Stunned by the physicians' alarming prognosis, Georgette fought through her shock long enough to find a pay telephone. Knowing that the family would want to see her husband one last time, she called Sima and also tried to get through to his son Michael, a nephew, Sidonie, Tibor, Olga, and Pips. "Marc is headed for open-heart surgery, and he might not survive," she informed them.

Georgette then returned home. Pacing back and forth through the now-dark apartment where only days before she and the rabbi had been planning for their parenthood, she began to sob. When Georgette reported unaccompanied to Dr. Bartsich's office for her next routine prenatal checkup, being unaware of Marc's medical setback, he inquired: "How's your husband?" "I don't know if he'll make it to the delivery room with me," she replied.

By Saturday the thirteenth, however, the rabbi seemed to be stronger, and so his surgery was put off until Monday. While he perked up during Sima's visits that weekend, when he and Georgette were alone, shaking his head, he would say over and over again, "I can't believe this is happening to me. Never in my life did I imagine that it would come to this—that I would have to go through heart surgery."

On Monday the fifteenth, early in the morning on a perfectly beautiful summer day, Georgette snuck past the hospital's security guards and made her way her to her husband's side. He was sitting up in bed, clutching his prayer book, serene as the zero hour for his surgery, 11:00 a.m., approached. He had written a note to Georgette, which he asked her to read once he had been taken to the operating room. Pressing it into her hand, he gazed into her eyes and said, "There's so much more I want to say, and I *will* say it."

Within minutes, Marc was on his way into surgery, Georgette at his side, holding his hand, until his gurney disappeared into restricted space. Then Georgette, in the company of family members and two close friends, Nancy Risser and Tom Freebairn, retreated to the hospital's visitor's lounge to await the surgeon's updates. Her spirits buoyed by the improvement in her husband's condition over the weekend, she was certain that she would see him by day's end.

At one point during the daylong vigil, Georgette retreated to the ladies' room to read the note her husband had pressed into her hand hours earlier. Dated June 15, 1992, 9:59 a.m. and addressed to "My Dearest Beloved Georgette," this missive contains the very passion missing in the anniversary card she had discarded weeks earlier:

It's about 9:50 a.m. In about an hour I will be going into surgery. I am hopeful that everything will go well and that I will come out of the operation stronger than before. Whatever happens, I want you to know I love you more than ever—and I have loved you completely, totally from our first day together. That's a great culture we've created together, and it will go on forever. I know Joshua will be nurtured in that love. I expect to come out of this better and stronger than before, and I expect and hope to love you and care for you for many years of our lives together. You have been the greatest gift and blessing of my life and I shall be forever grateful for our wonderful 10 years together.

After six hours of waiting, Georgette and Sima would be escorted to the recovery room, where the patient now lay, intubated but conscious. His clot had been removed and a new pacemaker installed. Sutures now ran the length of his chest cavity. In a precautionary move, the surgeon had at the last minute placed a stent in a trunk artery.

Relieved after days of anxiety and convinced that Marc was on the way to recovery, Georgette embraced him and exclaimed: "You *made* it! You're going to be fine!"

The rabbi continued to rally during the night—so much so that on Tuesday evening, he urged Georgette to keep her commitment to complete her degree at the Stonier Graduate School of Banking in Wilmington. She agreed to do so—if she could commute back and forth, so as to be with the rabbi every evening. To that end, her friends Nancy and Tom, in an extraordinary act of generosity, drove her to Delaware and back to New York each day of the course.

Other friends, as well as members of the couple's family, were recruited to visit the rabbi in shifts during Georgette's daytime absences. She asked them to bring the recovering patient the nourishing roast beef sandwiches that his physicians were now permitting him to have.

Later that week, Georgette would defend her thesis. It received the Stonier School's highest accolade: her thesis would become part of the collection at the Harvard Business School library. As always, the proud rabbi gloried in this latest distinction achieved by his determined partner.

He would be even more excited the following week. Having traveled the long road from academic sociology to finance, Georgette would return to New York, with a diploma marked "With Distinction." Despite her gnawing anxiety over the rabbi's health, she had graduated fifth in her class of 240.

But the family's high spirits would be cruelly short-lived. On the evening of Saturday, June 27, following the end of the Jewish Sabbath, Marc was feeling well enough to write the commentary for a WINS broadcast, a paean to Lenox Hill's medical staff. When he attempted to phone it in to the station, however, his voice was so weak that the engineer suggested, "Let's try again next week."

When the results of the culture taken on his excised blood clot revealed that it had been infected, Georgette rejoiced. She believed that it had caused her husband's many alarming symptoms. But despite Georgette's theory, her husband was growing more and more despondent, even to the point of doubting the medical staff's assertions that his recovery was progressing well.

"The infection is reversing itself," Georgette would assure him. "You're getting better." She would remind the discouraged patient that the dosages of the steroids that had been playing havoc with his emotional state were being reduced, and his depression-inducing diabetes was abating. Despite her encouraging words, Marc was, in fact, declining rapidly. The newspapers she brought him daily now lay unread, and he refused to allow the television set in his room to be activated. Was the inveterate news junkie now willfully severing his ties to the world beyond his hospital bed?

There would soon be another, even more troubling, sign of the rabbi's retreat from his surroundings. He was now refusing to eat. Realizing that in order for the rabbi to become stronger, he would have to gain back some of the weight he had lost, Georgette had begun to supplement his hospital fare with the deli sandwiches that he once loved.

One evening, she had put a roast beef sandwich in the drawer of the rabbi's bedside table. When she called him on the following morning, he assured her that he had consumed half of it for dinner and the rest on awakening during the middle of the night. But on visiting her husband later that day, Georgette would find that sandwich, still uneaten, exactly where she had placed it.

On Wednesday, July 1, while reading the New York Times, Georgette came across Ari Goldman's obituary of Rabbi Israel Mowshowitz, who had lost his long battle against cancer a day earlier. Should she tell her husband of his close friend's death? She thought this might be the very day that the patient decided to reconnect with the world. If so, he would certainly come upon his revered colleague's death notice, most likely when he was alone. Thus it was with great dread that Georgette decided that she must inform him of Israel Mowshowitz's passing.

As she did so on that warm summer day, Marc Tanenbaum let go of a bit of his own life. He chided himself for not having been able to visit his dying friend, as well as now being so unwell that he could neither attend the rabbi's funeral nor pay a shiva call on Libby Mowshowitz.

But there would be one bright moment for Marc Tanenbaum at that otherwise terribly sad moment. Days earlier, he had asked Georgette to purchase a card for his son Michael, whose birthday would occur on Independence Day. Then, poised on the edge of his hospital bed, with IV fluid dripping on the card, the rabbi had written the young man a warm greeting and asked his wife to enclose a cash gift before mailing it.

Now, on the evening of July 1, when the rabbi spoke with Georgette on the telephone, there would be a jubilant tone in his voice. "You'll never guess what just happened!" he exclaimed. "Michael called me and we talked for an hour!" The young man had even suggested that he might visit his father in the hospital.

On Georgette's return to her husband's side the following day, he said over and over again, while gazing constantly at the object of his deep adoration: "I'm so sorry. I'm so sorry. I love you." It was as if those words were all he had left to give her, she thought. Returning the rabbi's gaze, she remained silent, simply holding his hand. Georgette Bennett knew that during their years together, she and Marc had told each other everything there was to say. They had lived by a creed expressed in a verse often quoted by the rabbi: "If you love me, tell me that you love me. For the silence of the grave is long enough."

Later that morning, Georgette returned to her office before meeting a colleague for lunch. Then, following the cancellation of an afternoon appointment, she indulged in a leisurely stroll down Madison Avenue, something she had not done in many months.

At Lenox Hill, meanwhile, the rabbi was having a good morning. He was out of bed and walking with a nurse. She reported that the patient had greeted her warmly, as always, with a smile, and that "he seemed to be in good form." They chatted about his impending fatherhood, and he said that following his discharge from the hospital, he would come by to visit, leaning on his son's baby carriage for support.

But upon visiting the rabbi during the afternoon, Pips would find him in a different mood. Then, at four o'clock, a staff member reported that the rabbi wasn't feeling well—that he was having trouble breathing. Tests revealed the presence of metabolic acid as well as a low bicarbonate count in the patient's blood—indications that his heart wasn't pumping enough oxygen to supply his organs.

When Georgette returned home to change clothes before returning to the hospital, the rabbi called her: "I'm sorry I haven't called you sooner," he said apologetically, "but I've been throwing up." "I'll be there soon," she replied, regretting that she hadn't checked in with the rabbi before he called her.

Georgette arrived at Lenox Hill shortly after six o'clock. In her absence, the rabbi had become critically ill, his hospital gown soaked with perspiration and his breathing labored. Within minutes, the rabbi was being transferred to an operating room, where his wife's entry was barred, and she watched as her husband's gurney disappeared from view. Then a physician threaded tubes into his frail body and connected them to a heart monitor.

As Georgette waited outside, a Hasidic visitor from an adjacent room approached her and asked, "So is that *Mr.* Tanenbaum in there?" Recalling the frequent snubbing that her husband had experienced from parts of the Orthodox community because of his work with Christians, she pointedly replied, "No, it's *Rabbi* Tanenbaum."

She could hear what was happening within: a nurse was shouting, "Marc! Can you hear me?" The rabbi could not. He had stopped breathing. He regained consciousness, only to pass out yet again. His chest was opened and his heart massaged. As Georgette awaited the appearance of someone who could tell her what was happening, she heard the one word she had hoped against all hope would not be uttered: "Code!"

She was then told that the rabbi's breathing had been restored—that his new pacemaker was functioning. Much relieved, she now thought: I'll finally be able to see him. That would not be. Marc Tanenbaum would code once again. Despite being administered massive doses of restorative medications, one of the rabbi's physicians who left the ICU to brief Georgette said: "He's a very sick man, and I just don't know if he's going to make it."

So this is how it's going to end, Georgette thought. But after three hours of medical intervention, the patient's condition was stabilizing, and Georgette was finally allowed to be with him. There, Marc lay unconscious, with life-sustaining tubes streaming from his arms and throat. Placing one of Marc's large but gentle hands against the belly that still shielded their unborn son, Georgette murmured every loving word she could muster. And she begged him to hold on—for her sake and for Joshua's.

Once more, Marc Tanenbaum's body would begin to fail. Georgette would be asked to leave the cubicle where he lay, then brought in again. Finally, following five additional hours of medical heroics, the rabbi's physicians asked for permission to disconnect his life support apparatus. Georgette nodded her agreement.

Then, still clutching his hand, she embarked on her death vigil. Realizing that she was experiencing his physical warmth for the last time, she held onto the moment, knowing that she would have to live on that memory for a long time.

At 12:15 on the morning of Friday, July 3, the monitor connected to the heart of the great humanitarian who had filled his soul mate's heart with so much joy emitted several ominous beeps. Then the device, whose visual images of zigzags had affirmed the existence of life, flat-lined. As Georgette stroked his hair, she whispered, "Rest peacefully now, my love."

Her thoughts immediately following his marriage proposal in 1981 came rushing back. Ten good years is exactly what she had with Marc. He died one month after their tenth anniversary.

Knowing that she now stood alone after more than a decade of standing together with Marc, Georgette left the hospital. She now had to steel herself to organize the great rabbi's final journey.

CHAPTER 25

Of Blessed Memory

"Rabbi Tanenbaum's passing is the end of an era. He was a pioneer in Christian-Jewish relations and Catholic-Jewish relations in particular."

—Cardinal John O'Connor,
the Roman Catholic Archbishop of New York

"He was a great source of reconciliation and strength during moments of deep difficulty between our communities."

—Cardinal Edward Cassidy, president
of the Vatican Commission for Religious Relations with the Jews

"With Marc gone, there is no one with whom I can work."

—The Reverend Billy Graham

"Rabbi Tanenbaum spent his life attempting to strengthen healthy relations between Christians and Jews. He was brilliant and committed."

—The Reverend Jerry Falwell

THERE WAS AN OUTPOURING OF grief in the hours following Rabbi Marc Tanenbaum's passing. News bulletins interrupted local television and radio broadcasts. Newspapers ran long obituaries. And more tributes would follow during the rabbi's funeral three days later, on the morning of Monday, July 6, at the Park Avenue Synagogue. Within the walls of that magnificent Byzantine edifice, Marc Tanenbaum and Georgette had worshipped and been married. Decades earlier, the rabbi had served there as a guest officiator during High Holy Day services. Now there sat more than one thousand mourners to memorialize the man known as "the human rights rabbi."

Among those gathered for the service on this early summer day were some unexpected family members: the rabbi's former wife, Helga, and their three children. Among the many close friends from many walks of life were Mayor Giuliani and his wife, Donna Hanover; Rabbi Arnold Turetsky, a friend of twenty-five years' standing; and Roz Goldberg, the Jewish community activist who had brought her close friends together eleven years earlier. There were also Roman Catholic, Eastern Orthodox, Protestant, and Jewish clergy, as well as American Jewish Committee colleagues.

"Marc was always able to draw a big crowd," his widow observed as she eulogized her late husband. "But why couldn't he have died *after* his funeral?" Georgette posed the question: "Is it easier to lose a great man or an ordinary one, an imperfect love or a special one?" She would in the future conclude: "That depends on whether you focus on your loss or on the time you had together."

She then spoke of her loving relationship with the rabbi, many of her reminiscences infused with abundant humor. She recalled how she had encouraged her scholarly husband to expand his horizons, and of how he, in turn, "became my greatest motivator; there was nothing he didn't appreciate. We opened, rather than shut, doors for each other."

Other eulogists were Cardinal O'Connor, who brought a message from the pope; journalist Ari Goldman; State Senator Roy Goodman; Roz Goldberg; and Rabbi Turetsky, who said of his deceased colleague: "He risked his newly gained friendships with the highest-power Christians in the world. His mission was not to befriend Christians, but to bring his people to a sense of pride."

Judah Nadich, the officiating rabbi, spoke of how difficult it was for him "to find words to describe the void" in Georgette's life. Then, paraphrasing words of the prophet Jeremiah, he said: "Weep not for one who is taken from us, but weep for one who is still treading the path of life."

Following the services, a police escort of two cruisers and five motorcycles shepherded Marc Tanenbaum through the city's traffic, en route to his final resting place, the New Montefiore Cemetery, on Long Island.

In the days to come, tributes would continue to arrive from throughout the world. Weeks, months, even *years* later, Marc Tanenbaum's colleagues would still voice their appreciation of his life and deeds.

One of the most moving testaments to the legacy of Marc Tanenbaum would come to light little more than eight months after his death. Following Claire Huchet Bishop's own demise on March 13, 1993, her last will and testament bequeathed an antique menorah to the rabbi. When settling her husband's estate, Georgette would donate that precious article of Judaica to the Hebrew Union College, along with information on its provenance.

As Georgette continued to mourn her husband, she began the formidable process of organizing his papers—voluminous correspondence, diaries, and other memorabilia of his extraordinary journey of self-discovery and quest to ensure the well-being and security of the unfortunate among his fellow human beings.

Barely a week following Rabbi Tanenbaum's death, his exhausted widow, now eight months pregnant, would receive a telephone call from Rabbi Sam Dresner, a collaborator with writer Ed Kaplan on the definitive biography of Rabbi Abraham Joshua Heschel. Both writers were urgently requesting the rabbi's papers on Rabbi Heschel, to which they had been promised access.

Georgette responded that she was planning to send that material, included in 140 boxes of unsorted papers, to the American Jewish Archives, and that they could be reviewed there. But the writers sounded so desperate that she agreed to permit Kaplan to review the papers in the apartment she had so recently shared with her late husband. As she recalled:

For three days, Ed came over and we scoured all the papers but failed to find the documents for which he was searching. We finally both sat down on the floor among those heaps of papers, completely spent. For some reason, we both happened to look down at the same time. And there between us were all of the papers! I can't say I believe in Divine Providence. But there is no other explanation for the appearance of those papers where they hadn't been before!

As Georgette sought to get on with her new life as a soon-to-be single mother, two weeks after the rabbi's death, she had received a telephone call that would profoundly alter the future direction of her life.

Sir Sigmund Sternberg, chairman of the International Council of Christians and Jews, was on the line from London. He had worked very closely with the rabbi during the controversy over the convent at Auschwitz, among other issues. Now he was saying, "You know, Georgette, we really must continue Marc's work, and we must do something soon because people forget. I should like for you to be prepared to discuss this with me when I come to New York in November."

Georgette recalled, "I had just lost the love of my life, and being in my eighth month of pregnancy, I was not in the mood to think about starting an organization." Within weeks, however, she would experience what she regarded as an epiphany. "That's a strange word for a nice Jewish girl to be using," she observed, "but at that moment, it became very clear to me that nothing I had been doing in my working life was as important as continuing what *Marc* had been doing, and to try to build on his work."

By the time of Sir Sigmund's arrival in New York, she had already established an advisory committee including two prominent members of the clergy, Rabbi Balfour Brickner and the Reverend Theodore Hesburgh. Hesburgh, the distinguished president of the University of Notre Dame, would go on to serve as a founding board member of the resulting organization, which would be named the Tanenbaum Center for Interreligious Understanding.

Sir Sigmund, in turn, presented the center with a small gift, and other donations would be forthcoming. Initially, the Center was engaged in the type of activities in which Marc had been involved—focusing on intergroup dialogue and scholarly work. But wishing to do more than create a memorial to her late husband, Georgette sought instead to establish an organization that would build on the rabbi's life's work.

In time, following the Center's first board retreat and strategic planning session, four core areas of activity would be identified and pursued: education, including the development of curriculum and teacher training in order to reach schoolchildren before they learn to hate; the workplace, where adults spend most of their time; a spin-off of the workplace program, focusing on law enforcement and health care, namely, the religious dimension of health care, emanating from the recognition that there are certain areas in which a cultural gap between a provider and a client can have an enormous impact; and, finally, the role of religion in conflict resolution. In each one of these areas, the Tanenbaum Center would become a pioneer, as well as the field's leading resource.

Georgette, assisted by a part-time secretary, began the Center's operations in her home office. In time, Howard Milstein, then-chairman of Milstein Properties and later chairman, president, and CEO of the New York Private Bank & Trust, would provide the organization with a mail-drop address in Rockefeller Center, followed by a real suite of offices at 575 Madison Avenue. The Center would go on to occupy a full floor in a building across the street from Madison Square Garden. (Milstein's generosity continued when, inspired by her husband's deep commitment to refugees, Georgette founded the Multifaith Alliance for Syrian Refugees [MFA] in 2013. Early funding from Milstein helped to get MFA off the ground, and, as of this writing, the MFA offices are housed in another building owned by Howard Milstein.)

Georgette would go on to memorialize her late husband and settle his affairs in other ways. In 2002, for example, after recently released Oval Office tapes indicated that Billy Graham had been a party to

President Nixon's anti-Semitic remarks during a meeting in the White House, Georgette immediately dispatched a letter to the *New York Times* in defense of Mr. Graham. In that letter, published on March 19, 2002, Georgette acknowledged that Mr. Graham had "exhibited clear anti-Semitic attitudes in his 1972 conversation with President Richard M. Nixon." But, she noted, "evangelical Christianity is based on the premise that even the greatest sinner can be redeemed." She then noted the "many untold stories about Mr. Graham's support of Jews. Before leaving for any crusade in a Soviet-bloc country, he would call my husband, Rabbi Marc Tanenbaum, to ask what he could do for the Jews while overseas. And Mr. Graham worked behind the scenes to extricate a number of Jews from the Soviet Union."

Georgette added, "But perhaps the greatest untold story, which Marc related to me, is Mr. Graham's intervention during the 1973 war in the Middle East. Although others also intervened, it was only after Mr. Graham made a phone call to Mr. Nixon that the president finally sent a military airlift to Israel, which helped ensure that country's survival." In conclusion, she wrote, "Were he alive today, I believe that my husband would have come to his good friend's defense."

A few days later, on March 22, Mr. Graham sent a letter to Georgette in which he said, "Words cannot express my appreciation for your letter to the *New York Times*." He added, "It brought back so many memories of your husband Marc. His years of friendship and counsel to me is one of the greatest treasures in my memory."

Georgette would be brought into another of Marc's issues in 2012. A revival of *Jesus Christ Superstar* was being mounted in London, and a reporter for London's *Daily Telegraph* asked Georgette what she thought. She reminded the reporter, Matthew Sweet, that Marc had called the rock opera "a witch's brew of anti-black and anti-Semitic venom." In her interview with Sweet, and in a piece she wrote for the *Huffington Post*, Georgette called the rock opera "an equal opportunity offender" and said it was "part of a long tradition of Passion Plays that depict the suffering and death of Jesus Christ."

She drew a line from the Oberammergau Passion Plays, which

began in 1634 to Mel Gibson's controversial film, *The Passion of the Christ*. These retellings of the Easter story "bring a renewal of Christ's message of redemption," she said, but she added they also "have inspired far less noble passions that led to vicious pogroms against Jews." And she recounted the story of Marc's uncle, who was set upon by congregants in a small village in Ukraine when they were streaming out at the end of Easter services. They had been inflamed by a fiery sermon in which their priest railed against the Jews, and they pursued the first Jew they could find, Marc's uncle, and chased him into a river. She invoked Marc's question: "How can a gospel of love be turned into such a gospel of hate when it comes to the Jews?"

In the aftermath of Marc's passing, Georgette also sought to heal a breach with the American Jewish Committee, which had been Marc's professional home base for a quarter century. As his health declined, Marc withdrew from contact with the AJC. And none of his colleagues from many years with the organization were among those invited to speak at his funeral. Many years after his death, Georgette sought out AJC Executive Director David Harris, who started at the agency as Marc's deputy, to explain what had transpired. She told Harris that Marc had been "more ill than anybody knew—that his autoimmune response had not only caused his body to destroy platelets, but that the steroids he was required to take caused him to become depressed and convinced him that people were out to undermine him." As Georgette recalled, "David had no idea of what had been going on, so it was an important conversation."

In addition, Marc did not live long enough to see the signing of the Vatican-Israel accords. But afterward, Georgette received many congratulatory phone calls and letters from those who knew Marc's pivotal role in bringing those accords into being. Soon after, the new Tanenbaum Center for Interreligious Understanding organized the first post-Accords conference in Israel on Catholic-Jewish relations. History was made when one of the chief rabbis of Israel met for the first time with Catholic prelates.

And, finally, following a lengthy effort to organize Marc's

voluminous papers, Georgette would donate them to the American Jewish Archives in Cincinnati. The papers, recordings, and videotapes would all be digitized, and in the fall of 2015, the Rabbi Marc H. Tanenbaum Collection would go live on the American Jewish Archives website (https://fa.americanjewisharchives.org/tanenbaum/).

The archives would preserve Marc Tanenbaum's words and deeds, but, in fact, his real memorial would be very visible in a variety of places around the world: In the worldwide Catholic church, for example, which had made dramatic progress in obliterating centuries of painful ideas and practices regarding Jews. His legacy was also visible in the increased sensitivity many Christian denominations displayed in their relations with Jews. Indeed, his legacy could be seen in a host of causes and institutions that helped make the world at least a modestly better place for both Jews and gentiles.

But nearly two months after Marc's death, his true legacy would arrive: The birth of his son, and their only child.

CHAPTER 26

Will the Real Marc Tanenbaum Please Stand Up?

"The American Jewish Community's foremost Apostle to the Gentiles."

—*Newsweek*, November 9, 1970,
on Rabbi Tanenbaum's emergence as a leader in interreligious affairs

WHO *WAS* THE MAN WHOM *Newsweek* magazine dubbed "the American Jewish Community's foremost Apostle to the Gentiles"? Who was the man who was labeled the "human rights rabbi," the "interfaith rabbi," and "the Secretary of State of the Jews"? Who was the man whom a poll of religion newspaper editors had ranked number four among the ten most respected and influential religious leaders in America? (He trailed only Billy Graham, Martin Marty, and Jimmy Carter—who was a Baptist lay leader as well as president.) Who was the rabbi who had received fifteen honorary degrees—awarded by both religious and secular universities—and whose advice had been sought by Presidents Eisenhower, Carter, Reagan, and George H. W. Bush?

Was he truly a compassionate humanitarian, a brilliant mentor and teacher, an altruistic, deeply motivated, pioneering ecumenist? Or was

Marc Tanenbaum perhaps a bit of a self-promoter, a taskmaster who demanded deference, and a publicity seeker?

In some ways, he was all of the above, according to those who worked with him over the years. Eugene DuBow, who began his forty-seven-year-long career at the American Jewish Committee in 1966 as its Westchester area director, attested to the rabbi's friendly, caring, and nurturing nature, as well as to his intellect. An officer for eight years with New York State's Division of Parole before coming to the committee, DuBow initially knew very little about the inner workings of Jewish organizational life. After sitting in on several AJC meetings, he concluded that his new colleagues were very intelligent, "and Marc Tanenbaum seemed to me to be one of the most brilliant of them all." In fact, the rabbi was so impressive that the neophyte committee staffer thought of him as being a very large man *physically*. "He wasn't actually so tall; he was of modest height," DuBow observed, "but his aura was such that he appeared otherwise. I was terribly impressed with him. And I became even more so after a while."

DuBow said that Marc appreciated his staff's efforts. "In his speeches, he always thanked the people who worked on the programs *publicly*, and he did that with a lot of feeling," DuBow recalled. "I thought he was a really nice person. And he certainly took care of his junior colleagues."

Jerry Goodman, director of European Affairs, appreciated Marc's enjoyment of a good laugh. "His was a hearty one," he said, "and as important as he may have been—he had met with *the pope*, after all—Marc did not talk down to people. He was quite human and warm. I was a junior member of the staff, but he never made me feel that way. It was a peer relationship, in spite of our age and experiential differences."

Dr. George Gruen, the AJC's longtime director of Middle Eastern Affairs, whose career coincided with Marc's entire tenure with the agency, had a slightly different view: "He was very articulate, with a very commanding presence," Gruen recalled. "He was also eager to let other people have their share of credit—as long as *he* was number one. He liked to be in charge."

David Harris, who became the committee's executive director in 1990, first met Marc in 1979, when Harris was hired as a very junior AJC staff member. Assigned at that time to an office "quite close to the mail room," Harris was in awe of the rabbi, whose next phone call, he observed, "could have come from the pope, the vice president of the United States, or the *New York Times*, asking him to write an op-ed for tomorrow's paper." That was a bit intimidating to Harris. As he noted, "I was not getting calls from the pope in those days—and I haven't *since*. While the rabbi's aura was certainly inspiring and impressive, I wondered: What kind of relationship will we have?" Harris would be pleasantly surprised by what he found: "Marc was able to set aside those op-eds that the *New York Times* was clamoring for to be very empathetic. He always found the time—sometimes it was quite late at night when most of the building was empty—to have a closed-door, roll-up-your-sleeves, heart-to-heart schmooze." And all these years after Marc's death, Harris avers, "I still ask: WWMD (What Would Marc Do)?"

Howard I. Friedman, a California attorney who served as the agency's president from 1983 to 1986, said simply, "The Jewish-Christian relations of today are a monument to him."

The rabbi's mentoring was not confined to committee staff and lay leaders. Among those with whom he formed a close relationship were people like a newly ordained rabbi named Joseph Potasnik. Potasnik, like Marc Tanenbaum, attended Yeshiva University, and would become spiritual leader of Brooklyn's Congregation Mount Sinai, and later the head of the New York Board of Rabbis. But at the time, in September 1972, when he first met Rabbi Tanenbaum, he had just joined the New York Board of Rabbis. In the years to come, Rabbi Potasnik would reach out to Marc often—even going so far as to find out where he was speaking on a given day. Rabbi Potasnik acknowledged having been "dismayed by the lack of instant progress" concerning interfaith issues. But Rabbi Tanenbaum urged patience as well as persistence.

Perhaps more than any other Jewish leader of his day, Marc also reached out to gentile leaders. For example, Father John T. Pawlikowski was a graduate student at the University of Chicago when he first met the rabbi. At that time, the committee had decided to publish its findings on Catholic textbooks as part of a tristate committee project in conjunction with the Ford Foundation. Marc had invited the young Catholic theologian to New York to discuss the possibility of his editing and summarizing those findings for publication in book form. Thus began the warm, enduring relationship between the rabbi and the reverend. "There was a catching dynamism about Marc," his new Catholic colleague recalled. "He brought you into the fold. He was in many ways, at least in terms of interreligious relations, a consummate diplomat."

Pawlikowski added, "Marc was able to establish relations with a variety of Christian leaders—many of whom were not exactly on his wavelength—that would be quite conducive to change." He credited that feat in large part to Marc's personality. "People *liked* him," Pawlikowski observed. "He could give a great speech and he stirred them up in a good sense. He respected their viewpoints and perspectives. He was aggressive, but in a nonthreatening way. He didn't put down, or criticize, the other party."

There are numerous stories of personal favors and assistance, counseling, and mentoring, among Protestants as well as Catholics, and among Jews and non-Jews. To Liv Ullmann, "Marching for freedom with Marc Tanenbaum changed my life in a way that I cannot describe."

Just as Marc Tanenbaum was the caring teacher and mentor, he was also a highly skilled self-promoter. When he was advising filmmaker Vincenzo Labella on the television miniseries *A.D.*, he wrote to Labella on December 2, 1984, and asked, "If it is appropriate, I would welcome a credit line on *A.D.* as 'script consultant' or something like that." In support of his request, the rabbi noted: "I was given that on NBC's *Holocaust* production and it was helpful to me in my work." Moreover, during the rabbi's nearly four-decade-long career, he would excel in the cultivation of his extensive media contacts. He would be mentioned on more than ninety occasions by the *New York Times*, as well as 276 times in Jewish Telegraphic Agency dispatches.

This visibility, highly unusual for a staff member of a communal organization, reflected several factors. He had considerable skills in oral and written communication. He was a riveting orator and an interesting writer. But, most important, he knew precisely how to use those skills to garner the mass media's attention

Marc, a seasoned former PR man, and Mort Yarmon, the committee's Director of Public Relations, would prove to be ideally suited to work together. While the articulate, well-informed rabbi was given to rhetorical flourishes, the committee's taciturn publicist was an expert at crafting tersely written media handouts containing the essential "Who, What, Where, When" details.

Marc was always happy to put his aura in the service of the AJC and its priorities. "There was a period of time when there were a couple of stars at the American Jewish Committee, and Rabbi Tanenbaum certainly was the *leading* star," AJC lay leader Mimi Alperin observed. During Marc's many public appearances throughout the country, "He always drew a crowd," Eugene DuBow remembered. "The laypeople who listened to him always loved him. And he had a lot to say in those days; there were many questions about the Catholic Church, Christians versus the Jews, Israel, and Soviet Jewry. He was the 'great ambassador' to the Christians wherever he went."

David Harris added, "Marc would walk into a room and its chemistry would change. It didn't matter whether there were two people or two *hundred*. Most important, he could help sway a room in whatever direction he hoped for. And there were many who *needed* swaying in the 1970s." Noting that Marc "took on the big issues of our time," Harris said the rabbi was "the committee's ideal persuader."

Despite his own promotional skills, Marc gave his media maven free rein in promoting him and the committee. Thus Yarmon's frequent press luncheons were a must for major print and broadcast journalists. On those occasions, just as an actor "makes an entrance," Marc would stride into the agency's eighth-floor conference area, his tattered briefcase bulging with all manner of papers. And he would simply suck the air right out of the room. Dr. Thomas Bird, a longtime associate of

Marc Tanenbaum in Soviet Jewry advocacy, and a professor of Slavic languages at Queens College, in New York City, insisted the rabbi was very much aware of his own gravitas. "Surely, he understood that because the resonance was there and the response was there."

How much was this about Marc Tanenbaum's ego? Howard I. Friedman, a California attorney who served as the agency's president from 1983 to 1986, said, "Marc would be the first to tell you he had a big ego." However, he added Marc "was entitled to it." In any case, Friedman added, "He was never on an 'ego trip.' He was always concentrated on the importance of what he was doing, not on his own ego."

Noting that the rabbi's utterances "resulted in headlines, in new undertakings, new committees, new involvements, and new enthusiasm for the things he was promoting," Professor Bird said, "I didn't see egotism. I saw profound generosity and profound human commitment. He understood his own worth, but he also understood that other people respected him. When he addressed an issue from the podium, people sat up and took notice."

The rabbi was well aware of his effect on people, especially on the media, but he would often joke: "You can't believe your own publicity."

Perhaps the definitive word belongs to his wife, Georgette. "He was a master of publicity," she observed. "And boy did he *love* it! And boy did he *seek it out*!" But Georgette attributed the rabbi's publicity seeking only partially to ego. "Most of it was because he understood how much leverage it gave him in terms of effectively promoting his agenda," she observed.

For Marc Tanenbaum, the pursuit of publicity served a larger purpose: It enabled him to draw attention to his causes and attract allies to his side. In so many of his battles, his strategy was to build a coalition that made his side seem bigger and stronger and made his demands appear to serve more than the narrow needs of the Jewish community, however just its cause might be. Thus, the battle for Soviet Jewry was not simply about Jews trying to help other Jews. It was a *human rights* struggle, with *nuns* in leadership roles and *gentiles* introducing legislation in Congress.

As a prominent public figure, Marc had an impact on the leading religion journalists of his day, not only in the United States, but also abroad. Among the New York–based correspondents with whom Marc established collegial relationships was Peter Steinfels, who began his career with the Catholic publication *Commonweal* during the 1960s, before moving on to the *New York Times* as its senior religion correspondent and "Beliefs" columnist. Given Steinfels's background as the grandson of one Jew and three Irish Catholics, interfaith relations were an issue of long-standing interest, and he had "an emotional connection from both sides." As Steinfels pursued his journalistic career, he would be in touch with Marc regarding "any kind of story having to do with the Jewish community, most notably and memorably, Catholic-Jewish relations." He always found the rabbi to be "a font of moderation and of wisdom about evaluating things."

Ken Briggs was *Newsday*'s religion correspondent in 1973 when he met Rabbi Tanenbaum. His initial impression was of a "very cordial, very polished individual with an impressive style, and perceptive manner." On becoming the religion correspondent for the *New York Times*, Briggs would also be in frequent contact with Marc. "He could really get into the issues without rancor, or a hedge, of any kind," the correspondent recalled. "He was very good at concentrating on what was central to the issues, but flexible enough to accept the nuances that may not have thought of. And he was loyal to the causes he was involved in. He could go quite a distance in elaborating and debating various aspects of issues."

Briggs recalled that the rabbi was enormously helpful in sorting through the Jewish organizational minefield regarding interfaith matters, in which, the correspondent observed, "each group represented itself as *the voice*. Getting a balance in the middle of that was difficult. Marc Tanenbaum knew how to speak to that spectrum probably better than anybody else tasked with representing the Jewish community to the rest of the country. He had that gift."

Another appreciative journalist was Joe Berger. Like Briggs, he was first a reporter with *Newsday* and then spent four years as the religion correspondent for the *New York Times*. He covered Marc's activities beginning in the 1980s, and Berger recalled, "Marc understood the importance of newspapers and other media. He was very accessible and knew the importance of the media's getting the story correctly. So he was very interested in making sure that it would be told as truthfully, and as *accurately*, as possible."

While Marc Tanenbaum and the press had a long-term courtship, the rabbi's visibility would also be considerably enhanced by his well-crafted, incisive commentaries airing for more than two decades on WINS and other stations around the country. Similarly, his numerous articles in newspapers and magazines would also provide substantial visibility for the rabbi—and for the causes he supported. He was a highly visible representative of the Jews. He would be the first rabbi to address the World Council of Churches, speaking before some four thousand delegates at the group's Sixth Assembly in Vancouver in 1983. And he would sometimes be the first Jew anyone had met when he spoke to a few dozen people at local events all across the United States.

Whether dealing one-on-one with rabbis and priests, talking to senior government officials in the White House and assorted national capitals, or appearing on national television, Rabbi Marc Tanenbaum sought to speak truth to power, and to persuade others that the positions he espoused and the issues he cared about deserved to be heard.

He would live to see the fruits of his efforts in the Vatican and the Christian evangelical community, in the civil rights movement, and in the struggles to aid the oppressed and the dispossessed in Asia and around the world. He would not live long enough to see the signing of the Vatican-Israel accords in 1993. Nor would he live long enough to see the birth of his son.

L'dor Vador
(From Generation to
Generation)

Joshua-Marc Tanenbaum

"As I watch Joshua toddle around, I'm constantly amazed that his walking posture is just like yours—shoulders slightly thrown back, stomach slightly thrown forward. He has your walk."

—Dr. Georgette Bennett, speaking to her late husband of their nearly eighteen-month-old son via her audio diary, February 21, 1994

IN THE WEEKS FOLLOWING MARC'S death, Georgette organized and cleared Marc's papers out of his study in order to put the finishing touches on its new incarnation as a nursery for the baby boy she would name Joshua-Marc Bennett Tanenbaum. While Marc was alive, one of the couple's few ongoing sources of friction was the clutter caused by his omnipresent piles of papers, which consumed more and more space in their apartment. She used to tease him by threatening, "When you die, I'm going to wrap you up in your newspapers, like a Friday herring, and set fire to your study!"

Of course, now that Marc had died, every piece of paper was a precious remnant of his presence. So with great care—and with Marc's sister, Sima, and nephew, Adam, at her side—she had embarked on the monumental task of preparing his papers for *their* final resting place. Marc had willed his voluminous collection of papers to the American Jewish Archives at the Hebrew Union College, in Cincinnati. This collection, which initially comprised 140 boxes of material, would ultimately be available to researchers via the Internet, obviating the need to travel to Cincinnati in order study Rabbi Tanenbaum and his world.

Someday, Georgette's son would be able to peruse this archive and, his mother hoped, grasp the scope of his father's life and work. Sifting through Marc's papers helped Georgette endure what she assumed would be the last week of her pregnancy; her revised due date was August 31.

As Georgette Bennett rose on the morning of Monday, August 24, 1992, the new widow planned to spend the day going about her business, with a full schedule of meetings. She would soon find that she could not keep to that schedule. By early afternoon, she started to experience contractions, which she ignored, certain that they were false labor. Two weeks before, she had hired Pansy Campbell as a nanny. Certain that there would be no need for her to come in that day, and wanting to give Pansy more time with her own children before assuming her live-in schedule, Georgette had given her that day off. That proved to be a mistake, because that was the very day that she found herself completely alone as she went into labor.

When Georgette started to hemorrhage, she finally realized that the labor was real and that she needed to get to the hospital. She urgently tried to reach Richard Smith, a friend, who had agreed to be her birthing partner. But her labor was a week early, and he was nowhere to be found. Nor were any of her desperate messages returned. So she turned to Tom Reppetto, then-president of the New York Citizens Crime Commission and a former commander of detectives in the Chicago Police Department.

"Tom, your services are needed!" "I'll be there in twenty minutes!" he replied. But Georgette, not having anticipated Joshua-Marc's arrival so soon, requested that Reppetto stop at the nearest Duane Reade drugstore to pick up some tape for her camcorder and a few odds and ends to make her hospital stay more comfortable. In the meantime, she continued her packing and preparations.

An ever-more-anxious Tom Reppetto said, "Georgette, don't you think we ought to get going?" He finally urged her out the door and into a taxi, and no sooner were they on their way than her water broke. The two arrived at the hospital, where they were met by Georgette's cousins Olga and Pips. Her labor was progressing very quickly—too quickly. Joshua's umbilical cord was wrapped around his neck. The doctors who had made Joshua's conception possible, Doctors Zev Rosenwaks and Ernst Bartsich, huddled together, deciding on a course of action that would enable Joshua to be delivered alive.

Georgette needed an emergency cesarean section and was immediately put under with general anesthesia. She had arrived at the hospital at 5:30 p.m. Joshua-Marc was born at 6:05 p.m. The first people to welcome him to the world were Tom Reppetto, Olga, and Pips.

When Georgette awoke from the anesthesia in her room, the nurse placed her six-pound newborn in her arms. In great pain, the new mother quickly handed her little boy back to the nurse. Very soon, she would finally be able to hold Joshua-Marc in her arms—only to have him taken away just as she was starting to bond with him, because, within hours of his birth, he would become jaundiced. The treatment for that condition meant that, except for feeding times, he had to spend the entire day in an incubator, getting light and intravenous fluids.

Day after day passed, with no assurance that Joshua-Marc would recover in time for the circumcision ritual required of Jewish males on the eighth day of their lives. Having vowed to Marc that there would be a proper bris, Georgette's anxiety spiraled hour by hour—as did her loneliness. She was given very little access to her child. When she was allowed to hold him to nurse him, she was surrounded by happy couples getting to know their infants—a keen awareness of the emptiness by her side, where a beaming Marc should have been.

Finally, after a week in the hospital, Joshua-Marc was deemed recovered, and Georgette triumphantly took her baby home—just in time for his afternoon bris. The apartment was filled with friends, family, and colleagues.

Judah Nadich, David Lincoln, and Arnold Turetsky—the rabbis who had been the bookends around Georgette and Marc's marriage—officiated at Joshua-Marc's bris. As Georgette had vowed, he was circumcised at home, in the apartment she had so recently shared with his father. Robert Lewis, the baby's godfather, was the sandek, who had the honor of holding the baby as he was cushioned on his grandfather's and father's heirloom prayer shawl.

Marc and Georgette had agreed to name their baby Joshua, after her father. Now that Marc was gone, Georgette realized that under Jewish tradition, she could name the baby after his own late father. She would honor Marc's wishes by naming the baby Joshua but added the name Marc, after his late father. And she would refer to her son as Joshua-Marc.

In the days immediately following Joshua-Marc's birth, his mother's main challenge lay in coping with the deep sadness of her first Jewish New Year observance without her husband. Since Marc had conducted High Holy Day services at the Sutton Place Synagogue for many years, it would have been appropriate for her to worship there now with their infant son. But in this first year of widowhood, she could not deal with the reminders of attending the services Marc had conducted there She would instead carry Joshua-Marc the two blocks from their apartment to the Park Avenue Synagogue, the site of his father's funeral and where his parents had exchanged their very personal marriage vows only a decade earlier.

The next major Jewish holiday of Georgette's first year of widowhood, Chanukah, would begin on December 19. Joining Georgette and Joshua-Marc on that festive first night were Sidonie, Tibor, Olga, Pips, and some close friends.

Following her guests' departure, the hostess would record details of the evening's celebration in an audio diary. Addressed to her late husband on "The first night of Chanukah," she said:

It's my first Chanukah without you and my first Chanukah with Joshua-Marc . . . Joshua-Marc wore a little yarmulke, and I read to him from the booklet that you wrote for your record album on Jewish holidays. I wanted him to hear what his father had to say about Chanukah. . . . We managed to have an evening of hilarity, playing Chanukah music and playing with the baby.

Georgette would also note that the family viewed videos of Joshua-Marc, as well as that of her husband's funeral. Picking up the tape marked "Marc's Funeral," she began to play it, only to realize at once that it had been mislabeled. As she reported in her audio diary:

When I put it on, there you were! It was the video that I had made of you the day that we bought the camera so that it would be ready for the baby when he came. I had snuck up on you working at the dining room table, and you were vintage Marc. You were funny. You were loving. And you were surrounded by your papers. I fell apart when I saw that tape. I hadn't been expecting to see you. And my emotions broke. I sobbed and sobbed and couldn't stop. With these raw emotions, Chanukah was a special form of torture, because unlike other holidays that I've had to endure since your death, this one lasts eight days. But I lit the candles every night. I wanted to do it right. Sometimes I lit them alone. Sometimes I lit them with the baby.

The one bright star in her existence during that otherwise bleak winter was Joshua-Marc. He was beginning to resemble his father, especially along his jawline, his only bow to his mother's genetic heritage being his blue eyes—which the rabbi had always called "those Beitscher blues." In addition to his emerging good looks, Joshua-Marc was precocious. While new parents often join in the noting of their infant's every development in a "Baby Book," Georgette Bennett, absent a living husband, would be the sole chronicler of their beguiling son's milestone events.

By January 1994, the beginning of Georgette's second full year of widowhood, she was experiencing the need to reconnect with the various strands of her former life and, specifically, to communicate with her late husband. She described such an extrasensory experience as "spending time alone with Marc."

In the months and years to come, with their son's awareness of his surroundings increasing, Georgette would face the enormous challenge of raising him without a father. Uppermost in her thinking as she set about doing so were two crucial issues: explaining to Joshua-Marc that, while he didn't have a *living* father, he was not fatherless; and humanizing the public figure regarded as having been both "the Human Rights Rabbi" and "the Apostle to the Gentiles."

In Georgette's effort to balance the two aspects of the late rabbi's image, she understood that she would have to find a way to make his legacy "a blessing, rather than a burden" to Joshua-Marc. To that end, whenever the opportunity would arise to do so in a casual way, she would inform the little boy: "Your father did that." And when strolling in Greenwich Village, she would ask him: "Do you see that building? That's where your father and I once lived."

Joshua-Marc remembered those conversations. Later, he would say, "the first one was actually a one-way talk; I couldn't actually ground it in any one thing. But since I had been in prekindergarten, my mother had been very on top of telling me about my father, and putting me through the process of dealing with *not* having a father, but knowing who he is."

Despite his mother's efforts to humanize Marc to Joshua-Marc during his childhood, he still found it difficult to distinguish between the man and the public personality. But he did feel his father's absence.

Some of Marc Tanenbaum's great legacy would be transmitted to his son via the boy's thirteen years at the Abraham Joshua Heschel School, in Manhattan. Every year, on the occasion of Rabbi Heschel's yahrzeit (the yearly commemoration of the deceased's death), which occurred very close to Martin Luther King Day, there would be a special commemoration of both men of God. Georgette provided the school's administration with material about her late husband's relationships with Rabbi Heschel and Martin Luther King Jr. She explained, "This way, Joshua-Marc could be proud of his father, and his classmates would know that he *had* a daddy—not a live one—but a *daddy*, nonetheless—and that *his* daddy had done great things."

Another aspect of Joshua-Marc's awareness of his father came from spending time with the rabbi's colleagues, many of whom had been close friends as well, among them Archbishop Iakovos. The prelate welcomed Georgette and Joshua-Marc to his home many times, and their friendship lasted until the archbishop's death on April 10, 2005.

Others, too, would speak to Joshua-Marc of his father. "There is a general consistency in what people tell me about how great my father was—not necessarily the relationship they had with him, but about the work he had done independent of their relationship," he recalled, "so you live without the man, but you certainly get a really good picture of who he was."

One of Marc's colleagues who reached out to Joshua-Marc was Rabbi Joseph Potasnik. His son and Joshua-Marc had been close as children. They would go on to travel on separate paths, Rabbi Potasnik said, "but I used to look on them with such joy and pride: here was my son, playing with Joshua-Marc. He is an extraordinary young man. His father is *within* him." Meanwhile, Joshua-Marc described Rabbi Potasnik, his father's successor as a WINS radio commentator, as "one of the sweetest people I know. He made himself totally accessible to me. Every once in a while he would bring up a memory or two of my father."

In 2000, during the vacation week between Christmas and New Year's Day, the seven-year-old Joshua-Marc would be part of an event that altered his family life. His mother had been dating a widower, Dr. Leonard Polonsky, an American-born British entrepreneur who also maintained a home in Aspen, Colorado. And when they were all gathered in Aspen, Dr. Polonsky proposed to Georgette.

Leonard, born and raised in Bay Ridge, Brooklyn, had skipped several grades in elementary school and graduated from Townsend

Harris High School, one of New York City's select public schools, in three years instead of four. Like Marc, he started college at age fifteen. After earning his bachelor's degree in less than three years, and serving in the U.S. Army, he embarked on graduate work under the G.I. Bill.

After studying at both Oxford University and the Sorbonne in Paris, where he earned his doctorate, he obtained a three-year contract to teach in Heidelberg. Following their marriage, Leonard and his wife first lived in Frankfurt, then in Switzerland, just outside of Zurich, where their children were born, and finally in Britain. It was there that Leonard would establish his company, Hansard Financial Trust, an international financial services company that eventually became Hansard Global PLC. His affluence grew when he took his company public, and so did his philanthropy. He became a significant donor to charities in the UK as well as the United States and Israel. In June 2013, he would be named a Commander of the British Empire for his "charitable services."

After his first wife died in the 1980s, Leonard continued with his international life. Based in London and Monaco, and with a home in Aspen, he regularly traveled to Israel and elsewhere. Ironically, his London home (which he now shares with Georgette when in England) is located down the street from The Langham Hotel, from where Marc wrote his first love letter to Georgette in 1991.

Now on this December day in 2000, Joshua-Marc Tanenbaum, Leonard's brother, and a close family friend, Ann Kern, were relaxing in the hot tub of Dr. Polonsky's home in Aspen when Georgette Bennett joined them. "Leonard has just made a half-baked proposal to me," she said, "and now we all need to decide what I should do about it."

She had been introduced to Leonard a year earlier by a mutual friend, Al Freedman. As she recalled, "Al called me and said, 'I have a very good friend from London, and he's coming to New York. May I give him your phone number?'" Georgette recalled that she was "very, *very* reluctant" because she had a feeling that this caller would be an older man, and she at first demurred. But then her friend uttered the magic words: "I think he can be helpful to the Tanenbaum Center, he has *a foundation*." Not missing a beat, Georgette responded: "Yes, *by all means*, give him my phone number. I would love to meet him."

What had begun as mere donor cultivation, and Leonard's recruitment to the center's board of directors, would within eleven months become more of a personal relationship. Once again, Georgette was faced with the dilemma of being involved romantically with a man who was extraordinary in every way—and was also many years her senior.

Her change of heart had come about when Leonard called one day and said, "I'm funding scholarships at the Truman Institute for the Advancement of Peace at the Hebrew University, and they're letting me name them. Would you object if I named them The Rabbi Marc H. Tanenbaum/Young Truman Scholars?"

Wow! she thought: What a bigness of spirit in this man! And how extraordinary that he loves me and he's not threatened by my enduring love for Marc of which I've never made a secret. Despite never having met Rabbi Tanenbaum *in life*, Georgette said that "Leonard actually likes him very much. Leonard really feels he's got a *relationship* with Marc!"

Georgette Bennett and Leonard Polonsky would recite their wedding vows on June 10, 2001, in the City Council Hearing Room and hold their reception in magnificent rotunda of Manhattan's City Hall.

There, the bride, attired in a cream wool pants suit, would joyfully walk down the aisle to the strains of "Georgy Girl," escorted by Joshua-Marc and scattering sterling roses—the same flowers she carried in her wedding to Marc—from her bridal bouquet along the way. Following close behind, the bridegroom dispensed chocolate cigars bearing the words "It's a *We*."

Then, the couple stepped beneath the chuppah, their wedding canopy fashioned from the prayer shawl that had belonged first to Ignace Beitscher, then to Marc Tanenbaum, to be passed on to Joshua-Marc on the occasion of his bar mitzvah. They were joined there by the nearly eight-year-old Joshua-Marc; three Polonsky granddaughters; and the bride's matron of honor, the late rabbi's sister, Sima. There, in the presence of 180 guests, Rabbis David Lincoln of the Park Avenue Synagogue and Rabbi Arnold Turetsky performed the religious rites. Mayor Giuliani and Bishop Mark S. Sisk of the Episcopal Diocese of New York also participated in the ceremony. At the wedding, Rabbi Potasnik, one of the guests, observed, "Both he and Georgette are committed to Marc's preservation—not just the Tanenbaum *name*, but his real interfaith legacy."

Before long, Joshua-Marc would be addressing Leonard as "Daddy," distinguishing his new stepfather from Marc, whom he always refers to as "my father."

Regarding Leonard and Marc's unusual relationship, Georgette observed, "They get to share this boy, who doesn't seem the least conflicted about loyalties. I don't think Joshua-Marc feels that by loving Leonard, he loves Marc less. And Leonard is not troubled in any way by Joshua's trying to find his father—a journey that he is into right now."

Responding to his mother's observation, Joshua said that "the reality soon sets in—that my father is not *here*. That's the only time it's troublesome. But then my friends and I say: 'He did all of this.' That's a point of pride. As I grow older and discover more of myself, I think: look what you have and what you could do with this."

In Joshua-Marc's quest of self-discovery, he recalled having "licked envelopes at the Tanenbaum Center" during his first internship there, as well as having compiled chronologies of the organization's programs, tracing their roots back to his father's work.

"Going through different writings, manuscripts, and interviews—as well as my mother's constantly telling me what he had done, the people he interacted with, the things he stood for, what he stated, what he fought for—I understood more of what my father stood for," he said.

By balancing the many details of the rabbi's legacy, Joshua-Marc would discover the man his father had been: "a character, a very loving person with a great sense of humor, with complications in his life, like any other human being. He was very *human*."

Five years after the wedding, Joshua-Marc would celebrate his bar mitzvah. He would be called to the Torah at the Park Avenue Synagogue, on the very bimah where his father had once served as a guest officiator. This bar mitzvah boy's performance, unlike those of his friends, would be reviewed in the October 21, 2005, issue of the *New York Jewish Week* by no less a critic than Ari Goldman, a former religion correspondent for the *New York Times*, who wrote that Joshua-Marc possessed "the Tanenbaum cadence."

As Joshua-Marc matured, he would increasingly resemble his late father. But while admiring of Marc Tanenbaum's achievements, he understood that he must make his own way in the world. "I guess you could call it my first personal life crisis," he said of his search for self-identity. "But it was not just because of my father; it was actually due to having *three* over-achieving, very successful, parents, all of them major impact players." Thus, during Joshua-Marc's first year of college at George Washington University, he wondered: Am I actually doing things on my own merit? Or is everything happening because of one or the other of my parents' names?

Feeling burdened by his parents' reputations and accomplishments, he decided he needed to transfer to a school far, far away, and so he gained admission to the University of Melbourne.

Joshua-Marc's need "to find his own path," as his mother put it, convinced her and Leonard to permit him to matriculate at the University of Melbourne. "I'm sure that Joshua must realize that we went through months of very agonizing decision making," Georgette said. As Leonard observed, "Australia is not *next door.*" But "when Joshua-Marc said, 'I need to go someplace where nobody knows my father, where nobody knows Daddy, and where nobody knows you,'" Georgette noted, "Leonard and I thought that was absolutely great."

When he got there, "What did he do?" his mother asked rhetorically: "He organized interfaith activities—his father's area of concern; he took as his second major sociology—*I'm* a sociologist; and he took a minor in finance—his daddy's field." But, she noted, "Joshua-Marc came at it in his own way, starting with the application process for the University of Melbourne. And he did the whole thing on his own, without any intervention from us, from beginning to end." Joshua-Marc would also spend a year studying at the University College London before returning to Melbourne to receive his degree.

Reflecting on his chosen course of study, Joshua-Marc said: "I tried running away from what my parents had done for so long, but I actually bounced right back into it by establishing an association exploring the role of religion in the university setting." He would realize very quickly: "I can do all those things on my own; I can totally embrace what my parents had done—all *three* of them—and run my own race at the same time."

Among the activities in which Joshua-Marc would become involved while attending the University of Melbourne was philanthropy—a major focus of Georgette and Leonard. Describing his own approach, he said: "I essentially concluded that young people could become philanthropists before they even had the financial capacity to give. I started working in what I called 'alternative currencies.'" He explained, "I actually have a method of how young people can get involved in philanthropy. By the end of this methodology, they have a focus on how to create impact and how to measure impact—how to leverage and how to bring other people into that space."

Referring to Leonard's extensive giving, Joshua-Marc observed, "Dad has done philanthropy in a very romantic way; it's from the *heart*, it's out of *love*, but with the understanding that there needs to be a result—there has to be constant feedback in the process. There are many lessons learned from Dad in that area."

While in Australia, Joshua-Marc started a company, Local Vibes, that bridged a gap in the live music business but also included a social enterprise component that presaged his later work. The business was successfully exited in 2014.

After graduation, Joshua-Marc joined Korn Ferry, the world's largest executive search firm. There, he worked in Global Asset Management & Alternatives Practice and participated in the foundation of the firm's impact investing practice. Simultaneously, stemming from his experience at Local Vibes, Joshua-Marc started working with startups that had "scalable social DNA." He continues to invest in early stage ventures that bridge gaps in access to education, capital, and mobility for underserved and under-banked communities. In addition, he holds a number of leadership positions in the philanthropic world: he serves as vice chair of the Board of the Council of Young Jewish Presidents and is the youngest president ever elected by the America-Israel Cultural Foundation. He is a Young World Fellow of the Duke of Edinburgh's International Award Foundation and is active in the Nexus Global Summit as well as the Jewish Funders Network.

But as he pursued his many professional interests, he treasured his experience at the Tanenbaum Center and his exposure to his family's value system. "That affects my view of politics; the way I approach the problems I'm dealing with—and my attitude generally," he said. "I will always recognize what my parents have accomplished. But, in reality, I have become my own person, while, at the same time, constantly recognizing where it all comes from."

Joshua-Marc has embraced the heritage from his father in several ways. "One day when I was at the University of Melbourne, at Queen's College, I decided to throw a *farbrengen*, a gathering that typically happens after the Sabbath. Everybody comes together, sits around the table, has food and liquor, debates, sings songs, and tells stories." Being "very much of a mind that much of the world knows nothing about Judaism beyond typical stereotypes," Joshua-Marc observed that "Judaism is such a religion of life—it is *focused* on life—in celebration of life. People need to understand that, not *proselytizing*." Joshua-Marc realized that as his fellow students were about to do something outside their comfort zone, he had to establish "a safe space" so that they would know that "everyone is here to support you and I am here to help you. We will try it once. If you love it, maybe we will do it again." During the gathering, Joshua-Marc answered "a number of fundamental questions about Judaism and Jews. I put Jewish delicacies in the middle of the table so everyone could try them. And then I said, 'Now we are going to start singing.' I gave out books with transliterations."

By evening's end, Joshua-Marc reported: "You have fifty non-Jews singing these songs in Hebrew. It was fantastic. The college wanted to do more interfaith programs. It was a party—informal—people got immersed, having an affirmative view of Judaism, maybe for the first time in their lives. They *loved* it."

But long term, where does Joshua-Marc see himself heading? "I wouldn't say even now that I plan to spend my entire life in the shadow of my parents. Quite the contrary; I think I'm building very much my own identity." As of this writing, Joshua-Marc is at Cornell, working on his MBA. His ultimate goal is to build a career in venture capital and private equity with a focus on serving undeserved and marginalized populations.

Joshua-Marc Tanenbaum has expressed regret that his father's name is becoming less and less well known to younger generations of Americans. But he was heartened to learn that Ben Skinner, someone closer to his own age, whom he'd met at the Nexus Global Summit, was familiar with Rabbi Tanenbaum's accomplishments "He's the youngest person I've ever met who knows who my father was," Joshua-Marc said.

In the wee hours of the morning of Tuesday, May 27, 2014, Georgette would receive an excited e-mail from Joshua-Marc: "Thought you'd think this was amazing!" he wrote regarding his e-mail exchange a little more than an hour earlier with Ben Skinner:

Ben: Josh: Are you related to Rabbi Marc Tanenbaum, by any chance? He crossed my mind, given the pope's [Francis] visit [to the Middle East].
Joshua-Marc: How did you come across my father's name? I'm not used to people of our generation knowing his name.
Ben: He's in my pantheon of heroes for a couple of reasons— mostly interfaith reconciliation. My folks were in Nigeria during Biafra, as was your dad, I think. (My dad was a colonial administrator there, then started one of the largest universities in the country.)

More than a quarter century after his passing, Rabbi Marc Tanenbaum belongs to the pantheon of heroes who transcend time and space. His life, his legacy, and the lessons he imparted are sorely needed for this unstable time. He showed us, by example, that human responsibility means the ability to respond to human suffering.

There are many mysteries to his life. Why, like the Biblical Moses, did he not live to see the Promised Land of his youngest son's birth, the only child he bore with Georgette Bennett, his great love? Why did he not live to see the signing of the Vatican-Israel Accords in 1993? Why were he and Georgette granted only one decade of love and creative collaboration?

Rabbi Marc Tanenbaum lived many lives simultaneously. He defied the laws and limitations of the physical world. He was a dreamer; he was a doer. He was a rebel, a radical, and a role model.

His heart was great. He loved those nearest to him as well as those farthest away. He had a sense of mission that was unwavering. Above all, Marc Herman Tanenbaum was the rabbi who refused to stand idly by while the soul of humanity cried out to him.

List of Interviewees

The following individuals were originally interviewed by the authors for inclusion in the Rabbi Marc H. Tanenbaum Oral History Archive. That project was commissioned in 2012 by the Tanenbaum Center for Interreligious Understanding.

Mimi Alperin, lay leader, American Jewish Committee (AJC): January 23, 2013, New York, New York.

Neal Ball, Chicago businessman, member, International Rescue Committee (IRC) delegation to Southeast Asia, 1978; founder, 1979, and honorary chair, American Refugee Committee: January 4, 2013, by telephone.

Judith Banki, assistant director, ret., Department of Interreligious Affairs, American Jewish Committee: November 24, 2012, New York, New York.

Dr. Georgette Bennett, criminologist; sociologist; correspondent, NBC Television News; widow of Rabbi Marc H. Tanenbaum; founder and president, the Tanenbaum Center for Interreligious Understanding: September 11, 2012, New York, New York.

Joseph (Joe) Berger, journalist, *Newsday*, the *New York Times*: January 9, 2013, New York, New York.

Dr. Thomas Bird, professor of Slavic languages, Queens College, New York: December 17, 2012, New York, New York.

Ken Briggs, religion correspondent, *Newsday* and the *New York Times*: December 19, 2012, by telephone.

Eugene DuBow, long-term staff member, 1966–2013, American Jewish Committee: November 29, 2012, New York, New York.

Rabbi Myron Fenster, classmate, friend of Marc Tanenbaum, Yeshiva University and the Jewish Theological Seminary of America (JTS); rabbi, Shelter Rock Jewish Center, Roslyn, New York; rabbi emeritus, Shelter Rock Jewish Center: December 12, 2012, New York, New York.

Dr. Eugene Fisher, former executive secretary, Secretariat on Catholic-Jewish Relations, National Conference of Catholic Bishops (NCCB): December 7, 2012, and January 4, 2013, by telephone.

Roz Goldberg, Jewish community activist, retired investment banker, friend to Dr. Georgette Bennett and Rabbi Marc H. Tanenbaum: June 30, 2013, New York, New York.

Dr. George Gruen, director, ret., Israel and Middle East Affairs, American Jewish Committee: November 28, 2012, New York, New York.

David Harris, Executive Director, American Jewish Committee: December 12, 2012, New York, New York.

Rev. William Harter, Presbyterian minister; secretary-treasurer, National Christian Leadership Conference for Israel; coconvener, Presbyterians for Middle East Peace: January 23, 2013, New York, New York.

Rev. Theodore M. Hesburgh, President Emeritus, University of Notre Dame: August 27, 2012, by telephone.

Dr. Susannah Heschel, daughter of Dr. Abraham Joshua Heschel; Eli Black Professor of Jewish Studies, Dartmouth College: January 16, 2013, by telephone.

Vincenzo Labella, filmmaker; producer, *Jesus of Nazareth*, 1977; producer and cowriter, with Anthony Burgess, of its sequel, *A.D.*, for which Rabbi Marc Tanenbaum served as a consultant, 1985: December 20, 2012, by telephone.

Irving Levine, longtime American Jewish Committee (AJC) staff member; director, Cleveland Field Office, Education and Urban Planning, and Institute for American Pluralism: December 12, 2012, by telephone.

Ambassador Thomas Patrick Melady, US ambassador to Burundi, Uganda, and the Holy See; president, Sacred Heart University; author of sixteen books: January 10, 2013, by telephone.

Reverend John Pawlikowski, O.S.M., professor of Ethics, Catholic Theological Union, Chicago, Illinois: January 3, 2013, by telephone.

Philip Perlmutter, New England regional director, ret., American Jewish Committee: December 4, 2012, by telephone.

Rabbi Joseph Potasnik, senior rabbi, Congregation Mount Sinai, Brooklyn, New York; executive vice president, New York Board of Rabbis: December 27, 2012, New York, New York.

Seymour Reich, attorney, American Jewish community activist, B'nai B'rith; Anti-Defamation League (ADL); chairman, IJCIC (International Jewish Committee for Interreligious Consultations): January 9, 2013, New York, New York.

Rabbi A. James Rudin, assistant Interreligious Affairs director, American Jewish Committee, 1968–1983; National Interreligious Affairs director, 1983–2000; Senior Interreligious Affairs adviser 2000–present: September 12, 2012, New York, New York.

Dr. Neil Sandberg, director, Western Region, American Jewish Committee, 1962–1980: by telephone.

Abby Scherr, Rabbi Marc H. Tanenbaum's niece and daughter of Sima Scherr: January 7, 2013, Pikesville, Maryland.

Adam Scherr, Rabbi Marc H. Tanenbaum's nephew and son of Sima Scherr: January 7, 2013, Pikesville, Maryland.

Sima Scherr, Rabbi Marc H. Tanenbaum's sister: January 7, 2013, Pikesville, Maryland.

Dr. Donald Shriver, husband of Peggy Shriver; president emeritus, Union Theological Seminary, New York: December 13, 2012, New York, New York.

Peggy Shriver, wife of Dr. Donald Shriver; assistant general secretary, head, Office of Research Evaluation and Funding, National Council of Churches, New York: December 13, 2012, New York, New York.

Peter Steinfels, staff member, *Commonweal*, the 1960s; senior religion correspondent and columnist, "Beliefs," the *New York Times*, 1990–2010; author; visiting professor, University of Notre Dame, 1994–1995; visiting professor, Georgetown University, 1997–2001; currently professor, Fordham University: January 22, 2013, New York, New York.

Dr. Leonard Swidler, professor of Religion, Temple University: December 3, 2012, Philadelphia, Pennsylvania.

Liv Ullmann, stage and screen star; author; UNICEF Goodwill Ambassador; participant, with Rabbi Marc H. Tanenbaum, International Rescue Committee (IRC) Mission to Southeast Asia, 1978: February 25, 2014, Key Largo, Florida.

Archbishop Rembert Weakland, Milwaukee, Wisconsin, ret.: October 23, 2012, by telephone.

Dr. Marvin Wilson, Harold J. Ockenga Professor of Biblical and Theological Studies, Gordon College, Wenham, Massachusetts: February 7, 2013, by telephone.

Gordon Zacks, former chairman, American Jewish Committee, International Affairs Commission: January 4, 2013, by telephone.

Chapter Notes

Confronting Hate is based on information gleaned from the authors' extensive research as well as from their discussions with the interviewees listed in Appendix A. They are quoted either directly or on background. The sources of material not contained in the authors' interviews are noted below.

Abbreviations
American Jewish Committee: AJC
AJC Oral History Conducted by Mimi Alperin: AJCOH/MA
Jacob Rader Marcus Center of the American Jewish Archives
Hebrew Union College-Jewish Institute of Religion: MHT papers, AJA
Jewish Theological Seminary of America: JTS
National Conference of Christians and Jews: NCCJ
Synagogue Council of America: SCA
Morris B. Abram: MBA
Dr. Georgette Bennett: GB
Dr. Leonard Polonsky: LP
Abraham Tanenbaum: AT
Joshua-Marc Tanenbaum: JMT
Rabbi Marc Tanenbaum: MHT
Sadie Baumsiger Tanenbaum: SBT

Acts of Courage and Human Decency amid a Sea of Brutality
The refugee rescue in the South China Sea was recounted by MHT to
GB, who related it to the authors. The encounter with Nguyen Than
and his family in Jakarta is described in an MHT op-ed in *Newsday*,
November 1978.

Chapter 1
Baltimore: Living above the Store
A history of the Jewish presence in Baltimore may be found in *The
Jewish Community of Baltimore*, Arcadia Publishing, Charleston, SC;
Chicago, Il; Portsmouth, NH; San Francisco, CA, 2008. For a general
history of Baltimore, see *The New Columbia Encyclopedia*, Columbia
University Press, New York and London, 1975; distributed by J.B.
Lippincott Company, 1975, especially p. 220. Regarding SBT and
AT immigration to U.S., AJCOH/MA (entire AJCOH/MA in
MHT papers, AJA, Box 3, Folder 42). Regarding the family's early
years in Baltimore, see AJCOH/MA. The dollar value of 1850 Light
Street, 2013, Website, trulia.com/homes/Maryland/Baltimore/sold.
Prominent individuals born on October 13, 1925, MHT's date of birth,
including Margaret Thatcher and Lennie Bruce, are noted in *Chronicle
of the 20th Century*, Dorling Kindersley, London, New York, Stuttgart,
Moscow, 1995, Pages 344 and 951, respectively. Information regarding
MHT's family life and Jewish education may be found in AJCOH/
MA. A description of Baltimore City College and its distinguished
graduates may be found on Wikipedia.

Chapter 2
A Rebel in New York City
The history and architecture of Yeshiva College are recounted in
American Jewish History, Vol. 996, No.2, "Yeshiva College and the pursuit of Jewish Architecture," Eitan Kastner. Regarding MHT at Yeshiva
College, see AJCOH/MA. Ted Comet described MHT's impact in a
brief conversation with the authors in late 2013. Regarding MHT's
coursework, disillusionment with Orthodox teaching and practice,

see AJCOH/MA. The post-Holocaust pogrom in Kielce, Poland, is described in *Encyclopedia Judaica*, Vol. 10, P. 990, Ketar Publishing House, Jerusalem, 1972. MHT's initial postgraduation employment is discussed in AJCOH/MA. The views of Harold Shulweiss are recounted in his obituary, written by Bruce Weber and published in the *New York Times*, December 26, 2014.

Chapter 3
Seeking God in Morningside Heights and Beyond

The history of the Jewish Theological Seminar (JTS) may be found on its website, jtsa.edu. MHT's first night in residence at JTS is recounted in AJCOH/MA. JHT's poems may be found in MHT papers, AJA, Box 1, Folders 2 and 11. Descriptions of his academic life may be found in MHT papers, AJA, Box 8, Folders 12–14. Regarding MHT's early relationship with Rabbi Abraham Joshua Heschel, see AJCOH/MA; for additional material regarding Heschel's life and career, see Box 73, Folder 8. MHT's extracurricular activities and growing self-confidence are discussed in AJCOH/MA. His relationship with Rabbi Louis Finkelstein is discussed in ACJOH/MA; for additional material about Finkelstein, see Box 8, Folder 7. MHT's graduation from JTS is discussed in AJCOH/MA.

Chapter 4
The Return of the Prodigal Son

The MHT-Rockmore correspondence may be found in MHT papers, AJA, Box 9, Folder 4. The retreat to the mountain to write is discussed in AJCOH/MA. The MHT novel's synopsis is courtesy of GB. The appointment as SCA acting executive director is discussed in MHT papers, AJA, and in an SCA press release, March 4, 1954.

Chapter 5
Shaking Up the Synagogue Council of America

The Synagogue Council of America was dissolved in 1994. Its records may be found at the Center for Jewish History in New York. A brief history of the SCA may be found on Wikipedia. Regarding MHT's early months at SCA, see MHT papers, AJA, Box 19, Folders 4–6, including all SCA years. Helga Weiss's background and her marriage to MHT are recounted in MHT papers, AJA, Box 10, Folder 8. MHT's increasing out-of-town travel is described in, MHT papers, AJA, Box 10, Folders 5 and 6. Major SCA initiatives during MHT's tenure are discussed in MHT papers, AJA, Box 10, Folders 5 and 6. MHT's offer of a position with the American Jewish Committee, his resignation from SCA, and his testimonial dinner are described in MHT papers, AJA, Box 19, Folder 6.

Chapter 6
Arriving at the AJC at the Right Moment

The SCA veto of Jewish involvement in Vatican Council II is discussed in AJCOH/MA. The Protestant study, 1952–1959, was undertaken at the Yale University Divinity School by Dr. Bernhard Olson, a Methodist scholar, and published later by Yale University Press as "Faith and Prejudice"; a follow-up study by Gerald Strober in 1963 was jointly published in 1972, by AJC and NCCJ, as "Portrait of the Elder Brother." The Catholic studies discussed in this chapter were supervised by Reverend Trafford Maher, SJ, St. Louis University, and carried out by Sister Rose Thering, O.P, religious materials; Sister Rita Mudd, F.C.S.P., social studies materials; Sister Mary Linus Gleason, C.S.J., literature materials. These studies were later summarized by Reverend John Pawlikowski, O.S.M., in *Catechetics and Prejudice*, Paulist Press, 1973; additional research, French, Italian, and Spanish-language textbooks, Pro Deo University, Rome, and University of Louvain, later to be summarized by Claire Huchet Bishop, *How Catholics Look at Jews*, Paulist Press, 1974; Jewish study, Dropsie College, supervised by Dr. Bernard D. Weinryb and carried out by Dr. Daniel Garnick. All study details courtesy of Judith Banki, AJC.

Zachariah Shuster's consultations with Jewish and Christian experts and AJC's relations with Pro Deo University are discussed in MHT papers, AJA; additional material regarding Pro Deo University is in David Danzig, August 1958 Committee Report article, "Pro Deo," and AJC news release, January 20, 1962, which may be found in AJC Archives. The AJC audience with Pope Pius XII is described in the AJC Archive, "Audience with Pope Pius XII," 1957. A discussion of the AJC as a "breath of fresh air," Slawson's assurances, Blaustein's support, and the AJC skills of the staff are discussed in MHTOH/MA. Judith Banki's document, the first-ever submitted by Jewish organization to Secretariat for Promoting Christian Unity, may be found in MHT papers, AJA, Box 1, Folder 13. Claire Huchet Bishop's AJC Confidential Memorandum may be found in MHT papers, AJA, Box 95, Folder 3. See also "The Vatican Decree on Jews and Judaism and the American Jewish Committee: A Historical Record," August 28, 1964, MHT papers, AJA, Box 51, Folder 11. Jules Isaac is discussed in MHT papers, AJA, and *Encyclopedia Judaica*, op. cit., Vol. 9, Page 10. Rabbis Soloveitchik and Toaff's opposition to Jewish participation in Vatican Council II is discussed in MHT memorandum, May 10, 1961, MHT papers, AJA, Box 51, Folder 6. See also MHT-Soloveitchik correspondence, Box 51, Folder 6. AJC lay leader Herbert B Ehrmann's December 15, 1960, letter to Pope John XXIII and the pontiff's reaction may be found in MHT papers, AJA.

Chapter 7
1900 Years of Waiting:
Vatican Council II, Session One: October 13–December 8, 1962

The Shuster-Friedman September 1962 meeting with Augustin Cardinal Bea and other activities while in Rome are discussed in MHT papers, AJA, Box 51, Folder 11. Vatican Council II delegates' St. Peter's Basilica protest is discussed in *A Man Named John: the Life of Pope John XXIII*, Alden Hatch, Hawthorn Books, Inc., New York, 1963, Pages 245–46. Shuster report to John Slawson on the opening session of Vatican Council II is in MHT papers, AJA, Box 49, Folder 2; additional material: Shuster Memorandum, October 18, 1962, Box 51, Folder 5. American Agapé is discussed in MHT papers, AJA, Box 1, Folder 14; additional material: "A Proposal for an Agapé," Box 49,

Folder 1. The unprecedented AJC private symposium is discussed in MHT papers, AJA, Box 49, Folder 1; additional material: Cardinal Bea, April 1, 1963, New York Agapé address, "Civic Unity and Freedom under God," Box 49, Folder 3.

Chapter 8
Regarding the Arabs: A Political Tug-of-War
Vatican Council II, Session Two: September 29–December 4, 1963

Reports of anti-Semitism issue being dropped from the Council agenda due to Arab nations' opposition and Shuster investigation, MHT papers; see AJA, AJC Paris office memorandum, December 18, 1963, Box 50, Folder 1; additional material: Shuster memorandum to NY Office, December 9, 1963, Box 51, Folder 5. Regarding the receipt of "positive news," see MHT papers, AJA, Shuster memorandum to NY Office, September 11, 1963, Box 51, Folder 2.

Cardinal Bea's September 25, 1964, "Declaration Concerning the Jews and Concerning Non-Christians," Unofficial English Translation, adopted by Council, November 20, 1964, and reported in *L'Osservatore Romano*, November 30, 1964, MHT papers, AJA, Box 49, Folder 9; additional material: Box 49, Folder 9. Declaration, Chapter 4, MHT papers, AJA, MHT article, *New York Herald Tribune*, November 10, 1963, Box 50, Folder 5. AJC actions in anticipation of document's formal presentation to Vatican Council, MHT papers, AJA, Shuster to Slawson, November 16, 1963, Box 51, Folder 5; additional material: Shuster to Danzig, October 15, 1963, Box 51, Folder 3 and A.M. Sonnabend confidential memo, October 17, 1963, Box 51, Folder 3. Regarding Nahum Goldmann's 1962 announcement, see MHT papers, AJA, Box 51, Folder 11. Discussion of schema: MHT papers, AJA, Box 49, Folder 3; additional material: MHT article, *New York Herald Tribune*, October 10, 1963, Box 49, Folder 3 and MHT memorandum, November 13, 1963, Box 50, Folder 8.

Chapter 9
The Conservative Backlash

Distribution of *"Gli Ebrei e il Consilio—Alla Luce della Sacra Scrittura della Tradizione"* is discussed in MHT papers, AJA, Box 51, Folder 11. Shuster's seven-page analysis is in MHT papers, AJA, Box 51, Folder 5. Rabbi Soloveitchik firestorm, article: *Columbia Spectator*, February 26, 1964, MHT papers, AJA, Box 50, Folder 6. AJC leadership working privately to galvanize American prelates to action and global effort, MHT papers, AJA, Box 51, Folder 11. Papal audience with AJC leadership, the *New York Times*, May 31, 1964, MHT papers, AJA, Box 49, Folder 9; additional material: text, pope's statement to AJC leaders, Box 49, Folder 10. Rabbi Heschel learns conservatives will not allow votes on Document or religious freedom and intensification of AJC efforts, MHT papers, AJA, Box 51; Folder 11; additional material: Heschel: MHT, "Heschel and Vatican II," MHT papers, AJA, Box 4, Folder 11; article, "Heschel's Significance for Jewish-Christian Relations," Eva Fleischner, *Quarterly Review*, Winter 1984, MHT papers, AJA, Box 23, Folder 8 (in copy from author to MHT, she writes: "With much gratitude for your help"); and article, "The Spiritual Radicalism of Abraham Joshua Heschel," Edward K. Kaplan, *Conservative Judaism*, Fall 1973 (author's copy to MHT inscribed: "To Marc Tannenbaum [*sic*] with admiration and gratitude"), MHT papers, AJA, Box 23, Folder 8.

Chapter 10
Can't You Jews Agree on Anything?

MHT letter to Rabbi Soloveitchik, June 18, 1964, may be found in MHT papers, AJA, Box 51, Folder 6. Orthodox and Reform opposition is discussed in MHT papers, AJA, Box 49, Folder 3; additional material: MBA, draft letter, Rabbi Israel Miller, Box 50, Folder 9; *Day Jewish Journal*, February 5, 1964, Box 50, Folder 7; *London Jewish Chronicle*, February 7, 1964, Box 51, Folder 1; and the *New York Times*, August 18, 1964, Box 51, Folder 1. Goldmann episode, Cardinal Bea's reaction, and outcome is reported in the *New York Times*, July 13, 1964, MHT papers, AJA, Box 51, Folder 1.

Chapter 11
How Can a Gospel of Love Be Such a Gospel of Hate When It Comes to the Jews?
Vatican Council II, Session Three: September 14 – November 21, 1964

Pope Paul VI opening of session, *Vatican Council II*, Xavier Rynne, Orbis Books, Maryknoll, New York, 1968, Page 291. MHT and Heschel reactions to revised version of Declaration on the Jews, Religious News Service and *Jewish Chronicle*, September 11, 1964, MHT papers, AJA, Box 49, Folder 6; additional material: Heschel memorandum to Pope Paul VI, September 14, 1964, Box 50, Folder 6; Slawson to MHT, October 19, 1964, MHT papers, AJA, Box 49, Folder 7 and Shuster summary, Heschel-Pope Paul VI meeting, September 14, 1964.

MHT efforts bearing fruit, MHT papers, AJA, Religious News Service, September 28 and 29, 1964, Box 49, Folder 2; additional material: Box 50, Folder 6. Cardinal Bea, May 5 response, Jewish Telegraphic Agency, May 5, 1964, MHT papers, AJA, Box 51; Folder 1; additional material: article, "Pope Favors New Stand on Jews," *New York Post*, May 11, 1964, MHT papers, AJA, Box 50, Folder 6; on Cardinal Bea, Shuster to Slawson, October 16, 1964, MHT papers, AJA, Box 49, Folder 2 and Religious News Service, September 25, 1964, Box 49, Folder 2. MHT Loyola University address, MHT papers, AJA, Box 1, Folder 30.

Chapter 12
Ending Two Millennia of Contempt toward the Jews
The Decisive Fourth Session: September 14–December 8, 1965

MHT return to Rome and address, University of Notre Dame, 1966, *A Prophet for Our Time: An Anthology of the Writings of Rabbi Marc H. Tanenbaum*, Judith H. Banki and Eugene J Fisher, editors, Fordham University Press, 2002, Pages 75–98; additional material: AJC memorandum, "Summary of the Declaration on the Jews," October 12, 1965, MHT papers, AJA, Box 49, Folder 3. Description, promulgation ceremony, *Nostra Aetate*, Robert Doty, the *New York Times*, October

29, 1965, MHT recollection of October 28 in history, Website, www.
datesinhistory.com.

For additional material on Vatican Council II, see *From Enemy to
Brother: The Revolution in Catholic Teaching on the Jews, 1933–1965*, John
Connelly, Harvard University Press, 2012, Pages 239–272; MHT arti-
cle, "The Ecumenical Council and the Jews," *St. Louis Review*, MHT
papers, AJA, Box 1, Folder 27; The American Jewish Committee and
Vatican II: A Chronology of the Agency's Involvement, MHT editor,
November 27, 1984.

Chapter 13
Mr. Graham Comes to Visit

Preliminary AJC meetings with Billy Graham associates: MHT
papers, AJA, Box 21, Folder 1. Justice Goldberg letter draft, MHT
papers, AJA, Box 21, Folder 1. Philip Hoffman letter, MHT papers,
AJA, Box 21, Folder 1. Details of Graham-AJC meeting, June 23,1969,
MHT papers, AJA, Box 21, Folder 1. Ensuing MHT-Billy Graham
correspondence, MHT papers, AJA, Box 21, Folders 1, 2, 3, 4, and
5. "His Land" and response, MHT papers, AJA, Box 21, Folder 2,
Box 22, Folders 2–4. MHT-Billy Graham June 25, 1970, meeting and
attendance at evening's Shea Stadium Crusade, MHT papers, AJA,
Box 21, Folder 2. Bernstein suggestion re: MHT leave of absence and
rabbi's response, MHT papers, AJA.

Billy Graham call to President Nixon, regarding resupplying arms
to Israel is recounted in MHT papers, AJA, Box 22, Folder 9.

MHT-Graham correspondence re: Munich massacre and Yaseen
article, MHT papers, AJA, Box 21, Folder 3; additional material: Box
53, Folders 7 and 8.

"Key '73" controversy, MHT papers, AJA, Box 24, Folder 4, Box
27, Folder 7, Box 35, Folders 1–5, Box 36, Folders 1–4, Box 37, Folders
1–3. Graham-Nixon telephone conversation, MHT papers, AJA, Box
22, Folder 9. MHT-Graham Montreat meeting and thank-you notes,
MHT papers, AJA, Box 21, Folder 4. AJC follow-up press briefing
and MHT WINS commentary, "Billy Graham and Judaism," MHT

papers, AJA, Box 21, Folder 4. Follow-up MHT-Graham correspondence, MHT papers, AJA, Box 21, Folder 8. MHT Interim Report, Key '73, MHT papers, AJA, Box 21, Folder 4. MHT letter to Mel Bloom, MHT papers, AJA, Box 21, Folder 4. MHT-Graham correspondence, MHT papers, AJA, Box 21, Folder 7. AJC award to Billy Graham, MHT papers, AJA, Box 21, Folder 6. MHT memo to Bertram Gold, October 7, 1977, MHT papers, AJA, Box 21, Folder 6; additional material: Box 21, Folder 7; MHT and Billy Graham Honor America program, MHT papers, AJA, Box 21, Folder 2, Box 22, Folder 6. April 21, 1982, letter to Billy Graham, MHT papers, AJA, Box 21, Folder 7. Billy Graham joining honorary board, Campaign to Remember, United States Holocaust Memorial Museum and letter of acceptance, MHT papers, AJA, Box 21, Folders 8 and 9. Billy Graham April 19, 1985, call to MHT, re: President Reagan's planned visit to Bitburg cemetery, MHT papers, AJA, Box 22, Folder 1, Box 56, Folder 2. MHT-Deaver April 20, 1985, telephone conversation and Graham suggestion, MHT papers, AJA, Box 56, Folder 2. MHT's presidential speech draft sent to White House May 1 and Reagan's May 5 delivery, MHT papers, AJA, Box 56, Folder 2. MHT's 1989 participation in Billy Graham tribute, Los Angeles, MHT papers, AJA, Box 71, Folder 10. For a concise summary of Billy Graham and Jewish issues, see MHT book proposal, *Billy Graham, the Jews and Israel,* Box 22, Folder 9.

Chapter 14
The Jews' Foremost Apostle to the Gentiles

For AJC History, AJC Timeline, see *Let Us Prove Strong: The American Jewish Committee,* Marianne R. Sanua, *Brandeis Series in American Jewish History, Culture and Life,* 2007. Recruitment of Gerald Strober: coauthor's recollection. Jewishness of late Utah Governor Simon Bamberger, Jewish Telegraphic Agency, October 17, 1926. MHT-drafted remarks of lay leader Howard Friedman, February 14, 1985, to Pope John Paul II, MHT papers, AJA, Box 34, Folder 10 and pontiff's response, MHT papers, AJA; additional material: Box 100, Folder 3.

Chapter 15
Civil Rights: What It Means to Truly Overcome

Program details for the first National Conference on Religion and Race, MHT papers, AJA, Box 1, Folder 16 and Box 39, Folder 4. Declaration of Conscience, MHT papers, AJA, Box 39; Folder 5. MHT praised by Conference's executive director, MHT papers, AJA, Box 39, Folder 4. MHT arrest during civil rights demonstration, authors' telephone conversation with Rev. John Collins. MHT speech, Second Annual Interreligious Institute, Loyola University, MHT papers, AJA, Box 1, Folder 31. MHT arrest in Florida civil rights demonstration: authors' telephone conversation with Rev. John Collins. Speech, North American College, Rome, September 1965, op. cit., "A Prophet for Our Time," Page 4. MBA-Martin Luther King, Jr. correspondence: MHT papers, AJA, Box 84, Folder 14. MHT address, "The Moral Legacy of Martin Luther King, Jr.," Ecumenical Service: MHT papers, AJA, Box 3, Folder 40. IFCO controversy and MHT resignation: MHT papers, AJA, Box 24, Folder 2, and Box 95, Folders 2, 3, and 4. Conference on Black-Jewish Relations, Fisk University, June 1974: MHT papers, AJA, Box 79, Folders 6 and 7.

Chapter 16
Redeeming Soviet Jewry

Martin Luther King Jr., December 11, 1966, address reaffirming Soviet Jewry advocacy: MHT papers, AJA, Box 84, Folder 14. MHT founding Interreligious Task Force on Soviet Jewry, MHT papers: AJA, Box 72, Folder 1. Billy Graham's intervention, at MHT's behest, with Henry Kissinger on behalf of refusenik Ruth Alexandrovitch: recollections of Gerald Strober; additional material: MHT to Billy Graham, May 28, 1971, MHT papers, AJA, Box 21, Folder 2, Box 22, Folder 8.

CHAPTER NOTES • 369

Chapter 17
Defender of the Faith:
Combating Anti-Semitism and Defending Israel
around the World

For backgound regarding the Oberammergau Passion Play, Website: Ammergauer Alpen Oberammergau AJC/MHT efforts to achieve change in play's anti-Semitic content, MHT papers, AJA, Box 41, Folders 1–11; additional material: Box 95, Folders 2 and 4. Continuing AJC Oberammergau protests and initiatives, MHT papers, AJA, Box 4, Folder 2. MHT-Jesse Jackson debate, Queens College: MHT papers, AJA, Box 5, Folder 6; Box 84, Folder 3. AJC analysis, "Jesus Christ Superstar"; MHT/Billy Graham correspondence and AJC attempts to assist in film production: MHT papers, AJA, , Box 21, Folder 4. Regarding the Auschwitz Convent Controversy, see MHT papers, AJA, Box 11, Folders 12–16; Box 12, Folders 1–3.

Chapter 18
Do Not Stand Idly By

MHT concerns regarding South African apartheid and plight of Biafrans: MHT papers, AJA, Box 100, Folder 4; Box 101, Folder 1; Box 21, Folder 13; and Box 56, Folder 1. MHT consultant to NBC miniseries, *The Holocaust*: MHT papers, AJA, Box 3, Folder 38. AJC/MHT support to Southeast Asia's endangered populations: MHT papers, AJA, Box 60, Folder 6; Box 61, Folders 1, 2, and 6. IRC "March for Survival" mission and participants: MHT papers, AJA, Box 61, Folder 4. MHT accused of being "Israeli spy" and thus initially denied entry into Malaysia: GB recollection. Call to Billy Graham during Singapore Crusade: MHT papers, AJA, Box 22, Folder 9. AJC invitation to Liv Ullmann and response: MHT papers, AJA,Box 92, Folder 11.

Chapter 19
The Private Life of a Public Man

MHT eulogy for mother: audio tape, courtesy of GB. Courtship of Georgette Bennett: see GB, unpublished memoir.

Chapter 20
More Oy Than Joy—A Year of Indecision and Turmoil

Giving MHT "a hard time"; his telephone call and letters from London; GB's emotional tailspin, exhaustion, anxiety, and elevation of relationship to new plateau, GB, unpublished memoir; MHT's continuation of professional activities and ongoing tensions in relationship, derailment of relationship, trip to Pebble Beach, San Francisco nightmare, and acceptance of "extraordinary love affair," GB, unpublished memoir. GB-MHT marriage ceremony: audio tape, courtesy of GB. GB-MHT Honeymoon: GB, conversation with authors, December 1, 2014. Norman Lear thank-you letter, courtesy of GB. Postponed MHT surprise 60th birthday party: GB, conversation with authors, December 1, 2014. Dinner with Billy Graham, GB, conversation with authors, May 28, 2014.

Chapter 21
Denouement: A Decisive Personal Pivot

Details of MHT travel as AJC's director of International Affairs, MHT papers, AJA,Box 59, Folders 20 and 21; Box 60, Folders 1, 2, 3, and 4. Details of protracted MHT-AJC retirement negotiations, authors' inspection of pertinent documents, courtesy of GB.

Chapter 22
Kimpitur!

Learning of pregnancy, consultation with therapist, GB Diary notation of dreams, IVF procedures and pregnancy confirmation: GB, unpublished memoir.

Chapter 23
Trading a Life for a Life

Pregnancy details, GB, unpublished memoir. Killeen Lecture Series address transcript, courtesy Killeen Chair of Theology and Philosophy, St. Norbert's College.

Chapter 24
The Stilling of a Great Heart

The accounts of GB/MHT respective health issues, Passover Seder, New York Board of Rabbis ceremony, choosing a name for son and dreams for family's future, details of MHT hospitalization and surgery, MHT's last hours and death are all based on GB, unpublished memoir.

Chapter 25
Of Blessed Memory

Tributes to MHT, *New York Times* obituary, July 4, 1992. Losing a great man v. an ordinary one, GB, article proposal, "After a Great Love Dies." List of MHT eulogists and details of postfuneral police escort, GB, article proposal, "After a Great Love Dies." Postfuneral telephone call requesting access to MHT's Heschel papers, GB, note to authors.

Chapter 26
Will the Real Marc Tanenbaum Please Stand Up?

Based on authors' interviews with those cited in the text.

Coda:
L'Dor Va Dor (From Generation to Generation): Joshua-Marc Tanenbaum

Joshua-Marc Tanenbaum's birth, bris, and first Yom Kippur, GB article proposal, "After a Great Love Dies." Decision to forego Yom Kippur services at the Sutton Place Synagogue and worship instead at Park Avenue Synagogue, GB, article proposal, "After a Great Love Dies." Description of Four Seasons Hotel weekend: GB Audio Diary. Account of LP's proposal to GB: the *New York Times*, June 17, 2001. Loss of MHT's rings as omen from above: GB conversation with the authors, December 1, 2014. Bride's wedding attire, color video, courtesy of GB. GB-LP wedding procession, the *New York Times*, June 17, 2001.

Index